Yes, this **is** the book that was feature͏͏ in 1996. Following are extracts of som͏͏ ͏͏͏͏͏ ͏comments:

The
Astrology
of
Death

Richard Houck

**Groundswell
Press**

A Division of ARC Associates, Inc.

The Astrology of Death

Copyright © 1994 by Richard Houck

Published by: Groundswell Press
Post Office Box 8925
Gaithersburg, MD 20898 USA

Phone & Fax: 301-353-0212

Cover and layout by Christy Ridgell. Chapter collages by Paula Houck using extracts of copyright-free illustrations within the Dover Pictorial Archive Series with the permission of Dover Publications, Inc.

Printed tropical (round) charts are from the CCRS92 Program written by Mark Pottenger (Los Angeles, CA). Sidereal (rectangular) charts are from Haydn's Jyotish (v. 1.9) written by Haydn Huntley (Fairfield, IA) and slightly customized for this book.

ISBN 0-9641612-5-7

Library of Congress Catalog Card Number: 94-77043

Printed in the United States

First Edition

3 4 5 6 7 8 9 10 15 20 25

For Pavli

The kind Lace Maker
And Pool Shark

who lives to her standards
and was once referred to as
just a breeze passing through

ACKNOWLEDGEMENTS

Many of the best sources of inspiration for this book passed from my memory long ago and can therefore only be thanked from the equally leaking well of my unconscious. In addition, I am most grateful to the many individuals whose stories anchor this text, and provide classical metaphors for the tapestry of the human drama.

Meriting special thanks for their feedback on the draft are Kathy Campbell, Steve Chuhta, Dan Nusbaum, Lois Sheldon, and most especially, Jim Butler. James Braha also restrained me from writing quite a number of stupid things, although many still slipped through. Finally, I must recognize the insight, generosity and good heart of my long-time friend, Rebecca Mayo, who shoulders the blame as the first person to re-introduce me to how a professional astrologer actually thinks. Hopefully she still doesn't regret that.

I would like to further acknowledge the indulgence of those readers, with sensibilities more refined than my own, who may be disturbed by a strong, but ultimately harmless, point of view. It seems like I may manage to accomplish the normally difficult task of offending almost every engaged astrologer in at least some minor way, even though, from my own point of view, I'm only hacking away at a thicket of abstractions. As in all things, blame my natal chart! But in the end, this book will only help to further strengthen your own ideas about related matters, and I'm convinced it would have been a greater sin to bore you.

Speaking of sin, it also remains necessary to apologize in advance for the many sins of omission and commission that undoubtedly continue to populate this rather dense book. Any valid errors brought to my attention will be corrected at any subsequent revision.

TABLE OF CONTENTS

LIST OF CHARTS

"The reign of the fear of death is well-nigh ended and we shall soon enter upon a period of knowledge and of certainty which will cut away the ground from under all of our fears... This, our present cycle, is the end of an age, and the next two hundred years will see the abolition of death as we now understand that great transition... A new and better attitude to the phenomena of death is essential, is possible and near... In dealing with the fear of death, there is little to be done except to raise the whole subject onto a more scientific level.

"In the minds of those left behind the thought of sorrow will not enter and death beds will be regarded as happier occasions than births and marriages... Before very long this will be deeply so for the intelligent of the race, and little by little for all... The morbid attitude of the majority of men to the subject of death, and their refusal to consider it when in good health, is something which must be altered and deliberately changed.

"Death, as far as the human being is concerned, is increasingly due to the planned intent and planned withdrawal of the soul under the pressure of its own formulated intent... Death in the last analysis, and from the standpoint of the average human being, is simply disappearance from the... plane of appearances... (it) is an act of intuition, transmitted by the soul to the personality, and then acted upon in conformity to the divine will by the individual will.

"As humanity becomes soul-conscious... death will be seen as an 'ordered' process, carried out in full consciousness and with understanding of cyclic purpose.

"I conjure all of you to push the study of death and its technique as far as possible and to carry forward occult investigation of this matter.

"There is no death."

– Alice A. Bailey

FOREWORD

by James Braha

The Astrology of Death is a ground-breaking contribution to the world of astrology. Here, for the first time, is a comprehensive, exhaustively-researched text examining in detail the characteristic astrological factors indicating death. Richard Houck, a skillful and highly respected veteran astrologer, courageously confronts the most taboo subject in astrology. In doing so, he brings issues to the table that astrologers have repressed and ignored for many generations. The result is extremely enlightening.

By scrutinizing many case histories of deaths, the author provides all of us with the opportunity to view death differently, to see death as a natural phenomenon and even a valuable experience rather than something to dread. *The Astrology of Death* offers a wealth of astrological knowledge while simultaneously prompting astrologers to let go of their fears, both conscious and unconscious, about death. What astrologer would not leap at the chance to gain greater awareness and equanimity in this realm?

While *The Astrology of Death* reveals many different astrological factors connected with death, its final purpose is not to train astrologers to predict peoples' deaths. It is to shed light on the entire subject and finally deal with an important facet of our field. Certainly astrologers will find plenty of tools for predicting death, and many who carefully study this book will dramatically increase their ability to accurately predict death. I did. But that is neither the beauty nor the profundity of this work.

What is presented in the following pages is a plethora of practical astrological techniques, fascinating case histories, critical philosophical issues for all astrologers to grapple with, birthchart rectification procedures that work, and more raw data on the subject of death than any astrologer could hope for. This is a rich astrology manual to be read and re-read for years throughout one's journey on the astrological path.

Like others who may recoil at the subject matter of this book, I was initially put off by the topic. I simply have never desired to foresee death, except in dramatic instances such as, for example, those of John Lennon and Marilyn Monroe (whose deaths were *easily* predictable in their *Hindu* birthcharts). In those cases, the period of death was so obvious in their natal charts that their deaths must have been highly karmic and therefore, preventable.

Although one may wonder how an occurrence could be both karmic (fated) and preventable, the question is absolutely relevant to astrologers. If karma cannot be altered, why would we astrologers bother to foresee the future? And why would Hindu astrology, a completely predictive and fate–oriented system, offer *upayes* – powerful and effective antidotes to planetary afflictions in the form of gemstones, mantra chanting, and religious rituals – if not to alter one's upcoming undesirable karma?

Although I am not interested in forecasting death, as I read page after page of precise astrological analyses of death, I was struck by the cumulative weight and power of what I had learned. It became apparent that with minimal effort I could pick out two or three highly probable dates of my own death as well as those of loved ones. Worse yet, for one who has no desire to know such information in advance, I realized that with my newly–opened eyes, chances were high that someday I would inadvertently stumble across indications of these deaths in the course of my daily astrological practice.

What then is the purpose of a book on death for those who do not care to predict it? Why embark on a subject almost certain to open a Pandora's Box of difficult philosophical issues? Why not let well enough alone? The answer lies in the fact that nature determines the timing of much of our existence. Based upon current planetary positions, the time has arrived to deal with all issues pertaining to death. Let those who flinch from a comprehensive astrology text on death, or even those who wish to ignore the topic, argue with the stars.

For *The Astrology of Death* has arrived within months of Pluto's entrance into Scorpio in the *sidereal* zodiac. Pluto and Scorpio are the planet and sign that symbolize death. Accordingly, the years from 1993 to 2005 will bring much greater focus and research into the areas of longevity, immortality, and dying. There will be tremendous advances in genetic restructuring, and interest in death will increase significantly. What intrigues the world intrigues astrologers. Or consider what an Indian astrologer once asked Richard Houck: "How can you plan your life if you don't know when you're going to die?"

The Astrology of Death is not merely the best astrology text to date on the subject of death. It is a treasure chest of predictive techniques and penetrating astrological insights. The author uses all kinds of valuable astrological tools. There are natal and prenatal eclipses, transits, secondary progressions, Hindu dasas and bhuktis (planetary periods and subperiods), Hindu marakas (death-inflicting planets by virtue of house rulerships), stationary planets, catabolic planets, and on and on. These are the techniques the author uses in his private astrology practice, and they are what allow Richard Houck to offer many of his clients (especially skeptics) a double your money-back guarantee! As the following pages will demonstrate, Richard Houck is an astrologer who can put his money where his mouth is.

Perhaps the most important contribution of all lies in the author's explanation of tertiary progressions, a powerful technique that typically provides startlingly accurate results (and especially as he links it to the Hindu method of progression). Tertiaries are a system of lunar progression where the positions of planets each *day* after birth represent one *lunar month* of life. For example, to determine the tertiaries for a twenty-year-old, a person who has lived 240 months (20 x 12 = 240), look at the position of the planets in the ephemeris 240 *days* after birth. Each day that follows represents an upcoming month in the person's life (although a lunar month is actually about twenty-seven-and-a-third days, I used full months here, for simplicity).

Ever since discovering their usefulness, Richard Houck has been promoting tertiary progressions in articles, lectures, and to any who would listen. I am one who listened and am so favorably impressed that tertiaries are now a part of my daily astrological practice. As the author explains, unlike most other progression systems, tertiaries allow for significant activity involving the more slowly moving planets (Jupiter, Saturn, Uranus, Neptune, and Pluto). Further, tertiary planets often turn retrograde or stationary direct, signifying important effects in a person's life. Two recent personal examples of the power of tertiaries come to mind.

The first occurred on January 26, 1993, the day of my second marriage, when tertiary Jupiter was exactly conjunct my ascendant. The second was in February 1994, when tertiary Venus, the ascendant ruler of my birthchart, turned stationary direct, coinciding with publication of my fourth book (*How To Predict Your Future*). Interestingly, publication was scheduled for mid-1993 but kept being delayed. By the fall of 1993, I began to analyze my own horoscope to determine when the book might actually appear. Out of the many Hindu and Western techniques I routinely use, I was able to accurately predict the month of publication based solely upon the upcoming tertiary progressed stationary Venus.

One of the most important principles in astrology is to always analyze a birthchart as a *whole*. That is certainly what this book is about. Richard Houck rarely, if ever, makes a case unless there are numerous confirming factors. Indeed, in his professional practice he rectifies *all* birthcharts in order to verify the accuracy of the birthtime. The text in hand gives added weight to the astrological adage: "See an indication once and the outcome is a possibility. See it twice and it is a probability. See it three times and you can bet on it."

Richard Houck is passionate about astrology. Expect to be provoked by his strong opinions, entertained by his humor, and elated by many of his findings. I cheered out loud when he attacked the vague and worthless definitions commonly offered for intercepted houses. I had a good laugh at the story of a death–row inmate who based his legal appeal on the fact that his electric–chair execution would harm his future lives by damaging his "subtle body." And I wanted to thrash Mr. Houck about the neck when he asserts that only one zodiac (sidereal) could be correct.

But that is where some of the best learning takes place. The author questions all predictive techniques that do not, in his experience, produce accurate results. Using numerous examples, he also presents a compelling case for using Uranus, Neptune, and Pluto in Hindu astrology (where they are typically ignored).

Richard Houck is an astrologer to be taken seriously. For example, in November 1993, he wrote an article titled "The Clintons Cruise for Trouble" for a Washington D.C. based newsletter. A month later, he called to alert me to the fireworks that he expected to begin almost immediately. He began reciting innumerable details (the likes of which comprise this book) of Bill's and Hillary's current astrological indices. There were transits, tertiary progressions, secondary progressions, dasas, bhuktis, marakas, and an important solar eclipse that had recently touched sensitive points in both of the Clintons' natal and progressed charts.

Within *days* of our conversation, a month–long period began that saw the death of Bill Clinton's mother, a new embarrassment called "the state trooper sex scandal," the first subpoenas in the Whitewater scandal, a clash with North Korea forcing the president to issue a real threat of war, and the resignation of one Secretary of Defense and withdrawal of another!

The Astrology of Death is a book for those who seek the truth. Finding truth requires time, effort, and most of all – patience. Do not be deceived. The material in this text is demanding. It is rich and subtle, and deserves to be studied, not merely perused. For those who are willing, the rewards are great. The author uses many of the best techniques offered by both Western and Hindu astrology, and there are buried secrets everywhere.

Finally, let those who read this book give thanks for Richard Houck's profound commitment to astrology. *The Astrology of Death* is a self-published work. It is a text which intrigued major publishers (in their own words), but scared them in their wallets. After a lengthy period of indecision by the publishers, and to stay within his own timetable, the author recalled his manuscript and took action.

Eight years ago, I experienced the same predicament with my first book, *Ancient Hindu Astrology for the Modern Western Astrologer*. Most publishers were excited by the text but were afraid that Hindu astrology books could never sell in the West. Seven printings and 20,000 books later, it is safe to say that the publishers lacked courage and vision. Years from now, I believe the publishers who sat on this text will also feel that special tinge of embarrassment.

PREFACE

It's odd that nobody has ever written a book dedicated to a topic of potential interest to 100% of the general public that aspires to be astrologically literate. Death is sometimes hinted at and danced around in Western astrological books, but rarely addressed directly. Western astrological periodicals occasionally list birth and death data, but as a general rule without technical comment. Eastern books and journals will discuss it at length, but there do not seem to be any dedicated books on the topic. If it's true, as the old joke goes, that death is nature's way of telling you to slow down, then one would expect there to be more interest in being able to recognize some of its warning signals.

But there are other good reasons to write about this topic, and here are just a few:

1. *To Lower The Level of Morbidity* — Good astrologers invariably have an equally good sense of humor since this quality helps manage many of the anxiety–inducing ambiguities and paradoxes of language and life. Indeed, among the key characteristics alleged to distinguish humans from animals are a capacity for humor and an awareness of our own mortality. When you combine these two features you end up with an affection for morbid jokes which usually seems associated with people of exceptionally strong mental health!

I can understand why astrologers who have very solar charts have a problem dealing with, or even talking about, death since astrologically–trained physicians have noted that the bodies of highly solar people (e.g., Leo rising with the Sun in the 1st house) actually put out an increased amount of heat immediately after death. But for the rest of us, to confront a fear is often to loosen its illusive grip. In addition, your broader astrological perception should improve and, as a bonus, you shouldn't have to pay life insurance premiums until nearer the end.

Ignore the superstitious, and often smiley–faced, contingent who tell you that you shouldn't even look into this topic, lest somehow you become metaphysically "infected" and draw this King of Terrors down onto yourself. They often advise: Think Happy Thoughts, and Have A Nice Day. But you'll notice that they die much like the rest of us, and retroactively we usually think we can see some clues about it, either in their charts or in the charts of those close to them.

2. *To Decriminalize Fatalism* — Much "modern" astrology literature suggests that we should "rise above" forecasting, even though that is astrology's fundamentally distinguishing strength, and the mastery of time projection is historically what the world's population has rightly come to expect from astrologers. Instead we are now advised to counsel clients with New Age booster talk that lays out the client's alleged "constructive options." But the fact of the matter is that many of life's major events *do* seem to be quite inevitable (fated?) and can be neither redirected nor evaded. Death seems to be one of these. Actually, this ties into one of my favorite definitions of life which is that "life is what happened to you when you had other plans."

The 20th century Western trend towards "humanistic" astrology, including its tendency to attach itself to the latest jargon and fads within the therapeutic professions, has often been misused by weak astrologers to justify a collapse of rigor since their vague sign–oriented approach offers no effective methods to identify deficient techniques. And modern Western astrological assertions are typically packaged within a flow of myth–based symbolism said to assure "collaboration with the intent of universe" — as if many of these astrologers could objectively demonstrate claim to such knowledge.

But the use of non–objective referents is logically linked to the rise of an embedded Guru class of astrological authorities, the idea being that there must be somebody who can make astrology work consistently against its implied reputation; and worship, like any narcotic, can help overcome inner doubt about techniques. It's not considered good form to become too crabby about all this, but until astrologers agree to a certain standard of objective performance it will be hard to ever demonstrate that astrology is little more than what a Scorpio friend of mine has referred to as "cosmic masturbation."

Parenthetically, it's a pleasure to see Western astrology attempting to revitalize its fundamentals through Project Hindsight. Its "hard corps" of highly competent astrologers is attempting a complete retranslation of the entire body of relevant Greek, Latin and Arabic classics from ancient times through the Renaissance. This probably won't resolve the zodiac problem, but it is already revealing, via contrast with the large body of original surviving documents currently being uncovered, the shallowness of much what currently passes for popular Western astrology.

Oddly, the same Western astrologers who piously advise against forecasting nevertheless continue to show great interest in electional activity, and numerous articles in astrological publications still do retroactive "forecasts" to impress their readers. This magnetic attraction back to event forecasting reminds me of the wonderful remark of Jewish philosopher Isaac B. Singer: "We must believe in free will; we have no choice!"

On this topic of "fatalism," at least one major astrological publisher has actually advertised its unwillingness to even *consider* manuscripts that do not conform to what they consider to be the philosophically correct view in this regard. This censorship by allegedly Uranian people was documented yet again via some comments printed in *The Horary Practitioner*, a journal dedicated to propagating the accumulated horary techniques of William Lilly, the 17th century author of *Christian Astrology*.

In their 12th issue (January 1992), with its unusual focus upon horary questions related to death, astrologer C.J. Puotinen wrote that, "Matters of life and death fill our newspapers, mystery novels, movies and news broadcasts. In moments of high drama, they touch our lives. But among astrologers, death is often a taboo subject. My essays on the questions 'When will Emperor Hirohito die?,' and 'When will Ferdinand Marcos die?' were rejected by editors of astrological journals because of their 'inappropriate' subject matter..."

"If these men had not been world figures, and I had wanted to know when they would die in order to insure their lives while naming myself beneficiary (author's note: sorry, C. J., but that's not legal — if it were, there would probably be a lot more interest in astrology), that would be unethical and unprofessional. But sincere questions about...the health of others should not be dismissed categorically."

The correspondent went on to assert that more contemporary writers on horary (Watters, Goldstein-Jacobson, Barclay) generally reject the derivation of death from a horary chart, "Yet William Lilly, like his contemporaries, found death a riveting topic, and he wrote enthusiastically on such themes as, 'Who will die first, the querent or his wife?' and, 'How long will the querent live?', and 'What kind of death will the querent die?'."

3. *To Re-explore Techniques* — Many dozens of technical claims vaguely float "out there." We have, for example, the infamous House of Death

about which a lot is said — much of it contradictory. In any case, its actual location varies depending on who you listen to, as does its ruler. And, to the extent it is discussed at all, there is no agreement about what it actually means relative to the physical reality of death for the chart-holder himself.

We have accumulated various "Parts" of death (geometrically derived points) which are seemingly more tied to horary astrology. But these often refer to disputable house cusps, rulers, degrees and so forth. Maybe these constructs have consistent usefulness, and maybe they don't. But stimulating a more focused look at old concepts, by the simple process of presenting and analyzing a block of actual charts, should lead to stronger techniques that would benefit all astrological work.

Some astrologers suggest that if you want to estimate the moment of death it would be much simpler and easier to just monitor the chart of the person(s) most likely to be affected by the death. This position has merit, but it often derives from the un-demonstrated presumption that death is too subjective to register in the chart of the dead person itself and therefore, by definition, exceeds the parameters of what the chart could register. But many things that "should" work, don't — and vice versa. As usual, the problem is more typically with the deficiencies or biases of the observer and not with the observed, and this seems especially true regarding astrology.

4. *Society is Ready* — In October of 1993, Pluto made its third and final ingress into sidereal Scorpio. The power of the sidereal ingresses of the outer planets is not commonly recognized. Examples are the publication of both Freud's (sex) and Einstein's (atomic) theories which coincided with Pluto ingresses. The first Moon walk, the invention of the car and TV, the 1987 509-point stock market drop (and the 1993 100-point drop), and the entry of the U.S. into World War 1 occurred on Uranus ingresses (the latter three exactly). But if it's true that Pluto and Scorpio are about stripping the varnish off — about expulsion, separation, isolation, cancellation and repulsion — then this sounds like death to a lot of people. So Pluto's ingress into sidereal Scorpio seems like a more than appropriate period to focus further dedicated attention on this topic.

We have clearly begun to see the "mainstreaming" of what was once the rejected fringe — in this case, "new age" concepts related to death and dying. This involves the many areas popularized by people such as Shirley Maclaine (reincarnation), Elizabeth Kubler-Ross (hospices and death psychology), Dr. Jack Kevorkian (physician–assisted suicide) and the like. A book that explores life's final moments (*How We Die* by surgeon Sherwin Nuland) already has 350,000 copies in print as of mid–1994 and is receiving very positive reviews.

Indeed, the initially shocking "how to" book of 1991, *Final Exit*, has been out on cassette tape for quite a while, so that now you can learn the many practical ways to commit suicide even while driving to the office — presumably with modern commuter traffic itself contributing to the volume of sales. Indeed, speaking of cars, officials at San Quentin prison announced in January of 1990 that they were going to change the official hour of executions (10 AM) that had been in effect for 97 years due to the fact that rush hour traffic jams were being increasingly aggravated by visitors to the executions. So apparently something is in the air.

Toss into the pot 1) technology that frustrates the ability to define death's boundaries, 2) the billion dollar, 10–year genetic mapping project of the new NIH Center for Human Genome Research that will find the location and function of more than 100,000 human genes with the hope that flaws can be directly modified, 3) the overall de–emphasis on the body at death including a strong increase in cremation and organ donor programs vs. preserving corpses in indestructible cases[†], 4) hospital lawyers battling the exhausted elderly over ownership of their right to die, 5) the massive political struggle over abortion "rights" (actually an attempt to define by legislation when the soul takes possession of the body), and more and more, the question begs: *when* am I *supposed* to die? And astrology is at least as qualified to address this issue as any other existing discipline.

5. *To Cut The Convolution* — It's a Tower of Babel out there. We have the Draconians and the Heliotropes. There are astrologers justifying their observations using hypothetical planets or thousands of "personal name" asteroids, directing angles and planets by custom arcs of personal choice, doing a selective extraction of over 75 midpoints, or using orbs so wide they are statistically meaningless, and so forth. There are two dozen systems for deriving intermediate house cusps and almost as many minor aspects. And this doesn't even include the various repositories of direct revelation such as the Sabian Symbolists, nor the completely different

---

[†] *On the 1st Pluto ingress on 12/92, the American Funeral Service Museum opened in Houston, TX to "dispel myths about the business of dying and chronicle the American way of death."*

systems of "esoteric" or "hermetic" interpretation.

It goes on and on, and much of what sustains this is the amazing psycho-logical tendency that humans have towards selective perception and self-attribution. Those of a socially–inclusive temperament charitably refer to this as "Unity in Diversity." With stacks of "evidence," they all swear, "My stuff works!" — which, from a certain point of view, is somewhat possible given the prismatic charm inherent in astrology's ratios.

BUT, if you can't agree with the following nine points regarding life's major "transactions" then this book will probably be unable to gratify your metaphysical wanderlust:

- The most powerful explanations are the *simplest* and most obvious (the K.I.S.S. principle),

- *Consistent* tools and explanations should squeeze out inconsistent ones,

- Anything of consequence *must* involve the Angles, the Lights &/or the nodes,

- Maximum orbs of *one* degree should be used in *all* explanations (preferably much less),

- Houses and their rulers should *clearly* work, or drop them,

- Planets should emphasize their *plain* classical meanings,

- The simple *hard* harmonics (0, 2 & 4) preempt all others (that's conjunctions, oppositions and squares),

- All final "proof" is in successful *forward* forecasting,

- Everything else is *secondary* support.

This book cannot remotely pretend to investigate the massive number of variables involved with the apparent event called death. But, through a process of anecdotal commentary, my hope is to refine some productive factors that affect "fated" events. If it were not to be written, it wouldn't be.

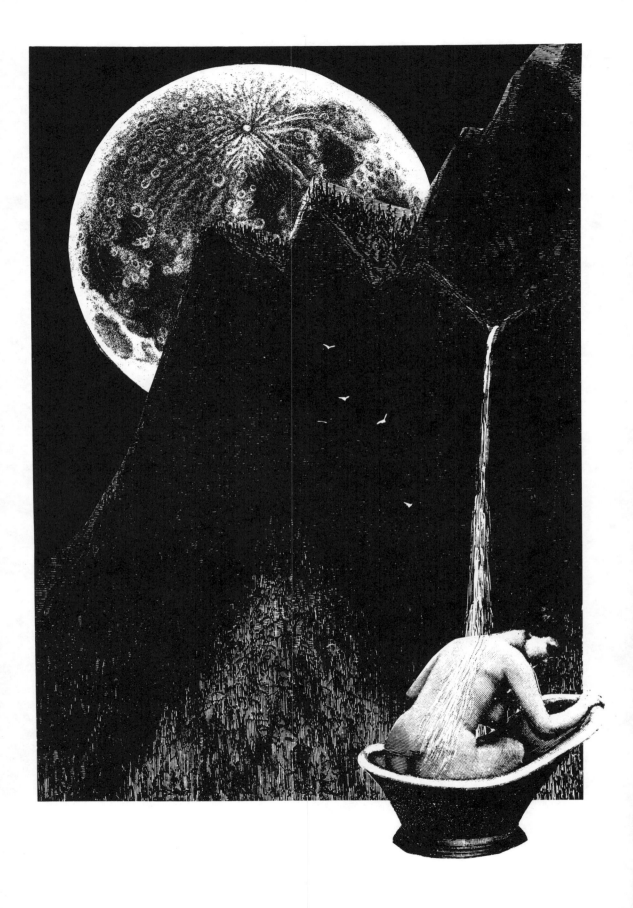

INTRODUCTION

Approach, Cautions & Notations

This book is much more of a 4th than a 3rd harmonic activity. Especially in the latter half, it can get quite data intensive. You will find that the case studies simply cannot be read; rather they must be studied in small doses since the data is quite compressed, and the inferences must be digested. If there were simple and easy answers, astrologers would know what they are. But they don't because the answers are a mosaic unique to each chart —although there is a unique logic to the making of mosaics. Nevertheless, you will find that the cumulative effect of all these cases is nearly rhythmical and quite compelling. The logic will eventually wear a groove in your brain.

Much of this book is argument combined with a significant amount of "new" (actually very old) material. It assumes the reader is at least familiar with basic Western astrological theory, and that s/he understands most of the core issues that Western astrologers typically debate among themselves. I would like to suggest that you read it from front to back.

Note that the charts and arguments in this book are *very different* from what a Western astrologer is commonly familiar with in at least six significant ways:

1) *Zodiac*: After about 15 years of intensive study I've concluded that, at least for my purposes, the tropical or Western zodiac is the "wrong," i.e., least productive zodiac. I now use the sidereal zodiac in all my conclusions, and that will be the fundamental viewpoint.

BUT: for the convenience of the Western reader, I will continue to show both Eastern and Western charts. AND PLEASE FURTHER NOTE THIS IMPORTANT FACT: throughout this book, when I comment on any house and its ruler, it is *sidereal* (unless otherwise noted). BUT all references to a specific sign-and-degree combination (e.g., 28-LI-35) are *tropical*. The latter action is purely a courtesy, so that the Western reader can easily follow along with a standard ephemeris which confirms eclipse points, and so forth. So: you should look at the *Western* chart when I make reference to any specific sign–and–degree combination, but at the *Hindu* chart when I make general reference to either a house and/or its ruler, or a plain sign reference (without degrees).

I know of no easier way to transition this dual situation, and *the examples will develop within you the ability to do a quick conversion in your mind if you persevere*. Eastern readers will probably have an easier time of this since many Hindu astrology books and periodicals often don't bother at all to display the planetary signs or degrees when they show sample charts. Later on in this text the Western reader will learn how this can be so.

These two zodiac signs still overlap roughly 25% at this time, and this is enough to aggravate the deductive confusion that won't exist about 400 years from now when the two zodiacs will actually be offset by one full sign. The confusion caused by the current 23–24 degree overlap is further aggravated by the fact that the meanings of planets, signs, houses and aspects in both systems also have significant areas of overlap. There will be further description and explanation of this issue in the chapter on Hindu Astrology.

This position will challenge some notions dearly held by the majority of Western astrologers such as their basic Sun Sign, (tropically) Void of Course moons, and many other things they believe they have "proven" to themselves (and which I thought I had proven to myself) to be "true" —including even the fundamental distribution of triplicities and quadruplicities. And for those astrologers who derive conclusions from the "obvious" symbolic linkage of zero degrees of Aries with the first moment of Spring, I can only suggest you spend April and May in Brazil or Australia and then report back your findings (hint: don't expect seeds to be asserting themselves).

This shift in main premises puts inordinate pressure on this book to prove itself, but generally the proofs will be found elsewhere and through your own open–minded investigation of actual charts over an extended period of time. Actually, the clear superiority of the sidereal zodiac is, in fact, much more obvious when *not* discussing death, which is an especially arcane arena.

This text can only do so much, and it is going to try and stay focused upon its main topic at a generally "popular" level. If you cannot even *consider* the implications of the alternative zodiac, then this book is *not* for you. After presenting some basic arguments, it will make no extended effort to "prove" theoretically the superior utility of the sidereal zodiac. More generally, it will assume it.

2) ***House Systems***: I have read arguments in many journals for well over a decade that have done a fine job of weakening the logical derivation of all the commonly used Western house systems. It's usually a Koch fanatic "definitively" whacking Placidus, but sometimes vice versa. The Regiomontanus crowd can also get pretty rowdy, and then there are the "quiche eaters" such as the Porphyries, Topocentrics and Alcabitiuians.

But only a few years of simple observation, even as a most junior astrologer, demonstrates that *no* set of intermediate house cusps works with any simple consistency. And I have observed how performance failures of this type quickly lead to a very sophisticated quality of rationalization. Rationalization increases gratuitous complexity, and this is to be deplored wherever it can be identified since astrology is difficult enough as is. However, it *is* perfectly clear, and very rarely disputed, that the angles *do* work with considerable power, although there is some legitimate argument regarding geographic vs. geocentric coordinates, precession, methods of progression, and closely related issues of that sort.

As a consequence, several years into my study I stopped considering intermediate cusps in favor of an unconsciously pseudo–cosmobiological approach. As the Beach Boys would sing, I was waiting for a "good vibration" to let me know which house I was really dealing with. Unconsciously, I was using a type of eight–cusp system waiting to see which way things would flop. It turns out that there have been strong eight house systems in astrology's deep past, and who knows: that may still be the best way to go.

Of course, related notions such as "intercepted signs" and their alleged meanings also had to be tossed. Doing charts for Alaska or Sweden, where apparently few people can have a life due to massive "interception," drives the entire issue to its most absurd unless one wants to get involved in some abstract intellectual gyration. As I have mentioned, space constraints do not allow this book to become involved in a futile refutation of ideas long held dear by various True Believers, many of whom will be reading this book. So excuse me if I ignore prized theories and just slog forward as best I can.

But having said all these crusty things, I will occasionally highlight intermediate cusp observations (using only the most common Placidus system) in deference to both my Western readers and my vast powers of fallibility. However, note the fact that although there will be hits to the Placidus 8th cusp, this is not "proof" of anything. There may be Koch hits also, and both of these could often turn out, in any case, to just be sensitive arc points located within the ancient Hindu "house" system I will be highlighting.

3) **House Reality**: Certain effective schools of astrology reject the idea that house systems function at all, and they have rebuilt their interpretative models on angles and related sensitive points. Or they may work with more purely harmonic charts, excluding house systems altogether. I am sympathetic to this, as long as they don't drift off into hyperspace, since their interpretative systems often seem to perform quite well.

Perhaps foolishly, I do accept the utility of houses, but this book will be highlighting 12 equal and full-sign houses starting with whatever sidereal sign is on the ascendant without regard to degree. Among other things, this means that the Hindu 1st house will often deeply infringe upon a space traditionally assigned to the Western 12th, i.e., part of the area above the "horizon" (the Ascendant / Descendant axis), and the Hindu 10th will often deeply infringe upon the traditional space assigned to the Western 9th. It is incidentally useful to note that this also definitely supports the key discoveries of the industrious French statistician Michel Gauquelin with regard to his power zones.

[I should further note that there is another more "modern" Hindu house system that uses the Asc degree to establish the center and "cusp" of the 1st (30 degree) house and which sets all subsequent (30 degree) houses. This is thought to work better for latitudes much more distant from the equator than India. But since it is not the one that ancient writings are based upon, it will not be used in this book. Therefore, this further means that any reference in *this* book to a "sidereal" or "Hindu" *cusp* is a reference to *zero* degrees of a sidereal sign and is the same thing as a Hindu house cusp.]

Using this text's ancient full-sign system, the Midheaven (MC) does not define the beginning of the 10th although it is usually found somewhere in the 9th or the 10th. But I do get a little twitchy when it is occasionally found in the 8th or 11th. When that happens, I used to resolve the matter by going for a cup of coffee. Now I just consider the MC as having to do with the "aspirational ego" and not "career" which remains a function of the 10th and its ruler. I play the MC in the house where it resides, and continue to progress it (with excellent results).

For purposes of this book it is also very important to reinforce that when we progress the "top" of the Meridian (the MC), we are also by definition progressing the "bottom" of the Meridian (the IC) although its progressed position is almost never printed on any chart. You will see that the progressed Imum Coeli (IC) often does have a close link to death. Further note that I will be emphasizing the progression of the IC itself and not its ruler. In any case, keep in mind that, since the natal IC will not necessarily be found in the 4th, this will have an impact upon any thoughts you may otherwise have about the ruler of the IC vs. the ruler of the 4th (which may now be different).

4) ***Zodiac/House Correspondence***: As long as I have thrown out, at least for my purposes, the correspondence of zero degrees of Aries with the first moment of Spring, i.e., the tropical zodiac, I'll also mention that I don't automatically accept any "natural" correlation of the sign Aries with the 1st house. In fact, I'm somewhat inclined to believe that the 1st has a more natural correlation with the sign of Libra *when* the subject under discussion (i.e., the 1st house topic) is death itself. I discuss this, and relevant implications, at greater length in the chapter on Marakas (death–inflicting planets in Hindu astrology). But lest you be concerned about this, be advised that this little bit of arcanery has almost no practical implications for the purpose of this book.

5) *"New" Systems of Forecasting*: In order not to totally lose contact with my likely reader, this book will continue to emphasize the commonly recognized Western techniques of secondary progression, transits, and the like. However, other fairly easy techniques will be introduced such as tertiary progressions and the Hindu Vimsottari Dasa/Bhukti system, both of which I use extensively. I also place significant forecasting emphasis upon other less commonly used factors that highlight the very important issue of planetary strength such as apparent velocity and brightness (magnitude).

[Other commonly held concepts such as combustion, the allegedly negative implications of retrogradation and the like are, however, rejected. I do believe in giving classical ideas extensive benefit of the doubt and, conversely, giving "new" ideas the "Missouri Look." So be assured that such rejection was not arrived at quickly or frivolously — if only because such rejections negatively impact the conventional shorthand and easy conversational assumptions of everyday discussions with my peers.

Having said that, I should comment that sometimes the Sun *can* damage an associated planet, but not by the simple formulas. And with regard to retrogrades, planets actually increase in power, for better or worse, as their velocity decreases. While their direction does not much matter for purposes of this text, I do think retrograde symbolism is important in horary work and under certain other circumstances. There is another special way that retrogrades function, and this is briefly discussed in the chapter on tertiary progressions.]

6) ***Pre-Natal Eclipses***: These are eclipses (3 – 4 on the average) that occur between conception and birth, and they are logically within the vicinity of the natal lunar birth nodes. Pre-natal eclipses almost invariably register as critical factors in any analysis of death, along with the natal nodes themselves and transiting eclipses before death — most particularly under certain circumstances that will be defined. Eclipses are clearly identified in any good astrological ephemeris or similar tables of planetary phenomena.

Shorthand Notation – Technical discussion of actual charts will sometimes reflect certain shorthand notations in order to pack more useable information onto a page and speed up its readability:

> ➤ P2   =   Secondary Progressed
> ➤ P3   =   Tertiary Progressed
> ➤ T.   =   Transiting
> ➤ PNE   =   Pre-Natal Eclipse
> ➤ TOB   =   Time of Birth
> ➤ TTM   =   To The Minute of arc (give or take a minute or two)
> ➤ Rx   =   Retrograde

Notes: ➤ Again: *All house* references will be based upon sidereal full signs (see the subsequent chapter on Hindu astrology)

➤ When they are almost perfectly exact, I will make occasional reference to *octiles* and *tri-octiles*. This is half a square (45 degrees) and one–and–a–half squares (135 degrees) respectively. It defines the 8th harmonic.

➤ *Nodes*: In every chart I've ever done I've inserted both the mean and the true node for study purposes.
I used to favor the classic *mean* lunar node and *not* the newer true node that you now see in most ephemerides. Now I ultimately remain uncertain since one or the other will often seem to work precisely to the minute (as will their midpoint), and I have been unable to discern any distinguishing rationale.

tNN	=	true north node
mNN	=	mean north node
tSN	=	true south node
mSN	=	mean south node

Rahu is the Indian word for the lunar north node
Ketu is the Indian word for the lunar south node

Approach

There is quite a variety of other productive factors I would like to have highlighted that relate, for example, to various fully–directed arcs, less common harmonic charts, true power midpoints, synodics, alternative coordinate systems and other aspects of local space, shadow points and absolute degrees, comets, converse directions and progressions, other planetary nodes, certain star clusters and even other planetary viewpoints[†].

Additionally, the vast extension of Hindu concepts is beyond any significant access in this book. But the new ideas introduced, and the specialized focus, will provide more than enough transitional material for

---

[†] *A point of potential fertility suggested by the Edgar Cayce material and now software–supportable — at least through the CCRS program that I use.*

any Western astrologer to digest. Hopefully this book will help stabilize the initial discussion platform for other interested authors to further evolve this topic to a more sophisticated level.

This book is specifically *not* designed to assure, let us say, a facile "marketable talent" in the forecasting of death even as much is insinuated, and despite the fact that it contains many excellent clues (including a few which are quite hidden!). Even well-developed, this would be a generally worthless talent. This text should be considered similar to the efforts of pure, vs. applied, mathematicians who develop ideas purely for their own charms and internal consistencies. And it can certainly be used to sharpen technique for other purposes.

But: if you are diligent enough to digest and synthesize this material, and then to carry forward many of its clues, I *can* guarantee that you should *at least* be able to discriminate between a death chart and a non-death chart if both are handed to you for that purpose. Just like countries that have The Bomb or people who earn very advanced status in martial arts, I'm making the hopeful assumption that any reader who puts in the necessary dedicated effort to investigate this topic is at, or will evolve into, a sufficient level of ethical development and sophistication to manage the obvious responsibility inherent in a "successful" technical meditation on this topic.

This book's focus is much more mechanical than philosophical. Like many of my likely readers, my personal library is full of texts that address, from every possible angle, the many metaphysical issues associated with death: its definition, process, meaning, reality, and so forth. I will touch on it, but I assume you already have your own ideas about these matters, and I have enough other axes to grind.

But certainly nothing focuses the mind and heart upon the definition and execution of an appropriate life as much as the certainty that it will be boxed up and labelled in the end. There is a growing school of thought that there are no "psychological" problems, only spiritual ones, and my feeling is that these problems are aggravated by, among other things, a failure to focus regularly, but softly and constructively, upon the reality of death.

The inevitability of death is life's most fundamental fact. Its acceptance, or avoidance, affects the fundamental quality of our anxieties and desires. These, in turn, affect the will and therefore our fundamental human behaviors. I would ask the reader to give some extended thought to how lives would be led if the moment of death was known to all from the moment of birth. My personal feeling is that such knowledge would be highly salubrious with regard to true spiritual development. But maybe not.

Parenthetically, back in 1989 I recall reading about a 66-year-old gangster named Anthony Antone who was on Florida's "death row" for a gangland murder. He filed a suit on the grounds that the 2,300-volt electric chair might jolt his "astral counterpart" and thereby "ruin any subsequent existences that he might have." This was probably based upon Article V of the U.S. Constitution which states in part that, "...nor shall any person be subject for the same offense to be twice put in jeopardy of life or limb."

It's heart-warming to see Mr. Antone now focusing upon the nexus between life and death. But, as an apparent convert to the theory of reincarnation, perhaps he should have wondered if he may have already used up his multi-lifetime budgeted quota of badness, so that there would really be little reason for him to return again in any case. This may also explain why, ever since the "New Age" movement began, judges are now giving multiple lifetime sentences to the same person "to be served simultaneously." But back to the main track...

Theological folklore says that only God knows the final moment of death. The extent to which that may be increasingly untrue, whether through genetic mapping or later generations of astrological artificial intelligence software, may be the extent to which we must necessarily, like it or not, assume the responsibility of becoming more God-like (as intended by mystics and not by egotists).

It's quite clear that God doesn't care one whit about apparent death since both the domesticated and undomesticated worlds are continuously saturated with it in every possible permutation of apparent cruelty. Therefore, from a certain spiritual perspective, and assuming a fundamental "benevolence" underlying all things, it is more than plausible to conclude that death goes completely unseen because it simply does not occur.

So I am not at all persuaded that the theoretical ability to accurately forecast form-based transitions is at all "bad" (although incompetent, immature and misdirected forecasting *is* bad). Such a skill would just shift mankind into a new "place," and it wouldn't be the first time. People can always find a way to misuse knowledge, but the knowledge keeps coming nonetheless.

Still, to be clear: as long as the fear of death continues to rule most hearts, you should not give a forecast of death to others despite whatever skills you may, in fact, develop in this matter. Here I would also add the caution that, as a result of reading this book, you will have a powerful initial tendency to "see" incipient death–related factors in every chart you pick up. That, of course, is a mistake of over–focus, and presumably you will learn how to shake it off and re–normalize your perception.

In the end, there is no need to worry about the misuse of knowledge because, if it is truly wrong (i.e., spiritually immature), it will inevitably self–correct. In thought, word, and deed, two choices always exist at any moment, and these choices co–build reality. One choice moves us toward alignment with our ultimate spiritual ideals, and the other moves us away. As long as you are moving away, you will feel the urge to move back. It may take 1,000 lifetimes but, in the end, through understanding, we choose to animate our will towards right choices which we will conclude are the only choices. Thus the definition and final fatedness of any free will upon this earth. In the interim, everything is always exactly as it should be.

Heaven exists, but not as advertised, nor in a spatial dimension. Hell exists, but only as a construction projected within illusion. Evil exists, but it is only sustained through false choice, and it is completely defined as separation from Unity and The Good. Good exists everywhere and only waits to be revealed and then animated. The Good, residing in Universal Time, will "wait" as long as it takes.

In the end, there is only Love which has essentially *nothing* to do with romance, sentiment, motive or ego. The best we can think of it is that it has something to do with a generally inaccessible quality of warmth without heat that is derived from a type of "music" whose unique combination of notes we have not yet heard, as described through mathematical equations that remain unformulated. This is indeed The Light Which Casts No Shadow. Totally impersonal, and sometimes vaguely felt in dreams, its indestructible inevitability permeates all things.

So. Have *fun* with this death book.

THE DEFINITION OF DEATH

"Either this man is dead,
or my watch has stopped."
— Groucho Marx

erhaps one of the problems in drawing astrological conclusions about death is that we really don't have a definition of it. Without this, it may not be possible to match up the proper flow of correlative symbols. Death often seems sudden and obvious, where the heart and the brain stop producing measurable output relative to the current performance thresholds of sensory–based instrumentation. But more often than not, a closer look indicates that death appears to be a sequence of subtle "events."

One set of these events has been popularized, in terms of psychological responses, by Dr. Elizabeth Kubler–Ross. I won't repeat them here because they don't seem very productive from the point of view of this text, and they also emphasize deaths that are self–aware. Alice Bailey describes at length the occult mechanism supporting the sequence of death events. It begins with the soul issuing a word of withdrawal followed by the glands secreting a death–dealing substance into the bloodstream that affects the heart where the life thread is anchored. A vibratory tremor then loosens the connection between the nervous system and its etheric counterpart. The rest of the process is explicitly described in an extract from her works titled *Death, The Great Adventure*.

As this process can begin significantly before occurrence of the last breath, it brings to mind the counterpart to this, and that is the problem of defining when "life" begins. Implied in all this is the key problem of actually defining life itself and indeed, recognizing certain assumptions about the definition and "behavior" of time itself. As there are perhaps few phenomena nearer to God than time itself, this issue (like the Sun) really cannot be viewed directly, although it receives a lot of basically metaphorical attention in occult Eastern texts.

The major abortion battle in the United States is, as was noted in the Preface, actually an attempt to define, through pressure groups, legislation and judicial precedent, the exact moment that "life" begins. At the purely material level, is it at fertilization, implantation (genetic stabilization), gastrulation (the technical establishment of singleness), quickening, thalamus development (permitting neural integration and the registration of pain), viability (basically the theoretical capacity for spontaneous respiration), or what? The list can go on.

Embryologists note that nearly half of all fertilized human eggs create embryos that are often referred to as a "survival mistake," and the female body will usually dispose of the error before she even misses her first period. Sometimes also a disorganized mass of tissue is formed (a hydatidiform mole) which is, in fact, genetically unique, but doctors trash it. A century back, the Catholic Church softened its stance on ectopic pregnancies, which are inherently dangerous, referring to the removal of such an embryo as the "treatment" of a "pathological organ." At the present time the Catholic Church, oddly enough, apparently does not take a clear position about when ensoulment begins.

And when does an individual become a person? Is it consciousness — which clever scientific tests of plants have repeatedly demonstrated? The ability to reason — which people in comas, and many institutionalized individuals, do not seem to have? The capacity to communicate — which the severely emotionally disabled do not seem to have? Self–awareness — which a one–year–old child does not seem to have? The U.S. Congress has held hearings on "fetal pain" and its apparent resistance to being aborted, although pain does not necessarily imply suffering nor the development of a cerebral cortex.

Science, of course, is totally befuddled on this point. Scientifically, it may even be an "unaskable" question. And so the definition of "life", from a social policy point of view, will apparently be established by which camp can generate the most political strength. Increasingly, we have a symmetrical development going on in the arena of death where politicians will be attempting to assert control over one of the soul's most spiritual and occult processes.

Although technically unnecessary, every astrologer I know assumes the existence of a soul. There is the further perception that life on the earth heavily partakes of the symbolism of Saturn, so that the soul can be constrained by the apparent linearity of the earth's time and its inertial qualities of space and matter (or, to put it in terms of a classic American bumpersticker, "Life's a bitch and then you die"). Occult texts argue that these distinctive earth qualities are exactly what the soul seeks in order to have the evolutionary experiences that it needs at this "time."

The Moment of Birth

Western astrologers use the moment the first breath is taken as the ensoulment base point for setting up the natal chart. This is due to the obviously occult nature of breathing itself and its support relationship to the equally occult closed river that is the bloodstream. It would otherwise seem that any moment in the overall gestation process could qualify as the key astrological reference point if that moment could be crisply defined and if rules were developed and applied consistently. But that seems neither possible nor practical.

At a point in the past, Western astrologers seemed to bias more towards the moment that the cord was cut, thus defining an independent blood stream. However, follow–up studies showed that this was not a working proposition. In addition, the first breath seems to work despite whether a birth was induced, Caesarian, premature or what have you[†]. The first breath has always been used in the East.

Pregnant astrological clients often ask what moment they should capture when their baby is being born. This introduces some interesting issues. I'm told that the amount of time difference between the first gasp and the first cry is usually less than a minute. The first breath can also be taken before the head has obviously emerged. The first cry is usually within five seconds but may not occur for many minutes, and regular breathing almost always occurs within two minutes. So even close observation does not necessarily yield a chart that would not benefit from modest rectification as angular events begin to unfold in the child's life.

An intriguing alternative for a birth moment might be when the eyes open so the pineal gland can be stimulated by light and thus initiate the process of independent growth. But this raises odd questions for children born blind, and it would otherwise merit a lengthy follow–up study. In any case, the remarkable behavior of the bones in the skull for several months after birth permits some absorption of light without necessary use of the eyes.

[†] *Michel Gauquelin concluded statistically that induced births did lose their hereditary effects, i.e., the loss of similar angular planets as the parents, and some astrologers argue that induced births charts do not perform.*

Many years ago I remember being startled upon reading a trance remark of Edgar Cayce that a soul takes possession of a body sometimes before, sometimes during, and sometimes after the moment of physical birth. I've lost the specific reference, but here are two specific examples to reinforce my recollection. First, in reading #826–8 for a 35–year–old male born March 2, 1901 near Patterson, MO, Cayce replied, in answer to a specific question, that the exact time of the client's soul birth was "11 p.m. central time, for this experience was two hours, lacking a few minutes, after the physical birth."

In the second example reading (#488–6) where he was asked for the inquirer's TOB (which the inquirer apparently knew but did not provide), Cayce replied, "This, as we find, as the record has been made of same, is near right to the second; and while at the entrance of the entity into the earth's plane the spiritual and physical birth varied little, there was the physical under one sign and the spiritual under another! Hence the doubts that often arise, from an astrological view."

This may partially explain why Indian philosophy places emphasis upon calculation of the pre–natal epoch. His statement is potentially alarming from an astrological point of view because it breaks the implied link between breathing and the soul — thus raising doubt about whether astrologers are just monitoring something at the biological / personality level vs. the soul / spiritual level. It also may help explain why some of Cayce's recorded comments about various individual's astrological tendencies are seemingly not supported by the information in either standard Eastern or Western charts, thus giving rise to the claims of "draconic" charts and the like[†].

The Moment of Death

But what is perhaps more interesting about Mr. Cayce's remark is an implied converse possibility that the moment of death may have a similar variability. Sensitive people who have dealt with those near death have often registered a moment when a subtle yet well–defined change seems to occur. When this particular "event" occurs, it has the quality of a departure. After that moment, the personality may carry on for a while, but it seems quite void. At the moment of the last breath, I understand

[†] *The draconic zodiac uses the north node of the Moon to define the point of zero Aries.*

there also seems to be a measurable loss of weight.

Easily reproducible Kirlian photographs clearly indicate the existence of something etheric. This appears as a type of radiant projection when, for example, part of a leaf is cut away, yet its original form outline seems to remain for a period of time. But the scientific community does not acknowledge the existence of the various "bodies" said by occultists to vitalize tissue through the absorption of solar "prana" thus causing personal radiation or what is sometimes referred to as "occult heat."

The famous channel Alice Bailey says that when the will to sustain the form nature departs then the radiant etheric body, as the giver of form, withdraws through the top of the head (and Hinduism asserts the existence of a tiny pin hole in the top of the head for this purpose). As a consequence, the physical framework loses all order, falls apart and disintegrates. This idea of a "form maker" may also help explain how good psychics can pick up the residual continuity of, for example, a war injury from a prior lifetime — although, strictly speaking, this is not due to etheric continuity.

But here the discussion gets even more arcane, since one purpose of all spiritual practice is to lessen ego affiliation with the lower spiritual energy levels — which include the etheric. Bailey asserts that within a century or so, most people will be able to perceive the etheric body and therefore will lose concern about the falling away of transitory structures such as the human body.

Why might the etheric body withdraw? Bailey says that the soul comes to earth with an objective, and works through a cycle with four qualities: chaos, experiment, experience and comprehension. At the achievement of comprehension, the ego loses desire and, as a result, is no longer attracted to its form on the physical stage. It decides to turn inward, reverses polarization and dematerializes, i.e., while all the atomic matter persists, the form does not. A death metaphor comes to my mind of atoms being dropped like marbles onto a perfectly flat glass tabletop. Hinduism mirrors this in its assertion that longevity is directly related to the nature and strength of past life karma, and therefore one literally cannot die until this karma has been fully exhausted through experience.

Even an animal's awareness and seeming acceptance of its impending death can often be easily observed, especially in the wild. On the domesticated side, and at the risk of being accused by sophisticates of anthropomorphizing, I should add that the apparent sadness, often including tears, of cattle lined up for slaughter has been "occultly observed" by certain sensitive individuals as being related more to the lack of respect at their death and the related unnecessary suffering of their friends since animals partake of a group soul.

For that matter, it is commonly known among people who work closely with domesticated pets that an animal will wait a very long time, sometimes patiently and sometimes not, for a missing companion who may have been killed. It is therefore actually recommended that the body of the dead companion be laid in front of the surviving animal. He will immediately observe the departure of his companion's spirit, and will wander off, apparently with the concern for his companion's safety fully allayed.

The clear irritation of the very elderly at attempts to needlessly prolong their lives gives evidence to this thought about the loss of desire to sustain the form. In this regard, I vividly recall a letter written several years ago to an astrologers' magazine, *The Mercury Hour*, from the elderly wife of a fatally ill husband. They were fairly pleading for some knowledge or assistance in knowing when his long ordeal would finally be over. To an astrologer studying the topic of death, I expect there is a profound research clue in this moment when the soul loses form desire. To the extent it could be ascertained anecdotally through "occult" vision it would be interesting to compare that astrological moment to the more apparent last breath.

As far as records go back, astrology theory makes a tight connection between sex and death, and psychoanalysts regularly repackage this concept. Salmon die almost immediately after reproduction, and praying mantises are notorious as the most extreme example of this in that the male is consumed by the female while actually having sex — leading to even more psychoanalytic theory and many a symbolically derived Hollywood movie theme[†]. Adult humans generally wait to die until after they have at least raised their children. In any case, it is certainly true that only organisms that reproduce sexually leave a corpse (except for a certain class of "virgin birth" insects...).

[†] *In the year this book was started, an example was "Fatal Attraction."*

As I mentioned in the Preface, it's also getting harder and harder to define when the full set of life forces have truly surrendered. It still happens in modern Western hospitals that people "return" to life after being pronounced dead. People are also now regularly resuscitated who, in the past, would have been pronounced clinically dead. A good example is people who "drown" in icy waters (some for over an hour), people who have heart attacks, and many other situations with which the reader is undoubtedly familiar.

This has lead to extensive modern discussion of the phenomena of "near death experiences," and the apparent decision of the life forces, or soul, not to withdraw after all (often characterized with regret in the face of a duty). And in many primitive cultures, extensive rituals surround a transition period of from days to years between death and burial. For example, in Bali a corpse can only be cremated exactly 42 days after apparent bodily death.

You might think this issue has been settled in modern scientific countries, but this is not so. In the early 1970's a neurologist developed a device much more sensitive than an EEG. It was tested against several dozen people who were pronounced dead by the EEG standard developed only a few years earlier. As it turned out, several of these people were revived without any brain damage.

On the flip side of this, a Canadian doctor in the mid–1970's did an EEG analysis of a lump of lime–flavored Jell-O in an intensive care ward. Apparently all the trash signals from the maze of nearby electrical devices created readings that seemed to signal "life." I think this was supposed to prove something about the limits of instrumentation, but to me it just proves what so many of us have suspected all along — which is that Jell-O really IS alive.

By the way, the legal definition of death varies from state to state within the United States, so you may want to relocate to get the best deal in this matter. It also varies from country to country. Using the criteria of a flat wave on the EEG, Russia gives you five minutes, the United States gives you 24 hours, and France gives you 48 hours, so you sure don't want to get hypothermia in Russia. All this admitted arbitrariness is probably what leads to science fiction horror movies with titles such as "Nightmare of the Living Dead."

Death And Planetary Symbolism

The following sequence has a lot of logical charm:

If	Pluto	=	Conception (magical explosive atomic creation)
and	Neptune	=	Gestation (undifferentiated aqueous dream state)
and	Uranus	=	Birth (shock trauma into a new dimension)
and then	Saturn	=	Life on the Earth (struggles through space/time)
might	Jupiter	=	Death?

Novice astrologers have a somewhat instinctive tendency to view death as a Saturnian experience, not only because death has something to do with "badness" from the viewpoint of a form–oriented observer, but also because of its clear linkage to time, which Saturn rules. In Chinese astrology, Saturn is considered an earth planet and specifically governs the growth of virtue, while Jupiter, the wood planet, rules death. And indeed, more experienced observers of many death charts find that Jupiter is often highly prominent.

At the death of former President George Bush's young daughter, for example, even though transiting Saturn was exactly on his true Ascendant, transiting Jupiter was also stationary (in his 9th). Often when humorists die, Jupiter is clearly involved. For example, when Jim Backus (the comic voice of Mr. Magoo) died on 7/3/89, the transiting Saturn/Neptune conjunction was exactly on his Jupiter (his DOB is 2/25/13).

I have also been initially startled to see a natally stationary Jupiter in the chart of more than one successfully suicidal person and, because it seems so counter–intuitive, I will therefore give an example or two in the section on suicide. It's also true that when Vincent Foster, President Clinton's lifelong friend, apparently killed himself on 7/21/93 not far from the White House where he had been working, transiting Jupiter was exactly conjunct President Clinton's tertiary progressed Neptune exactly to the minute (we will be giving a lot of attention to tertiary progressions later in this book). It's interesting that President Clinton's almost immediate reaction was to feel that the true rationale behind the death would never be uncovered.

Jupiter is a royal planet. Its worst characteristic is to bring too much of something, but intrinsically it tends toward relief and blessing. Therefore the above sequence hints that death is hardly a dark event, and all true psychics powerfully support that view. I will note here that intrinsically benefic planets can become functional malefics in the Hindu system depending on placement, rulership and so forth.

Certainly death could be viewed as a malefic event from a mundane and temporal perspective, or at least occur under circumstances associated with the negative side of a planetary benefic. Without doubt, the transition to death can often be very traumatic, and the loss of companionship is often very real and not to be trivialized. But death might otherwise be viewed as a transitional event liberating the ego from earthly space/time constraints. And this Jupiterian attitude is why death in some spiritually–sophisticated cultures is a cause for extended celebration. For example, when Tibetan Buddhists honor the lives of noteworthy people, they hold the ceremonies on the anniversary of the person's death, instead of birth as is common in the West[†].

In looking for death in the charts of people related to the deceased, the question is how these people are likely to process the death. In the charts of some people it won't show up at all, suggesting no true connection despite outward circumstances or appearances. Otherwise, in those charts of others where death is known to be reasonably certain within a fixed period of time, all you have to do to accurately estimate the period of death is monitor the key planet(s) that matches the symbolism of the likely response of those left behind. And this would not necessarily exclude Jupiter if the person has a magnanimous attitude towards death.

---

† *An exception to this Western rule is Saint Patrick's day, which celebrates the day of his death, and which has inexplicably evolved into what one disgusted observer has characterized as "maudlin and puerile sentimentalizing, cloying cuteness, and a bacchanal of bathos, booze and blarney." So much for Saint Patrick's conversion of the "pagan" Irish chiefs!*

A VERY BASIC INTRODUCTION
TO HINDU ASTROLOGY

As noted earlier, the technical level of this book must necessarily assume that its reader is at least familiar with the basic elements of Western astrological thinking. But with this as a baseline, it is important to add that throughout this book you will observe many statements and thought processes that may initially strike you as quite odd. It is strongly suggested that you make an attempt to absorb, rather than criticize, this adjusted way of thinking since the objective of these statements is to guide you more towards the basic Hindu approach to analyzing a chart. When I first entered into this topic I myself recall writing some critical remarks that ultimately proved to be more a function of my ignorant assumptions and biased point of view than of the new subject matter itself. Eventually your mind will "flip" into an understanding of this revised perspective.

To me there is little doubt that the Eastern system is more productive than the Western. Some astrologers argue that this is only true from a forecasting point of view, but I find it equally superior for psychological commentary as well. What possible rationale would have the seasons producing "personality," but the stars producing event "karma?" How strangely schizophrenic to suggest that inner and outer realities should, or could, somehow be separated! For the reader, the plain evidence you need to see will not be found in a book with this type of dedicated and esoteric focus. After learning this methodology, you can easily evolve the proof yourself over time simply by studying the verified natal and event charts of public individuals and your daily associates.

This chapter will be a type of "Cliff's Notes" to Hindu astrology since the comments will be compressed to the brink of near simple–mindedness. Its purpose is to give you a basic shell for puzzling through my subsequent remarks, although many training–related comments and arguments are further distributed throughout the book. To those who wish to learn more about the many initial subtleties of this topic, the book I recommend as a first book is *Ancient Hindu Astrology for the Modern Western Astrologer* by James Braha (Hermetician Press). I have many others, but I'm convinced that this is still the most practical first primer. This is especially so since many of the subsequent books you may read will really be quite weird, eccentric or even wrong in many of the things they say. Conversely, that doesn't mean that I always agree with James and, in any case, we all evolve over time in terms of our understandings.

It is very much recommended that you purchase some Hindu astrology software, all of which is relatively inexpensive. This book will not teach any calculation methods as many other books do. Using your own software against actual cases will help you to make much better sense of the theoretical material that follows. Various packages are coming onto the market ranging from simple to extensive and sophisticated, and some are listed in the "resource directory" in the back of this book.

So without further ado, let's just plunge right in.

ZODIAC

As already noted, we'll be emphasizing the sidereal one where zero degrees of Aries is based upon a fixed star position, rather than the first moment of Spring which moves forward relative to those star positions (this is at a rate of about one degree every 72 years due to precession of the equinox). This accumulated difference is currently out of alignment with the Western zodiac by about 23–24 degrees of longitude. In about 400 more years the two zodiacs will diverge by one full sign. And that will be very interesting indeed. Perhaps I should note here that I have never seen an astrologer move from the sidereal to the tropical zodiac, but I have seen an increasingly large flow in the opposite direction.

The degree of difference between these two zodiacs is called the "ayanamsha," and there is much argument about this (the argument is actually about what year the two zodiacs first exactly overlapped). Western siderealists tend to favor the Fagan/Bradley one, but I can assure you that, all the excellent theoretical arguments aside (such as expressed by the late Neil Michelsen in the introduction to his sidereal ephemeris), Fagan/Bradley is useless when it comes to the interface with the key Hindu forecasting tool called the Dasa System, which is the Indian equivalent of Western progression (within this chapter, Dasas are defined under a later sub-heading titled "Transits and the Dasa/Bhukti System").

Another ayanamsha that I see referenced, but rarely used, is by the prolific author and publisher B.V. Raman. The best runner up is called Lahiri and is supported by the government of India. This was developed by a government commission that is rumored to have pushed Lahiri into a slight compromise in coming to a supportable conclusion on this rather contentious matter.

In my opinion, the nearest correct ayanamsha with a name attached to it is called Krishnamurti (you may see several spellings for this and, in fact, you may see creative spellings for many terms in Hindu astrology). Its value is derived by subtracting only 5 minutes and 47 seconds from the Lahiri ayanamsha. Before I ever heard of Krishnamurti I had reached the point where I was subtracting 5 minutes and 10 seconds from Lahiri, and this is what I still do to this day since almost no case has driven me to consider a wider deviation.

At this point, you may be comforted to know that the initial practical consequences of the differences between Lahiri, Krishnamurti and me are almost nil. Later you will notice that Lahiri often still has you in the prior Dasa for a week or two when new Dasa events are obviously happening and, as a general rule, this is most especially observable when someone has moved into a new Mars Main-Period (Dasa) or Sub-Period (Bhukti). By the time you have developed to the point that this becomes important to you, you will have evolved your own hardheaded opinion on this matter.

*Secretly running around with Death's girlfriend, Dr. Jack Kevorkian unfortunately did **not** realize that he had been relying upon the **wrong** ayanamsha.*

TABLE OF AYANAMSHA VALUES

Following are the ayanamsha values used in this book. They are 5 minutes and 10 seconds "shorter" than the values developed by the Lahiri Calendar Reform Committee. These values are generally within about a minute of the popular Krishnamurti ayanamsha, but they may differ significantly from the values developed by other Indian authorities and Western siderealists. Western astrologers should subtract these values, calculated for the first day of each year, from all Western planets and angles in order to match the same sidereal values that this book refers to.

1900	22	22'	45"		1920	22	39'	27"
1901	22	23'	33"		1921	22	40'	13"
1902	22	24'	20"		1922	22	40'	58"
1903	22	25'	05"		1923	22	41'	42"
1904	22	25'	49"		1924	22	42'	27"
1905	22	26'	34"		1925	22	43'	12"
1906	22	27'	19"		1926	22	43'	59"
1907	22	28'	05"		1927	22	44'	48"
1908	22	28'	53"		1928	22	45'	38"
1909	22	29'	43"		1929	22	46'	31"
1910	22	30'	35"		1930	22	47'	25"
1911	22	31'	28"		1931	22	48'	20"
1912	22	32'	23"		1932	22	49'	16"
1913	22	33'	19"		1933	22	50'	12"
1914	22	34'	15"		1934	22	51'	08"
1915	22	35'	11"		1935	22	52'	02"
1916	22	36'	03"		1936	22	52'	54"
1917	22	36'	59"		1937	22	53'	45"
1918	22	37'	50"		1938	22	54'	33"
1919	22	38'	39"		1939	22	55'	20"

1940	22	56'	06"	1971	23	22'	06"
1941	22	56'	51"	1972	23	23'	01"
1942	22	57'	35"	1973	23	23'	54"
1943	22	58'	20"	1974	23	24'	45"
1944	22	59'	06"	1975	23	25'	34"
1945	22	59'	54"	1976	23	26'	21"
1946	23	00'	43"	1977	23	27'	07"
1947	23	01'	34"	1978	23	27'	52"
1948	23	02'	27"	1979	23	28'	36"
1949	23	03'	22"	1980	23	29'	21"
1950	23	04'	17"	1981	23	30'	07"
1951	23	05'	13"	1982	23	30'	54"
1952	23	06'	09"	1983	23	31'	43"
1953	23	07'	04"	1984	23	32'	34"
1954	23	07'	58"	1985	23	33'	27"
1955	23	08'	50"	1986	23	34'	21"
1956	23	09'	39"	1987	23	35'	16"
1957	23	10'	27"	1988	23	36'	12"
1958	23	11'	14"	1989	23	37'	08"
1959	23	11'	59"	1990	23	38'	03"
1960	23	12'	43"	1991	23	38'	57"
1961	23	13'	28"	1992	23	39'	49"
1962	23	14'	13"	1993	23	40'	40"
1963	23	15'	00"	1994	23	41'	28"
1964	23	15'	48"	1995	23	42'	15"
1965	23	16'	38"	1996	23	43'	00"
1966	23	17'	30"	1997	23	43'	45"
1967	23	18'	24"	1998	23	44'	29"
1968	23	19'	19"	1999	23	45'	14"
1969	23	20'	15"	2000	23	46'	01"
1970	23	21'	11"				

PLANETS

Planets generally retain their old classic meanings as used in the West. A very key distinguishing point however, which is very important, is that in the Hindu system planets *accumulate strength or weakness*. For example, they build strength roughly in this sequence (by being):

1)   located in certain exact degrees (I'll note this),
2)   exalted (shown on chart printouts with an "E"),
3)   nearly or actually stationary,
      (shown with a "D" for "stationary" direct,
      i.e., under 10% of normal), or an "S" for
      moving very slowly, i.e., under 20% of normal)
4)   in certain ruling degree zones,
      (shown with an "M" for moolatrikona),
5)   in rulership, i.e., own house (shown with an "O"),
6)   in a "friendly" house (discussed further below),
7)   in a good or strong house (discussed further below),
8)   aspected by a benefic (natural or functional – see below),
9)   in the same sign in both the main chart (rasi) and the
      9th harmonic one (navamsha), or
10)   in a sympathetic house either of the same class (such
      as the rulers of angles in other angles), or with the same
      general symbolism (such as the Moon in the 4th or
      Venus in the 7th).

You can correctly imagine that weakness develops as a general reverse variation on all this – fallen placements, "bad" degree zones, involvement with "bad" houses, etc. Therefore, note carefully that, as opposed to the Western orientation, the Hindu use of signs goes well beyond being merely descriptive of the *mode* in which planetary energies are deployed[†].

With this strength or weakness, they dominate (or are dominated by) their planetary associates, and they strengthen or weaken the affairs of any particular house. With experience, this composite information gives the power to make excellent forecasts. Also: for each Ascendant, when

---

[†] *On the chart examples, I suggest you ignore any qualitative descriptors that are assigned to the nodes (exaltation, friendship, etc.) since this is subject to significant dispute. However, you may wish to adopt the commonly suggested attitude that, since the nodes are so instinctive and "brainless," they do better in Mercury–ruled signs.*

certain good combinations of two planets come together, basically as a result of ruling certain combinations of good houses, this is called a "rajayoga" (royal union), and it typically brings excellent benefits to its house. It will be shown as an "R" on the printouts. Usually there will be two "R" designators in such a house, but note that in the case of Venus–ruled Ascendants, Saturn by itself creates a rajayoga, and in the case of Cancer rising, Mars by itself creates a rajayoga (an example of this is Mars in Leo in the 2nd house of billionaire Mike Milken's chart).

The lunar nodes are generally treated like planets, yet clearly they are in a special class, and they receive much more attention in the East than in the West. My Western work always gave a lot of attention to the nodes, so I was especially pleased when I happened onto the extensive expansion on this topic, and the improved perspective, that the East provides. The nodes will be further discussed shortly, but I should reinforce here, strictly as an astronomical observation, that they have supporting applicability wherever eclipses are discussed.

By the way, I briefly mentioned the notion of planets residing in the houses/signs of their friends or enemies. This simply means that certain planets are friendly to each other, while others are not. As a single example, it does help to explain why so many extremely rich people (Mike Milken, Donald Trump, Jack Kent Cooke, Bill Gates,etc.) often have very tight hard aspects between Venus and Saturn which would initially seem to imply poverty rather than wealth. However, these two planets are actually friends in the Hindu system, and part of the clue for this may be found in Saturn's exaltation in Libra which Venus rules.

As a general proposition, the Sun, Moon, Mars and Jupiter are usually friends. Mercury, Venus and Saturn are also usually friends. Planets in each group are usually not friends with planets in the other group. Friendships can also flow one way but not the other. To simplify this whole issue, on the Hindu printouts a friendship relationship will be shown with a "+" sign, great friendship with a "++", and enemies will be shown with minuses. Considering everything else to be absorbed, don't focus too hard on this at this time, but read about it elsewhere at your leisure.

Here are a few other brief but relevant notes that will become more clear as we develop examples and their supporting commentary:

 Full Moon: It is considered better and better as the Moon gets brighter and brighter. Therefore a full Moon is considered very good and has no symbolism of inner estrangement. As I will repeat elsewhere in this book, keep in mind that all such generalizations are subject to extensive qualification. For example, a Moon in Scorpio conjunct Mars and the north node would arguably be even further damaged by being lit up.

 Yoga karaka: On the Hindu charts you will note designators of "T" or "R". These will represent the fact that a planet either rules the positive 5th or 9th houses (thus a "trikona"), or that the planet is a rajayoga karaka ("karaka" means "indicator"). As already mentioned in the earlier discussion of rajayoga, a planetary condition of rajayoga typically brings excellent status to its house location based upon rulerships and other types of positive strengths that it has gained and weaknesses that it has avoided.

 Navamsha Chart: Hindu astrology always gives primary emphasis to the main (rasi) chart, but they review any potential modulation of its message through a primary supporting chart called the "navamsha." Westerners would call this a 9th harmonic chart. It is an important chart that is often used in compatibility work, but this is primarily because it has a closer affinity to the soul than the main (rasi) chart which is related, in a sense, more to the ego personality of this particular incarnation.

A useful clue as to its use is found in this statement: if the rasi is strong but the navamsha is weak then the ego personality is strong but the soul is weak. Conversely, if the rasi is weak but the navamsha is strong then, while the current incarnation presents many challenges, the soul is easily up to the challenge. Simply to control the span of discussion I will make only very modest reference to the navamsha, but it would be false to interpret this as a suggestion on my part that it is unimportant.

To keep the concept alive in your mind I will make occasional reference to the navamsha, but there is insufficient space to show it. Remember that all harmonic charts require quite an accurate time of birth[†].

[†] *The navamsha is more extensively defined in the Longevity chapter.*

HOUSE SYSTEM

The ancient system used full sign houses (bhavas). To understand this, take your tropical natal ascending sign and degree and subtract the ayanamsha for the year you were born from the table that was just given. Whatever sign results is the sign for your 1st house, and your 1st will span from 0–29 degrees of that sign (with the ascending degree placed somewhere in the 1st house based upon the subtraction). The 2nd house is the next full sign, and so forth. A review of the many charts shown in this book will rapidly make this clear.

The 10th house is therefore ten signs from the 1st, and has no necessary connection to the MC. I do personally recommend subtracting the ayanamsha from the MC and then putting the MC into whatever house is associated with its new sign (note that just like the Asc, it will not be the beginning cusp of the new house). Western astrologers should note that, since Hindu signs and houses always exactly overlay each other, there is no such thing as interception, i.e., it cannot be possible for the same sign to be on two different house cusps.

If you find that your new (sidereal) Asc is within a degree or two of zero, be very careful and attempt to revalidate your birth time, because if it really is 29 degrees and 50 minutes of some particular sign, then it will be a great error to round up to the next sign since the new chart will be totally wrong. For example, all the planets will be in the wrong houses, and almost all the house rulers will be wrong. I will use the chart of Casper Weinberger at the end of this chapter to illustrate this and some other related points.

HOUSE RULERS

Only the seven visible planets are used as house rulers and sign dispositors. In fact, the outer three planets do not exist in the ancient system (even though the ancients did seem to be aware of them). Therefore, two houses/signs always share an original classic ruler except, of course, Leo (Sun) and Cancer (Moon). I personally recommend that you continue to insert Uranus, Neptune and Pluto into their appropriate full sign houses (after subtracting the ayanamsha, of course), but do not assign them any rulerships. Begin by correctly assuming that they have an effect in the houses where they reside, upon any other planetary residents, and upon the house opposite from it.

In my personal mixing of Eastern and Western systems, I have found that the outer planets are, in fact, animated whenever an inner planet becomes activated by Dasa or Bhukti, *and* the two planets are conjunct natally or in tight hard aspect (the tighter the aspect the more apparent the effect). Some of the examples in the second half of this book will give many further clues about how all this works.

HOUSE GOOD GUYS AND BAD GUYS

There are gradations of "goodness" and "badness" assigned to each house. Some is inherent, and some accumulates. Planets ruling a good house (and sometimes those in it) usually carry positive energy. Conversely, the more defective a house, the more trauma its ruler provides and its residents experience. Remember that all planets except "the Lights" (Sun and Moon) will share the rulership energy of two different houses, and this complicates overall logical reduction. Here are some very broad thoughts on the matter keeping in mind that, as you might expect, there is much exception by case:

   Fire (dharma) houses (1,5,9) are unreservedly good and have to do with life purpose as revealed through the personal projection, the karma and the general good fortune.

   Earth (artha) houses (2,6,10) have to do with wealth, practicalities and the public projection. The 6th is the defective of the set, but it has constructive possibilities and improves over time.

   Air (kama) houses (3,7,11) have to do with life's desires as seen in the general quality of adventure/courage, sexual passion and the opportunities that support ambition. Considerations related to the 7th are very dominant in the life, and the 3rd and 11th improve with effort over time.

   Water (moksha) houses (4,8,12) have to do with inner realization and spiritual liberation. They present the opportunity for converting mundane weaknesses into spiritual strengths. But the rulers of the 8th and 12th are considered damaging for purposes of the practical day–to–day, and planets actually in the 8th or 12th are almost always considered injured. Conversely, certain placements can help these houses.

Angular houses (1,4,7,10), called "kendras," are the most powerful. They therefore tend to do a better than average job of making constructive use of often overbearing factors such as the Sun, Mars, Saturn or the lunar north node. This is especially so if these planets are well reinforced by sign, aspect, and so forth.

ASPECTS (Drishtis)

There are many issues here that are very important:

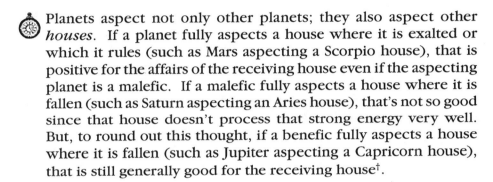 Planets aspect not only other planets; they also aspect other *houses*. If a planet fully aspects a house where it is exalted or which it rules (such as Mars aspecting a Scorpio house), that is positive for the affairs of the receiving house even if the aspecting planet is a malefic. If a malefic fully aspects a house where it is fallen (such as Saturn aspecting an Aries house), that's not so good since that house doesn't process that strong energy very well. But, to round out this thought, if a benefic fully aspects a house where it is fallen (such as Jupiter aspecting a Capricorn house), that is still generally good for the receiving house[†].

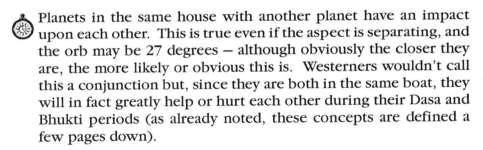 Planets in the same house with another planet have an impact upon each other. This is true even if the aspect is separating, and the orb may be 27 degrees — although obviously the closer they are, the more likely or obvious this is. Westerners wouldn't call this a conjunction but, since they are both in the same boat, they will in fact greatly help or hurt each other during their Dasa and Bhukti periods (as already noted, these concepts are defined a few pages down).

However: do not confuse these wide natal orbs with the tight transiting and progressed orbs I will be using in the many examples used throughout this text. Excluding error on my part, transit and progressed data will only reference applying orbs, and 95% of the time these will be within only one (1) degree of being perfectly exact. This is an especially necessary discipline that I think should be a minimum standard in all astrological forecasting. And well over 95% of the time these aspects will only be

---

† *This being said, don't lose track of the more simple general proposition that benefic planets cast good aspects, and malefic planets cast harmful aspects.*

the standard classical conjunctions, oppositions and squares (the 1st, 2nd and 4th harmonics).

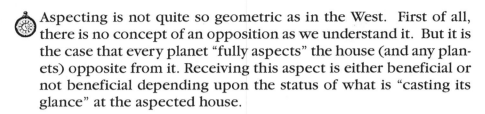

Aspecting is not quite so geometric as in the West. First of all, there is no concept of an opposition as we understand it. But it is the case that every planet "fully aspects" the house (and any planets) opposite from it. Receiving this aspect is either beneficial or not beneficial depending upon the status of what is "casting its glance" at the aspected house.

For example, Saturn exalted in Libra in the 1st can be good for the 1st, bringing out the positive side of Saturn, but as a generalization, the person may find him or herself lonely during the run of its Dasa or Bhukti period. This is because the 7th is damaged by the strength of a strong Saturn aspecting the sign (Aries) where Saturn is fallen. Approximately the same generalization could be made for someone who has Mars exalted in Capricorn in the 1st.

Conversely, if someone has Saturn and Mars (fallen) in Cancer in the 1st, such as the current U.S. Vice President Al Gore, it strengthens the 7th where Saturn rules and where Mars is exalted. But meanwhile the 1st house person gets accused of being wooden (negative Saturn) and over-bearing (negative Mars). The person may still secure a good spouse, but will have marital problems, and the 7th house person tends to get the upper hand over the 1st house person.

For purposes of this book only three more basic aspects will be mentioned. Three planets cast additional aspects which are also considered "full":

➤ Mars also aspects the 4th and the 8th forward from the house it occupies (counting that house).

➤ Jupiter also aspects the 5th and the 9th from itself (note that, of all the planets, only Jupiter can cast a trine), and

➤ Saturn also aspects the 3rd and 10th counting forward from itself (the former seems to imply more of an octile (45 degrees) than a sextile (60 degrees) relationship).

➤ Parasara, one of the most famous ancient astrological authorities, wrote that the lunar nodes also cast aspects on the 5th and 9th from themselves. But, for whatever reason, most practicing astrologers do not make use of this assertion in their daily work.

 Aspects tend to activate depending upon the Dasa and Bhukti in effect. For example, if Jupiter is natally in the 2nd, and a Jupiter Bhukti kicks into effect, the trinal aspect will also become more animated. This means that not only will the 2nd more apparently benefit (depending on the sign Jupiter is in, other planets in the house with it, and so on) but also the 6th and the 10th which are the houses that Jupiter aspects.

Here is an example of this "distributed benefit" from natal aspecting. Let's say Jupiter is natally in Scorpio in the 2nd. This is an okay sign placement for Jupiter in the 2nd (all other factors excluded), but by being placed there, Jupiter will actually be much better for the 6th (Pisces) and 10th (Cancer). That's because that is where Jupiter rules and is exalted respectively. And this beneficence will be especially apparent depending upon where Jupiter is transiting during its Dasa or Bhukti period. For example, if Jupiter were transiting the Cancer 10th house during a Jupiter Dasa or Bhukti, career matters should boom (as usual, excluding any other considerations).

 Mutual receptions work very powerfully and obviously in Hindu astrology. It will be immediately apparent that the planets really will reflect the exchange of sign rulers. If they also happen to aspect each other, the effect is even more greatly enhanced (especially as the aspecting gets tighter by degree). Mutual receptions will be represented on the Hindu chart examples by a double squiggle that look a lot like the symbol for Aquarius.

A COMMENT ON WHAT A HINDU CHART LOOKS LIKE

There are two kinds of Hindu charts, but I will only be showing and discussing the rectangular one. There are only two main differences in this chart compared to the Western one: 1) signs run clockwise, and 2) signs are fixed in position instead of houses. One of the houses is just marked as being the 1st. As Westerners look at the examples, their eye will become conditioned to this.

If you look at the example on page 86, you will see that the rectangular chart is quite logical in terms of rulerships. Moving from left to right, the top and bottom houses are each ruled by the same planet (Jupiter, Mars, Venus and Mercury respectively which is their actual sequence in the sky). At the right side, the Sun and Moon-ruled houses oppose the two Saturn-ruled ones — which you will recognize as having its own inner symmetry (basically the same time duration for transiting Saturn, the secondary progressed Moon, and the tertiary progressed Sun). Once these sign locations are memorized, the ability to make practical connections becomes much more rapid.

TRANSITS AND THE DASA/BHUKTI SYSTEM

Throughout this section, I have made some premature reference to the (Vimsottari) *Dasa/Bhukti system*. This is the fundamental and powerful Hindu predictive tool. I could easily fill a book with great stories related to just this. While it is the approximate Eastern equivalent of Western progressions, it provides a declarative certainty and sure-footedness that progressions, which are somewhat more speculative in their possible effects, do not. It also provides more precise timing parameters.

Imagine that there is a continuous loop of tape, and on that tape are marked 120 years. These years are broken down into main planetary segments in a fixed sequence, but the lengths vary depending upon the planet. The sequence, and length in years, is as follows: Sun (6), Moon (10), Mars (7), lunar North Node or "Rahu" (18), Jupiter (16), Saturn (19), Mercury (17), lunar South Node or "Ketu" (7) and Venus (20). These are referred to as the various "Dasa" periods.

Inside each of these periods is a set of time periods in identical sequence that are in the same relative time proportions to each other but adjusted to be in the same proportion to the varying length of each Dasa. These are referred to as the "Bhukti" periods (there are even further sub-breakdowns from this that follow the same logic, but we won't be discussing them). Later examples will make this more clear.

When you are born, you enter onto this fixed "tape" loop at some point, and your life then proceeds forward from there. Since you are unlikely to live 120 years, you will never get to experience some of the Dasa periods during this particular lifetime, although normally you will get to experience all the Bhukti periods multiple times within the context of various Dasa periods. The Dasa period generally prevails as a backdrop while the Bhukti factor is in the foreground providing more immediate modification and coloration to the Dasa factor.

As you can see, one of the odd "cruelties" of this system is that Saturn always follows Jupiter and, as a general rule, this is often like being lifted up for 16 years and then all of a sudden dropped. This is especially so during the first few years of the Saturn Dasa when it is "pure" Saturn, i.e., there is no possible relieving Bhukti period. The intensity of the differential will depend upon how positively Jupiter was situated and how negatively Saturn is situated.

It is definitely possible to have a very strong positive Saturn and a very debilitated Jupiter (and some examples will be discussed in this book), but it doesn't seem to be the norm. In general, most of my clients who have gone through this transition would agree with the bumpersticker philosophy on this problem (weak Jupiter/strong Saturn) which says that "a bad day fishing is still better than a good day working."

As you will see in the many examples, when a natal planet "clicks on," it becomes the key factor in play during the run of its period. We assess its complete status to see what the planet will, in fact, do from where it is located *natally*. The Hindus then give further attention to transits that will further ripen and animate the class of events that now become possible. I add tertiary progressions to get even better timing, often down to the day. The Dasa/Bhukti page basically lays out the fundamental cycles of your life's karma.

Note that a good Bhukti can offset theoretically awful transits. As an example, in March of 1993 my wife, who has Jupiter in the 1st (almost exactly square her Sun), was in a Jupiter Bhukti when transiting Pluto at 25–SC was exactly square her fixed natal Sun while transiting Saturn was exactly conjunct it at 25–AQ. Although she was working very hard during this time, there were no ill effects at all. Western astrologers all around were expecting catastrophe because they didn't have the underlying context, i.e., that natal Jupiter was activated by the Bhukti and protecting the Sun (although not by Hindu aspect).

The reverse can also be true. One of the most extreme examples I have seen of this was found in some astrological work I did for a presidential candidate outside of the U.S. He was able to secure the birth data on his opponent including some prior life events for validation. It turns out that his opponent lost the last presidential election when transiting Jupiter was exactly to the degree on his Midheaven! Why? Because among other reasons: 1) he was in a Saturn Bhukti, 2) Saturn was in a mutual reception with Mars and aspected it (frustration), 3) natal Saturn was closely conjunct the natal south node, and 4) Saturn was exactly stationary that month by tertiary progression (this concept will be discussed in the next section).

So Jupiter brought him right up to the election pinnacle, but could not deliver the prize. It is *very* rare to see the Dasa system working in such severe counterpoint to transits — indeed they almost invariably give off highly synergistic messages — but my point is that the Hindu indicators invariably prevail. There was a complex message in this transit for this individual.

Example: Jim Bakker

Let me now close with two simple examples to illustrate the function of the information given above. The first example concerns the "televangelist" Jim Bakker. The following extract of commentary is taken verbatim from Lois Rodden's *Data News* newsletter of December 1991 (see chart # 1):

"James Orson Bakker was born January 2, 1940, 11:00 AM EST, Muskegon Heights, MI, 86W.15, 43N.12, from the B.C. quoted by Genevieve Edwards in *American Astrology* July 1990... (He) was born to a strict Christian family... Jim was ordained in 1964, he and Tammy began as traveling evangelists through the American bible–belt, but were in the right place at the right time to move directly into evangelical television. They launched the 'Jim and Tammy Show' on TV religious networks in 1965, tearfully pleading for money and followers.

"Their rise to wealth and power was phenomenal... They built the PTL (Praise The Lord) ministry into a $129 million a year business, and lived like potentates with cars, jewels, mansions and jet travel.

"In May, 1987, the bubble broke. An investigation began with the claim of a 1980 seduction by church secretary Jessica Hahn, and led to accusations of homosexuality on Jim's part... and of siphoning some $3.7 million from the ministry for personal use. On the fourth day of his trial facing 120 years in prison and a $5 million fine on 24 counts of fraud and conspiracy, Jim broke down on August 30, 1989, curling into the fetal position on the floor and crying."

2nd Pisces Mars Jupiter　　　　　　　O	3rd Aries Saturn　　　　　fe Ketu Dx ♒	4th Taurus	5th Gemini
1st Aquarius Ascendant 12th Capricorn Venus　　　　　T++	RASI CHART for JIM BAKKER		6th Cancer ♇ 7th Leo
11th Sagittarius Mercury　　　　Te+ Sun　　　　　　++	10th Scorpio	9th Libra Rahu Dx　　　++	8th Virgo Moon　　　　++ ♆

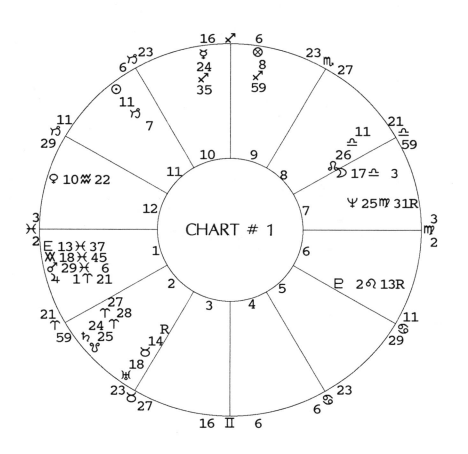

CHART # 1

Dasha Periods for Jim Bakker

```
MARS      Jupiter   beginning on 01/19/1941 at age    1y  0m 17d   for 11m  6d
MARS      Saturn    beginning on 12/25/1941 at age    1y 11m 23d   for 13m  9d
MARS      Mercury   beginning on 02/04/1943 at age    3y  1m  2d   for 11m 27d
MARS      Ketu      beginning on 02/01/1944 at age    4y  0m 29d   for  4m 27d
MARS      Venus     beginning on 06/28/1944 at age    4y  5m 26d   for 14m  0d
MARS      Sun       beginning on 08/28/1945 at age    5y  7m 26d   for  4m  6d
MARS      Moon      beginning on 01/04/1946 at age    6y  0m  2d   for  7m  0d

RAHU      Rahu      beginning on 08/04/1946 at age    6y  7m  2d   for 32m 12d
RAHU      Jupiter   beginning on 04/16/1949 at age    9y  3m 14d   for 28m 24d
RAHU      Saturn    beginning on 09/10/1951 at age   11y  8m  8d   for 34m  6d
RAHU      Mercury   beginning on 07/16/1954 at age   14y  6m 14d   for 30m 18d
RAHU      Ketu      beginning on 02/04/1957 at age   17y  1m  2d   for 12m 18d
RAHU      Venus     beginning on 02/22/1958 at age   18y  1m 20d   for 36m  0d
RAHU      Sun       beginning on 02/22/1961 at age   21y  1m 20d   for 10m 24d
RAHU      Moon      beginning on 01/16/1962 at age   22y  0m 14d   for 18m  0d
RAHU      Mars      beginning on 07/16/1963 at age   23y  6m 14d   for 12m 18d

JUPITER   Jupiter   beginning on 08/04/1964 at age   24y  7m  2d   for 25m 18d
JUPITER   Saturn    beginning on 09/22/1966 at age   26y  8m 20d   for 30m 12d
JUPITER   Mercury   beginning on 04/04/1969 at age   29y  3m  2d   for 27m  6d
JUPITER   Ketu      beginning on 07/10/1971 at age   31y  6m  8d   for 11m  6d
JUPITER   Venus     beginning on 06/16/1972 at age   32y  5m 14d   for 32m  0d
JUPITER   Sun       beginning on 02/16/1975 at age   35y  1m 14d   for  9m 18d
JUPITER   Moon      beginning on 12/04/1975 at age   35y 11m  2d   for 16m  0d
JUPITER   Mars      beginning on 04/04/1977 at age   37y  3m  2d   for 11m  6d
JUPITER   Rahu      beginning on 03/10/1978 at age   38y  2m  8d   for 28m 24d

SATURN    Saturn    beginning on 08/04/1980 at age   40y  7m  2d   for 36m  3d
SATURN    Mercury   beginning on 08/07/1983 at age   43y  7m  5d   for 32m  9d
SATURN    Ketu      beginning on 04/16/1986 at age   46y  3m 14d   for 13m  9d
SATURN    Venus     beginning on 05/25/1987 at age   47y  4m 23d   for 38m  0d
SATURN    Sun       beginning on 07/25/1990 at age   50y  6m 23d   for 11m 12d
SATURN    Moon      beginning on 07/07/1991 at age   51y  6m  5d   for 19m  0d
SATURN    Mars      beginning on 02/07/1993 at age   53y  1m  5d   for 13m  9d
SATURN    Rahu      beginning on 03/16/1994 at age   54y  2m 14d   for 34m  6d
SATURN    Jupiter   beginning on 01/22/1997 at age   57y  0m 20d   for 30m 12d

MERCURY   Mercury   beginning on 08/04/1999 at age   59y  7m  2d   for 28m 27d
MERCURY   Ketu      beginning on 01/01/2002 at age   61y 11m 29d   for 11m 27d
MERCURY   Venus     beginning on 12/28/2002 at age   62y 11m 26d   for 34m  0d
MERCURY   Sun       beginning on 10/28/2005 at age   65y  9m 26d   for 10m  6d
MERCURY   Moon      beginning on 09/04/2006 at age   66y  8m  2d   for 17m  0d
MERCURY   Mars      beginning on 02/04/2008 at age   68y  1m  2d   for 11m 27d
MERCURY   Rahu      beginning on 02/01/2009 at age   69y  0m 29d   for 30m 18d
MERCURY   Jupiter   beginning on 08/19/2011 at age   71y  7m 17d   for 27m  6d
MERCURY   Saturn    beginning on 11/25/2013 at age   73y 10m 23d   for 32m  9d

KETU      Ketu      beginning on 08/04/2016 at age   76y  7m  2d   for  4m 27d
KETU      Venus     beginning on 01/01/2017 at age   76y 11m 29d   for 14m  0d
KETU      Sun       beginning on 03/01/2018 at age   78y  1m 29d   for  4m  6d
KETU      Moon      beginning on 07/07/2018 at age   78y  6m  5d   for  7m  0d
KETU      Mars      beginning on 02/07/2019 at age   79y  1m  5d   for  4m 27d
KETU      Rahu      beginning on 07/04/2019 at age   79y  6m  2d   for 12m 18d
KETU      Jupiter   beginning on 07/22/2020 at age   80y  6m 20d   for 11m  6d
KETU      Saturn    beginning on 06/28/2021 at age   81y  5m 26d   for 13m  9d
KETU      Mercury   beginning on 08/07/2022 at age   82y  7m  5d   for 11m 27d
```

Without going into the intricacies of it all (especially as the TOB may be rounded off), I just want to use this brief commentary to demonstrate some "big picture" Dasa/Bhukti considerations. Watch the chart and Dasa listing during this review:

🕐 He was born during a Mars Dasa (ruler of 3 & 10 — public communication) and Rahu (NN) Bhukti[†]. Mars picks up the energy of religious Jupiter, strong in its own sign of Pisces, and the North Node is direct in the 9th house of religion. But we note that the ruler of the religious 9th is itself dumped into the undoing 12th, and Jupiter is damaged by its association with Mars. In the supporting navamsha (which I will not be showing due to lack of space), Jupiter is also with the Sun in the 9th house.

🕐 The 9th house North Node (Rahu) period consumed his young adult life to age 24 — religious development.

🕐 Age 24 he moved into his Jupiter Dasa and was ordained. Jupiter is not only in its own sign in the 2nd; it also rules the financial 11th (ruling public income as the 2nd from the 10th and generally "money by any other means"). Jupiter is made aggressive by its close association with Mars, but is greatly undermined by a full aspect from an almost stationary Neptune. Financial income from the public is supported by the aspect from the moon to Jupiter noting also that the 8th house rules the resources of others. Financial opportunities abounded during this period. By the way, note that, in the Western chart, Saturn and the South Node are in the 2nd hardly promoting wealth potentials, and Jupiter, ruling the 1st, is in the 1st in Aries hardly explaining his obvious diminutiveness — which a very slow Saturn, ruling the 1st and conjunct the South Node, does explain.

🕐 In 1980 Jessica Hahn was allegedly seduced. At this point the Jupiter period had just ended, and this was the beginning of his Saturn Dasa — and apparently the beginning of his subsequent unraveling. As Saturn rules his 1st house (and 12th), he now meets himself. Saturn had very little velocity at birth and is fallen not only in the main (rasi) chart but also in the navamsha. It is closely

---

[†] *All Dasa/Bhukti listings begin with the first Bhukti shift after birth, in this case into Jupiter.*

conjunct the "weird and undoing" South Node, and this is also true in the navamsha. Saturn also aspects Venus (women) in his 12th since Saturn aspects the 10th house from itself. But the Venus issue remained hidden until...

May, 1987 is when he actually moved into the Venus Bhukti thus revealing the Saturn aspect link to the 12th house Venus issue. Issues associated with the almost stationary Neptune in the 8th also became animated: fraud with regard to other people's money and allegations of homosexuality. Note again that Saturn's own dispositor (the malefic Mars) is conjunct his 2nd house Jupiter. The trial and breakdown also completed during this period. Saturn hardens the quality of the 12th which it not merely aspects but also rules.

The important thing to note here is how this commentary flowed so easily and completely without regard to transits, progressions or any other considerations which would have brought in even much more precision and confirmation. And it is generally deducible from your current basic knowledge of Western planets, signs and houses. There can be some significant differences in house meanings, but I will try not to emphasize them as they will generally not be necessary for the narrow purpose of this book.

Example: Casper Weinberger

I will use a second final example to reinforce some of the points noted above. You may recall that, on Christmas Eve 1992, former President Bush pardoned former Secretary of Defense Casper Weinberger from continuing his battle with the congressional special prosecutor over what was referred to as the Iran–Contra Scandal or "Contragate."

Officially, Weinberger was born on 18-Aug-1917 @ 3:10 PM PST in San Francisco, CA 37N47 & 122W25 (see chart # 2). This gives a natal MC of 12-LI-51. On the day he was pardoned, T. (transiting) Jupiter was at 12-LI-51 — thus seemingly presenting an open and shut case for the perfection of his birth time. But there was one big problem: when I reviewed the issue from the point of view of the Hindu chart, it simply wasn't likely that he could be pardoned until near the end of 1993!

A TOB of 15:10 clearly gives Sagittarius–rising tropically and just barely (by only minutes of arc) sidereally. When I saw this chart years ago I

5th Pisces	6th Aries	7th Taurus	8th Gemini
		Jupiter 16°03'	Ketu Rx 17°17' Mars 21°48' ♇

4th Aquarius	JUPITER Ketu	beginning on 11/11/1981	9th Cancer
	JUPITER Venus	beginning on 10/17/1982	Saturn 14°24'
	JUPITER Sun	beginning on 06/17/1985	
	JUPITER Moon	beginning on 04/05/1986	
	JUPITER Mars	beginning on 08/05/1987	♆
	JUPITER Rahu	beginning on 07/11/1988	

3rd Capricorn	SATURN Saturn	beginning on 12/05/1990	10th Leo
	SATURN Mercury	beginning on 12/08/1993	Sun 2°47'
	SATURN Ketu	beginning on 08/17/1996	Moon 15°48'
	SATURN Venus	beginning on 09/26/1997	Mercury 29°45'
	SATURN Sun	beginning on 11/26/2000	
♓	SATURN Moon	beginning on 11/08/2001	
	SATURN Mars	beginning on 06/08/2003	

2nd Sagittarius	1st Scorpio	12th Libra	11th Virgo
Rahu Rx 17°17'	Ascendant 29°55'		Venus 3°06'
	USING 3:08 PM		

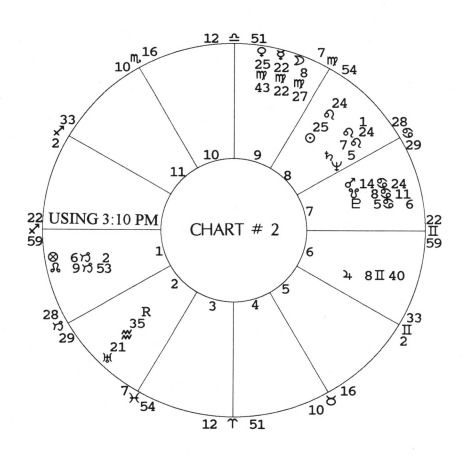

thought, oh well, he's a lawyer ruled by Jupiter, etc. However, using Hindu full-sign houses this would put Saturn in his 8th (note: this chart is not shown). By the rules of Hindu aspecting, this would put a clear block on his 10th (3rd from itself) —especially during its Dasa or Bhukti period. Even using any nearby TOB, Weinberger went into his Saturn Dasa in early 1991, and he could not yet have moved into any potentially offsetting Bhukti period. So pure Saturn was definitely in effect, and this should have blocked a pardon.

My initial thought was: oh well, a block on the 10th makes sense with the prosecutor's assault on Weinberger's prestige and status, etc. But as I looked at it, I began to think: given the somewhat mediocre look of this chart, how could Weinberger *ever* have achieved the long career of status and prestige government positions that he indeed held — and with good reputation. Indeed a close reading of the political press finds his many presidential patrons repeatedly extolling him as a key player behind the scenes who helped various administrations achieve many of their more memorable accomplishments. In fact, the Western chart has no planets in the 10th, the ruler of the MC fallen in the 9th, the ruler of the 1st feebly placed by sign and house, etc. etc. Perhaps there was a cometoid named Capstar somewhere that explained it all?

But getting back to the real world, if you backed up his TOB by only 2 minutes (to 3:08 PM) then you get sidereal Scorpio-rising (and this made me think of his OMB nickname of "Cap The Knife"). See the revised Hindu chart # 2 on the same page (original Hindu chart not shown). This gives an MC 32 minutes earlier of 12-LI-19. Then I discovered that the White House had asked Weinberger's attorneys a week before Christmas eve to send them a letter requesting that he be pardoned. At *that* time, T. Jupiter was on Weinberger's new MC exactly to the minute.

As you now know, changing a rising sign in the Hindu system puts every single planet into a different house and changes nearly every single house ruler. Could he have Scorpio-rising? Without doubt. For now what jumps out is the fact that Weinberger has a relatively rare "rajayoga" condition. In the case of a Scorpio-rising, this only occurs when the Sun and Moon occupy the same house. Not only is this true for Weinberger, but they happen to join in his 10th. And not only is it in the 10th; the Sun is in its own house in the regal Leo which it rules (and the Moon is vargottama). Any Hindu astrologer would immediately declare his public fame from this formation alone. Mercury is yet a third planet in his sidereal 10th.

This 2 minute TOB difference would define Weinberger's exceptional career reality where sidereal Sagittarius-rising simply would not. Additionally, because natal Saturn is now in the 9th and not the 8th, it takes its block off of Weinberger's 10th (thus not precluding the pardon) and puts the block onto his 11th where he natally has a fallen Venus. Weinberger has never been a particularly wealthy man as a result of dedicating himself to government service (an example of how a good planet can be a good news/bad news joke when it is fallen), and the financial pressure of defending himself was part of Bush's motivation for the pardon. Saturn also now aspects Weinberger's 6th house (10th from the 9th), and Weinberger's health was further cited by Bush as part of his motivation.

You may recall that pre-natal eclipses were mentioned in the Introduction, and I will be extensively referencing them in later sections. As a "warm up" to what we will soon be getting into, here are some supplemental Weinberger facts (other than T. Jupiter noted above) as of the pardon date:

> 02-CP-44 = the first eclipse after he was conceived
> 02-CP-28 = the transiting eclipse on the day of the pardon
>
> 24-LE-14 = the last new moon the day before he was born
> 24-SC-21 = transiting Pluto on the day of the pardon
>
> 17-CA-29 = another pre-natal eclipse
> 17-CA-26 = George Bush's Venus
> 17-CP-12 = transiting Uranus on the pardon date
>
> 18-CP-05 = transiting Neptune on the pardon date
> 17-CA-47 = his tertiary Midheaven (see next chapter)
>
> 18-GE-10 = the last transiting eclipse before the pardon
> 18-GE-47 = his secondary Moon on the pardon date
>   (natal Moon exactly squares Jupiter)
>
> 27-GE-39 = another pre-natal eclipse
> 26-SA-14 = his secondary Midheaven on the pardon date

Closing again on the main topic, Rudolph Nureyev also died around the time of Weinberger's pardon (DOD: 06–Jan–93). He was born on a moving train on 17–March–1938 thus raising the question of whether his astrology chart would look blurred, but certainly his life was a blur of motion and rootlessness. This highly energetic dancer, famous for his leaps, who was almost thrown out of school for his inability to keep still, has tropical Mars in Taurus (remember: sluggish? rooted?), but sidereal Mars in Aries.

The only possible Western argument is that Mars is within 6 applying degrees of being conjunct Uranus (also in "Taurus"), but that hardly fits. One reviewer of this draft suggested that perhaps it was due to a cometoid named Rudy in sextile to the midpoint of two imaginary planets, but I'm inclined to think that perhaps he was just kidding. Actually, from this point forward I will generally stop making invidious comparisons of Eastern to Western charts, but I encourage you to pay attention to these types of issues.

The last quarter moon before Nureyev was born was 18–GE–08 and the first quarter moon after he was born was at 02–CP–45. The last transiting eclipses before his death matched exactly at 18–GE–10 and 02–CP–28. Due to his worldwide fame, it's even possible that he may have been conceived on a further matching eclipse at 17–GE–36 (on 08–June–37). He also had another pre–natal eclipse at 25–TA–35; transiting Pluto at death was at 24–SC–46. You will see a lot of this in the last half of this book.

Exalted and Fallen Degrees

Throughout this book you will see occasional reference to a planet being on, or very near, its most exalted, or most fallen, degree position. This is a reference to the degree of longitude where a planet can achieve its very best results, or conversely where a planet is least able to function well. The maximum exaltation degree (sidereal, of course) for each planet is as follows. The exact opposite degree is where that same planet would be most deeply fallen. And applying towards its exaltation degree is always better than applying towards its fallen degree.

SU	MO	ME	VE	MA	JU	SA
10-AR	3-TA	15-VI	27-PI	28-CP	5-CA	20-LI

Here is a re-summary of planetary condition codes that you will find on the Hindu charts:

D	—	Direct at less than 10% of normal speed
e	—	Close to the Edge of a sign (just a warning)
E	—	Exalted sign
F	—	Fallen sign
M	—	Moolatrikona sign
O	—	Own sign
R	—	Raja Yoga karaka
Rx	—	Motion is Retrograde
S	—	Moving Slowly (less than 20% of normal speed)
T	—	Trikona
+	—	in a Friend's sign
++	—	in a great Friend's sign
-	—	in an Enemy's sign
--	—	in a great Enemy's sign

A "squiggle" shows a mutual reception

Let's now move on to a quick review of tertiary progressions.

AN INTRODUCTION TO
TERTIARY PROGRESSIONS

For many years I've used tertiary progressions ("P3") as a very fundamental tool in my astrological work. I remain utterly amazed that there continues to be almost no reference to it in the astrological literature although there is some long out-of-print German material from the 1950's on "tertiary directions" by E. H. Troinski. For clarity, I should note here that my understanding of what Troinski did (dividing the year by the sidereal month and using each of these blocks of 13-14 days as representing a year in the life) may, in fact, be related to what will be explained in this chapter and used throughout this book.

I've considered writing a separate book about it myself, but I'm convinced that all I would end up doing in the end is little more than listing hundreds of client examples (the literary equivalent of sputtering and flapping my arms) because the results, when viewed directly, are so crisp and often startling that explanation is generally gratuitous. And, when it is used in conjunction with the Hindu Dasa system, it provides a level of technical assurance that has allowed me to guarantee certain aspects of my work — including double-your-money-back guarantees under the appropriate circumstances.

I should note here that I don't actually use full tertiary charts per se; what I do use are the tertiary planets and tertiary solar arc'd MC (and derived ASC) as they hit the natal chart. That doesn't mean that I've rejected use of the full tertiary chart itself, I've just never felt much of a need to look into it — particularly since I've never had much interest in Western intermediate house cusps to begin with.

Here is a beginning definition: If you understand what a secondary progression (P2) is, where each day in the life starting at birth is symbolically equated to each subsequent year in the life, then just think of a tertiary progression (P3) as being a simple variation on this, i.e., a day in the life (or ephemeris) is equal to a lunar *month* in the life (i.e., a little less than an average calendar month).

For example, the 12th day of life has a symbolic linkage to the 12th lunar month of life. What this immediately implies is that P3's move at a rate about 12 times faster than P2's. This eliminates the most annoying problem associated with P2's which is that nothing seems to move at all except the Moon, and it isn't exactly whipping along.

Sometimes it seems you have to wait half your life just to get a P2 angle to conjunct or oppose a natal planet. That may be fine for outlining "big picture" life cycles, but it's fairly useless for the finer level of granularity at which most people lead their lives. Put another way, most people live their lives from month to month and not from year to year. Tertiary progressions provide a lively and accurate tool to map this reality. They essentially plug the previously vacant middle ground between secondaries and transits.

Historically, the Moon has always had much more of a reputation as a timing mechanism than the Sun. Anyway, the Sun hardly goes away in the P3 system. In fact, it continues to progress at about the same rate as the common P2 moon, i.e., roughly a degree per month. The really ancient Arabic, Chinese and Hindu zodiacs were actually lunar, with 27–28 "lunar mansions" (sometimes referred to as "nakshatras", "asterisms", "manzils", "sieu", or "constellations") basically equal in length to the daily mean motion of the Moon as opposed to the more modern derived concept of "signs" of the Sun.

Nakshatras are often clustered into types, but not contiguously. Although I didn't mention it in the last chapter, in Hindu astrology the derivation of what Dasa and Bhukti one is born into is based upon what nakshatra or constellation the Moon occupies at birth, and which planet rules it. Currently in India, nakshatras are heavily used in electional work including the arrangement of marriages. This book will basically not discuss nakshatras at all although I will make some occasional references just to keep the concept alive in your mind.

This lunar emphasis was further highlighted by Rodney Collin in his excellent *Theory of Celestial Influence*, and by A. T. Mann in *The Round Art* and his later works. They articulated the concept of the "typical" life as having 1,000 months from conception. They broke this down into four logarithmic stages, each of which is subjectively experienced as being of equal duration through time: conception (month 1), end of gestation (month 10), end of childhood (month 100) and end of life (month 1,000) all of which, as it turns out, is equal to one transiting Uranus cycle, i.e., about 84 years. The number 84 is an interesting multiple of 7 and 12, the harmonics of which we again otherwise find driving numerous key "occult" cycles.

[By the way, ancient Vedic texts indicate a belief that the natural un-degraded human life span is actually 120, and not 84, years. In the hugely popular American movie "Terminator 2", it was therefore amusing to hear Arnold Schwarzenegger, while acting the role of a robot, describe his own design parameters as including a life span of 120 years — al-though, just like most humans, he managed to terminate it well ahead of time.

As yet a further aside on these "occult" numbers, you may recall that the human spine has 7 cervical (neck-related) vertebrae and 12 thoracic (mid back-related) vertebrae. Chiropractic theory holds that each vertebra has a direct link to specific functional areas of body systems (glandular, eliminative, nerve, digestive, musculoskeletal and circulatory). Many readers are probably aware of the numerous other "occult" design fea-tures of the human body.]

If we assume you will live to be 84 years old (i.e., about 1,000 "regular" months), then by P3 you will have worked your way through about 1,100 lines in the ephemeris which is a point about 3 years from where you started. This will produce facts such as that P3 Mercury will have com-pletely circled your chart over twice, and all by itself will give you per-haps 20 P3 lifetime stations.

If you have Gemini or Virgo rising (sidereally, of course), this will, with-out doubt, define 20 significant life reversals. Venus will do about the same, especially for Libra rising, but will provide fewer stations (maybe 5), and so forth. In general, you could easily get over 50 P3 planetary stations, roughly 10 progressed eclipses, and lots of progressed sign changes (again speaking sidereally). Using only P2 you may get almost none of this thereby missing all the true action.

The implications of tertiary stations, eclipses and sidereal sign changes are *profound* since they identify, to the month, the fundamental shifts and amplitude fluctuations in a person's life. This does not even con-sider the second layer of fundamentals which include exact hard aspect hits by P3 angles and planets to natal planets and angles. To be very clear: *this stuff works*, and if you don't use it, you are significantly asleep at the switch in terms of predictive potency.

Even more amazing, I have found a very close correlation of this activity with the Hindu Dasa system even though the official word on the Dasa system is that India's best mathematicians have yet to figure out when, where or how it was derived. For example, I've often noticed that P3 Saturn will go stationary during a Saturn period, Jupiter during a Jupiter period, or Mars during a Mars period. Alternatively, for example, Mars may go stationary during a Mercury period. Typically they will be tightly involved natally, and this will have a profound effect upon Mercury.

Considering that there is no documented crossover between these Eastern and Western systems that I am aware of, I find this correlation *very* interesting indeed. For lack of a more charming label, let's modestly call it: *Houck's Law*. To be explicit about Houck's Law: there will often be an "appropriate" correlation between the current Bhukti (or Dasa) planet and a corresponding progressed planetary station, particularly at death. You will have the opportunity to see many examples of this.

Earlier I noted that tertiary progressions, as I use the term, are based upon a "lunar month," and this is the tropical equinoctal moon (zero Aries to zero Aries). Its value is 27.321582 — very close to the non-precessed sidereal moon (27.321661). Despite being a "siderealist," I use the tropical (vs. sidereal) lunar month since, practically speaking, this has nothing to do with zodiac issues per se. In addition, I do not worry about precession since the practical impact of both, particularly as it applies to progressions, is quite inconsequential[†] (7 seconds of clock time monthly).

I happened into tertiary progressions through Mark Pottenger's default settings as programmed into his technically-excellent CCRS software. He calculates lunar returns before and after the date being inquired about in order to have an exact lunar month instead of an averaged, or mean, one. The MC is progressed by solar arc with all other cusps calculated from that.

This is not the same as moving all points by a value equal to the solar arc ("arc directing"), and also should not be confused with two other common methods of progressing the MC which are 1) Quotidian (true day-for-a-year angles that move the MC about 361 degrees every 24 hours), and 2) Naibod in RA (referred to within CCRS as Right Ascension of the Mean Sun) which moves the MC about 1 degree every 24 hours.

[†] *Although, if I were to begin discussing lunar returns, which I won't, I favor and recommend use of the sidereal zodiac.*

Further, none of this is to be confused with a "minor progression" where each lunar month after birth is equated to a year in the life. Reputable people speak well of this technique, but I have not found it useful. If any confusion remains on these technical points, full chart data is provided for all the cases I discuss. So you have an opportunity to either attempt a simulation of the many progressed points I will clearly identify, or to experiment in a more knowledgeable way with the other alternatives.

Returning to matters of application, the practical upshot of all this is that the P3 Sun and MC move around the chart at about 1 degree per month with the P3 Asc typically at a very slight variation on this. This therefore has the P3 angles in their respective signs/houses about 2 & 1/2 years (about as long as transiting Saturn spends in a sign/house), and the P3 Sun will take about as long to circle the chart as transiting Saturn. The P3 Moon moves roughly 1/2 a degree per day; therefore it will spend about 2 months in each sign, and take about 2 years to circle the entire chart.

Exact Timing of Events Using Tertiaries

Another key point to note is that tertiaries are, to me, the single most rapid and useful tool in minor rectifications. Unlike secondaries, at major life events you can *routinely* expect tertiary angles and planets to be in a perfect 4th harmonic aspect (conjunction, square or opposition) to relevant natal factors. Read that: *to the degree* (if not to the minute).

A simple rule of thumb is that a one–week error in the occurrence of an angular life event is equal to about one clock minute of birth time error. For example, did a client get hit by a bus when the P3 Asc was still one full applying degree from being conjunct N. Mars? This is the same as saying that she got hit about a month before she "should" have. Add four minutes to her TOB, and watch the rest of the chart lock more firmly into place. Watch transits perform with more precision, and so forth.

Let me now show an example of this (see chart # 3). This person was born on 13–Dec–1964 in Rahway, NJ (40N36 & 74W17). She said she was born at "3:00" PM EST. Since I'm inclined to think that "nobody" is born right on the hour, this made me a little nervous because it could mean 2:45 or 3:15 if not worse. This could cause months of error using my methods. In May of 1993 she inquired about a major job promotion she thought her company could be considering her for. Keeping my worry in mind about her TOB, I could still tell her, with reasonable certainty, that she was not likely to get a promotion until "around January" 1994. In fact, she received a huge promo-

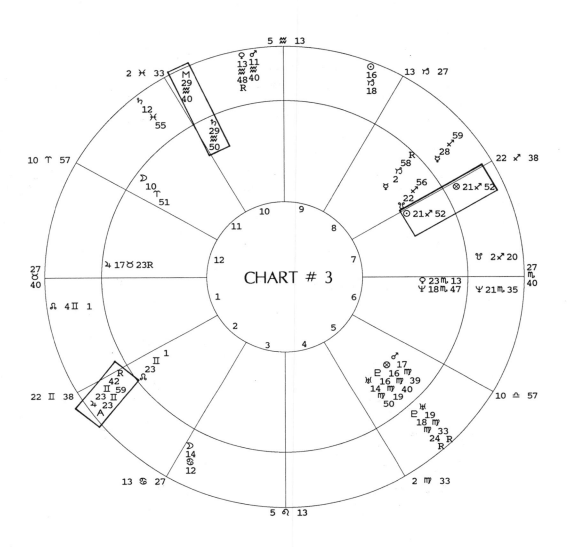

TERTIARY PROGRESSION EXAMPLE

A MAJOR PROMOTION

Natal Inside; Tertiary Outside

tion on 1/24/94, making her the youngest person ever to hold such a high position in this "household name" corporation (P3=1/7/66).

On January 24, her P3 Asc was conjunct her P3 Jupiter (within 17 separating minutes), and her P3 MC was conjunct her N. Saturn (within 10 applying minutes). Two initially seductive adjustments would have been to make it 2:56 when her P3 Asc would conjunct her P3 Jupiter TTM, or 2:58 when her P3 MC would conjunct N. Saturn TTM. But clearly we are dealing with a phenomena that constrains her TOB, without any doubt, into a zone of 2:56 PM to 2:58 PM. I finally settled on an adjusted TOB of 2:57:20 PM (which is the one shown) for two reasons: 1) it has her P3 Part of Fortune (P3 Asc + P3 Sun – P3 Moon) conjunct her N. Sun TTM, and 2) it also has T. Pluto conjunct her Desc TTM. Notice that natally she has Pluto conjunct her Part of Fortune.

By the way, there were two other planetary signals confirming January:

> Saturn: N. Saturn has status being in its own sign in the 10th house. She was now having an exact Saturn return, with T. Saturn at 29-AQ-30. Her 10th house is also a strong house by a Hindu pointing system (called Ashtakavarga) which allows it to absorb and deploy this strong Saturn rather than being victimized by it.

> Venus: She had tertiary progressed just into the P3 date of 1/7/66. You will note that this makes Venus essentially stationary and, in Washington D.C. where she works, N. Venus is upon her relocated Desc to the exact same degree, thus being exceptionally well-received by her Taurus Asc (yes, she is also very pretty). And, at this point, you shouldn't be surprised to find out that she is also in a Venus Dasa thus making all this possible.

Let me mention how tertiaries initially caught my eye. When unknown clients would call me out of the blue, I'd record the date and time of the call, and then would begin to crank out what was my former set of standard materials. Working at the computer one day, I decided to see what an exotic thing called a "tertiary progression" would produce.

When I ran the client's P3, I noticed that his P3 Asc was exactly conjunct my Sun. Interesting coincidence, I thought. Anyway, as you probably expect, and to make a long story short, a variation on this happened with almost every single client that I've subsequently had, i.e., their progressed Sun, Moon, Asc, Equatorial Asc or MC was exactly, to the same sign and degree, conjunct a similar factor (although never exactly the same factor as the client's) in my chart — or vice versa.

This still happens to this day. A woman who has recently become a very good friend of mine (born 18–Jan–1967 @ 01:01 AM EST per BC in Mt. Vernon, NY 40N55 & 073W50) was told (Mercury) about me on 11/3/92 when her P3 Sun and Mercury were both at 6–CP–43 (which is my tropical Asc to the minute), and she subsequently met me a short while later when the P3 ruler of her 1st (Venus) was exactly conjunct the natal ruler of my 1st (Jupiter) at 26–SC. As an exercise, you can verify this yourself by looking up the date her chart had tertiary progressed to (call it her "P3 date") which was 12/29/67 (to reinforce: the number of days between this date and her birth date is the number of lunar months she has experienced since birth).

The Clarity of Tertiary Symbolism

Tertiaries can be dramatically informative in client counselling. I will give this example, but I need to mask the overt data for obvious reasons. In August of 1993 I had an astrologically–literate client referred to me who had a number of major things going on in her life, but she just couldn't see it either in the western natal chart nor via standard western methods of timing. Even before she arrived, I knew that one of the key things we would be discussing was the fact that her P3 Mars was exactly conjunct a P3 Saturn that had itself gone totally stationary. Her 12th house Saturn ruled her 7th and 8th, so I assumed there would be a total blockage concerning these matters. This was confirmed by the Hindu data indicating that this was the month she was moving into a multi–year Saturn Bhukti. Further, T. Saturn was at the cusp of her 8th.

It further turned out that her tertiary progression date (within 1946) as of the month of our consultation was, in fact, the exact month, day and year of her husband's birth (she spotted this on my computer printout, and pointed it out to me). Unknown to her, she had progressed by P3 to her husband's exact date of birth. Without going into a lot of supportively interesting technical detail, one of the key discussion topics was his sexual withdrawal and apparent impotence. Go back to what I just wrote, and you can see how this fits perfectly. Tertiary progressions give these kinds of obvious clues all the time, and progressed stations are invariably motivating and clinically informative.

Here is a different kind of case of a woman born 3–Aug–1948 @ 6:47 AM (central STANDARD time) at 37N59 & 87W33. She was in a Saturn Bhukti, and Saturn rules her 7th. She came home on 6/17/92 and was astonished to find that her long–time boyfriend had taken all his possessions and moved out. When you run the tertiaries, you find that her P3 Desc was exactly conjunct natal Neptune (as a precision note: if her TOB had been recorded only seconds earlier, this progressed conjunction would have been exact to the minute. Instead, there was 10 minutes of applying arc deviation which erroneously suggested that this event would not have happened for 3 more days).

Part of the energy for a male disappearance from her home is arguably found in the fact that natally her Mars, as ruler of her 4th, is exactly conjunct Neptune. The T. Uranus/Neptune conjunction was exactly conjunct her P3 Moon (which was also exactly opposing her N. Moon), but the angle progression best told the story of the disappearing mate (P3 Desc conjunct Neptune). Her P3 Uranus was also only a few days from its own station, and other interesting features supported this event.

I have another sample on the same theme, and it reinforces how the Dasa and Bhukti will set up the situation, and the tertiary progressions will give the exact timing to set it off — in this case, right to the day. This is the case of a divorced female who was born on 20–Sept–1943 @ 1:03 PM CWT at 35N28 & 97W31. If you run this chart, you will see that it is generally very unstable in relationships with Uranus almost totally angular at the Desc and further agitated by Mars only a few degrees away.

On 9/21/92 she had a major shock when her boyfriend told her that he was seeing someone else. In the Hindu system this was during a Saturn Dasa and Sun Bhukti. In the Western system this date turned out to be the exact day that her P3 Sun was conjunct P3 Saturn if you add only 15 seconds to her given birth time (her P3 Moon was also conjunct N. Uranus). The link of these two planets to her relationships is that her (Bhukti) Sun is perfectly square to her (Dasa) Saturn, and this Saturn is only five degrees from her 7th house Moon. When the perfect natal square became an even more perfect P3 conjunction, the inherent symbolism manifested during their Dasa and Bhukti periods.

Progressed stations also have terrific applicability in political analysis. In the Summer of 1993 I was solicited to write an extensive article for an international astrological publication that would primarily address the question of which U.S. chart was the correct one and then to do some national forecasts. I concluded to my own satisfaction that the United States was actually "born" 14–15 days before 04–July–1776, and this whole argument was fundamentally reinforced primarily through the use of progressed stations on truly major events in the history of the U.S. I now use 6/19/1776 at 11:53:50 AM in Philadelphia, PA, and have found considerable effectiveness in my regularly documented political forecasting work. As far as I can determine, this date means nothing historically.

You can watch the twists and turns of politicians, and even other countries, through this same mechanism. People wondered: how in the world did Dan Quayle, a political "nobody", get picked for Vice President in the 1988 election? The answer is that he was having a P3 Jupiter station the month he was picked (and George Bush was selected for Vice President the year he himself was having a P2 Jupiter station). Saddam Hussein attacked Kuwait on the exact month he was having a P3 Pluto station. We retaliated on the exact month that Saddam's P3 Mercury went stationary (as I forecast in writing five months ahead of the fact). Kuwait itself was having an exact P2 Neptune station the year it was attacked, and so on.

Speaking of former President George Bush: in a widely distributed newsletter article postmarked 12/10/91, I wrote that it was "at least safe to say that something critically personal *will* happen to George Bush between 01/04/92 and 02/24/92 that will have an impact on the country as a whole...(and)...this reminds me of a cerebral hemorrhage or something spasmodic." In fact, he vomited and blacked out at a formal dinner in Tokyo on 01/08/92, and the televised images caused significant concern within the United States about his overall health.

My forecast article gave detailed reasoning for this unequivocal assertion, but for purposes of this chapter, a key component was the fact that George Bush would be having three (!) P3 planets going stationary during that period. First was Uranus (which natally squares his Sun), second was Mars, and third was Mercury (which natally squares Mars). Following are a few other examples of the effect of progressed stations in the charts of politicians.

President Richard Nixon was expelled from office the year he was having a P2 Pluto station (and you will see how he died on a P3 station). Boris Yeltsin was elected the first President of Russia on the exact month when he was having both a P2 and a P3 Pluto station. He got into a position of extreme weakness at the end of Sept 1993, which I had forecast (almost to the week) in writing well ahead of time. This was because his P3 Neptune had gone stationary exactly at that time. And that's when he had to barricade himself in the Kremlin and make deals with the military to keep the parliamentary coup plotters from taking over the government. Bill Clinton will be having a P3 Neptune station the exact month of the 1996 U.S. election. Much more goes into it than this, but hopefully I am capturing your attention on this point. Tertiary stations contribute the issue of *amplitude*, and its implications, to all chart considerations.

I have another more refined observation on the "twists and turns of politicians" mentioned above, but of course this will apply to anyone. I'm not a big "believer" in the concept that, when transiting Mercury goes retrograde, the entire world goes haywire with regard to Mercury matters. Unbiased observation shows that simply is not true — except perhaps around the day of the reversals themselves. But, in the chapter on Hindu astrology, you already learned a clue about what personalizes planets over extended periods (the Dasa/Bhukti system).

This is the unseen "Factor X" that actually controls the true malfunction of transiting retrograde planets. If, for example, someone is in a Mercury Bhukti period, and transiting Mercury goes retrograde, then Mercury really will malfunction in a sustained and obvious way. The limit of malfunction is related to the extent of natal strength or weakness of the planet, and what the planet rules.

What if Mercury goes retrograde by tertiary progression (as will happen many times in a normal lifespan)? Even if the person is not ruled by Mercury, there will still be a noteworthy reversal of direction in their thinking. Alternatively, something obviously mercurial will become dominant in their life. For example, many people win awards on progressed Mercury stations.

If a person's chart is actually ruled by Mercury, such as current U.S. President Bill Clinton or Ross Perot, then there will be an obvious reversal of direction in their intentions, plans or direction on the month of the progressed station. If they are also in a Mercury Dasa or Bhukti, the effect is magnified all the more. Remember that progression systems, whether East or West, personalize what are otherwise impersonal transits.

In the last half of this book a high volume of symbolically appropriate tertiary considerations will be presented for your consideration. These will all be within one degree of orb and usually much less. 95% will be simple conjunctions, squares and oppositions, i.e., those aspects which incite activity. Although I will be graphically showing and discussing the base data, I will not be showing the progressed and transiting data in order to prevent visual overload. Therefore, these latter chapters cannot be outright read; they can only be studied. Of course, I will be providing and discussing the data in great detail.

If you have the software to recreate and display tertiary progressed chart data (relative to natal chart data), I recommend that you do so because the pattern is much stronger when visually observed rather than merely described. Additionally, your chart data should match the data that I will be describing. If it doesn't, and excluding descriptive errors on my part, you should attempt to find out why it does not.

By the way, as a result of reading the first printing of this book, Das Goravani (see page 359) has implemented a report listing a lifetime (120 years) of tertiary progressed stations, and he has matched these stations on the report to the Dasa/Bhukti periods. This is quite unique.

MARAKAS

"Killer" Planets for Each Sidereal Ascendant

This section raises the theoretical question of whether we can know, from the Hindu natal chart, what planetary factors make a more direct contribution to our earthly transition. Does any planet achieve functional "killer" status (i.e., become a "maraka" or death indicator) in a natal chart and, if so, how did it get that way?

Of course, this imputes a causal vs. synchronous metaphysic, but I will be addressing this question more from a Hindu point of view, and they are not "into" Carl Jung. So here we enter into a kind of topsy turvy world where good planets (such as Venus and Jupiter) can easily "go bad" or become functionally malefic.

> "It's so hard to understand, officer;
> he always seemed like such a *nice* boy..."

RULE # 1: A planet becomes a potential killer simply by virtue of ruling (primarily) the 2nd or (secondarily) the 7th house. As this is generally without regard to the inherent nature of the planet, it is an argument for environment over heredity, and is contested by those who completely reject even the possibility of Jupiter ever becoming a killer, or of Mars ever being rehabilitated. But we often see a prominent Jupiter in death situations, and we are all aware of deaths that have a Jupiterian quality — if only by being heavily trined which Jupiter itself symbolizes.

Rule # 1 also raises the initial question of what planet rules the 2nd house. This implies the need to correctly determine the true ruler of the 1st. So what will now follow is some background on the topic that further supplements what was given in the Hindu chapter. My key objective over the next few pages is to sneak up on you and rearrange your brain cells with an argument that hopefully will "flip upside down" your current understanding of the 1st, 2nd, 7th and 8th houses. But be aware that this inversion of house meanings is only applicable to the discussion of death. Here we go.

Determining The True Ascendant

When a Hindu astrologer asks your sign, he is asking for your Ascending sign, and sometimes the Moon sign, but *not* your Sun sign. While acknowledging the life-giving creative quality of the Sun and a certain number of other positive astrological attributes, Hindu astrologers nevertheless lump it, in a preliminary way, into the category of "bad" planets. Unlike the West, they give no abnormal focus to your Sun sign, although it is one of the indicators of the soul. If India had not been located at such a hot latitude I sometimes wonder whether their solar symbolism would have taken such a bad hit.

Since the Hindu culture is not as aggressively self-referential as the West, your rising sign is not much used to make statements about the alleged qualities of your personality, developmental attributes, "mask" or whatever. Their real reason for wanting to know your Asc is basically to discover what planet rules it, what house it occupies plus all its aspects and relationships. The planet ruling the sidereal Asc has a much stronger hold over the entire chart than that attributed by a typical Western astrologer.

As you recognize by now, I've become convinced that Western astrology has become so "sign-oriented" because it allows for vague statements that are hard to refute, and this encourages a high degree of selective perception and self attribution. If you are said to have Cancer rising, a Western astrologer could declare you "moody," and this would direct your attention to all the times you had, in fact, been moody. But if you had Cancer rising in the Hindu system, the astrologer would immediately look for the Moon. If it is (exalted) in Taurus (in the 11th), and conjunct Venus (in its own sign), this would lead to very specific positive statements about 11th house-related matters, assuming other factors did not contradict.

[However, let me counterpoint here that there are some Western astrological texts of a psychoanalytic or psycho-therapeutic nature that are outstanding in the quality of their commentary. An example might be Liz Greene's classic book on *Saturn*. What I heartily suggest is that the reader take the commentary from books such as these, and apply it directly to the Hindu signs and houses. I think you will be very favorably impressed by the improved applicability. For example, if I have a client coming who has Saturn in the Western 11th but Hindu 12th, and this person has just moved into a Saturn period, my clear experience is that he or she would respond absolutely better to Liz Greene's 12th house, rather than 11th house, commentary.]

As already noted, the Hindu rising sign has only about a 25% chance of being the same one calculated by a Western astrologer. The arguable gap between the Eastern (sidereal) and Western (tropical) zodiacs, called the "ayanamsha" and caused by the precession of the equinoxes, is now approximately 23 to 24 degrees depending on whose arguments you accept and which year you are discussing. Speaking approximately, this means that if your Western Asc is less than about 23 degrees of a sign, the Hindu Asc is actually the prior sign. If the Western Asc is above 23 degrees then the sign is likely to remain the same. See the ayanamsha table on page 40 for more precision.

Therefore, for example, if you have 20 degrees of tropical Scorpio rising, your chart is actually ruled by Venus (because Libra is actually rising); if your have 25 degrees of tropical Scorpio rising, your chart is ruled by Mars (because Scorpio actually is rising). Note that Pluto cannot rule a house (neither can Uranus or Neptune). They are not identified in the ancient Hindu system which, however, does assert the existence of "seven visible and five invisible" planets (including the two lunar nodes).

Practically speaking, this absence of the three outer planets seems to be quite an oversight because I have repeatedly seen this deficiency cause extremes of interpretive rationalization that often exceed even those of the West. But over time you will find that the Eastern use of five planets to rule ten signs (excluding "The Lights," i.e., the Sun and the Moon) does present an increasingly attractive and useful symmetry. To resolve this matter I therefore assign no house rulership to the outer planets, but I do leave them in their houses for what they so obviously are and do.

True House Rulerships

The second house is simply the next sign after the first. So, for 20 degrees of tropical Scorpio rising, the second sidereal house would simply be Scorpio; for 25 degrees of tropical Scorpio rising, it would be sidereal Sagittarius. All houses are full sign; therefore there can be no interception. This is no loss as Western astrologers could never make a remotely objective or measurable statement about intercepts in any case. I put it in the class of superstitious concepts where one can "see" what one wants to see.

[Parenthetically, I believe this rulership discrepancy plays interesting havoc with Western horary astrology. In the example above, 20 degrees of tropical Scorpio rising would actually have Venus, and not Mars, ruling the Asc. Mars therefore rules the Desc. A chart of 30 minutes later would produce a complete flip: the first house would have the same ruler tropically *or* sidereally (Mars) with Venus now ruling the 7th (Taurus). Under these two alternate circumstances, suppose Venus were separating from Mars and a relationship question was asked about which party is moving away from the other. Excluding luck, I would argue that a Western horary chart starts out with only about a 25% chance of answering correctly depending upon whether the degree rising is higher or lower than 23 degrees.

As far as I know there is no objective evidence to disprove this likelihood. If Western horary astrologers will open their minds to this possibility and perform some simple tests, they will find that the sidereal zodiac flushes out much of the convoluted mirroring and overlay mechanisms that have muddied their art to an incredible degree. Horary and electional work in the sidereal system has the quality of being more demonstrably clear and straightforward.]

In my experience, a strong "proof" of the sidereal zodiac is the consistently and objectively demonstrable power of its exaltation, rulership and fallen placement guidelines. A close reading of most common tropical astrological literature clearly reveals that there is very little *consistent* interpretive use of these powerfully practical qualities for the simple reason that they *don't work* tropically in a consistent and objectively demonstrable way — except where they also happen to overlap the sidereal zodiac.

For example, Venus in Aries is supposedly a "detrimental" placement being opposite the sign that it rules[†]. Yet it is hard to speak badly of this Venus placement because, as a practical matter, people with this placement usually do very well with Venus–related matters (especially what it rules and where it's placed) because Venus actually has a "75%" chance of being exalted in sidereal Pisces. I'm not talking about states of mind or temperament that are subject to selective perception and soft interpretation. I'm saying its beneficial function is clearly observable in their daily life by others around them. The same could be said of Venus in the first

---

[†] *There is no concept of "detriment" in the Hindu system.*

23 degrees of tropical Scorpio, which is actually sidereal Libra, and many other similar combinations.

For example, if someone has Gemini rising (and therefore a Pisces 10th) with Venus (exalted) in the 10th, then career matters should *objectively* be quite fine excluding all other considerations. Another example might be a former powerful executive I know who tropically has Aquarius rising and Uranus, its Western ruler, in his 3rd. How did he rise up with this? But when you look at it sidereally, you see Capricorn rising with Saturn exalted in Libra in the 10th. I've seen this type of simple but vast discrepancy way too many times to ignore. My decision to use the sidereal zodiac is therefore not particularly scholarly, historical, personal or philosophical. It derives from the School of Looking Around.

Now let's return more directly to our discussion of the 2nd house...or almost.

House–Sign Symbolism

The question may now be raised as to how a house (the 2nd) known primarily for its relationship to income could generate such a killer (on the other hand, maybe that's why there's big money in organized crime!). Let me start the argument by putting this question to the reader: what vast amount of money did the world's vain population spend last year on cosmetics? Is not one of mankind's most fundamental desires to *present* an *attractive* image to the world and the "significant other?" If you agree, then might the Presentation House (the 1st) have more of a natural affinity with the sign of Libra than with the aggressive sign of Aries?

Having made this observation, let's shift momentarily to the 7th. Should not the inherent nature of the key symbol of the opposition aspect (the 1/7 axis) imply the likelihood of Mars (enemies) ruling the 7th (Aries) since Venus partakes more of conjunction than opposition symbolism? So if, as you see me arguing here, Libra actually has the natural affinity to the 1st and not Aries, then Scorpio, ruled by Mars and long associated with death, would have the affinity to the 2nd by succession — and we know that Mars is the plain and simple killer of ancient astrology. So...might the 2nd house have to do with death?

Let's layer on another fact. In the Hindu system, the 3rd and the 8th houses are the two key *life* houses (plus, of course, the 1st) having much to do with desires and vitality respectively. If Taurus, as I am arguing, has the natural affinity to the 8th then Venus should be very strong when placed there. And indeed simple observation will show what powerful life vitality people demonstrate who have Venus in the sidereal 8th house — and which logically must not be true if the 8th were truly Scorpionic, i.e., where Venus would be in detriment. You can further observe that this vitality is not consistently observable when Venus is in the 2nd (unless the 8th house is owned by one of Venus' rulership or exaltation signs and can thus most favorably receive the benefit of Venus' full aspect).

And, keeping the symbolism simple, since the 8th is associated with sex and regeneration (life), should it not have the classical link to seductive Venus instead of Mars (let alone Pluto)? While Mars may rule vascularity, it takes a lot of stretching of its original fundamental mythology to render it sexy. Mars would see sexual conjugation in terms of power and would therefore probably have, at best, the classical motivations of a rapist. Sexual (re)creation is an anabolic activity from a social policy point of view, and Venus is absolutely anabolic — sometimes too much so.

If this 1/2/7/8 house argument (linking Mars "naturally" to the maraka 2nd and 7th) is tentatively accepted, then even further observe that the 2nd and the 7th would be the respectively-derived 12th houses from the 3rd and 8th, and would therefore serve to "secretly undermine" the key function of the life houses. This is definitely an Eastern idea but not purely so. It can be seen in many older Western texts that death was indeed somehow associated with the rulers of the 2nd and the 7th. For example, Alan Leo spoke of it, and Manilius referred to the Descendant as the "Portal of Death" since it is, after all, where the source of all earthly life is "extinguished" every evening.

Actually, this reveals a more hidden reason we temporarily flip the zodiac upside down to discuss death theory. Saturn, the natural karaka (indicator) of death, has its greatest strength when exalted in the sign of Libra. Saturn also becomes a rajayoga karaka all by itself since it rules two good houses (the 4th and 5th). Therefore, this would be the natural configuration to give Saturn maximum status. The sense of Libra as a weakened sign undoubtedly derives from the pervasiveness of Western Sun Sign astrology since the Sun is fallen in Libra. But Saturn can "flourish" for a Libra–rising person.

As a further comment on another "portal of death", the Hindu god of death is Yama, and he is said to reside in the rectum. All ancient systems of healing emphasize fundamentally two things for life to be properly sustained: there must be the means for true nutritional assimilation and vitalization (the intake side), and this must be fully balanced by the effective disposition of waste (the output side). Therefore, in purely physical terms, death is often characterized as a simple result of either deficiency or toxemia. Western culture, with its fear of death (Yama), gives scant attention to the latter half of the equation.

Parenthetically, it is interesting that the registered trade name for a longstanding Western plumbing product is "Sani Flush," since "Sani" is the Indian word for Saturn. Does this help make the point? Actually, the human organism originally evolved from tube–like structures (sea anemones). In further fact, pre–tubelike organisms absorbed nutrients diffusely, but expelled them through a specifically–defined orifice. So the elimination process actually has historical claim to a more structurally–sophisticated ancestry than the digestive process.

Anyway, suffice it to say that the modern simplistic symmetry of Mars–with–Aries–with–the–1st–house, etc. leads to a lot of retroactive "forecasts" and to "happy talk" counselling — for what else can it do? Certainly it has very little to do with the actual origins of astrological thinking. This urge for simple symmetry has helped scramble the meanings of signs and houses and, through these warped constructions, has actually begun to feed backwards, like the bad plumbing I've just mentioned, into a deteriorated understanding of fundamental planetary symbolism.

Signs and houses should never contribute to the definition of planets, but don't we see this all the time? The attempt to somehow render Mars or Pluto "sexy" because of their link to Scorpio (because of its alleged link, in turn, to the 8th house) is an example of this, as is the occasional attempt to assign a temper to Taurus because of its association with bulls (the true symbol has to do with fertility and not bullfighting).

What often seems to drive this reverse engineering of ancient planetary meanings is the felt need of tropical astrologers to explain why, using the example of this latter sign, so many of history's maniacs, and so many policemen, have tropical Taurus Sun signs (sidereally they are usually Mars–ruled Ariens). Please don't tell me they like to keep the peace! Well, this diversion is actually an argument for another day, but I need to at least scorch the trail a little bit for purposes of subsequent commentary.

The Eighth House

In general, much further clarification is also needed about the 8th house per se. One Hindu school thinks it has to do with where the soul goes after death, but I will generally avoid this class of occult speculation if only for its lack of practical applicability. It's also easy to find Hindu authorities who contradict almost any particular metaphysical speculation (for example, I've seen both the last prior life and the immediate future life assigned to the 12th house).

I would like to make the preliminary suggestion that the 8th, as a general rule, provides information about death–related *issues* and the *concept* of death rather than timing the actual death of the chart's primary referent. It can therefore be tested, along with its true ruler(s), toward this purpose.

For example, the 8th house can perhaps be used conceptually to derive a response to a death–related question in a horary chart, or to discuss abortion in a natal chart (e.g., a strong malefic as ruler of the 5th in the 8th or vice versa). It may give clues about the cause and nature of death, and also give some information about deaths occurring in the environment of the chart's primary referent. And if the ruler of this key vitality house is under major stress, then death is elevated as a potential consequence. But in this case, the ruler of the 8th would usually be the *object*, and not the agent, of a planetary transaction.

Put another way, the ruler of the 8th would rarely function as a maraka, but could certainly be acted upon by (other) maraka planets. More fundamentally, the 8th has a lot to do with *life* and longevity. For example, Saturn in the sidereal 8th generally promotes longevity. Whether this longevity is desirable derives from a more extended analysis of the chart. Intrinsic longevity is further discussed in a later chapter.

Speaking of subjects and objects, it is certainly odd that the 8th is alleged to rule both death *and* the possessions of the dead (wills and legacies). If indeed the 7th has more of the affiliation with death, especially those that occur somehow as a result of the action of others, then the 8th, as 2nd from the 7th, makes sense as a "wills and legacies" house, and the contradiction disposes of itself.

In the end, I think the only reason death has any kind of a link to the 8th house is because the 8th is extremely "occult," and death (like sex) is clearly in the class of occult events. But the 8th is *not* a fundamentally morbid or terminal house. Having completed our discussion of Rule #1, let's move on to...

RULE # 2: Rule # 1 isn't quite accurate. Some writers argue that the ruler of the 2nd (and then the 7th) is not necessarily the strongest maraka. Many worthy authorities assert that the strongest maraka is a planet that is conjunct the ruler of the 2nd. An interesting example is if Jupiter rules the 2nd but is exactly conjunct or opposed by Saturn, especially a strong Saturn, and the person goes into a Jupiter Dasa or Bhukti. The result is typically very negative. Note again that this would be during a Jupiter Bhukti and *not* a Saturn Bhukti[†].

Finally, occupants of the 2nd (and 7th), if malefic and strong, are often considered more deadly than its owner since they directly assault the vital 8th (and 1st) with what the Hindus refer to as a full aspect, but what Western astrologers call an opposition.

It is important to have such a general priority sequence, since some authorities assert that death simply cannot occur except in the Dasa and Bhukti periods of planetary marakas. There is even a third level of factors in the very unlikely case these marakas never have a chance to become Dasa and Bhukti planets. An example of this is Saturn conjunct one of the potential marakas. This is because each house has an inherent planetary associate ("karaka" or indicator) and, in the case of the concept of death (an 8th house topic), this indicator is Saturn.

Therefore, a Saturn period, in the example being discussed, could bring about the same consequence as the maraka itself even if the maraka never actually became activated by Dasa or Bhukti. If the karaka Saturn were to conjunct a live maraka, the focus would be compounded (again, depending upon all other considerations).

Parenthetically, Saturn rules time, and this helps explain why the Chinese word for both "clock" and "death" — "zhong" — is exactly the same. This has a further interesting symbolic linkage into follow-up studies of people who have had near death experiences, and who consequently lost their fear of death. One interesting discovery is that a significant

---

[†] *This book will demonstrate many similar examples of the concept of damage by affilial invocation.*

percentage of these individuals are no longer able to wear a watch, i.e., their watch will not keep "correct" time.

Sample Rulership Marakas for Selected Sidereal Ascendants

PISCES	ARIES	TAURUS	GEMINI
AQUARIUS			CANCER
CAPRICORN			LEO
SAGITTARIUS	SCORPIO	LIBRA	VIRGO

With this as some brief background, and using the blank chart above, let's examine half a dozen sidereal Ascendants to pick out some preliminary rulership marakas based upon some commonly-given rules. Just for emphasis, I will highlight normal "good guy" planets. Theory notwithstanding, later in this book we will review real cases for what *really* works.

Aries — Lovely Venus rules both death-inflicting houses (2 & 7), so how lovely can she be? However, some astrological authors do not believe that this Femme Fatale can become a maraka under this rigged circumstance —although I've seen plenty of evidence to suggest she certainly can, and many other good authors agree with me. Perhaps they think it's too obvious, or perhaps, unlike myself, they've just never met that kind of girl... Anyway, some look more to Mercury (ruler of the health house) and karaka Saturn (ruler of an angular house in square to Aries). As I have already pointed out, Venus has the odd quality of being a planet that thrives in the 8th house, as both are vitality factors, and this is especially true when Venus is well reinforced by sign.

Death, however, might occur in a Venus period for an Aries-rising person if Venus is otherwise under exceptional stress, for example in tight natal opposition to Pluto or, in another example, if Venus is natally in the 8th combined with another stressed-out planet (or the ruler of the 1st), and the Dasa/Bhukti of both planets is in effect. This gives a flavor for how this works, so I won't repeat it for the other example Ascendants.

Taurus — Here Saturn is constructive because it rules both the 9th and the 10th so, excluding all other cumulative considerations, its periods won't hang you out to dry. Mercury rules the 2nd, but Mercury is a *very* poor assassin unless it associates with bad friends, and anyway it rules the good 5th. Mars would seem to be a killer as ruler of the 7th and 12th but, for reasons unclear to me, I only sometimes see it flagged as such. So oddly enough Venus, as joint ruler of the 6th and the 1st, is often blamed. But I have found Mars to work as might be more simply expected.

In support of my own observations, I want to note here that many contemporary Indian authorities on this topic will also dutifully list the official marakas as passed down from ancient times, but then, in effect, also say, "well, not really!" For Taurus, Jupiter is also sometimes flagged as a maraka.

Virgo — Here Jupiter could be a problem as the ruler of two houses in a 4th harmonic relationship to the 1st. If Jupiter, for example, as ruler of the 4th and 7th, were to be natally square to Mercury, which rules the other two houses in the harmonic, a Mercury/Jupiter or Jupiter/Mercury Dasa/Bhukti could be highly problematical depending on the usual: natal status, any associates, other aspects, progressions, transits, eclipse patterns, and so forth. Mars, as ruler of the two vitality houses, is also monitored for vitality malfunction.

Scorpio — Venus rules the 7th and the 12th and so again can be a maraka. Some of these deaths could come through Venus-related illnesses and disease such as diabetes, sexually-contracted diseases or problems picked up while in a hospital. As usual, other factors must confirm.

Sagittarius — Mars is generally a good guy as ruler of the 5th, but Venus (6th ruler) is a potential killer again, and I have often seen it happen that

Sag-rising people die during Venus Dasa or Bhukti periods. Venus often kills via cancer as Venus has to do with cellular growth, and under natal and/or transitory stress it always has the potential for cellular disorder (as, for that matter, does the Moon but to a much lesser degree). But I don't want to get sidetracked into medical discussions. Here karaka Saturn can also be a maraka depending on its overall formations.

Pisces – Supposedly these people won't die during a Mars Dasa or Bhukti because Mars rules the wonderful 9th – even though it also rules the 2nd. Yet again Venus bears watching because it rules the two life houses (3 & 8) and has a link, through exaltation, to the 1st. If Venus comes under exceptional stress, which a Western astrologer can easily observe via outer planets and progression techniques, then caution is in order – especially if Venus is poorly placed by sign and/or house. Just as with the other Jupiter-ruled sign, Saturn is also treated as a maraka since, among other things, it is a karaka with the power to undermine the 1st.

Here are marakas I've often seen listed for the remaining six Ascendants, but as already mentioned above, common sense and simple experience would generally *not* seem to support them.

For example, for Libra-rising, Mars rules both the 2nd and the 7th. Given its own nature, it would seem like the ultimate maraka (and a good example of that will be seen in the case of Luis Donaldo Colosio discussed in the assassination chapter). But I have seen it absent from some maraka lists. That is quite clearly wrong, and other good authors agree. Your own study is the best resource, and there are plenty of cases later in this book to aid you, but do keep in mind some of the sometimes odd, but not necessarily wrong, logic noted above.

Gemini	—	Mars and Jupiter
Cancer	—	Mercury and Venus
Leo	—	Mercury and Venus
Libra	—	Jupiter
Capricorn	—	Mars and Jupiter
Aquarius	—	Mars

As I periodically remind, never lose track of the fact that the material in this and any other chapter is dedicated to a very narrow aspect of this topic, and forms just a part of the overall mosaic. Since astrology is synthetic and inductive, it ultimately needs an experienced practitioner to reflect an accurate feel for how these various components prioritize and fit together. Let's now go on to the final rule, which is that...

RULE # 3: Rule # 2 isn't quite complete. Some Hindu texts further refer to the rulers of both the vitality houses (3 & 8) and the ruler of the 11th in the identification of death agency. There are also a lot of other considerations and combinations, but here the discussion gets even more arcane. Those readers who are interested in this can springboard off the baseline concepts suggested in this book to a further investigation via Hindu astrology books themselves.

But I did want to expand the range of your thinking on this issue by getting across my key points that, in general, death has more to do with sidereal 2nd (and 7th) house issues than with the 8th, and it also has fundamentally to do with assaults upon primary vitality rulers and associated weak points. By the way, this stating of the rules followed by the apparent "unstatement" of them is somewhat typical of how many Hindu astrology books read. It ties into the paradox of all generalizations having the quality of being both true and false, especially as applied to specific cases. You've probably already noticed that life, and death, often carries quite a bit of paradox.

Concluding Maraka Miscellany

In keeping with the symbolism of the 8th house and 8th harmonic, here are eight more miscellaneous maraka–related points for your consideration. As you might imagine, there are many more.

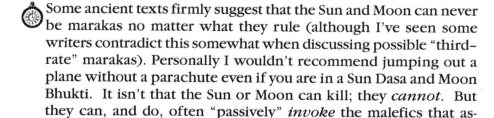 Some ancient texts firmly suggest that the Sun and Moon can never be marakas no matter what they rule (although I've seen some writers contradict this somewhat when discussing possible "third-rate" marakas). Personally I wouldn't recommend jumping out a plane without a parachute even if you are in a Sun Dasa and Moon Bhukti. It isn't that the Sun or Moon can kill; they *cannot*. But they can, and do, often "passively" *invoke* the malefics that aspect them during their periods, and death will result. You will have the opportunity to see plenty of these cases later in this book.

It is also the case that if any planet that would otherwise be a maraka, such as being a malefic and ruler of the 2nd, shares joint rulership with the 9th then it cannot function as a maraka (further evidence, by the way, that they think more highly of the 9th than the 5th since this rule is not applied to the 5th). In general, I have found both of these assertions to be true, but only speaking causally.

When a malefic planet shares rulership of the 3rd and 8th (e.g., Mars in the case of Virgo rising) this does not carry vitality energy despite what may seem to have been implied to this point. As a malefic ruler of two life houses, its strength can sometimes be elevated depending upon what sign and house it is in, whose energies it may share, and the like. But in general it tends to function as a maraka.

Before even concluding on the topic of marakas, Hindu astrologers first make a determination about general longevity. If longevity indicators are generally quite good, but an apparently strong maraka period occurs early in life, it can usually be ignored (at least with regard to death) and will instead perform its function during a comparable, but later, period when the body is less resistant and also less likely to be battling with comparable "death challenge" symbolism in the outer world. The next two chapters will give more information on this.

Rulers and tenants of the 12th (which "secretly undermines" the 1st) if involved with a more true maraka, should also be watched if any of them suffer obviously severe defect with little compensatory support. In general, note that a maraka typically will not perform if it is weak except in a recessive, invoking or implosive manner. Its weakness invites destruction rather than being a more active agent. Somewhat conversely, if a natural benefic has maraka status and also rules an angle, it has more power of release and hence becomes more dangerous.

Certain types of exchanges between Saturn, the 1st and 8th (e.g., Saturn in the 1st and the ruler of the 1st in the 8th) can confirm Saturn as a maraka. Therefore, a Dasa/Bhukti combination of it and another malefic would merit observation. But do not confuse this with Aries or Libra–rising without the Saturn factor; the ruler of the 8th cannot be a maraka when it is also ruler of the 1st unless there are other strong negative factors.

It is said that the ruler of the 22nd decanate, or planets associated with it, can become a maraka if sufficiently dominant. This is an obscure point for those who may have a special interest in the concept of decanates (which breaks each sign down into three equal sub–components).

 Throughout this book I will make very little reference to the quinc-unx (150 degree) aspect if only to control the range of discussion. But if you further review the sample charts on your own, you will find that it is not at all irrelevant depending upon the nature of the death. From the point of view of the 1st house, the nature of the quincunx implies 6th and 8th house issues, and the fact that Hindu Mars by definition casts an aspect on the 8th house from itself further reinforces this point, as does the fact that the two maraka houses are themselves quincunx. Consequently, if you'd like a little brain teaser, it is sometimes suggested that if the ruler of the 8th is in the 8th, death can therefore occur during the period of the 1st house ruler.

 Hindu astrology does other similar types of perspective shift-ing. For example, they frequently look at a chart (especially a female's) as though the house containing the Moon were the 1st house. Therefore the two marakas would be the 2nd and 7th from this house and so forth. Similarly they might tempo-rarily look at karaka Saturn or known marakas as if they de-fined the 1st and monitor other planets that have an quincunx relationship to them. They also watch any malefics that are in a 4th harmonic relationship to the Moon since it participates in the regulation of energy flow.

As you can see, once you drift away from the fundamentals you can enter into a maze of considerations that challenge your ability to maintain logi-cal order and priority. Like anyone else, Hindu astrologers can draw wrong conclusions from death charts, and some of these rationalizations can end up being codified over time. This is especially so since I have ob-served that many Indian astrologers seem to express only modest con-cern about working with wrong charts. Since each chart pattern is ulti-mately very unique with hundreds of interlocked considerations, there are two challenges to the reader.

First, as in all this work, you need to work towards developing the least number of rules with maximum generic applicability. And second, in order not to deceive yourself, you need to test those rules against actual charts ahead of time rather than after the fact (and one success does not make a rule). In the end, there is no other way than to study individual patterns.

Perhaps I should make a few final comments about the lunar nodal axis since each node has its own Dasa and Bhukti periods, and the nodes are clearly linked into life's karma (as a reminder, Indians call the NN "Rahu" and the SN "Ketu"). Chinese astrology asserts that the Moon's NN "is the evil aura of Mars," and the Moon's SN "is the evil aura of Saturn." Hindu astrology sticks with the same assertion but reverses the planets (the NN having the quality of Saturn and the SN that of Mars), but either way you get a malefic attitude about this axis. At this point you should probably be able to derive much of the logic yourself, but some of the considerations that establish maraka status for the nodes are these:

> Is the active node across the 1–7, 2–8 or 6–12 axis?
> What is the status of its dispositor? Is it sharply involved with malefics?
> Are any planets in a hard harmonic relationship to it — esp. to the exact degree?
> What is the link of the nodes to the ruler of the 1st? Are any of them highly incompatible with that ruler?
> What is the nature of any linkages to the rulers of the 2nd, 3rd, 7th and 8th?
> Are any nodes (natal or progressed) at zero degrees of malefic houses?
> Check both mean and true. For Western astrologers, does the nodal axis lie directly upon a relevant intermediate house cusp, especially one with malefic status, while involved with a significantly malefic factor?

In drawing conclusions about death indicators, Western astrologers will definitely want to use the outer planets, declination, and any other factors they have established are supportive. The consideration of compatibilities and incompatibilities alluded to above should actually lead into a discussion of constellational issues (nakshatras or lunar mansions) which are also very fundamental to this whole topic. But this will also be ignored to manage the span of discussion — although the reader should consider it worthy of further personal investigation.

PLANETARY DEATH YOGAS & INDICATORS OF LONGEVITY

"If the Sun is in the 8th, the Moon in the 1st, Jupiter in the 12th and a malefic in the 4th, the native may die as a result of falling from a cot."

"If the Sun is in the 4th, the Moon is in the 10th and Saturn is in the 8th, the native may be hit accidentally by a log of wood and die."

"The native's wife will die within three days of marriage due to a snake bite if the native has Rahu in the 2nd and Mars in the 7th."

"If the 6th, 7th and 8th are in their order occupied by Mars, Rahu and Saturn, the native's wife will not live long."

uotes similar to the above can often be found in many leading Indian astrological texts whether ancient or modern. While we may suspect that odd examples such as these reflect a database of approximately one case (and there are many stranger examples having to do with death at the hand of supernatural beings, the fate of corpses, and the like), they still serve to introduce the important concept of planetary yogas.

Yogas, sometimes referred to more generically as rules or aphorisms, are brief combinations of planetary factors that are said to identify various predictable consequences. I've read that over 400,000 have been identified in the East (although other texts make reference to 400,000 stanzas, each of which would not necessarily translate into a combination). This could make a remarkable project for an artificial intelligence program, and would certainly broaden the marketability of what currently requires a prodigious human memory. Towards this end, there is at least one Hindu astrology program currently on the market that will scan a chart for almost 2,000 applicable yogas as defined by the sage Parasara (see the resource appendix).

By the way, a key reason these stanzas are "easily" memorized by the thousands is that Sanskrit has a structural affinity with the human mind, and it actually has the quality of strengthening memory. It is said that if these stanzas had to be memorized in their very diminished English form, that it would not be possible except by individuals who have abnormally capable memories to begin with.

E Pluribus Unum

The yoga thought process is a productive one, and is insufficiently appreciated and developed in the West. The West tends more towards the analysis of each individual variable in isolation. Yet you may have noticed that the better astrologers are often those who have a gestalt response to the chart as a whole almost upon picking it up. The objective of yoga thinking is to always see *at least* two variables in a meaningful relationship at any particular analytical moment. Perhaps it is tautological to say that the "gestalt astrologers" are essentially performing a large reductive act of astrological yoga.

The study of yogas develops this quality of synthetic thinking. This is important because yogas provide a disciplined tool for resolving the accretion of paradox and apparent contradiction that characterizes astrology. New students with well-developed analytical minds often become quite frustrated with the astrological maze (actually if they read many of the old Hindu astrology books too early in their careers, they would soon be mainlining Prozac). Practicing synthetic meditation, an opportunity that yogas provide, strengthens the ability to intuitively resolve symbolic issues that cannot otherwise be penetrated through standard deductive methods applied against single variable explanations.

Keeping with our topic, this section will identify some classical yogas for death. Undoubtedly (one might almost say "as usual") you will see many yogas that apply to your own sidereal chart. Does this mean that you will die? Yes. Does this mean that you will die because of these yogas? No. As you should have surmised, yogas themselves must be further synthesized within the context of numerous other "pro–life" yogas that also apply to your chart. Any particular yoga is just another meta–fragment whose purpose is to inform and stimulate meaningful thinking about the larger coincident mysteries that any chart presents.

For example, here is one of many exact examples from an ancient seminal text that applies directly to my own chart: "Early death will be inflicted on the native if decreasing Moon is in the ascendant while malefics capture the 8th and an angle. There is no doubt about that." Well if I'm dead nobody has told me, although some mornings I increasingly have to wonder — although by "capture" the author may mean "own" rather than "occupy" in which case I don't qualify. But this is to reemphasize the warning that if one were to take quite literally the massive collection of Hindu astrological assertions (many of which are quite certainly false), one would be a basket case in short order. Indeed, you should see the material that I am *not* passing along.

The better approach is just to let it wash over you, assume that many single statements are wrong in isolation, but that the aggregation, if properly absorbed, structured and applied in a more or less common sense way, will lead to an accurate gestalt. This further assumes, of course, that one has the chart of someone who could become a competent astrologer in the first place.

As a very high level observation, any time two or more planets that suffer from significant "defect" are located in the same house or are otherwise tightly linked, this juncture should be regarded as a locus of energy difficulty and therefore a potential pathway to death. This would be particularly so during the Dasa/Bhukti of the afflicted or afflicting factors. Many charts commonly suffer from significant defect, and this can be determined through a variety of methods identified throughout this book. For example, it can be through ownership of potentially "bad" houses (i.e., 2, 3, 6, 7 and 8), residence in them, or various other fallen conditions by sign, association and so forth.

For those who may already be exhausted by the mere thought of yogas, here is a simple single variable statement I've seen now and them. The cause and mode of death is derived by finding the ruler of the 8th house, determining what nakshatra it was in at birth and then analyzing the dispositor of that nakshatra. But since that won't quite do it either, let's now look at...

Longevity (Ayurdaya) Indicators And Calculation

> "Why is it that a death may occur early or late, the healthy may die and also the diseased? What rules this onslaught of death?... It is a special kind of Karma that brings on the event of death in the case of everyone. The passage of time cannot and does not kill. It brings about only growth, stagnation or decay. That is one reason why astrology is able to foretell when a man will die in accordance with this special Karma.

> "It must be valid to accept this category of Karma for how many

of us have not seen a bright and sprightly young life snuffed out for no apparent physical reason or old men, however weak and suffering from long chronic diseases, continuing to live and of others, destitute and suffering from the most obnoxious diseases, laying on pavements for years, not dying in spite of total lack of medical care, food and other necessities...the death–dealing Karma will strike an individual irrespective of age, health, medical care or any other factor...

"How did some men manage to live so long? The scriptures say 'Not inflicting harm, truth speaking, not harbouring hatred, always acting in accordance with the words of the Guru, respecting the old, purity, not doing what is forbidden, taking only what is wholesome as food — all these qualities and modes of living lead to long life. Such long–lived people become strong by ascetic penances,...' Now that we have the secret of long life, any takers?"

These August 1992 remarks were written by someone called "Agastya" who writes a charming column titled "As It Strikes Me" for India's venerable *Astrological Magazine*. His third paragraph reminder of the benefits of virtuous living clearly applies over numerous lifetimes. In any particular lifetime the remarks of the first two paragraphs have the more compelling applicability, and that was his point. It reminded me of the well known American automobile bumper sticker that says, "Eat Properly — Exercise Regularly — Die Anyway."

Agastya's simple but true remarks tweak the billions and billions of foolish dollars put into many ultimately dubious schemes, no matter how "scientifically" blessed, to promote longevity (the U.S. spends almost a trillion dollars a year on health care). Better sanitation, better diet through the ability to preserve foods, a handful of wonder drugs such as penicillin, and the reduction of toxic environmental agents have provided the bulk of mankind's statistical gains in longevity. It would seem that the best any individual could do for any particular lifetime would be to improve its quality rather than its "quantity."

Parenthetically, the U.S. government lists the leading causes of death, in order, as: heart disease, cancer, stroke, unintentional injury, chronic lung disease, pneumonia and influenza, diabetes, suicide, liver disease and cirrhosis, and AIDS. However, valid countervailing statistical studies of the underlying causes of these official designations show the following in order of priority: tobacco smoking, defective diet and inactivity, alcohol, microbes, other toxic agents, firearms, sexual behavior, illegal drugs, motor vehicles and then "all other."

It's interesting how many items on the second, primarily behavioral, list emphasize the rulership of Neptune as compared to the first list. And when a drunk or an addict accidentally shoots himself or drives his car into a wall, is that a Mars problem or a Neptune problem? It's also remarkable how many terminal problems with microbial infections are acquired while in a hospital (12th house).

Three Score And Ten?

The East gives a lot of preliminary attention to the question of longevity (called ayurdaya) since, if you are not going to live long in the first place, there is no point in a more detailed analysis. Shortly I will list two sample extracts from the many generic assertions made for long and short lives that one will find throughout their literature. I've tended to emphasize those that I've seen repeated in multiple sources and which seem to make a reasonable amount of common sense.

These rules basically apply to adults since Hindu astrologers tend to see infant mortality, i.e., generally to about age 12 although some say to 24, as an issue controlled more through the "sinful" karma of the parents' charts (although a portion of that period they ascribe to the prior life sins of the child himself). This does not strike me as implausible. Since we inherit through karmic invocation a portion of the physical genetic flaws of our parents, why should we not equally inherit a portion of their spiritual genetic flaws? "The sins of the father are visited upon the son..."

By the way, ancient Hindu astrology texts regard many birth patterns as "evil." They have various highly elaborate procedures to "remedy," "provide relief," or "escape" the consequences which even open-minded Western astrologers would find somewhere between deeply strange and unacceptable (the ritualistic smearing of cow dung, and the like). On the other hand, the West absolutely does need to learn more about the East's remedial use of sound vibrations, gem therapy, their attention to closed-loop "neural" systems such as chakras and meridian energies, ayurvedic healing techniques, and the like.

But this still reinforces the cautionary note that many Eastern judgmental assertions are somewhat unique to their reality and often cannot be taken literally in the West where, in any case, they are likely to be misunderstood. Also Hindu philosophy typically asserts that locations, as well as people, have karma. In the context of this book, this is perhaps a little interesting in light of the fact that Washington, D.C., for example, consistently runs a rate of infant mortality that is more than double the national average, and it exceeds that of several Third World countries. Along this same line, Finland has a very high level of suicide that is otherwise very difficult to explain through any standard effort at statistical correlation.

Note that there is some minor dispute in the Eastern literature about what constitutes the boundaries of the different longevity categories but, in general and excluding the more extreme commentators (that address "supernatural" life spans of 1,000 years and "limitless" longevity that exceeds that), "short" is up to 32–36, "medium" to 64–72, and "long" is anything beyond that.

There is an essential core triad of the Sun, Moon and Asc which contributes to the overall maintenance of life energy (and note that none of these are ever marakas). The Ascendant rules the physical body per se. The Sun rules the soul, and therefore its intentions towards the body. And the Moon, since it reflects the Sun, rules the innermost core of the mind (also Mercury, as ruler of the nervous system and the overt aspects of the mind, typically makes a very weak maraka).

Therefore it is said, as a general proposition and exclusive of specific considerations related to marakas and the like, that problems related to the Asc have general rulership over longevity considerations until the early 30's. The mid–life period until the mid 60's would emphasize problems related to the Moon. And problems related to the Sun are emphasized in old age.

While I don't emphasize it in this text, the Part of Fortune, which is an Arabic construction from these three factors, often shows up very strongly in death charts by progression and the like – assuming the time of birth is very accurate. You will therefore see me making occasional reference to it as the "Part of (Mis)fortune." And all these factors are affected by the important question of what was seen and what was hidden at birth, i.e., whether the birth was before or after sunrise.

The most common Dasa system (Vimsottari) runs to 120 years which is alleged to be about how long someone should live once they subscribe to the rules for proper living. As a variation on this thought, in September of 1993 I had my first opportunity to briefly discuss this issue with Dr.

Vedavyas, a respected scientist, astrological author, lecturer and researcher based in Hyderabad, India. I understood his opinion to be that 72 years was about a proper life span since, at that point, one loses creativity as a result of having precessed off all of one's original birth degrees. One is dispossessed of one's platform, so to speak.

As you get into the following material, what if you find almost the same assertion being made within two mutually–exclusive categories, or what if this material seems to partially contradict some of the other material in this book? Well, you can say one of two things to yourself: 1) "That's India!", or 2) "I will contemplate this apparent paradox until I am able to synthesize it at a higher level of understanding." Or you could take an aspirin and read a comic book — perhaps thereby contributing to the eventual achievement of option two. But for Westerners, with our cumulative exclusionary logic, the achievement of satisfactory synthesis is often more elusive than that.

For those heavily into immortality, here is a very ancient definition of what it takes to live "until the end an age": "One born in Cancer ascendant will live till the end of the yuga if Jupiter is in an angle and be in Gopuramsa while Venus is in a trine and be in Paaravatamsa." To live the life span of a sage: "Jupiter in Simhasanamsa being in the ascendant, Saturn in Devalokamsa and Mars in Paaravatamsa — if these are so, one will enjoy the life span as due a sage." Got that? Well, there are a few other hidden qualifiers in any case...

As promised above, following are 40 standard yogas for different classes of longevity. I'll just be showing long and short combinations, since the middle is basically "all other." Don't get so fixated that you forget the "all other" offsetting considerations. Also be aware that these listings will exclude the innumerable even more specific yogas such as, "Danger through water will have to be feared during the 5th and the 9th years if the Sun is in the 6th or 8th while the Moon is in the 12th from the Sun."

In fact, momentarily stepping outside the concept of death yogas per se, here is an example of an even more complex yoga: "IF the lord of the 10th is in the 5th, Mercury is in a quadrant, the Sun is strong in its own sign, Jupiter is trine the Moon, and Mars is trine to Mercury, or Jupiter is in the 11th from Mercury" THEN you have something called "Sharada Yoga." These many specific yogas for blindness, deep poverty, hypocrisy, incest, stage fright plus generosity, genius, vast wealth, sexual strength, and the like are among the key performance features of Hindu astrology.

The lists below will be followed by the introduction of several concepts used for more precise calculation of the life span. You may wish to compare the approach of these ideas to an equally fated Western method called the Life Span Revolution (LSRev) developed by astrologer Ross Harvey and which is very briefly discussed in the next chapter.

Long Life Yogas:

01. Saturn in 8th (esp. with ruler of 8th in 6th or 12th).
02. Saturn exalted, in its own house or a good friend's house.
03. Ruler of 8th in 8th, exalted, otherwise powerful or well aspected.
04. Ruler of 8th in a kendra of a trikona (i.e., in the 1st, 4th, 7th or 10th from the 5th or 9th) aspected by, or with, benefics.
05. Ruler of 8th in 3rd or 11th in a benefic's sign and sharing other benefit.
06. Ruler of the 9th & 10th both in the 1st (just Saturn for Taurus rising).
07. Strong moon (by accepted methods) aspected by, or with, benefics.
08. Ruler of 1st in the 1st, and Ruler of 8th in 8th (preferably exalted).
09. Ruler of 1st in the 1st, and the ruler of the 10th in the 10th.
10. Ruler of 1st & 8th in 6th or 12th and aspected by a benefic.
11. Ruler of 1st, 8th & 10th all strong, involved w/benefics and no Saturn.
12. Ruler of 1st and 10th aspecting the ruler of the 5th.
13. Ruler of 1st and 10th in any angular house.
14. Ruler of the 10th exalted in the 5th.
15. Ruler of 1st and 9th in the 1st aspected by the ruler of the 5th.
16. Benefics in the 4th & 8th houses aspected by Jupiter.
17. Every planet loaded into the 3rd, 4th and 8th houses.
18. Rulers of both the 6th and 12th houses in the 1st.
19. Ruler of 12th strong and with, or aspected by, one or more benefics.
20. In general, if the Asc, and the ruler of the Asc, the Ascendant's nakshatra (and navamsha) plus Saturn and the Moon are all very good, the person will have a long life. If they are moderate, then the length of life will be moderate.

Short Life Yogas:

01. Few rulers of 1st, 8th or 10th strong and receiving benefit.
02. Ruler of 1st in 8th while the ruler of the 8th is under major stress (with or aspected by a malefic, in the 6th, in a very incompatible

sign, etc.).

03. Ruler of 8th in 6th or 12th along with a malefic, and esp. if ruler of the 1st is weak.
04. Ruler of the 8th disposed by a malefic.
05. Planets in the 12th when other negative combinations conspire, and positive combinations do not support.
06. A generally weak Sun within a generally weak chart (unless the Sun clearly rules the father).
07. Moon in any really bad house and aspected by a malefic (esp. if the Moon is darkening, defectively placed by degree and so on).
08. A Rx benefic in the 6th, 8th or 12th aspected by a malefic while there is no positive support to the 1st.
09. Harsh malefics aspect the Asc while one of the lights is conjunct the NN.
10. Mars in the 7th, Sun in the 9th with Venus and Jupiter in the 11th.
11. Moon in the 6th and Mars in the 7th with Saturn in the 10th.
12. Saturn in the 1st and Jupiter in the 3rd with Moon in the 8th (you may unravel the two benefics in the life houses).
13. Moon or Asc in the last navamsha of a water sign (called Gandanta).
14. Birth in the 72 minutes before the Sun rises or after it sets.
15. All malefics on the eastern side while all benefics on the western side... and you have Scorpio rising... and Mercury is unafflicted.
16. Malefics in the 1st and 7th while a malefic is conjunct the Moon without offsetting good aspects.
17. Moon in the 1st, 7th, 8th or 12th and bracketed by malefics.
18. A harsh malefic in the 7th with a weak Moon in the 1st.
19. Malefics are in angles unsupported by benefics, and the Asc lord is weak.
20. Good houses are loaded with only weak planets.

General Lifespan Categorization

Before showing some more detailed calculation methods, let me mention a method that is commonly seen for lumping a chart into one of the "Big 3" lifespan "buckets" (short, medium or long). Notice the following three groupings:

> #1: Signs occupied by rulers of the 1st and 8th.
> #2: Signs occupied by the Moon and Saturn.
> #3: Signs of the Asc and hora–lagna ("hour ascendant").

In these groupings the only concept that should require further explanation is the "hora lagna". This is a sign–and–degree longitude composed of that of the Sun at sunrise (at the birth location on the day of birth) plus one sign (and any residual degrees) for each hour from sunrise until the actual time of birth. Subtract 12 if the sum of the sign additions exceeds 12. If you had converted everything to degrees for purposes of calculation, now convert the final total back to a sign and degrees.

Now: for *each* of the three groups, select one of the following:

A. Long life if both factors are cardinal, or
     one is fixed and one mutable.
B. Medium life if both factors are mutable, or
     one is cardinal and one fixed.
C. Short life if both factors are fixed, or
     one is cardinal and one mutable.

If you end up with two or three A's then life will be long, two or three B's then life will be medium, etc. If you end up with an A, B and C then defer to the conclusion from grouping #3. There are two considerations that override these conclusions: 1) if an undamaged Jupiter occupies the 1st or 7th, you can bump up B or C by one category, and 2) for group #2, if the Moon is in the 1st or 7th, ignore Saturn and just use the Asc sign for categorization. Now I will add my own thought which is that if you see any other powerfully overriding factor(s), you may want to consider a further adjustment.

These three conjugal groupings should inspire a certain amount of additional insight into Hindu thinking about longevity. In group #1, since the 1st shares logic with the 8th, clearly the 8th has to do with sustaining life as I have argued all along (i.e., it can only be a "death house" by inversion). Regarding group #2, we already know that the Moon and Saturn share similar cycles but at different "octaves," and this implies a mysterious life sustaining link between the two. In group #3 there is a further life cycle clue associated with this mysterious adjustment to sunrise on the date of birth — especially when we keep in mind that the Sun is "extinguished" daily at the maraka descendant. The mathematically-inclined are invited to give further contemplation to this paragraph.

If you think you can get a fix upon your general longevity category (and common sense might factor in the more obvious genetic considerations and relevant lifestyle behaviors), it has been further said that if one adds up the longitudes of the Sun, Moon, Jupiter and Saturn, divides the result by 12 and then identifies this sign and degree in the natal chart, that death will occur when Saturn transits this point its first time (for a short life), its second time (for a medium life) and its third time (for a long life). The reader may wish to play with this idea or even test various alternatives such as substituting the Asc for Jupiter.

More Detailed Calculation Of Longevity

There are any number of precise systems for calculating longevity down to the minute, and this information is freely available to anyone with the stamina to search for it. In keeping with my position of not using this book to supply such perfectly precise methods, and in order to encourage the study of Hindu astrology, this section will only present some of the *concepts* associated with these calculations.

Over 31 methods have been catalogued from various classical works, but three methods are most commonly used: *Pindayu*, *Nisargayu* and *Amsayu*. Pindayu is more generally recommended, and software currently exists to perform the calculations for all three methods. It has also been recommended that the first thing you attempt to do is discern whether the Sun, Moon or Asc is the strongest in your chart. Whichever is strongest, you use the respectively corresponding method. If two factors seem equally strong, you use both corresponding methods and then average the results. If all three seem about the same, then average the results of all three methods. The comments below will give a type of composite view of various related ideas.

The baseline concept behind *Pindayu* is that each planet makes a contribution to a person's longevity. Its ability to optimize this contribution depends upon its strength and status in the many ways this can identified. Here is the greatest number of years that each planet can possibly contribute: Sun (19), Moon (25), Mercury (15), Venus (12), Mars (15), Jupiter (21) and Saturn (20). This adds up to 127 years (excluding a contribution sometimes said to be made by the Asc), so you don't have to worry too much if several of your planets are fairly wrecked. It is based upon the impossible assumption that every natal planet would be found in a condition of deep exaltation. These signs and degrees were given in the Hindu chapter (such as the Moon at 3 degrees of sidereal Taurus) and their most fallen positions are exactly opposite those most exalted degrees.

Given the impossibility of having across-the-board super-exaltation, we now start whittling away at your lifespan. After performing this if you ultimately find that you have gone into negative numbers, you can assume that either you have over–whittled, or else you are currently leading one of your past lives. To try and keep you out of your past life, be advised that a planet can only lose its single worse case scenario. You do not roll up all of its negatives.

Here are the various criteria typically given for reduction:

A) If any planet is in deep fall, it only gets half its allocation. Since most planets are somewhere between, a proportional reduction is taken based upon the arc from where the planet actually is relative to its most exalted point. This gives the maximum basic contribution from which the further reductions are taken.

B) Any planet eclipsed by the Sun, i.e., combust by the more detailed Hindu rules of combustion (excluding Venus and Saturn) loses half its contribution.

C) Deduct 33.3% if the planet is in a defective sign for itself (unless it is Rx). Ignore Mars in an enemy's sign and any planet in a neutral or friendly sign.

D) If standard malefics (including a waning Moon) are in the visible portion of the zodiac (based upon a Bhava chart), the proportional reductions for each planet in that house are: 12th – 100%, 11th – 50%, 10th – 33.3%, 9th –25%, 8th – 20%, and 7th – 14.3%. Benefics in the same houses lose only half of that. If multiple planets are in a house, only do a reduction for the single worse factor for that house.

E) For a malefic in the 1st, do a 50% reduction. But if a benefic aspects the Asc under this circumstance, only deduct 25%.

F) The Asc itself makes a contribution based upon the number of signs it is from Aries and the number of degrees the Asc gained in its particular sign (30 degrees is equal to a year). For example, if Cancer rises, add three years. Within the ascending sign, for every 2 & 1/2 degrees from zero to the actual degree rising add an additional month. Use the

ruler of the navamsha Asc for all this if it is stronger that
the ruler of the main chart (unfortunately this will result
in a slightly different computational rule).

The second method of *Nisargayu* is roughly the same as that given above.
The big difference is that the number of initial years allocated for deep
exaltation are as follows: Saturn (50), Sun (20), Venus (20), Jupiter (18),
Mercury (9), Mars (2) and Moon (1). This adds up to 120. If you have a
strong Moon, you'll probably favor Pindayu. However, if you have Saturn
around 20 degrees of sidereal Libra (tropically that's around 13 Scorpio)
you'll clearly have a warm spot in your heart for Nisargayu. Here the
Moon is only one step above dirt which is very odd considering the
preferential biases of the Hindu system.

The third method of *Amsayu* allocates years corresponding to the number of navamsas counted from Aries. 3 and 1/3 degrees equal one year.
Divide that into a circle and you get 108. So you multiply various planetary longitudes by 108 and expunge multiples of 12. You convert the
final result to years and months. Instructions about this system tend to
be less clear, but planets also go through a similar reduction process. It
is uniquely additive in that some writers recommend doubling and tri-
pling the calculated values under certain circumstances.

A Fourth Method (Navamsha–Based)

Since I can assure you that these three standard ancient techniques do
not seem to work, I thought I would consult a more contemporary authority. Earlier in this chapter I mentioned "Dr. Vedavyas" in a passing
reference to his remark that one degree of precession would seem to
define a "normal" life span. In the Fall of 1993 I was charmed during
lunch by one of his questions to me at a lecture of his I was attending.
Not knowing I was working on this book, he expressed to me his curiosity about what techniques Western astrologers use to forecast death. He
was quite amazed when I told him we had none.

He said, "Well, if you don't know when you are going to die, then how do
your plan your life?" From my point of view, that is one of the key implied questions of this book. He subsequently agreed to describe an
ayurdaya technique that was easy to understand, but he says that this
technique will only describe the *minimum* ayurdaya to be expected.

As for some brief background on Dr. Vedavyas, he has a Masters degree in Zoology, and was awarded a PhD in Sanskrit for his complex multi-disciplinary research work titled *The Astronomical Dating of the Mahabharata War* (which includes a foreword by the Dalai Lama). This in-depth study of the Vedic astronomical calendar attempts to subsume and critique all known scientific research on the Hindu calendar.

Its purpose is to establish the first moment of the "Kali Yuga" era (which he has concluded is 18-Feb-3102 BC) upon which all astrological calculations depend, including precession of the Equinox. This knowledge is vital to the accuracy of many predictive calculations — including the Dasa system and ayurdaya. Suffice it to say that Dr. Vedavyas has been intensively studying and teaching the Vedas and Puranas all his life.

Beyond this, he has published over 60 books in four languages including the 700-page *Hinduism in the Space Age* which has sold over 30,000 copies. He is also the discoverer of 45 missing slokas from the *Bhagavad Gita*, although the importance of this is lost on the typical Westerner. He has been a consultant to three Presidents of India, and has spoken under a variety of academic auspices and at the United Nations. Since retirement from his position as Secretary of State in Andhra Pradesh, he has devoted a large part of his efforts to establishing a "University of the Vedic Sciences" in Florida.

As a Westerner, I enjoy talking with Dr. Vedavyas because, with his scientific background, the logic of his thoughts is completely open to challenge. He views the Puranas and Vedic scriptures as actually a body of highly scientific knowledge as opposed to a "religion of conversion, cult or belief" centered on a single person or author. Consequently, his attitude is that it either stands on its merits, or it does not. To that extent, and to that extent only, he makes Hinduism interesting to me.

With this as some background, following are the written remarks of Dr. Vedavyas.

Ayurdaya Determination: An Example (written by Dr. Vedavyas)

Many Western students who have had a chance to consult the palm leaf "Nadi Granthas" texts can understand the uncanny accuracy of event forecasts and their timing — especially when they happen exactly as predicted. Even though they were written over 5,000 years ago, these scriptures contain the prophesy of your birth, details of your horoscope, even the name of your parents and your town of birth. Of course, they are only written for people who are destined to consult these books in the first place. The prophesies begin from the very hour the consultation commences. That also means that they describe the life events of specific people who are yet to be born.

These revelations are based upon knowing how to calculate not only the length of life but the events scheduled in your life history and their timing. The secret lies in the calculation of the life and length of chapters of your life. The simplest technique is based upon the sub-division of each sign of the zodiac into nine equal parts of 3 degrees and 20 minutes each called the "navamsa."

The "strength" of the planets at birth invest the child with the vitality to live exactly in proportion to their (a) strength or weakness by sign, and (b) their favorable or unfavorable location by house-related aspect. This being the axiom on which the length of life can be calculated, it is measured by the strength of a planet by sign and sub-divisions of each zodiac sign occupied at birth. The latter is measured by the navamsa position of each planet and the Ascendant. Let me explain.

Whereas Western astrology only has a main positional chart which we in India refer to as a rasi chakra (rasi = zodiacal sign; chakra = chart), there is a second chart called the navamsa (or "amsa" for short). This is based upon a 1/9th division of the rasi chakra. Each sign or rasi of 30 degrees is further sub-divided into nine equal parts.

	Beginning Position	Fire Signs	Earth Signs	Air Signs	Water Signs
1.	00-00 — 03-20	AR	CP	LI	CA
2.	03-20 — 06-40	TA	AQ	SC	LE
3.	06-40 — 10-00	GE	PI	SA	VI
4.	10-00 — 13-20	CA	AR	CP	LI
5.	13-20 — 16-40	LE	TA	AQ	SC
6.	16-40 — 20-00	VI	GE	PI	SA
7.	20-00 — 23-20	LI	CA	AR	CP
8.	23-20 — 26-40	SC	LE	TA	AQ
9.	26-40 — 30-00	SA	VI	GE	PI

In the table above you can see a pattern. These 1/9th sub-divisions begin with fire sign Aries navamsa in Aries sign and run through each of the nine sub-divisions. The next earth sign Taurus begins its first sub-division with Capricorn and continues through. The same is true for Gemini and Cancer. Leo goes back to column one (the same as Aries) and goes through the same cycle. Just like Taurus, Virgo goes to the second column, and so forth. Therefore, one interesting feature is that watery signs all begin with Cancer and end with Pisces navamsa, and so on.

How do you use this table? You want to find which navamsa, or 1/9th sub-division, of each sidereal sign that each planet occupies. So, for example, if a planet is situated at 19 degrees in Leo you go down to row six which begins with 16 degrees and 40 minutes. You go over to the fire sign row which is the first row. Thus 19 degrees of Leo will be Virgo in the navamsa. You do this for all seven planets, the north and south nodes of the Moon and for the Ascendant. Remember that this is based upon niryana (or sidereal) zodiacal degrees.

We shall now work out an example: find the navamsa position of each planet and Ascendant for the date of birth of 13-April-1947 with an Ascendant of 13 degrees of Sagittarius. You may follow along in the table given above.

	Rasi Degree	Navamsa	Sign
Sun	29-PI-07	9th	PI
Moon	26-SA-10	8th	SC
Mars	07-PI-43	3rd	VI
Mercury	02-PI-37	1st	CA
Jupiter	03-SC-07	1st	CA
Venus	22-AQ-50	7th	AR
Saturn	08-CA-53	3rd	VI
Rahu	10-TA-15	6th	AR (anti-clock)
Ketu	10-SC-15	6th	LI (anti-clock)
Ascendant	13-SA-41	5th	LE

Following are the rules for longevity:

Rule #1: Each planet gives as many years as the number of navamsas travelled by it in that sign. Accordingly are the years of life-span contributed by each planet. Planet in 1st navamsa gives one year, and that in the 8th gives eight years. Fractions give proportionately.

Rule #2: The planet in its exaltation or moolatrikona sign gives three times the ayurdaya as the number of navamsas travelled in that sign. Accordingly are the years of life–span contributed by each planet.

Rule #3: The planet in its enemy's sign reduces by half the ayurdaya given normally by it under Rule 1.

Rule #4: Planets in retrogression give three times the ayurdaya of what they normally give for that navamsa.

Rule #5: Planets in fallen signs reduce their longevity by half. Planets in extreme inimical signs reduce by 1/3. Planets combust the Sun according to special Hindu rules get zero ayurdaya.

In the example given, when you add up the navamsas, the total gross, or estimated, life–span is 49 years (9 + 8 + 3 and so forth).

Then we make these corrective refinements:

1. Mercury is in an enemy sign.   Subtract 4 months (i.e., reduce 1/3).
2. Jupiter is exalted and Rx.   Add 2 years (i.e., multiply X 3).
3. Venus is in enemy sign.   Subtract 2 years and 4 months (i.e., reduce 1/3).
4. Saturn is in a friend's sign.   Add 1 year.

Therefore, the net adjustment to the base of 49 years is to add 4 months. This gives a minimum ayurdaya of 49 years and 4 months which is 13–Aug–1996 A.D. Let us wish the subject many happy returns beyond the guaranteed minimum, just as we would expect a building or bridge to live beyond its estimated design life. Many outlive the minimum, and happily the Rishis also give us the means to enhance it by yoga!

This concludes the remarks of Dr. Vedavyas. It's interesting to me that he didn't really apply a qualitative weighing factor to individual planets — unlike the other three ayurdaya techniques just reviewed.

Does *this* ayurdaya technique work? I should point out five initial problems:

1. His rasi Moon calculation was actually four degrees too low relative to what is currently generated by standard software, yet he arrived at the correct navamsha sign. So I assumed an error on his part in recording

the Moon degree (otherwise he would have recorded a Libra navamsha), and adjusted it to standard computerized output.

2. A navamsha Moon in Scorpio is clearly fallen. Dr. Vedavyas wrote me that a reduction is not taken for this, but he did not explain why. I don't know if this is because the Moon is in the 4th house (a good position for the Moon), or just because it's the Moon. But there is some unstated rule here.

3. He also added a year for Saturn being in a friend's sign, but none of his five rules suggest this. Possibly the rules on friends are the reverse of enemies.

4. He seemed to flag some kind of anti-clockwise rule on the nodes to derive the navamsha, but he came up with the normally derived navamsha. Perhaps he is just stating that the nodes move backwards through the zodiac, which is true.

5. Since Venus is in an enemy's sign, it would seem like the reduction should be half (per rule #3). But this may just be a calculation error as Dr. Vedavyas rushed to put his comments together for me.

Due to communication difficulties, these five questions were unresolved as this book went to press. But it doesn't really matter since the objective was just to communicate the concept. I have studied and applied this technique to various deaths, and I encourage the reader to do the same. It *seems* to me to be yet another example of a technique that does not work. Or else it produces a result that is not very useful. For example, apply it to Richard Nixon (chart # 31) who died at age 81.

A Fifth Method (Ashtakavarga–Based)

I can mention yet a fifth method derived from a more generically pervasive and effective Hindu technique called *ashtakavarga* which literally means "the group of 8 things." It examines planets and houses from 8 different points of view and ultimately assigns a numerical value to each. It is more generally used to measure the relative strength and vitality of a house through its net accumulation of bindus (benefic points) and rekhas (malefic points).

The ancient sage Parasara stated that the grand total of this pointing system should always equal 337 (although some astrologers also add points for the Ascendant ashtakavarga, and there are other variations). Consequently, each house should average around 28 points. If a house ends up with less points, it is weak relative to its own potentials and also weaker than other houses. Conversely, once a house goes above 35 points it gets quite strong. This has special forecasting relevance as transiting planets pass through these houses since it influences the "amplitude" of their responses.

Now a key fact about the ashtakavarga methodology as specifically applied to mortality calculations is that, while most authors go through a sample procedure, they almost invariably add a concluding statement to the effect that it really doesn't work! This is further confirmed by one of India's most respected astrologers, Dr. B. V. Raman, who notes, in his book *Ashtakavarga System of Prediction*, that Indian astrologers very typically make assertions about longevity based upon their more general faith in ashtakavarga with insufficient regard as to whether their mortality forecasts actually manifest. It is the opinion of Dr. Raman that the performance of ashtakavarga as it applies to ayurdaya is generally unreliable — although he considers the possibility that it may be due to an inadequate understanding on the part of modern practitioners.

A second problem is that there are actually multiple mortality methodologies based upon the ashtakavarga. Suffice it to say that there are entire books written on this topic alone for those who wish to further pursue it. One useful point to note, however, is that if any particular house has an abnormally low bindu count in general, that IS *highly* relevant to death timing *if* maraka factors related to that house are otherwise impelling the ayurdaya logic.

In the end, although ashtakavarga will give you an attractive matrix that looks a lot like a Lotus spreadsheet, and which will give the time of death down to the minute, more contemporary authorities will assert that such precision, based solely upon a single mathematical model, is not possible.

What is the point of all these ayurdaya methods if their precision fails? Other than the fact that they are fun, I think the answer is that there are intriguing elements, or hints of the truth, in all of them. Each of them contains good *clues* to a foundation worth building upon. It is also simply to show what continues to be propagated in India to this day, even by worthy experts with significant claims to authority. It may just be to keep alive known elements of an ancient tradition.

However, it does seems that, in reality, many general practitioners actually default back to more classic synthetic judgements looking for an accumulation of confirming indicators based upon the structure of the natal chart, the relevant Dasas and Bhuktis, applicable yogas and certain other custom formulations that generally emphasize the nakshatras.

Nonetheless, I want to be clear that this does not imply that the moment of death cannot, in fact, be derived through a single methodology. There are even more obscure methods which yield good results to assiduous researchers and analysts. But these methods, being built upon a different foundation, are not in the mainstream of Indian astrology, and would therefore unnecessarily complicate the more modest objectives of this text.

OTHER FACTORS — Odd, New & Classic

To further evolve your tool kit, this chapter primarily highlights the function of *eclipses* at death. But before doing that let's take a little "side tour" into some "other" considerations related to death. This includes a brief look at the eccentricity of statistical mortality studies and a more serious look at an interesting fatalistic diurnal.

The Killer Alphabet

In 1987 Dr. Trevor Weston, a London physician and hospital consultant, performed a quite large study of a decade's worth of British mortality statistics. To his shock, he discovered that people whose last names begin with the letters S through Z died a dozen years earlier than the national average. They were also twice as likely to get ulcers and three times as likely to have coronaries.

His theory was to blame the schools, i.e., that the strain of waiting to be called on, and otherwise being last in so many things, made this subset of people morose and introspective. With apologies to my readers across the sea, my personal pet theory is that the correlation relates more to the strain of being the last in line to eject the dross of British food from their systems!

He presented this thesis at a medical association meeting which should mean that astrology still has a chance in the halls of legitimacy. But in any case, it's not a bad fallback when you are working with S–Z clients who are also morosely inclined. Just tell them "the stars" have revealed that they will die 12 years ahead of the national average, and they will go away "happy."

This also reminded me of a similar large study that popped up in the United States in the early 1990's. It showed that left–handed people have a mortality disadvantage of approximately the same magnitude as Dr. Weston's S–Z population. In the end, my suspicion is that studies of this type will probably just demonstrate the statistical quirks associated with slicing any random population into more than one piece based upon some random criterion and then comparing the two. I only mention these because there is a message of caution here for astrologers who like to do large number statistical studies. And, speaking of whom, let's move on to a type of study that's closer to our celestial hearts.

Sunspots

An intriguing mortality study was published in the March 1993 issue of a peer–reviewed scientific journal called *Radiation Research*. It was performed by Barnett Rosenberg, a biophysicist who has set up his own research institute in a field he calls "mortality theory."

What he found was that if the Sun was at a maximum in its 11 year sunspot cycle then the children of mothers born at that time would die an average of 2–3 years sooner than the children of mothers born during the sunspot minimum. He and a colleague studied members of Congress born between 1750 and 1900 who were chosen primarily because their birth and death data were considered likely to be quite accurate.

Rosenberg discovered a clear cycle in the life spans sliding down and climbing up the 11 year cycle, and this basically overlaid the sunspot cycles of 20 years before. He then studied similar data from deceased members of the British House of Commons and alumni of the University of Cambridge, and found the same correlation. You will recall that all of a female's ova ("eggs") are formed by the time she is born. It's logical that they would all be radiation–sensitized at that time thus affecting genetic "fatedness."

The question now concerns what kind of radiation is responsible: electromagnetic (gamma, X and UV) or charged particles (protons and electrons)? To get the answer he will be studying populations in the northern vs. southern hemispheres since magnetic waves travel in a straight line (and are therefore most intense in the south), but charged particles bend due to the earth's own magnetic field (and are more intense towards the north).

Well, large–number mortality studies regularly continue since they draw the intense interest of the world's insurance actuaries. But while interesting, at this time they would seem to be of marginal practical use to an astrologer. So instead let's look at some considerations contained within the key object of our affections, the standard natal chart.

A Perfect Closure Cycle?

In an exchange of correspondence I had with *Data News* publisher Lois Rodden, she made the remark in July of 1993 that she was on a "quest for the perfect diurnal." She had just given a lecture on the very rare topic of the Dynamics of Death (Pluto having just reentered sidereal Scorpio the month before) where I understand she discussed a type of locational diurnal, working with the local time zone, latitude and longitude but the natal TOB (I would like to have presented the basics of her ideas, but mutual deadline constraints did not allow sufficient time for preparation of the necessary materials). So like surfers in an eternal quest for "the perfect wave," some astrologers, presumably including serious readers of this book, search for an arc of periodicity, perhaps based upon the axial rotation of the Earth, that will summarize the life span.

I think it typifies something that lurks in the minds of many good astrologers: that a circle, as a perfect and fully closed construction, should necessarily have an ending perfectly implied in every beginning. It's yin and yang if you will, or perhaps the more human presumption that all world class dramas should come to perfect closure.

Ronald Davison in his book *Cycles of Destiny* had a chapter titled "The Phenomenon of Time." He wrote, "Occultists state that before the reincarnated ego finally comes to birth, there will stretch out before him a picture of the whole life about to be lived out on the physical plane. Usually the ego is given a choice of lives, so that even at this stage there is no absolutely rigid pattern to be followed. Lives offer opportunities, which may be capitalized upon or squandered."

This fairly well conforms to my feeling on the matter which is that "free will" is much more extensive at the soul level, such as when it makes choices that may indeed, repeatedly and severely, constrict and channel "choices" and opportunities at the more material level of personality. This seems quite obvious to anyone who cares to notice. I work from the assumption that the chart itself is chosen — basically to seize its qualitative cycles — so any other discussion about "free will," while useful enough, is much more mundane astrologically.

And that leads us to the LSRev.

Ross Harvey's Life Span Revolution (LSRev)

In Volume VII Number 2 of the magazine *Considerations* published in 1992, editor Ken Gillman decided to publish the preliminary research of astrologer Ross Harvey who lives in Australia. It is Mr. Harvey's contention that he has discovered a fundamental mechanism that will invariably reveal anyone's age at death — generally within a few months although, under various conditions, it may by incorrect by a year or two. This will attempt to summarize his key points:

 Death is fully pre-programmed at birth without regard to cause.

I had a roommate in college who thought that everyone had a specific allocation of heartbeats. As it turns out, the vast collection of ancient Indian writings that Westerners have collectively called Hinduism address this topic at length. This includes the concept of "kundalini" whose "job" in each individual body is to count each breath, pulse and heartbeat. When the body's pre-allocation is met, the heart stops since the heart chakra is said to be under the control of Rudra, who later became Siva or Shiva ("The Destroyer"), and who represents the essence of the catabolic function in nature. While my roommate used this theory to justify the elevation of lethargy to an art form, Mr. Harvey shares a comparable idea which is, in effect, that we each burn personal time at a different rate. I like to think of this as "metaphysical metabolism."

To figure out this "burn rate," he initially anchors each person's life to one full revolution of the earth after birth. Death occurs when all angles return to their original positions (see top of p.121). This is true whether viewed directly or conversely since the experience of time at the soul level is arguably omni-directional (and there are some important death clues in this concept).

For each individual chart, the objective of his method is to develop a rate of personal directed motion such that the angles will always hit a symbolically appropriate natal planet at major life events. He does his initial fitting by a hit-and-miss procedure that starts the search based upon a rate for the average life span (if the average lifespan is 72 years, then the average annual rate allocation would be 5 degrees). Ultimately he averages out the true hit rate. He then merely divides it into 360 to get the life span.

As a secondary alternative to directing the MC by right ascension (RAMC refers to the degree of right ascension from zero Aries — normally eastward — along the plane of the celestial equator), one may substitute the annual 360 degree motion of the transiting Sun in longitude in the year before and after birth. Therefore, to some extent, this theory can even be applied where the TOB is uncertain.

What *does* need to be known is a reasonable number of important events in the person's life since these are the keys to the system. Since they must already have occurred, Mr. Harvey says that the system would generally not be very useful to about age 30 unless that early period was both significantly eventful and documented. He uses standard biographical happenings many of which, in my opinion, may mean more to the social outer world than the personal inner world. I suggest use of rectification events of the type recommended in my Rectification chapter. But even though he is basically forced to use biographies of well-known individuals to test and demonstrate his concept, he seems to get quite good results nonetheless.

To gain some skill with this technique, you could easily start with relatives who are already dead because then the "burn rate" would already be known. For example, let's say you have three siblings and your mother died at age 69 years and 144 days (69.395). Just divide 360 by 69.395 and you will have her personal directed annual rate of 5.188. With regard to events, you already know that she at least had four children whose birth dates are known. Direct the angles to those birth dates (forward and backward) using those rates. This theory would assert that at least one of the axes should be conjunct an appropriate natal planet (my comment: it may very well be a stress planet if its symbolism accurately describes either the child or the lifelong relationship with the child). Then add more major life events to confirm.

Let's look at how he applied this to John F. Kennedy. He uses a rectified TOB for Kennedy only one minute deviant from the 3:15 standard which I use but, as he notes, it really doesn't matter for his purposes (see full JFK chart data in the chapter on assassination). Some of the following table is abbreviated, but it should be self-evident. The "trust fund" reference is to his inheritance of a million dollars on his 21st birthday. I don't know why the birth of his son was not included. Note that the small "d" means direct in motion, and the small "c" means converse.

EVENT	AGE	ASPECT	RATE
Trust Fund	21.000	cASC–0–VE	7.442
Graduated	23.063	cASC–0–JU	7.654
Congress	29.600	dASC–0–PL	7.463
	29.600	cASC–0–UR	7.791
Senate	35.430	cASC–180–PL	7.695
Married	36.290	dASC–0–UR	7.823
Daughter	40.497	dASC–0–MO	7.763
	40.497	cMC–0–MO	7.681
	40.497	dMC–0–VE	7.809
President	43.337	dMC–0–PL	7.691

The average of all 10 events is 7.681 degrees per year giving a projected life span of 46.869. He was assassinated at 46.484, and Mr. Harvey considers this as having been easily predictable by the time Kennedy was no older than 35. After reading my later comments on Kennedy's assassination, hopefully you can see how even further refinement (and certainly confirmation) can be brought to bear upon this concept. I suspect that Mr. Harvey will have more to publish on this matter, so I will leave out many of his further caveats and refinements.

Overall, this seems to be a useful technique once one gets the hang of correctly selecting and retrofitting events to an initially unknown rate of motion. I leave the reader to contemplate a final cryptic remark on my part, i.e., that there is other material in this book to inspire the diligent analyst to some impressive further understandings built upon Mr. Harvey's concept. For example, you can often quite accurately *assume* the significant manifestation of either an objective or subjective event at certain types of progressed stations — especially where other factors confirm. If you learn how to nail down those dates, you can establish a rate of "metaphysical metabolism" that is fully independent of any specific "event knowledge" whatsoever.

ECLIPSES

Eclipses have been known throughout history as powerful factors associated with death, and this may be partially related to the fact that they have measurable effects upon the earth's magnetic field. They often signal reversals in a variety of mundane cycles. An eclipse is a conjunction (or opposition) of the Sun and the Moon at the same (or opposing) declination. Essentially the Sun and Moon must be in alignment with the lunar nodal axis where the orbits of the Sun and Moon intersect. Older astrology books refer to the Sun and Moon as "The Lights," and an eclipse, by definition, has to do with the lights "going out" from the point of view of some location(s) on the earth.

There is extensive mythology surrounding the original motivation behind the unrelenting efforts of the "evil" lunar nodes to extinguish the lights. The nodes are treated as shadow planets (the 8th and 9th) and as strong dark forces in the East. There is argument about whether they can cast aspects or not. Regarding this "evilness" both East and West agree on the negativity of the Descending Node (SN). The West thinks there is a lack of growth at the descending end, and the East emphasizes its stupidity, weirdness and psychic involution — but with spiritual and concentrative potentials. Yet, unlike the West, ancient Hindu texts assert that the North Node is definitely the worse of the two.

The Ascending Node (NN) is mostly denigrated in the East due to their perception of its allegedly insatiable and grasping materiality. It gets much better treatment in the West where such a quality is more likely to be regarded as a "success" factor and therefore a virtue. Thus, for a person to have a billion dollars and want still more is considered to spring from a reasonable level of motivation. Its highly sensory tendencies would therefore be exaggerated, for example, by a natal conjunction with Venus. This is perhaps illustrated by the world–famous exhibitionistic rock star, Elvis Presley, who ultimately died of various excesses.

Eclipses can be either partial or total. For purposes of this topic, my observation suggests that the reader not be concerned with very minor partial eclipses nor with eclipses, no matter how total or observable, that have no strong and *exact* link into the natal chart (and/or its Dasa/ Bhukti periods). The second half of this book will be emphasizing (through perfect conjunction, opposition and square):

> ➤ Transiting and progressed eclipses to sensitive chart points,
> ➤ Transiting and progressed nodes to the same points,
> ➤ Stress transits and progressions to eclipse–sensitized points,
> ➤ The last lunation (generally not eclipses) before birth, and
> ➤ Pre–Natal Eclipses ("PNE's").

PNE's are the (typically) 3–4 eclipses that occur between conception and birth as identified in any good ephemeris. I tend to put critical ones into the chart and watch activity to them just as with any other planetary factor. And if they happen to land right on a subsequent natal planet — watch that planet! They seem to have something to do with the activities of the soul even before it takes possession of a particular body. As two technical points, note that it is possible for there to be a solar eclipse even though one of the lights is up to 18 degrees from the Moon's nodes, and the nodes move about 11 degrees during the pre-natal period.

Eclipse activity is always occurring in charts so, as usual, all the other issues in this book must be woven into the final equation before death becomes a real consideration. It's also useful to remember that there can be various levels of "death" including a project, an ideal, a pet, an anticipation, etc. Further, keep in mind that the NN can only intercept the Moon, and the SN can only intercept the Sun, although any other planet can potentially be afflicted by its contact with these "eclipsing" factors. As an example variation on this, if a person has a Mercury-ruled Asc and Mercury is exactly eclipsed pre-natally, that point will typically produce *at least* one extreme response during the life to certain key progressions and the like.

Note that eclipses are not always "bad." For example, you will often see them just before big lottery wins — although I must add that research studies have shown that big lottery wins, by totally intercepting prior life patterns, are often ultimately perceived as very undesirable indeed.

As a further comment in this regard, in August of 1989 there was a big lunar eclipse at 24-AQ-12 that was fully visible on the East Coast. My wife has her Sun at 25-AQ-47. As the eclipse arrived, I dragged her onto the front porch and pointed her right at the eclipse through its full occurrence. I told her, "Stand here; I want to see if you're going to die" (that's okay, she's a true Aquarius, and they relate well to laboratory experiments).

The net result is that nothing ever happened. One reason is that the orb was slightly over one degree. The other is that nothing else of note was going on in her chart. So don't let eclipses panic you unnecessarily. In fact, don't let them panic you necessarily either. It only encourages them.

Relationship Karma

It's a very odd oversight that almost no books on eclipses make explicit reference to the fact that an eclipse point often has a basic connection to other critical *people* in a person's life. It can be fairly well assured, for example, that if you have several PNE's in, say, your 8th house plus, as is therefore quite likely, the natal lunar node, then there will be key people in your life who have, for example, their Lights, Saturn or Meridian (MC/IC axis) exactly on this point, and they will be involved in some of your key regenerative life issues. And so on with the other houses. It will also often feel quite strange when you relocate your chart to their place of birth (as though you were born where they were) and then you discover that at least one of your nodes or PNE's becomes exactly angular. This actually has much to do with prior life linkages with others.

This is not an astrological "cookbook," and it will not address the alleged "lessons" implied by each sign and house placement of eclipses, the alleged meaning of the direct (i.e., reversed or stationary) nodal cycle, and the alleged differences between the effects of solar vs. lunar, etc. since I have found most of this material to be thinly speculative at best.

However, A.T. Mann, deriving a certain amount of further inspiration from Rodney Collin, has developed some interesting concepts on the pre-natal period and, in fact, gives a third of the natal chart to mysteries related to this period of experience[†]. Hindu literature also has extensive commentary on all this. Generally though you will learn much about eclipses and nodes by simply watching them closely.

A key reason eclipses are so fundamental to death is that they are so fundamental to life. Since they solely involve the Sun/Moon interplay, they have to do with the father/mother archetypes in all their permutations, and all issues of growth vs. habit. For me, one of the key questions about eclipses has been whether they represent a planetary interrupt or planetary intermediation. A lot of metaphysical cookbooks seem to derive their logic from one or the other of these two assumptions. For purposes of a book on death, the concept of an interrupt seems to be more productive.

This idea of an interrupt can be illustrated with the example of Albert Gore, the current U.S. Vice President, who was born on 31-March-1948. On 3/7/89 there was a solar eclipse at 17-PI-10. This was right on his natal 8th house Mercury of 16-PI-54 which rules his transport 3rd and squares his 5th of children. Less than a month later on 4/3/89, as T.

[†] *As an extension of this, A. T. Mann is also doing some of the best astrological work in reincarnation theory that I have seen.*

Saturn was conjunct his P3 Mercury to the minute, his son was hit by a car in Baltimore, MD and knocked about 30 feet. This resulted in serious injury to the child but not his death.

Mr. Gore himself was uninjured because, if you use his given TOB of 12:53 PM, his own angles were completely unaffected either by transit or progression. The effects were basically planetary such as his P2 Moon was conjunct P2 Uranus, Tipper Gore's Mars had gone stationary by P3, and so forth. However, the sole point I want to make here is the fact that Albert Gore has spoken repeatedly about how this (5th house) event totally intercepted (eclipse) his prior thinking (Mercury) about life (the 8th).

Only on the last day or so before a lecture I gave on pre-natal eclipses, at a regional conference sponsored by the National Council for Geocosmic Research (NCGR) in the late 1980's, did I decide to look up my own mother (b. 05/29/22). Many of my lecture points were easily confirmed even though I've never had her time of birth.

For example, the last new moon three days before she was born was at 04-GE-41; at my birth 25 years later, the mNN (mean North Node) was at 04-GE-44. She had two pre-natal eclipses at 23-AR and 21-LI; my Sun is at 22-AR-32. Her last solar eclipse before my conception was exactly on my Desc of 6-CA-43; only seconds of birth time error for me would make it exact TTM.

Indeed 6's and 22's were repeated new- and full-moon "theme" degrees during her pre-natal period. Even before her own conception the last eclipse was at 01-SC-38, and my MC is at 01-SC-55. Her last solar eclipse before that one was at 08-GE which is my wife's exact mNN. My wife's immediate family has multiple exact planetary conjunctions to my angles, and on and on it goes. Since I see these precision patterns all the time in birth relationships, it seemed logical to look for them in death relationships. This concept is briefly discussed in a later chapter on karmic links.

One thing that will become very clear throughout this book is that eclipse sensitization is generally required before a death will occur. One can be having the most horrible transits, but without the necessary supporting eclipse action, death will typically not result. All the examples in this book are based upon fully timed charts, but following are some simple untimed examples to illustrate how much you can sometimes observe with regard to the possibility of death even without the necessary progressed angles, house rulers, and so forth that a TOB would supply.

River Phoenix

As I was working on this chapter, a popular supporting movie actor by the name of River Phoenix stepped outside of a nightclub in Los Angeles, CA around 1 AM on 10/31/93 and just dropped dead on the sidewalk at the age of 23. It eventually turned out that this was drug-related, but that is of no particular relevance. The newspaper on the next day said that was born on 23-Aug-1970 in Madras, OR. He was born with N. Mars at 23-LE, and this was square N. Saturn at 23-TA. This is not a particularly uncommon configuration, except we do take note of the fact that it was exact and at zero degrees of the sidereal signs.

On the day he died, T. Saturn was forming a perfect T-square at 23-AQ, and it had been fully stationary only three days before. T. Pluto was at 24-SC (with Mercury having stationed only a few days before Saturn at 22-SC). All this set up a perfect grand cross at zero degrees of the sidereal fixed signs. While this was an extraordinarily intense pattern in its own right, the real hidden factor that fed into this as a potential death pattern was the perhaps unobserved eclipse that occurred only six days before he was born. It was at 23-AQ-49 thus sensitizing all four of the fixed house cusps that were now being set off.

In addition he also died the year that a P2 eclipse was occurring in his chart, i.e., on the 23rd day after he was born (at 22-PI). Finally, there was yet another eclipse that occurred eight days after he was born, and P2 Mars now at age 23 had moved up to be exactly conjunct this prior eclipse point at 08-VI. Now all the other factors that fully define a death pattern would have to be in place before death could be suggested, and this would require his TOB. But the point of this commentary is to demonstrate how, even without a TOB, applicable elements can quite obviously be seen. Certainly if we bothered to look at the progressed data, we would see even more. But that is for later chapters.

Federico Fellini

As I have already mentioned, the nodes are a simple astronomical variation on eclipses. Now it turns out that River Phoenix was not the only movie person to die on 10/31/93 — so did Federico Fellini of cardiac arrest. Fellini was born on 20-Jan-1920 in Rimini, Italy. When he was born, his tSN (true South Node) was at 22-SC-40 which once again tied it tightly into the transiting factors noted just above. He also had a PNE at 23-SC-09. This was exactly square the PNE of River Phoenix, and therefore it fully tied Fellini into the same transient pattern — again, without any further considerations. Note, by the way, that although Fellini was condemned by the Vatican, "The Universe" seemed to smile on him since he died on a P2 Jupiter station.

These eclipse patterns are an extremely common phenomena. I could sit here and list page after page of examples. The reader may want to review just untimed birth and death dates for Ferdinand Marcos, and many other publicly known personalities, whose mere birth date will give you the exact same message. I encourage you to insert your PNE's into your own chart and observe activity to these points. Some will be much more dominant than others, and this will be seen through theme linkups — such as repeating patterns in the prior or subsequent lunations around birth, involvement with certain hard harmonics or midpoints, and the like. Any activity exactly on a natal planet or angle is critical, of course.

David Koresh

I've spoken of the sensitivity of PNE's, but I would now like to add a qualifier. If you happen to have had one or more P2 eclipses in your chart within roughly 70 days *after* birth (such as noted above for River Phoenix on the progressed year equivalent of his death) that should also be monitored as the *most* sensitive of the eclipse set. Let me use this year's (1993) example of David Koresh, leader of the Branch Davidian compound in Waco, Texas that was assaulted by the U.S. Government, the first of the two times, on a Rx Pluto station on 2/28/93. The compound and most of its inhabitants were ultimately destroyed by fire 51 days later.

Koresh's mother has given his birth data as 17–Aug–1959 @ 8:49 AM CST in Houston, TX (29N45 & 95W21). Using my common methods of progressing the angles, what I saw made me initially reluctant to accept the accuracy of this TOB, and my tendency was aggravated by an awareness that she is said to be an anti–astrology religious fundamentalist. However, there is an extremely supportive factor, and that is the fact that he had a P2 eclipse three days/years before this assault at 23–PI–24 (see 9/17/59). This actually started to draw the attention of authorities to the issue of his many wives and children since it hit exactly upon his sidereal 7th house cusp if this TOB is correct (and remember: this is also one of the maraka houses).

So at the assault where do you think the "end of the matter" P3 IC was (the P3 date was 11/7/60)? Exactly conjunct the prior P2 eclipse at 23-PI-32, and thus again suggesting almost no birth time error. Natally, (death karaka) Saturn is only one degree from his IC, thus further high-lighting his IC's ultimate future involvement. The accuracy of this TOB could be considered further confirmed by the fact that, at the assault, his P2 IC was itself also square his natal Neptune TTM. But my key objective here is to highlight how any P2 eclipse that may occur during a life can become a critically sensitive point depending upon its natal placement and the nature of what may subsequently be applying to it.

Since eclipses are "just" a variation on the nodal axis, here I want to make explicit something that you will note in the later sample charts and in any charts that you may study on your own. Whenever you run across a case that has a natal planet(s) within a degree or so of the nodal axis (particularly if the declination confirms) that planet will usually behave as though it were eclipsed. That is, it typically will reflect extreme sen-sitization, and it will very often be a final active factor in death. This will clearly be so when any classic maraka factors further confirm.

Telly Savalas

As a clear example of this, let's take a quick look at popular actor Telly Savalas who died of prostate cancer in Los Angeles, CA on January 22, 1994. Despite acting in over 60 movies, he was most remembered for his role as the gruff, gritty but oddly–likeable detective "Kojak." Accor-ding to his mother's memory he was born at "5" AM EST on 20–Jan–1924 in Garden City, NY 40N44 & 073W58 (chart not shown). I backed this chart up about 4–5 minutes to get Scorpio–rising with Mars strong in its own sign in the 1st (he mostly played policemen and tough guys) along with Jupiter.

This sign adjustment (not to be confused with a true rectification) is plausible from many other points of view including, for example, the fact that he received his first movie role during a Jupiter bhukti, and achieved his greatest fame (1st house) as Kojak during a Jupiter bhukti (Jupiter would be in his 1st). In any case, data in the following two paragraphs will make my simple point.

Savalas died during a Venus dasa and Rahu Bhukti. Natally Venus is, in fact, conjunct his nodal axis (the tSN) within slightly over a degree (in the 4th with Uranus). Further, Venus is a maraka since it rules his 7th (and 12th), and this nodal/bhukti Venus is also in a mutual reception with an exalted Saturn in his 12th. Saturn aspects and strengthens his 3rd house Capricorn Sun. At his death, this P3 Sun (ruler of his 10th) was tightly conjunct N. Neptune and perfectly square P3 Saturn TTM.

Prostate cancer is supported by the fact that P3 maraka Venus was conjunct P3 Neptune within a quarter of a degree (cellular chaos). Natally, he also has the Moon exactly conjunct Pluto in the 8th. This links back to the nodes again since P3 Pluto was conjunct his P3 NN at death. A final nodal link is the fact that his N. Mercury (ruler of his 8th) is in his maraka 2nd, and his P3 SN was conjunct this planet at death.

Before leaving this idea I just want to bring to your attention to a related notion, and that is the concept of "occultation." It is somewhat like an eclipse, but is more generic in that it pertains to the temporary visual blocking of any body in space by another. For example, certain fixed stars are quite regularly occulted and this includes, for example, Regulus, which is said to have an association with leaders. The reader may wish to further investigate the function of occultations as a type of eclipse – particularly since the study of fixed stars can be extremely productive in the analysis of fated events.

Astrologer's Death Experience

I have a very interesting summary case to pass along that will illustrate, by its extreme nature, a number of these related points. After this book was about 90% done, I met an astrologer and hypnotherapist who expressed a great interest in its topic and asked to review the draft. After she saw my continuous heavy emphasis upon eclipses she went back to her own chart and was astonished to discover that she was born right in the midst of one! In addition Mercury was caught up with this at the same sign and degree (both longitude and declination), and Mercury is in a mutual reception with the ruler of her 1st (Venus). See chart # 4 (b. 30–May–1946 @ 4:33 PM EDT in Cobleskill, NY 42N41 & 74W29).

She then came back with this story. As it turns out, she somewhat secretly carries two charts. The second is for an event almost 25 years ago in Camp Springs, MD (38N48 & 76W54) on 3/13/69 when she believes she died, and a new soul took over. She was driving on the Washington D.C. Beltway when she was knocked completely off the road and into the back seat of her Volkswagen beetle. She went through all the now over-popularized phases of the near death experience. She felt herself being gripped in a vice-like embrace that felt like a cocoon. She rose

6th Pisces	7th Aries	8th Taurus Mercury T≈++ Moon M Sun Rahu Dx ♓	9th Gemini Venus ≈++ Saturn RTe++
5th Aquarius	MARS Jupiter beginning on 08/27/1953 MARS Saturn beginning on 08/03/1954 MARS Mercury beginning on 09/12/1955 MARS Ketu beginning on 09/09/1956 MARS Venus beginning on 02/06/1957 MARS Sun beginning on 04/06/1958 MARS Moon beginning on 08/12/1958		10th Cancer Mars f ♇
4th Capricorn	RAHU Rahu beginning on 03/12/1959 RAHU Jupiter beginning on 11/24/1961 RAHU Saturn beginning on 04/18/1964 RAHU Mercury beginning on 02/24/1967 RAHU Ketu beginning on 09/12/1969 RAHU Venus beginning on 09/30/1970		11th Leo
3rd Sagittarius	2nd Scorpio Ketu Dx --	1st Libra Ascendant e	12th Virgo Jupiter Rx -- ♆

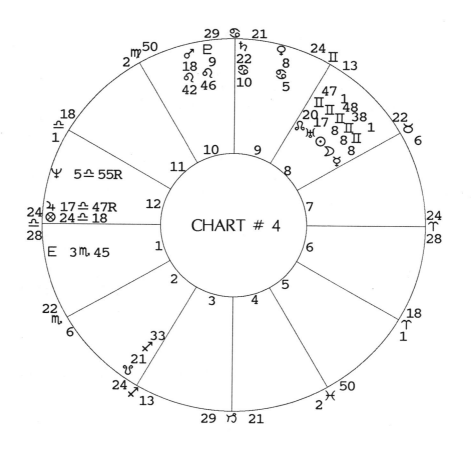

above and looked down upon herself. She had the experience of the white light, the choice to stay or leave, and she heard a voice tell her to relax and that she was going to be fine.

Later in the hospital she had a cardiac arrest resulting in a second out of body experience. The upshot of all this is that she immediately became psychic. When she would go into a room, all the objects in the room would be animated. It became so disconcerting that she chose to shut down this faculty. The fact that she had begun a practical career as a CPA undoubtedly contributed to the stress. She consulted several psychics about this trying to pin down the exact time of the new soul birth, and she had a dream in which a big clock showed the time of 8:10 AM EST. The psychics independently confirmed 8:10.

I'll go into this a bit more below, but right now I want to pass along a comment that is very relevant to the concept of eclipses as interceptors and disconnectors. And that is that the psychics told her that her soul had *always* been tenuously connected to her body in the first place, and if she hadn't died at that time, she would have died anyway not too long after.

Going back to her chart, what we see is that her original eclipsed birth occurred when the Sun, Moon, Mercury – plus Uranus and the NN – were all in the 8th house. "Death" ultimately occurred during a Rahu Dasa and Mercury Bhukti – thus animating all the 8th house factors including the birth eclipse which Bhukti Mercury is conjunct. Again, you will recall that Mercury is also in a mutual reception with the ruler of the 1st; it is further at the same natal declination as her 8th house Uranus (as is Saturn). To strengthen the pattern, note that this natal eclipse was repeated in the 8th house of the navamsha chart which also had Libra rising.

Natally, Saturn is with the ruler of the 1st which itself disposes the 8th. Not only is Saturn the death karaka; in this case it is also the atma (soul) karaka since it is the natal planet at the highest degree. Therefore, let's take a quick look at some precipitating data starting with five main Saturn factors:

> ➤ T. Saturn was right on the maraka Desc at 24–AR. For anyone born on a new Moon, let alone an eclipse, the Part of (Mis)fortune is always right on the Asc, so this transit compounded the effect on the 1st.

➤ P2 Saturn (at 24–CA) was also exactly square the horizon (the Asc/Desc axis).

➤ P3 Saturn was essentially stationary (see 3/31/47) and exactly octile to Uranus.

➤ P2 Bhukti planet Mercury, natally caught up in the eclipse, was conjunct N. Saturn (at 22–CA).

➤ The T. Moon at 22–CP perfectly opposed N. Saturn.

Since she was in a Rahu Dasa, let's look at some nodal factors:

➤ The T. tNN (true North Node) was at the cusp of the Placidus 6th (01–AR) conjunct the P2 Moon (this was opposite a T. Jupiter/Uranus conjunction at 02–LI).

➤ The P3 mNN (05–SA) was square the P3 Asc (05–VI) with T. Mars at 06–SA.

➤ P3 Mars was square the natal nodes within half a degree.

Some other factors contributing to a disconnect was T. Pluto at the cusp of her sidereal 12th, and the fact that her P2 Sun (the more general indicator of the soul) was exactly opposing P2 Neptune that year. One factor contributing to her protection was the fact that T. Venus, ruler of her 1st, was going stationary Rx within just a few days, and this was applying back to T. Saturn within 2 degrees. Protection factors are discussed in a later chapter. Considering that Mercury was her Bhukti planet and was caught up in the birth eclipse, it is perhaps of speculative interest that she may have been conceived on a Mercury station (see 8/30/45) since this station was at 21–LE, and her P2 MC at the accident was at 21–LE.

Finally, for those, including myself, who may be disinclined to accept that a new soul may have taken over this body (in the psychic literature this is often referred to as a "walk in"), note that this person had a huge unexpected flood on the evening of 11/27/93 in the basement of her home in a Washington, D.C. suburb. There was a second flood a week later. There is, in fact, absolutely nothing going on with regard to transiting Mars, Uranus or Neptune in her first chart.

Common sense, and the fact that I have seen other home flooding charts, indicate that that is clearly impossible. Investigative readers may notice there was an eclipse the night *after* this event somewhat over one degree from her natal eclipse. Alas, time on the earth is specifically designed to be experienced linearly, so that doesn't count! And even then, obvious common transits would have to animate and clearly reinforce the event. Many other very strange things were happening in home and career. And, as a final comment in support of this argument, when transiting Neptune returned to her Moon, she spontaneously abandoned her home and moved to California with no visible means of support, etc.

But: when you look at the rebirth chart (see chart # 5) it is quite clear:

➤ Her new P3 Asc was conjunct the prior T. eclipse within one degree.
➤ The flood occurred only two days after entering a Jupiter Bhukti, and natal Jupiter is exactly conjunct natal Uranus. Only seconds of birth time error would have made this new bhukti period correspond exactly with this event.
➤ Finally we see that T. Uranus and then Neptune were exactly on her MC those two weekends. This is commonly seen in home flooding charts as these two planets push their symbolic energies down along the Meridian.

Interestingly, the new chart has Aries (vs. Libra) rising, with its ruling planet strong in Scorpio in the occult 8th (hence the rebirth with psychic capabilities). There is still somewhat of a Libra–rising effect, however, since the new chart has a nearly stationary Venus in the 1st. Venus will clearly be a maraka factor her next time around since it rules both the 2nd and the 7th and is conjunct a fallen Saturn.

This will close out my introductory comments on eclipses and the nodes. By the end of this book, you will see enough 1) to convince you that these are key factors in death determination, 2) to know what the pattern tends to look like, and 3) to develop a feel for the extent to which a chart will demonstrate more or less sensitivity to nodal and eclipse factors as versus other factors.

12th Pisces Rahu Rx —	1st Aries Saturn fe Venus s– Ascendant	2nd Taurus	3rd Gemini
11th Aquarius Mercury + Sun Te	MARS Mars beginning on 03/05/1984 MARS Rahu beginning on 08/02/1984 MARS Jupiter beginning on 08/20/1985 MARS Saturn beginning on 07/26/1986 MARS Mercury beginning on 09/05/1987 MARS Ketu beginning on 09/02/1988 MARS Venus beginning on 01/29/1989	4th Cancer	
10th Capricorn	MARS Sun beginning on 03/29/1990 MARS Moon beginning on 08/05/1990 RAHU Rahu beginning on 03/05/1991 RAHU Jupiter beginning on 11/17/1993 RAHU Saturn beginning on 04/11/1996 RAHU Mercury beginning on 02/17/1999	5th Leo	
9th Sagittarius Moon e+	8th Scorpio Mars 0 ♇	7th Libra	6th Virgo Ketu Rx E Jupiter Rx T–– ♅ ♇

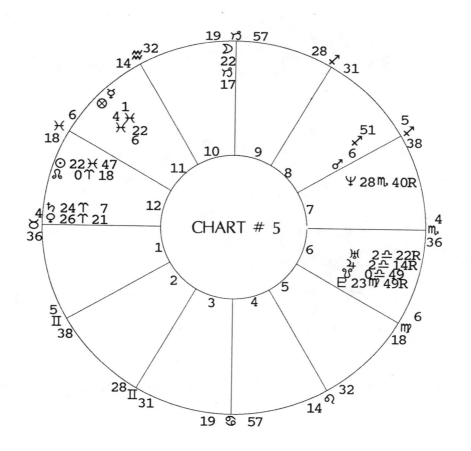

CHART # 5

RECTIFICATION VIA DEATH

It may seem odd to transition into the more technically "applied" phase of this text via the topic of rectification which normally is considered difficult. But I want to do two things. First, I want to impress upon you how some of the new techniques you've just learned can make the rectification of a chart much easier and more certain than you would otherwise have thought possible. Second, via these first half dozen cases, I want to begin to illustrate that death occurs with as much precision and clarity as any other event albeit with its own requirements. Recall that this book will generally be working strictly with conjunctions, oppositions and squares that have a maximum orb of one degree.

The extensive availability of accurate birth and death records, particularly on well-known personalities, provides an excellent opportunity to repeatedly test these new techniques. However, much caution is in order. Data on movie stars are especially to be doubted because the entire industry is Neptunian to begin with. For many reasons there is much inventing of new, and typically more useful, truths. This caution applies not only to data in biographies and from their relatives and friends — it even applies, without doubt, to alleged birth certificates.

I recall being amused by a friend of mine who is the publisher of a major "personalities" magazine. He published in passing the birth date of an aging household name "sexpot" that was quite older than the one on her driver's license. After being harassed by her attorneys for this offense, he eventually had to up the ante by advising them that if they didn't leave him alone he would publish her *real* birth date. So that's often how it is.

Bad birth data is a key factor that really damages the development of forecast confidence. This further impacts the reputation of astrologers in general. I can't tell you how many wrong charts I've seen, many of them immortalized in the books of well-known astrologers, used to retroactively explain, with impressive certitude, some particular phenomena. There are even bad data in the fine research work of the Gauquelins that was supposedly all based upon birth certificates (possibly just errors in transposition).

I've even caught myself entering bad birth data into this book. In fact, it is statistically certain that there continue to be data error and defective commentary in this book (and this is without even considering that much of it was written under very hard Neptune transits and progressions). A close monitoring of the literature also shows that other people in the astrological community who have developed reputations specifically in the area of research will themselves sometimes publish contradictory birth data that each claims is from a primary source.

Even Lois Rodden, who represents to me the pinnacle of care in this area, often publishes corrections, and sometimes these are to prior corrections. If you keep up with them it's fine, but if not, it presents obvious problems depending upon where you enter the data stream. Ms. Rodden has a quite rigorous contamination philosophy which currently presents the best model for other researchers.

These introductory remarks are therefore not intended to cast stones, but rather to indicate how slippery the entire topic is, and how you must keep track of where your data has been. Astrologers who insist upon working with nothing but the highest quality data will find themselves internalizing less convoluted "explanations," i.e., the astrological equivalent of nervous tics, and their ability to pick out defective charts will greatly improve.

If at all possible, I recommend validating every single chart you delineate by using two or three *angular* events that were *out of the person's control*. This includes any shocks to the body such as broken bones, house floods or fires, unexpected career gains or losses, death of parents, shocks to or from the spouse (this will also validate the true, i.e., sidereal ruler of the 7th), and so forth. Over time you will go much less wrong than if you use ceremonies such as marriage or divorce, most children and money issues, issues that develop over time, what they do for a living, parental information, looks, attitudes, alleged personality characteristics, and the like.

The point of all this is that if the life patterns cannot be correctly established astrologically, then neither can the death. This is especially so when very sensitive sub-charts are used such as various harmonic charts (the example of Amy Fisher will be mentioned below) or lunar returns. Not too long ago I told a resistant person that she could not have broken her leg in the week she claimed if she was born at 6:06 as she insisted. I told her it had to be 6:02 or 6:03. Several months later she accidentally discovered she was born at 6:03.

Don't rationalize charts and don't accept wrong information. On the flip side, don't insist a written birth time is wrong because it won't match your theory — unless you can prove your theory over and over again against the nine criteria noted in the Preface. Let me start out fanning the flames of controversy with a couple of quite significant adjustments. After these cases, it will only get easier.

CASE 1 (Elvis Presley)

I have dozens of significantly conflicted charts in my files of famous people. Let's start here with one of the worst, that of the most popular singer/performer in world history based upon total number of records sold (including 45 gold records and success in 20 consecutive movies). At age 42 on August 16, 1977, if you can believe his coroners instead of his fan clubs, Elvis Presley died. This was said to be from heart failure related to prescription drug abuse. In July of 1981 a copy of his birth certificate was sent to *The Mercury Hour* magazine. It said he was born on 8-Jan-1935 at 4:35 AM CST in East Tupelo, Mississippi (34N15 & 88W43). This would give an Asc of 12-SA-21.

In July 1989 another contributor wrote that the birth certificate on display at Graceland indicated he was born in Tupelo (34N16) at 3:37 AM. This would give tropical 00-SA rising. There is further documentation to indicate that Elvis himself, when asked, gave his own TOB as 3:25 AM to one astrologer and 3:30 AM to another. For all four of these birth times, the main Hindu chart will remain the same, with Scorpio rising and his death occurring in a Saturn/Moon period (with both planets natally in his 4th) although subcharts, such as the navamsha, will greatly differ (see chart # 6A arbitrarily set up for the 4:35 time).

I've also found an old birth time of 12:20 PM in a 1972 book titled *The Circle Book of Charts* (and elsewhere I've read that someone in Elvis' family supposedly commissioned a chart for this TOB). But the chart looks rigged, and the compiler of the book made no claims about its source and validity, so I will ignore it. But it does show that the issue is really up on the air. Let's now begin the arguments.

The heart problem was revealed by the applying P2 Sun, ruler of the 10th, conjunct the stronger P2 Saturn within 12 minutes at death (the Dasa planet Saturn was stronger in its own sign). Perhaps a hint of his fame could be suggested by the fact that the T. Sun was entering his 10th on the day of his death. The P2 node was exactly conjunct the ruler of the (maraka) 7th. This was Venus, and the tightest 8th harmonic aspect

5th Pisces	6th Aries	7th Taurus	8th Gemini
	♓		
4th Aquarius Saturn　M Moon　T-	JUPITER Ketu　beginning on 08/08/1956 JUPITER Venus　beginning on 07/14/1957 JUPITER Sun　beginning on 03/14/1960 JUPITER Moon　beginning on 01/02/1961 JUPITER Mars　beginning on 05/02/1962 JUPITER Rahu　beginning on 04/08/1963 SATURN Saturn　beginning on 09/02/1965 SATURN Mercury beginning on 09/05/1968 SATURN Ketu　beginning on 05/14/1971 SATURN Venus　beginning on 06/23/1972 SATURN Sun　beginning on 08/23/1975 SATURN Moon　beginning on 08/05/1976 SATURN Mars　beginning on 03/05/1978	9th Cancer Ketu　　-- ♇
3rd Capricorn Venus　++ Rahu　++			10th Leo ♆
2nd Sagittarius Sun　++ Mercury　e+	1st Scorpio Ascendant	12th Libra Jupiter　T	11th Virgo Mars

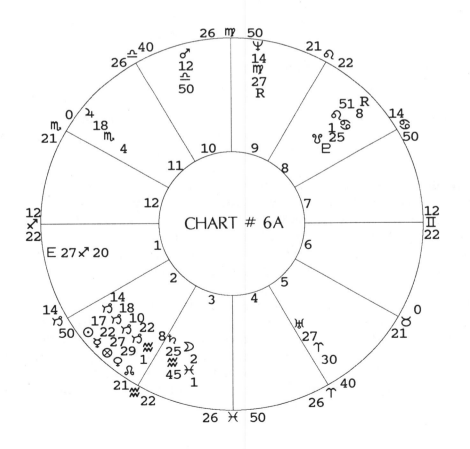

in his natal chart was its tri-octile (135 degrees) to Neptune (drugs).

At death, T. Neptune (drugs) was also Rx at 13-SA thus beginning the argument for the 4:35 chart which has an Asc of 12-SA-21. Parenthetically, I've seen other heart failures with Neptune on the Asc due to its highly lethargic impact upon the body's entire energy output (of course, other factors are also required). This could also imply the issue of drugs. P2 Pluto was also square P2 Mars TTM, and T. Pluto was exactly conjunct natal Mars (ruler of his 1st). Most of these factors are just a background since they would be true regardless of the TOB.

The Graceland 3:37 chart would initially seem to have something really going for it because the P3 MC was square the P3 nodes, and P2 Mars was conjunct the P2 MC within 3 minutes. But in the end I regard this TOB as unlikely because there are no tight transits to angles (natal or progressed), nor does adequate eclipse activity present itself.

Elvis was one of those people whose birth was itself bracketed between two eclipses. The eclipsed new Moon three days before birth was at 13-CP-57. The powerful eclipse full Moon 11 days after birth was at 28-CA-39 (for that matter, oddly enough, the very next new Moon was also an eclipse). The last eclipses right before he died were at 14-LI and 28-AR, exactly square the bracketing birth set. With that in mind, we would expect definite further action with regard to those hard numbers (esp. the more powerful 28's), yet the 3:37 Graceland chart has nothing at those points.

Therefore further argument for the 4:35 chart comes from the fact that the P3 Asc was at 28-CA (having just passed over P3 Pluto at 27-CA, and with P2 Uranus at 28-AR). Using this TOB we find that the P3 MC was conjunct the natal Sun within 2 minutes (remember, he was called "The King"). Recall that the N. ruler of the maraka 7th was also at 29-CP which is only a degree off this eclipse.

Jupiter at death was generally discussed earlier. Here we see P2 Jupiter Rx at 14-SA, i.e., conjunct the Asc as may especially be expected for a famous singer who died of excesses since JU rules both, and Jupiter is a maraka since it rules his 2nd. So we see that the 4:35 chart reflects the powerful 28's while the 3:37 Graceland chart does not. In fact, the 4:35 P3 Asc (28-CA-28) was a perfect harmonic of the pre-birth eclipse (28-CA-39) and the pre-death eclipse (28-AR-17).

So, sound good? Are you persuaded? Well I'm not. There is a small problem here and also a massive one. The "small" one is his marriage on 1 May 1967. The Graceland 3:37 chart would have his P3 MC conjunct N. Jupiter to the same degree, and his P3 Asc conjunct N. Venus to the same minute! This is utterly classic, and the 4:35 chart has none of this.

But that's just the small problem. The really *big* problem is with the overall chart itself. None of these charts give the slightest hint of his massive fame and near immortality. How can this be? Here is a man who everyone referred to as "The King", who travelled with an huge entourage, who lived in the equivalent of a castle, and so forth. But there is no denying the fact that his chart is utterly mundane. Let me dare to say that no Hindu astrologer would pick up this chart and declare fame at all, let alone Presley's level of fame.

So here is what I think. What Hindu word means "king?" Raj, right? So why does this chart not have (at least) a rajayoga? What would it take to get a rajayoga? Only one thing — that he be born at any of these exact same times, but in the PM! I recognize that this is a large proposal, but I'll explain why. Meanwhile I ask the reader to please recall how long it took for him or her to get straight on the meaning of these latin initials (AM/PM). Presley was born in the 30's in a small rural town in one of the most educationally backward states in the nation. It would not strike me as implausible at all that the AM–PM designator could have been recorded incorrectly.

What happens if we assume PM? First, Mercury moves into the same house with Venus since, over the course of the day, Mercury actually changes signs sidereally. Second, this would give him Gemini-rising (see chart # 6B arbitrarily set up for 4:35 PM), and Elvis was a twin whose brother died at birth (allegedly at 4:00). Also, whenever a Mercury-ruled sign rises, we get the relatively rare rajayoga condition if Mercury and Venus are in the same house. That would now be the case with Presley.

Further, this rajayoga is in the 8th, and this highlights a startling similarity. Coincidentally, there are two other famous singer/performers noted in this book. One is Karen Carpenter who sold a massive amount of records (see chart # 45), and the other is Eric Clapton who has won every award the music industry has to offer (see later chart # 11). What you see in both of their charts is that each has the exact same rajayoga, i.e., Mercury and Venus are combined in the 8th for a Mercury-ruled

10th Pisces	11th Aries	12th Taurus	1st Gemini Ascendant
	♓		
9th Aquarius Saturn MT Moon –	JUPITER Rahu beginning on 05/13/1953 SATURN Saturn beginning on 10/07/1955 SATURN Mercury beginning on 10/10/1958 SATURN Ketu beginning on 06/19/1961 SATURN Venus beginning on 07/28/1962 SATURN Sun beginning on 09/28/1965 SATURN Moon beginning on 09/10/1966	2nd Cancer Ketu ––
8th Capricorn Mercury Re+ Venus RT++ Rahu ++	SATURN Mars beginning on 04/10/1968 SATURN Rahu beginning on 05/19/1969 SATURN Jupiter beginning on 03/25/1972 MERCURY Mercury beginning on 10/07/1974 MERCURY Ketu beginning on 03/04/1977 MERCURY Venus beginning on 03/01/1978	3rd Leo ♇
7th Sagittarius Sun ++	6th Scorpio	5th Libra Jupiter	4th Virgo Mars ––

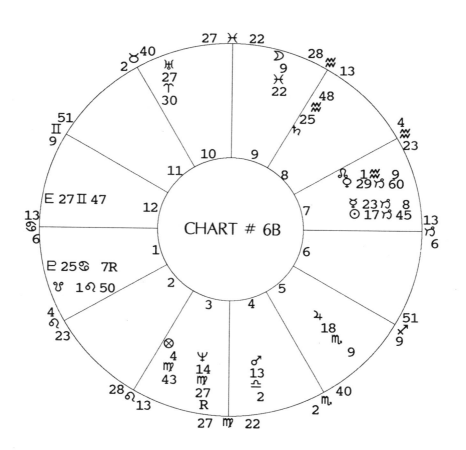

CHART # 6B

Asc. Try seeing those kinds of "coincidences" in their three Western charts! Notice that all these rajayogas also include the ruler of the 1st.

But Presley was far and away the most famous of the three. Why? Among other reasons, it is because his rajayoga was extremely animated by an opposition from N. Pluto, and a square from a stationary N. Uranus. So now a second question arises: does his navamsha confirm his status, and can a PM chart accommodate his marriage and his death? The answers are yes to all. Let's start with the navamshas.

A 3:25 or 3:30 PM TOB would give a Scorpio rising navamsha, with the Sun, as ruler of the 10th, in the 1st being directly aspected by Jupiter from the 7th. As ruler of the 9th, the Moon is a trikona and is well placed in the 4th. Venus was exalted in the other trikona (the 5th) and in a mutual reception with Jupiter. Mars was fallen in Cancer in the 9th, and he had problems with his father. Saturn was exalted in Libra in the 12th thus suggesting some ultimate problems with his health (the 6th). Note, however, that little of this pattern would be true if he were born five minutes later.

A 4:35 PM TOB also produces an impressive navamsha. Aries rises, and its ruler is fallen in Cancer in the 4th, but this gives power to the 10th where it would be exalted. Mercury (main chart ruler) is in the 10th in the same sign as in the main chart (a positive condition called "vargo-ttama"). The ruler of the 10th is exalted in an angle. The ruler of the 2nd is Venus, and it is in a mutual reception with Jupiter which is actually in the 2nd (thus contributing to his great wealth). Note that the AM navam-shas had none of these types of powerful patterns that should be typical for a life such as Presley's.

Regarding his marriage, a 3:30 PM TOB would have his P3 IC conjunct N. Jupiter (R. of his 7th) suggesting a past–life link (as did his P2 IC con-junct P2 Neptune within a degree) but, in any case, these are totally appropriate angle connections. His P3 Moon was only a few applying degrees from P3 Venus, while his P2 Moon was opposite N. Jupiter (R. of the 7th) within 10 minutes. A 4:35 PM TOB hangs in there with his P2 MC square N. Venus within 12 minutes while his P2 Moon is still oppo-site N. Jupiter within a degree.

The PM charts also support the death itself. He would be in a Mercury Dasa and Bhukti if born at 3:25, 3:30, 3:35 or 3:37 PM. Mercury is ruler of the 1st and 4th and is in the 8th. P3 Mars was opposing this N. Mercury from the maraka 2nd within about 1/2 of an applying degree. 3:25 PM would have his P3 Asc (as opposed to his N. Asc discussed in the AM series above) exactly conjunct the almost stationary T. Neptune. As noted above, Mercury is natally opposed by Pluto and squared by a stationary Uranus (which had just been eclipsed). A 3:35 PM chart would have the P3 Moon (ruler of the maraka 2nd) exactly conjunct his P3 NN, and T. maraka Jupiter exactly conj the Asc.

But I think I'll settle for the 4:35 PM chart. Natally, this would give 13–CA rising with N. Mars at 13–LI (among other things, he needed this strong Mars energy to the horizon to perform so hard). At death, T. Pluto at 12–LI was conj Mars and therefore square the Asc, and brings us right back at the eclipse series discussed at the beginning of this case (13–CP and 14–LI). This reemphasizes the importance of the eclipses in his chart and, in fact, using 4:35 PM he would be in a nodal (SN) Bhukti (Dasa planet in the 8th; Bhukti "planet" in the 2nd).

[Despite Elvis' super 8th house, it was still tremendously weak by a numerical weighing system called the ashtakavarga which I already mentioned in the discussion of longevity calculation methods. That is a key part of the explanation for an ongoing susceptibility to death when the other necessary factors move into position.]

A confirming final thought for a PM TOB (driven primarily by the Mercury/Venus rajayoga logic) is that, at his death, P3 Mercury and P3 Venus were exactly conjunct, and this could form part of a symbolic argument for his continuing cult status almost 20 years later.

CASE 2 (George Bush)

Another example of rectification via death is the chart of former president George Bush. To this day, almost every astrologer in the world uses an unproven birth time somewhere between 11 and 12 AM EDT, and many well-known astrologers have taken firm written positions of 11:00, 11:05, 11:30, 11:38, 11:45 and others. This is because this was supposedly his mother's recollection and also because some alleged "Washington Insiders" had told the late D.C. astrologer, Barbara Watters, that this was so.

As is so typical, all these charts were based upon subjective judgements that astrologers made about the President or just upon a couple of events, but it even extended to drawing inferences about his alleged "astrocartographic karma" in various countries as judged by various practitioners who adjusted his chart accordingly. Regrettably, there was never any concerted effort to fully account for *all* major personal events in his life that were out of his control. The angles (including progressed) should be involved in every single instance with a maximum orb of one degree, and the symbolism should be simple and appropriate.

Years ago I published a dated list of 25 qualifying events including activities such as being shot from his plane (9/2/44), Reagan's attempted assassination (3/30/81), Bush's heart fibrillation (5/4/91), when he was accidentally tear gassed in Panama (6/11/92), when he won and lost various elections, his appointments, birth data on all his children, and many more. Using the above data and constraints, it became indisputably clear, at least to me, that he was actually born at 3:45:30 PM EDT on 12-June-1924 in Milton, MA 42N15 & 071W05 (see chart # 7).

The reader may speculate why the President's friends and family were circulating wrong information. The bottom line is that this gave him a tropical Asc of 28-LI (his sidereal Asc therefore remains LI). This would have Venus, his natally *stationary* chart ruler, conjunct Pluto in the 9th, an exalted Saturn conj his Asc, and so forth. This would also give an MC of 03-LE. For purposes of this book, his correct MC is especially relevant because decades before he became President both a young daughter died (10/11/53), and his father died (10/08/72).

These deaths fully helped confirm the rectification because the last lunar eclipse (7/26) immediately before his daughter's death was at 03-AQ (Bush's IC — and with transiting Saturn exactly conjunct his correct Asc of 28-LI at the death). The last lunar eclipse (again on 7/26) immediately before his father's death was also at 03-AQ. And, for that matter, before his family ancestral home (IC) on the Maine coast was "killed" by a hurricane (11/2/91), with family heirlooms floating out to sea, the last lunar eclipse was again on 7/26 at 03-AQ. These three are the *only* eclipses at 03-AQ in the 20th century.

Parenthetically, I mentioned above the attempted assassination of President Reagan (who also has no certified TOB). The simple power of eclipses again becomes evident because the last solar eclipse (2/4/81) before he was shot was at 16-AQ which is exactly his natal Sun.

6th Pisces	7th Aries	8th Taurus Mercury T≈++ Sun e	9th Gemini Venus Dx ≈++ ♇
5th Aquarius Ketu Rx Mars – ♓	SATURN Sun beginning on 03/09/1973 SATURN Moon beginning on 02/21/1974 SATURN Mars beginning on 09/21/1975 SATURN Rahu beginning on 10/30/1976 SATURN Jupiter beginning on 09/06/1979 MERCURY Mercury beginning on 03/18/1982 MERCURY Ketu beginning on 08/15/1984		10th Cancer ♆
4th Capricorn	MERCURY Venus beginning on 08/12/1985 MERCURY Sun beginning on 06/12/1988 MERCURY Moon beginning on 04/18/1989 MERCURY Mars beginning on 09/18/1990 MERCURY Rahu beginning on 09/15/1991 MERCURY Jupiter beginning on 04/03/1994		11th Leo Rahu Rx
3rd Sagittarius	2nd Scorpio Jupiter Rx ++	1st Libra Saturn Rx ERT Ascendant	12th Virgo Moon

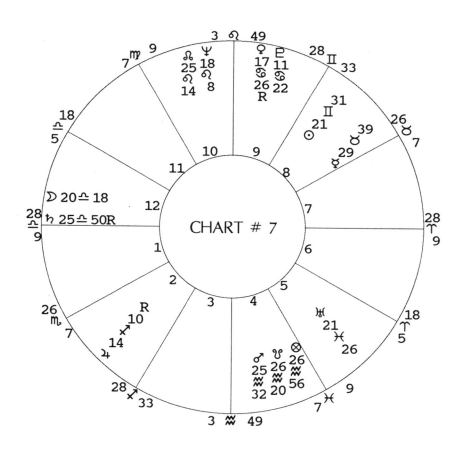

CASE 3 (John Connolly)

Continuing with politicians, while I was writing this chapter former three-term Texas Governor John Connolly died in Houston, TX of pulmonary fibrosis at age 76 on 6/15/93. His given data is: 27-Feb-1917 @ "2:00" AM CST in Floresville, TX 29N08 & 098W09. This time of birth has been rounded which will be demonstrated here, and this rectification will be further validated in the chapter on assassinations since he was seriously injured in the same car with former President John Kennedy when Kennedy was killed on 11/22/63.

A month before he died, Connolly had been admitted to the hospital on 5/17/93 with breathing problems. The P3 date for this was 12/13/19 and, only 1/2 a day/month before this, Mercury went stationary by P3. Mercury, of course, rules the lungs. In the main chart, Saturn is in the house opposing Mercury, and in the navamsha chart Saturn is in the same house with Mercury. T. Mercury was at 18-CA which natally is conjunct his tSN.

I have corrected Connolly's TOB from 2:00 AM (16-SA-07 rising) to 01:47 (see chart # 8) for three main reasons, and not yet counting the assassination factors. See if you can agree (especially after you finish this book):

⏱ His new Asc would be 13-SA-18, and the last eclipse only 11 days before his death was at 13-SA-55.

⏱ Using this TOB, both his P3 Asc and P3 Mars would be perfectly conjunct TTM at his death at 07-LI-28.

⏱ The P3 MC and P3 Pluto were both at 07-CA (as was the progressed Part of (Mis)fortune), so the two progressed angles were exactly caught up in the exact P3 Mars-Pluto square (per point 2). The angles and the eclipse would all be uncoupled by several degrees from this phenomena (indeed, any phenomena) using the original TOB. So clearly it is not functional.

Just to build perceptual strength, let's document three other non-angular (i.e., non-rectificational) considerations:

⏱ T. Pluto was at 23-SC; this is not only his P3 mSN and the cusp of his sidereal 1st; 23-SC was also the last new Moon before he was

5th Pisces	6th Aries Jupiter T++ Moon Te+	7th Taurus	8th Gemini Ketu Rx E ♇
4th Aquarius Venus e Sun -- Mars -	SATURN Saturn beginning on 11/29/1972 SATURN Mercury beginning on 12/02/1975 SATURN Ketu beginning on 08/11/1978 SATURN Venus beginning on 09/20/1979 SATURN Sun beginning on 11/20/1982		9th Cancer Saturn Rx e ♆
	SATURN Moon beginning on 11/02/1983 SATURN Mars beginning on 06/02/1985 SATURN Rahu beginning on 07/11/1986 SATURN Jupiter beginning on 05/17/1989 MERCURY Mercury beginning on 11/29/1991 MERCURY Ketu beginning on 04/26/1994	10th Leo	
3rd Capricorn Mercury - ♓	1st Scorpio Ascendant	12th Libra	11th Virgo
2nd Sagittarius Rahu Rx -			

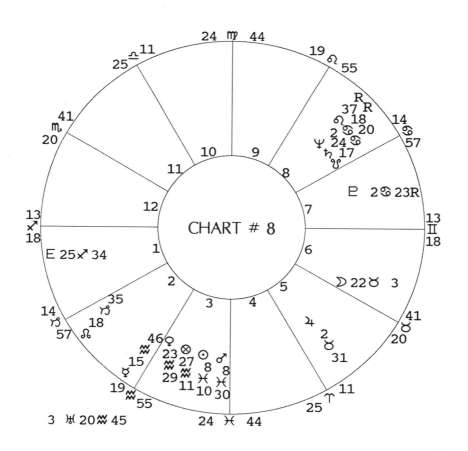

CHART # 8

shot in Dallas. His natal Moon links into this at 22-TA.

⏱ He was still in a Mercury Dasa (thus activating the associated Saturn, Uranus and Neptune factors), and Mercury is in Saturn's sign. Mercury rules his 8th (and the nakshatra of his Moon). In turn, his P2 Moon was at 00-PI-27 while T. Saturn was very slow at 00-PI-18. P3 Pluto was octile his natal Moon TTM.

⏱ The T. Sun (ruler of his 10th) was at the cusp of the 8th, and T. Mars (ruler of his 1st) was at the cusp of the 10th. N. Mars and the Sun are exactly conjunct in the 4th. The P2 Sun was at 23-TA (cusp of the sidereal 7th and one degree from the N. Moon) square to P2 Uranus at 23-AQ (cusp of the sidereal 4th and conjunct N. Venus), and opposite T. Pluto at 23-SC.

You might note here that he had quite a fated life. The three eclipses which occurred in just the last two months before birth were all exactly on a natal factor: one PNE at 02-AQ opposed Neptune (02-LE) and squared Jupiter (02-TA); another PNE at 17-CA overlaid the final nodal axis within nine minutes, and the third PNE at 02-CP sensitized N. Pluto at 02-CA. Indeed, the tropical "theme degrees" of 2 and 17 held firm for all the new and full moons in the four months preceding his birth.

A favorite of Presidents Kennedy and Johnson, and a Treasury Secretary under Nixon, Connolly also built quite a financial fortune (Jupiter in the 6th aspecting the Sagittarius 2nd) followed by a declaration of complete financial bankruptcy in January of 1988 (same Jupiter, exactly square to Neptune natally, now aspected by Saturn Dasa with other related factors at work). This "boom and bust" pattern illustrates how major Dasa/Bhukti shifts cyclically animate pre-existing, and even contradictory, conditions within the birth chart.

CASE 4 (Amy Fisher)

This case could as easily have been put into the chapter on murder except that the murder attempt did not succeed, and it is more useful as a quick rectification example. For non-American readers, fascination with Amy Fisher dominated the U.S. media in late 1992. She was designated "Lethal Lolita" by a major personality magazine because, at the age of 17 on 5/19/92, she walked up to the front door around noon and shot a woman who was married to Fisher's 36-year-old lover. Fisher was an indulged only child and a rebellious runaway from age 11 who had been sexually assaulted at age 13. She had been making significant amounts of money working as a part-time prostitute during her off-school hours.

Newsday quoted her birth data as: 21-Aug-1974 @ 9:26 PM EDT in Oceanside, NY 40N38 & 73W38 (see chart # 9). I want to show how easy it is to rapidly point out what is wrong with this chart, and then we can look at some secondary points of interest. One thing you notice immediately is that while her N. Mercury is at 3-VI-16, and her P3 Mars opposed it at 3-PI-24, her P3 IC is *beyond* that axis at 4-PI-15. This unacceptable one degree angular overshot is particularly disturbing when you notice that her P3 Venus is also at 2-PI-44 square her P3 SN at 3-GE-1. Therefore both of these were also overshot.

So I just pulled back her TOB by 4 minutes to 9:22. Now her P3 IC would be at 3-PI-19, and thus perfectly caught up in the complex. To fully confirm this speculation, this also now puts her P3 Asc at 21-SC-23. So where was T. Pluto on 5/19/92? — at 21-SC-23, perfectly conjunct her P3 Asc. Clearly notice that if you did not use P3 angles, this T. Pluto would not have much of a connection to anything, yet here it is perfect by "coincidence." This also pulled her N. Asc back a degree to 11-AR, and T. Mars was at 10-AR.

As long as we are on the topic, let's digress briefly to some of the considerations that might motivate a Fisher to murder. We've already seen above the formation that progressed into a perfect T-square involving Mercury, Venus, Mars, the Meridian and the Nodes. The P2 Sun was also only 20 minutes from being conjunct her N. Mars, and P3 Pluto (natally in the maraka 7th) has about the same negligible orb from being perfectly square her Meridian.

At the murder attempt, Fisher was in a Rahu Dasa and Moon Bhukti. The NN is with Neptune and they are both disposed by Mars. That she was totally clueless about the likely consequences of her action is seen in the fact that her P2 Moon (Bhukti factor) was opposite P2 Neptune (Dasa node affiliate) TTM. She probably thought that she and her boyfriend were going to ride off into the sunset and live happily ever after. Instead he tried to argue (ultimately unsuccessfully) that he didn't even know her.

Actually, this P3 moon was in Taurus and the Neptune/NN was in Scorpio which, yet again, brings up the Venus/Mars issue (recall the P3 "T-Square" noted above). Natally she was born into a Mars Dasa and Venus

1st Pisces Ascendant	2nd Aries	3rd Taurus Ketu Rx ++	4th Gemini Saturn ++
12th Aquarius Jupiter Rx —	MARS Sun beginning on 04/29/1975 MARS Moon beginning on 09/05/1975 RAHU Rahu beginning on 04/05/1976 RAHU Jupiter beginning on 12/17/1978 RAHU Saturn beginning on 05/11/1981 RAHU Mercury beginning on 03/17/1984		5th Cancer Venus ≈
11th Capricorn	RAHU Ketu beginning on 10/05/1986 RAHU Venus beginning on 10/23/1987 RAHU Sun beginning on 10/23/1990 RAHU Moon beginning on 09/17/1991 RAHU Mars beginning on 03/17/1993 JUPITER Jupiter beginning on 04/05/1994		6th Leo Sun M Mercury Mars T
10th Sagittarius	9th Scorpio Rahu Rx ♆	8th Libra Moon T≈+ ♅	7th Virgo ♇

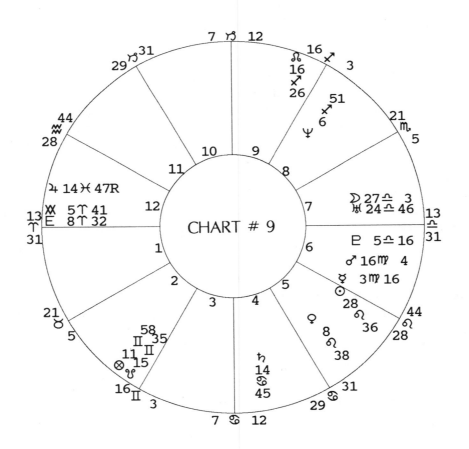

CHART # 9

Bhukti (the respective rulers of her 8th and 2nd). In her main chart, Venus is in the 5th in a mutual reception with the Moon (current Bhukti) in the 8th, and the Moon is also only 2 degrees from Uranus (so the Moon picks up that unstable energy).

In her navamsha, Venus is in the 12th picking up the defective energy of a fallen Mars–ruled Moon, and Venus is in another mutual reception — this time with Mars. So this just fully confirms the primary chart — and the sexual intensity of a sidereal Venus/Mars mutual reception, especially when other factors confirm and support.

In the primary chart Jupiter, as ruler of the 1st and the 10th, is in the 12th (potential imprisonment) and fully aspected by strong malefic energy from the 6th. It is interesting that the 4 minutes of rectification did cause all the houses to shift within the navamsha. This further confirms the validity of the rectification through the following typical piece of Hindu logic. The original 21:26 TOB had Capricorn rising, but its ruler is in the same house as Jupiter, so Saturn should have benefitted from the association. The revision to 21:22 now has Sagittarius rising, so its ruler is now conjunct a fallen Saturn. Therefore, her correct chart ruler is damaged by association with a defective malefic. The point is that the ruler is treated initially as neutral, and we look to see what happens to, and influences, it.

CASE 5 (Heart Attack)

This is this chart of a respected sidereal astrologer who died of a heart attack at age 62 on 4/26/91. I never met this astrologer but simply ran across his data in a professional periodical. This case provides an interesting variation since it had already been rectified by the highly significant amount of almost two hours. We will see if it works against the death which ultimately occurred.

He had apparently rectified his own TOB from 9:45 AM PST to 7:55 AM PST. The rest of his data is 17–Dec–1928 at 38N07 & 122W15 (see chart # 10). Let me state up front my personal conclusion which is that his rectification is either perfect or short by 3 minutes (i.e., it may be 7:58). Other life events would give the final answer.

Following are the maraka factors:

> ➤ Saturn as ruler of the 2nd (and dispositor of the Moon) and Venus

4th Pisces	5th Aries Jupiter Rx ++	6th Taurus Rahu Rx	7th Gemini Mars Rx T--
♓			♇
3rd Aquarius Moon +	SATURN Ketu beginning on 07/17/1970 SATURN Venus beginning on 08/26/1971 SATURN Sun beginning on 10/26/1974 SATURN Moon beginning on 10/08/1975 SATURN Mars beginning on 05/08/1977 SATURN Rahu beginning on 06/17/1978 SATURN Jupiter beginning on 04/23/1981	8th Cancer	
2nd Capricorn Venus ++	MERCURY Mercury beginning on 11/05/1983 MERCURY Ketu beginning on 04/02/1986 MERCURY Venus beginning on 03/29/1987 MERCURY Sun beginning on 01/29/1990 MERCURY Moon beginning on 12/05/1990 MERCURY Mars beginning on 05/05/1992	9th Leo	♆
1st Sagittarius Mercury - Sun T Ascendant	12th Scorpio Ketu Rx -- Saturn e--	11th Libra	10th Virgo

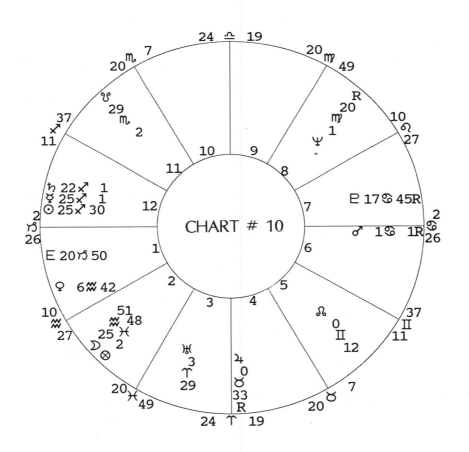

itself in the 2nd,

➤ Mars, not only in the 7th but almost totally angular, it assaults the 1st containing Mercury and the Sun, and is itself square Uranus in the 4th (but with a wide 2 degree orb),

➤ Mercury itself is ruler of the 7th, and

➤ Pluto (although it doesn't exist in the Hindu system and hence cannot technically be labeled as such).

While we will see that *all* these planets become perfectly involved, elsewhere I have stated my agreement with an ancient assertion that the Sun, Moon and Mercury generally do not have the inherent status to be marakas. But I would like to again make the distinction that they *can* be victims, as opposed to death agents, during their periods, and this is a good example of it.

This astrologer was in a Mercury Dasa and Moon Bhukti. Therefore, let's first focus in on Mercury. As noted above, it rules the maraka 7th, and being in the 1st it is under harsh natal assault from a powerful Mars in the 7th. By P2 (2/18/29) Mercury was at 9-AQ-2 and was within 1 day of being full stationary. So where was the very last T. eclipse axis before his death? — conjunct this progressed maraka station at 9-LE-51. This eclipse was also well within a degree of his 2/8 Placidus cusps.

Where was P3 Mercury? Only 5 minutes from being conjunct his IC and, to me, this is the best death argument for the perfection of his rectification. Where was T. Mercury? Well it was also stationary at 18-AR and perfectly square to Pluto which was itself also stationary by P3 (03/31/31) in his maraka 7th at 18-CA. So Dasa Mercury at all three levels was tightly bound into the death complex. What about the Sun ruling the heart? His Sun is perfectly conjunct Mercury, so it is inevitably linked to any Mercury-related activity. And anyway, his P2 Sun (28-AQ-53) was itself square to his mean nodes at 29-TA/SC-2.

Now may be the time to note why I see three potential death arguments, using nothing but the angles, in favor of a rectified time of 7:58:

⏱ While his P2 MC (27-SA-42) was within less than one applying degree of P2 Saturn (28-SA-29), it would have been perfectly conjunct using a TOB of 3 minutes later. Since this also brings in the IC, that would be classic.

⏱ His P3 MC/IC was at 8-LE-24. Using a TOB of 3 minutes later it would have been at 9 degrees of LE/AQ. This would have put it exactly upon the P2 Mercury station discussed in the paragraph above and would therefore have the P3 IC hitting the exact prior eclipse degree of 9-LE. That would also be completely classic.

The P3 Asc is at 29-TA-41. Using a TOB of 3 minutes later, it would be at 0-GE which, in fact, is his tNN. P2 Neptune, at 0-VI, was also now perfectly square this conjunct of the natal nodes and the progressed angles. So the Asc is just a wee bit short.

What about the Bhukti Moon carrying the vitality status of his 8th? His P3 Moon (03-VI-15) was conjunct P3 Neptune (03-VI-30). It's also a fact that the P2 true nodes (25-TA/SC-44) had moved back to now perfectly square his N. Moon (25-AQ-51). T. Saturn below gets even further attention since it is the dispositor of the Bhukti Moon.

Here are four final supporting considerations:

➤ P3 Mars, now at 0-LE-15, had moved from the cusp of the maraka 7th to now exactly square the N. ruler of the 1st (Jupiter at 0-TA-33).

➤ P3 Uranus, natally square Mars, was now at 14-AR-59 thus conjunct the P3 mNN at 14-AR-53.

➤ Any progressed planet at 22-23 tropical degrees would be conjunct a sidereal house cusp. P2 Mars was at 23-GE-37 (the cusp of his maraka 7th), and P3 Saturn was at 22-CP-23 (the cusp of his maraka 2nd).

➤ N. Venus was located in his maraka 2nd in a Saturn-ruled sign. T. Saturn, now stronger in its own sign, was exactly conjunct it at 6-AQ.

CASE 6 (Eric Clapton)

Eric Clapton, award-winning singer and rock guitar stylist, was the victim of a major life tragedy when his 4-year-old son fell to his death from the 53rd floor of a New York City apartment building on 03/20/91. In a later chapter on unexpected deaths in one's own chart I discuss the child's chart itself. In yet a later chapter (on death as seen in the charts of others), I review the death from the point of view of the child's mother, Italian actress Lory Del Santo. This chapter will use this as a rectification event as applied to the chart of the father.

Eric Clapton was born on 30-March-1945 in Ripley, Surray, England 0W20

& 51N30. His grandmother has said that he was born "between 8:30 and 9:00 PM" which is DT in zone 0 (caution: the following preliminary discussion pertains to a Libra–rising chart which is not shown; the chart I have settled on for Clapton is discussed and shown a little further down). Based upon that given time, I just selected an initial test time of 8:45, which amazingly produced an immediate hit: his P3 IC was conjunct N. Neptune at death.

This was such a classical angle hit that I thought I'd have no problem wrapping it up. This hit was especially apropos due to a hidden link that would go completely unseen by classical Hindu astrologers. He was in a Saturn Dasa (and Rahu Bhukti), Saturn ruled his 5th, and his N. Saturn (in the same house with the NN) was exactly square to N. Neptune in his 12th (that's the hidden link). Note also that, without regard to angular considerations, P3 Neptune was also opposing his N. Sun.

N. Mars is in the 5th of children (and only a degree from the Placidus 5th cusp), while it is a double maraka as ruler of both the 2nd and 7th. N. Uranus was in the 8th which would also be symbolically relevant to this type of death — especially since, at the death, P3 Mars (20–SA–57) opposed P3 Uranus (20–GE–04).

For a musician it would also be appropriate to have the Moon, as ruler of the 10th, in the 1st receiving a perfect full aspect from Venus which indeed rules the Libra 1st. Finally, this gave 23–LI–42 rising, and his last PNE was perfectly square to this at 23–CP–41. Further, at the death, this P2 Desc would be conjunct his P2 Sun within 11 minutes.

Considering all the above, it sure looked like a wrap to me. But never happy to leave well enough alone, a few things nagged at me. For example, he was abandoned as a child. This would be during a Rahu Dasa (the same as his current Bhukti) if you use a TOB anywhere near this one. It's true that Saturn is with the NN, but Saturn is a rajayoga karaka for Libra rising, and this chart would have it in the highly favored 9th. Saturn would rule the 4th, but karmic mother/father issues wouldn't seem to be so bad with the ruler of the 4th in the 9th. Although Pluto is in the 10th and square to the Moon, the Moon receives the full aspect of Venus (which admittedly Pluto also squares). By the way, his P3 Saturn at the death was conjunct N. Pluto at 08–LE.

I decided to try again and eventually ended up with 8:20 PM which was only a few minutes before his grandmother's recollection, and this did not change the Dasa/Bhukti planets (now see chart # 11). It has both the 1st and 10th being ruled by Mercury. Mercury is now in the very special rajayoga with Venus (in the 8th). Venus coming to this Mercury via a rajayoga would bring great strength to a songwriter and his career. I've already suggested this in the rectification of Elvis Presley's birth, and it is later demonstrated in the uncontested chart of Karen Carpenter.

Venus rules his 2nd, fully aspects the 2nd, and is perfectly aspected by the Moon in the 2nd — all of which could produce wealth related to the communication of beauty and emotion. And, as I mentioned, the mother of his child was a well- known actress, and this chart (that of the father of the child) has the Sun in the 7th in a mutual reception with Jupiter.

Neptune would now be in his 1st receiving the perfect square from Saturn in the 10th (along with the 4/10 nodes), and this would present a stronger picture of an abandoned child. Indeed, if you have ever seen a picture of him, he looks like Neptune being squared by Saturn! I don't know what year he was abandoned, but the exact Moon/Venus opposition axis was only about 5 and 1/2 applying degrees from T-squaring his N. Pluto and, by his 4th year, the revised ruler of his 1st was going Rx by P2. So, if I had to guess, I'd guess somewhere around 4 or 5 which is also the same age his own son died. Note that T. Neptune was also at 16-CP-31 thus opposing Eric Clapton's P2 Moon at 17-CA-07.

The ruler of the benefic 5th remains Saturn (now CP vs. AQ), and this new TOB put Saturn in the 10th with the NN. This is good for his career and, indeed, he has been winning his greatest awards during this Saturn Dasa period (however, to complicate the argument, the other chart has Saturn alone as a rajayoga karaka in the 9th, and the 3/9 axis generally rules musical performing). He also began playing in public with a group called "The Roosters" when he was 17, and this was also during a Saturn Bhukti (arguing back again for Saturn being in the 10th).

But these various points are only supportive of why I picked 8:20 PM in the first place which is that this TOB arguably brings even more angular perfectibility. Now two perfectly descriptive death patterns are that:

> ➤ 20-SC-26 = his P2 Asc while
> 20-SC-11 = T. Pluto, and

7th Pisces Sun ≈	8th Aries Mercury R+ Venus Rx RT+	9th Taurus ♓	10th Gemini Saturn T++ Rahu Rx E
6th Aquarius Mars −	JUPITER Moon beginning on 02/15/1971 JUPITER Mars beginning on 06/15/1972 JUPITER Rahu beginning on 05/21/1973 SATURN Saturn beginning on 10/15/1975 SATURN Mercury beginning on 10/18/1978 SATURN Ketu beginning on 06/27/1981 SATURN Venus beginning on 08/06/1982	11th Cancer ♇	
5th Capricorn	SATURN Sun beginning on 10/06/1985 SATURN Moon beginning on 09/18/1986 SATURN Mars beginning on 04/18/1988 SATURN Rahu beginning on 05/27/1989 SATURN Jupiter beginning on 04/03/1992 MERCURY Mercury beginning on 10/15/1994	12th Leo Jupiter Rx ≈	
4th Sagittarius Ketu Rx −	3rd Scorpio	2nd Libra Moon −	1st Virgo Ascendant ♆

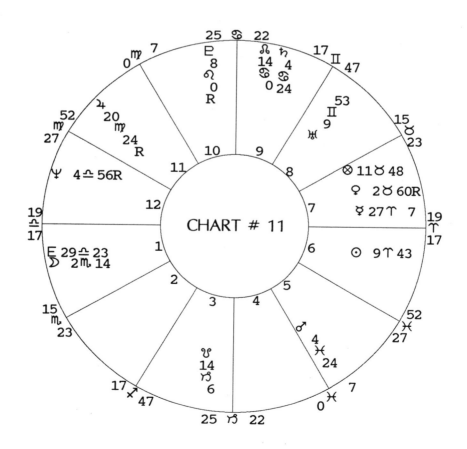

➤ 25-CP-22 = his natal IC while
25-CP-15 = his P3 Desc (child or child's mother) and
25-CP-20 = the last T. solar eclipse before death.
(This was further bracketed by two PNE's at 23-CP and 27-CA)

Compared to most, this is a difficult rectification. But overall I favored the latter time of 8:20 PM. You will develop more of an appreciation for why I feel that way as you work your way further through this book. Having more or less drawn my conclusion, I called Lois Rodden to see if she had any later data that would shed further light. She had information that Eric Clapton had himself been giving out two entirely different birth times: 8:45 PM and 4:30 AM, so maybe he does have Neptune in the 1st (8:20 PM)! I'm not even going to run the 4:30; I'll leave that to the reader.

Since he was also in a Rahu Bhukti, let me close by highlighting a few nodal/ eclipse observations that are independent of the TOB rectification issue.

➤ 14-CP-00 was his N. tSN
➤ 13-CP-58 was a PNE that further reinforced this point
➤ 13-CP-27 was T. Uranus at the death

➤ 07-CA-47 was a PNE
➤ 08-CA-01 was P2 Saturn (his Dasa planet)

➤ 11-SA-46 was his P3 tSN
➤ 12-SA-39 was his P3 Sun

FINAL CASE 7 (Ingrid Bergman Challenge):

Ingrid Bergman died of cancer on 8/29/82. Here is conflicting birth data (with DOB, TOB and source) compiled by Sylvia Tobias from 1978 through 1987 from the pages of *The Mercury Hour* magazine. It is only agreed that Ms. Bergman was born in Stockholm, Sweden (59N20 & 18E03). If you can figure this one out based upon her death you are well on your way to mastering a talent that you shouldn't apply! Keeping in mind that it may *all* be wrong, here it is:

Date	*Time*	*Source of Information*
08/29/09	Bef. Sunrise	Laura Breska, I.B.'s Astrologer
1915	not given	*Celebrities Register 1973*

08/28/15	not given	Hans Genuit
08/28/15	03:00 pm MET	*Das Neue Zeitalter*
08/29/15	not given	"files of Ingrid Bergman"
08/29/15	not given	Chryss Craswell per M.P.
08/29/15	not given	Birth Record Office B.C.
08/29/15	03:30 am MET	Data at Forste Stadslakaren
08/29/15	03:30 am MET	Birth Record per Wilhelm Nilsson
08/29/16	03:15 pm CET	Birth Certificate per Mark Penfield
1917	not given	*Index To Women*
08/29/17	not given	*Celebrities* by Kaye & Cakavell
not given	Not on B.C.	per Steinbrecher

In the later sample charts, I will occasionally be making slight corrections to the recorded times of birth — typically from 1/2 a minute to perhaps as much as 5 minutes or so. In every case where I do this I will let you know, so that if you'd rather go with the documented TOB you are welcome to. My slight adjustments would typically have no discernable effect upon either the Eastern or Western natal chart itself. In many cases, my correction will be justified by subsequent confirming "hits" to certain key points in the chart exactly to the minute (TTM).

And this will often be the case where the correction would result in more than one exact hit TTM. For example, upon adjustment the case might have transiting Saturn TTM on the natal Asc at the same time that the revised tertiary Asc was now conjunct some equally relevant planet exactly TTM. I have seen the behavior of enough correct charts to know that these micro–adjustments are not out of line and are, in fact, exactly revealing of the true time of birth. There is rarely any countervailing argument in favor of the original TOB.

KARMIC DEATH LINKS

As you have already realized, the fundamental approach of this book will be relentlessly empirical since clear events with repeatedly clear data themes cannot be denied. It is therefore with some hesitation that I insert this chapter to briefly touch upon chart connections that are, at least to me, suggestive of past life linkages. I hope to sensitize the reader to: 1) how a death chart can possibly be used for "karmic" rectification, and 2) how a certain amount of karmic inter-connectivity can arguably be inferred from various charts.

Actually, we undoubtedly interface with hundreds of souls from past lives, but we could generally expect that only a few of these have special death-related linkages. I'm inserting this chapter here, rather than at the end of the book, since many readers might prefer, as a break in method, a more personal speculation on how I think about some of these things. But because of its speculative nature, you may easily skip this chapter with no particular loss of continuity in development of the main objectives.

This is basically the only place where I will be using my own chart in an illustration. Since this is an approach I typically disdain, I solicit the reader's temporary indulgence. Not many people think about and capture this type of information, so these anecdotes, as well as any, address the two modest objectives of this chapter which, in the end, are only suggestive, and unlike the remaining chapters, obviously cannot make claim to any kind of proof. Some readers will finds it intriguing and useful; others will not. My data is 13-April-1947 @ 12:51 AM CST in Des Moines, IA 41N35 & 93W37 (see chart # 60 at the back of the book with the author's biosheet).

In early 1992, I went to see a palm reader at the enthusiastic recommendation of a friend of mine who works at the Pentagon. The palm reader is actually a revered Vietnamese physician who regularly cures "incurables." He was returning to Vietnam within two weeks because of his inability to speak English, and because he was not allowed to apply his medical skills in the United States.

Through an interpreter, he gave the most factual reading I ever received. This included excellent timing remarks that closely tracked the shifts and turns in my lifetime Vimsottari Dasa listing. Among other things, he said that I should have had surgery twice in my youth on an area above my neck. This was true (and no, it was not a lobotomy).

Then he said the kind of thing that Western astrologers never dare even if they knew how. He said I would have three children, two would die, and the third would move away in my old age. In the context of his more general accuracy, this was certainly strange because I've been married almost 25 years to someone my same age (47), and we have no children. My mind spun out a variety of possible scenarios, including symbolic, but overall I just filed it away. I also thought that one of the "death children" might be this book which was already beginning to quicken. But very shortly after, an odd event unfolded.

Let me begin by noting two sidereal facts: first, the ruler of my 8th is in my 1st (the Moon), and that's not true tropically. Hindu astrology specifically states that this fact is not inherently harmful — but remember the Moon. Second, Saturn (and Pluto) is in my 8th and therefore aspects my 5th (children) since Saturn always aspects the 10th from itself. Both of these planets were quite slow around my birth.

At the time of the palm reading I was in a Saturn Bhukti thereby putting what Indian astrologers often refer to as a "check" or block on "issues" (certainly, at least, during its period). Several months after this reading, the first modern Uranus/Neptune stationary "conjunction" applied within minutes of my natal Moon (which generally rules fecundity). This was in mid–April 1992 at 18–CP.

I have a female friend going back about 15 years who used to help me produce a computer security newsletter, but I hadn't seen her for many years since she had been living thousands of miles away. We basically communicate at Christmas. She is now married and has a young daughter. From her last Christmas note, she was expecting another child in May.

Over 10 years ago on 10/21/82 I had ordered a chart for her from a well–known chart service. Although my friend was born in August (17–Aug–1956 @ 4:59 AM in Elmhurst, IL 41N53 & 87W56), the chart they produced for her was set up for CST. This seemed odd, but Illinois did have some odd time changes, so I assumed the company knew something I didn't.

In May 1992 we received from my friend what we expected was a birth announcement, but instead it was a death announcement. For some reason, this struck me quite hard. Her son was delivered two weeks early on 5/5/92 @ 1:13 PM in Colorado Springs, CO by an emergency C-section because of a slowing heart rate. He did not have a heartbeat for the first 15 minutes of birth, and was kept artificially alive for about a day. All the tests were negative.

[Parenthetically, I mentioned this birth trauma to a neighbor of mine, and she said: "You know, that happened to my mother twice. Two of her children died at birth, and did you know that my brother ended up marrying a woman born on the exact same month, day and year that one of those babies died."

Readers of Edgar Cayce and similar material would immediately surmise that this particular soul was fundamentally seeking an opportunity to have a relationship with my neighbor's brother. Apparently it spotted a "better deal" at the last moment to ultimately be the brother's wife instead of sister, and it abandoned the body in motion via my neighbor's mother. This could help to explain why diagnostic tests often register no explanation. There was nothing there to animate the body's occult faculties. Now back to the main line of commentary...]

Using the original CST, her own chart demonstrated basically nothing with regard to her natal angles at the death of her child, and that seemed completely unacceptable since her own body was involved. When I corrected it to CDT (per the listing of an alternative atlas), the correctness of the new birth time leaps out as will be shown (see chart # 12).

In addition, the precision of her tertiary progressions clearly suggested only a 20 second correction to her given birth time for two reasons. First, this would have her P3 Uranus (12/7/57) perfectly conjunct her corrected Asc to the minute (at 11-LE-28), and second, her P3 Asc in turn would also exactly square it to the minute (at 11-SC-28). This total perfection of angularity is very simple and powerful symbolism that needs no explanation.

By the way, the mother's P2 Asc was exactly conjunct (but minutes beyond) her N. Jupiter. This could again argue for Jupiter as a death indicator (see comments elsewhere), but I have two objections. First, the application of the Asc to Jupiter was the anticipation of the birth — especially with Jupiter ruling children in the Hindu system. The Asc was now minutes *beyond* the conjunction to Jupiter. Second, I have seen

9th Pisces
  Mars Rx   SRTe
	10th Aries	11th Taurus
		  Ketu Rx ++
			12th Gemini
			  Venus ++

8th Aquarius	MOON Jupiter beginning on 02/07/1981 MOON Saturn beginning on 06/07/1982 MOON Mercury beginning on 01/07/1984 MOON Ketu beginning on 06/07/1985 MOON Venus beginning on 01/07/1986 MOON Sun beginning on 09/07/1987	1st Cancer Ascendant	

7th Capricorn	MARS Mars beginning on 03/07/1988
	MARS Rahu beginning on 08/04/1988
	MARS Jupiter beginning on 08/22/1989
	MARS Saturn beginning on 07/28/1990
	MARS Mercury beginning on 09/07/1991
	MARS Ketu beginning on 09/04/1992
	MARS Venus beginning on 02/01/1993
		2nd Leo
		  Sun Me
		  Jupiter T
		  Mercury	

6th Sagittarius
  Moon   −
	5th Scorpio
	  Saturn −−
	  Rahu Rx −−
		4th Libra	3rd Virgo

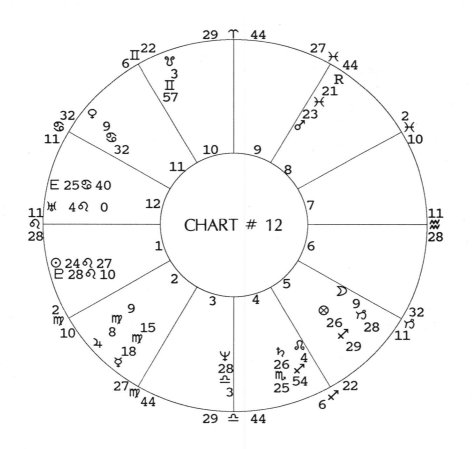

CHART # 12

other cases of a contradiction indicated by a simultaneous progression of a factor to P2 Jupiter but P3 Saturn. In one case, the person was fired, but there ended up being a clear silver lining in the firing.

I found the chart for the child to be most uninteresting since I don't think the soul was ever there. Since his heart was not beating for the first 15 minutes this raises doubt about any independent respiration, and if true independent respiration never occurred then I'm not sure what chart, if any, may be appropriate for him. It's likely that the soul just withdrew its intentions. As I wondered about the meaning of this for my friend, I recalled the comments of the palm reader — and the period that I was now in with regard to children. I wondered if it could be the case that I have some kind of strange karmic link to my distant friend. And here I was writing a book on death.

My friend's revised natal chart now has two major factors in the exact same sign and degree as in my natal chart: my sidereal 8th house Pluto is exactly conjunct her corrected Asc (11–LE) while her Saturn continues to exactly conjunct the ruler of my chart (Jupiter at 26–SC). And we know that Saturn and Pluto are the two classical "karma" planets with Jupiter having "rulership" over children. But this is still a little thin and impersonal, so let's see if there was more to this by looking at her planetary placements on her P2 date of 9/22/56 and her P3 date of 12/7/57 for this birth trauma.

What you see in her chart are six progressed positions that are in *exactly* the same sign and degree as one of the key factors in my natal chart. Consider that for *each* one, there is a somewhat low probability of its being there. For this to occur 6 times out of 12...?

HER PROGRESSED	=	MY NATAL	AT
Mercury (P3)	=	Ascendant	(06–CP)
Uranus (P3)	=	Pluto	(11–LE)
Mars (P2)	=	Venus	(15–PI)
Part of (Mis)fortune (P2)	=	Mars	(01–AR)
IC (P2)	=	Lunar SN	(04–SA)
AND Moon (P2)	=	Sun	(22–AR–32)

The IC/SN connection is especially informative, but to emphasize the apparent absence of randomness in this pattern of "meaningful coin-cidence" note that her P2 Moon is not only exact to the same sign and degree as my Sun; it is even exact to within one *minute*. As the P2 Moon takes roughly three decades to circle a chart, it is only in one particular sign and degree for about a month. It is only on any particular sign-degree-minute for about *1/2 a day out of this 30 year cycle*. Yet her P2 Moon was on that point during the half day that this child failed to thrive. So you can see how the palm reader's forecast arguably manifested in some strange way — although this may raise questions about what we think we know about the apparent "ownership" of children.

More Karmic Links?

Although it deviates from death-related karmic links per se, I'll add sev-eral personal asides here that might be considered suggestive of a past life link. This same month, April 1992, was the month of UAC'92, the large astrology conference (1,500+ attendees) that occurred in Washing-ton, D.C. About a year and a half earlier I picked up an international "pen pal." This was a French businesswoman living in London who accidentally spotted, in an executive's waiting room, a lengthy astrology article I had written in 1989 for an international business magazine (it was featured on their cover as "Advanced Astrology for CEO's").

She wrote me a letter in early 1992 indicating that she would like to come to D.C. for the conference but asked if I could help find her a less expensive hotel. We invited her to stay with us, and she agreed. As a reminder, Uranus and Neptune were stationing on my Moon. They were also stationing in exact square to her Sun. In looking at her chart, I noticed that the last new Moon before she was born (08-LI-34) was an eclipse within 1/2 a degree of my Neptune (09-LI-05). The first full Moon after she was born was (you guessed it?) at 22 degrees and 32 minutes of Aries — again, my Sun exactly, and the P2 Moon of my friend out West.

Anne was born on 12-Oct-1959 @ 8:47 PM in Toulouse, France 43N36 & 01E26. I was shocked to discover that when I relocate my chart to Toulouse, perfect double angularity occurs: Saturn is exactly on my 4th house cusp, and Jupiter is exactly on my 7th house cusp. Not knowing this, my house guest, with whom I had instant rapport, commented that she always thought she was a dancer (Jupiter) in a prior life. Further, her Jupiter is exactly on one of my PNE's (01-SA) while her Moon is on my Karmic Asc (the KA is your Sun/Moon midpoint). We would laugh when people at the UAC lunch table would look puzzled and say, "Are you sure you two don't know each other?"

To repeat the same theme, one of my oldest friends (b. 23–Nov–1951 @ 21:56 CST in Monterrey, Mexico 25N40 & 100W19), now living on the west coast, has her Sun at 01–SA (my same PNE), her NN conjunct my Karmic Asc, and an MC at (you guessed it?) 22 & 1/2 degrees of Aries – again, my Sun exactly. As you see, these were a repeat of the same numbers, and she was also a dancer for over 10 years (in fact, her 120 year Dasa pattern also exactly overlays mine with only about a week of deviance, so we ride exactly the same waves through this life).

Yet another person who had a major impact upon my life was born in Mendoza, Argentina. When you relocate my chart to Mendoza, my normally 12th house Jupiter, ruler of my 1st, is exactly conjunct my MC as is my Part of Fortune. So these angle linkages do rather go on and on. The overall patterns I'm trying to emphasize *must* involve the angles in *exact* hard aspect as they interplay with either the Sun, Moon, Saturn, Pluto and/or lunar nodes. My feeling is that the more exact hits to these that there are, the more likely there was a strong past–life connection.

I suspect this can happen even with people we never will meet in this lifetime. For example, I went to a lecture in March of 1994 by an astrologer who has been tracking three of her early childhood friends for many decades as a research project since all four of them were born within two days of each other. In her lecture, she mentioned that in early childhood one of the women had led her into a woods while chattering, in the way that children do, about a massacre by American Indians that had wiped out their families. This comment made me sit up and pay attention since, as you will see several pages down, I carry within myself a fundamental personal myth that concerns being involved in an Indian massacre in an immediately prior life.

When the speaker displayed this woman's chart (19–April–1946 at 10:47 AM EST @ 42N47 & 86W06), I was startled. The chart's Asc was less than a degree from my Moon, and her Saturn was only a few minutes (not degrees) away from my Moon. Her Neptune was only 3 minutes (not degrees) from squaring my Asc. Her Moon was exactly conj my SN. Her Jupiter opposed my Sun within less than a degree. Her Mercury is conjunct my Mars within a degree, and so forth. When she got married (4/26/68), there were numerous exact hits to my chart, including the fact that T. Venus was (you guessed it?) at 22 and 1/2 degrees of Aries (my Sun again). Now it could be argued that people with exactly similar compound degree themes simply labor under similar Indian massacre delusions — which would actually be interesting in its own right. But is this really any more plausible than the suggestion of a past life connection?

It is difficult to argue that these various people I've listed have a past life link. Why could they not merely be considered important in this life because of all the linkages? Because the exactness, the angularity and the nature of the specific planets involved creates a very unusual "knowingness." For further contrast, let me note that any female born in June of 1966 can typically galvanize my attention simply because her Uranus/Pluto conjunction exactly opposes my Venus. But, in general, there is nothing karmic at all about this type of Venus connection. It's just energy, and it would take other significant and personal astrological factors to support the suggestion of a past life connection.

This might also be further compared against two high-level corporate executives with whom I was forced to jointly engage in a pitched battle for over a year. One was born on 1–Dec–1944 and the other on 18–Dec–1934. The former had his Mars right on my SN, and his own SN right on my Moon while the latter had his SN right on my Saturn (with other connections, of course). Despite the absence of extensive planetary connections, I sensed these as karmic connections, and generally you can feel the difference at the spiritual level.

As a final point of perspective, consider the following case which every professional astrologer has experienced more than once. Not too long ago an unknown client drove three hours (one way) for an astrological consultation. I wondered to myself: why in the world would she want to do that? But when I ran her chart (21–Sept–1956 @ 3:40 PM EDT in Baltimore, MD 39N17 & 76W37 — chart not shown), I could see: 1) my Moon is one degree from her Asc, 2) her Moon is 4 applying degrees from my Sun, 3) her Mercury is exactly conjunct my Neptune, 4) her Mars is exactly conjunct my Venus, 5) her Jupiter is exactly opposing my Venus, 6) my Pluto is 3 degrees from her Venus, 7) her Saturn is 2 degrees from the ruler of my 1st, and so forth.

These were cumulatively strong connections, and they were felt as such. But was it a past–life connection? I rather doubt it because most of the conjunctions were purely planetary, and some of these were not exact. The conjunction of my Moon to her Asc was fractionally over one degree (the point at which I start to preclude it as a karmic factor). There really wasn't any nodal involvement (our nodes are flipped, but off by a few degrees). And while it's also true that my Pluto exactly squared her MC, I feel that conjunctions are more typically the rule in angular past-life connections. My simple point is that it's certainly possible to have strong present-life connections without converting all these into past-life connections.

Returning to the more specific topic of karmic death links, my final personal reference concerns a woman I met at the prior (1989) UAC conference in New Orleans (UACs seem to bring out more than normally weird happenings). I had no "romantic" or physical attraction to this woman at all, and she was definitely not my "type." But we walked right up to each other as if we knew each other perfectly well. A weird "force dynamic" set itself up almost immediately, and within but a few hours, I was overcome by the irrational fear of becoming separated from this person.

Understand that I am not one to go binging on "soul mate" nonsense, most particularly as popularized, misunderstood and overdone (actually, the lonely soul we seek to mate with is our own). I also didn't even care to discover whether I liked her or not. I have had a lot of strange experiences in my life, but this was abnormally so, and it's very difficult to quickly characterize in an adequate way.

When I returned to D.C. I had an intermediary (as a buffer) call the only psychic in whom I have developed great confidence in order to ask her who this woman was to me. The psychic said we had been married three times, all resulted in divorce and one in a suicide (the woman's data is: 01-July-1958 @ 7:10 AM CST 33N38 & 96W36).

Again we have a case of exact double angularity with her Asc exactly on my 8th house Saturn, and her MC exactly on my Sun. If you add 4 minutes to her unvalidated birthtime, and she suspected it may not be quite correct, both connections are exact to the same *minute* of arc. Well, I often have the urge to call this person, but I never have the urge to speak to her!

[As a further link in this chain, it is of peripheral interest to me that when I relocate my chart to a certain place in India, my own Saturn is exactly upon my own Asc while my own Sun is exactly upon my own MC. Since this is a repeat of the joint pattern above, it could fuel an initial speculation about the location of any such past-life involvement with this person. But I'm too far out on a limb here already.]

Other than the fact that it is the indicator of the soul, one may further wonder why my Sun specifically keeps showing up in these various cases. I expect the answer partially has to do with the fact that my Sun is actually in a "finishing degree" — the last half of the last degree of the sidereal zodiac.

Other Past-Life Continuity

I expect we are almost always attracted to souls with whom we died in a prior life, no matter what the circumstance, as a subconscious validation of continuity and also because it gives us a chance to put a good spin on things and to consummate unfinished business. I would expect an exception to this if we were murdered by someone, but even then it would probably depend on the underlying karma, emotions, intentions and the like. What sets up a high energy attraction is the prior intensity of mutual experience, as opposed to temporal judgements about the event-related qualities of prior experiences.

As an example of this, I have a couple I monitor over time for a variety of studies (him: 06–Aug–1957 @ 10:05 AM EDT at 38N43 & 075W04 — her: 28–FEB–1964 @ 01:05 PM EST at 38N49 & 077W06). They have quite a number of intense direct connections — including the fact that her Pluto is exactly conjunct his Venus. In trying to solve a complex issue that puzzled me, I sent the woman to the psychic in whom I have a lot of confidence. The psychic, knowing nothing about my question, told my client that a relevant consideration in her relationship was they both had drowned together in a prior life.

When I ran their composite chart, it had sidereal Cancer rising with a Moon/Neptune conjunction at the IC (all three factors within less than 3 degrees), and Uranus 2 degrees from the Asc. Since her chart remains questionable up to 5 or 10 minutes (his does not), the angularity of Uranus and Neptune could have been even tighter. The IC, of course, has a lot to do with "up from where you are coming" in this particular life, and natally they both have 4th house Moons.

Continuing support of the drowning conjecture, they met when T. Neptune hit her Desc, his P2 Asc was conjunct N. Neptune, and his P3 lunar SN, an excellent karmic flag, was exactly conjunct her Venus. They were dating for about a year before they went to the beach together. I asked her to let me know how they felt about it. I was wondering if there would be any kind of fear memories or related anxiety. She said it was one of the best experiences they ever had together.

This, and many similar cases, only confirms again my tendency to think that the soul has an actual attraction to its prior methods of transition if those methods functioned to stimulate the spirit. Guided past-life regressions often produce self-commentary that closely tracks the astrological chart symbolism of the person being guided. While this can argue for the validity of the link between astrology and the individual's unconscious (whatever that is), it can usually prove nothing about the actual reality of any past life claim — or indeed of any past lives at all.

When I first went to the psychic whom I later began using for referral, she said that in the prior life most affecting this one, I had died of a liver problem caused by an inability to process grief. Allegedly, during a fairly violent Indian incarnation, a night time lapse of vigilance made me feel culpable for the death of many — including my family (my chart now has the Moon, as ruler of my 8th, in my 1st, Saturn is slow in my 8th along with a slow Pluto, the ruler of the 7th is conjunct Mars which mutually receives the ruler of the 1st, and so forth). By the way, for my own curiosity, I did go to the library and validate, in a major Indian encyclopedia, that there was a tribe by the name she gave, in the location she gave, for the year of death she gave. And I still keep a gun at bedside.

The psychic mentioned in passing that the witch doctor had told me to eat wheatgrass since the raw chlorophyll was very "pro-life." Completely unknown to the psychic, I had been growing wheatgrass in my basement window for months based upon my strong interest in the work of Ann Wigmore at the Hippocrates Health Institute in Boston! It was also based upon my conviction, insupportable by medical data, that I have a weak liver. It turns out that Jupiter (as ruler of both the liver and my sidereal 1st) is with the SN in my 12th which would, in fact, flag a potential liver problem, or at least a problem with the blood[†].

It strikes me that "power psychics," who usually have little clue about astrology, are essentially reading, via their intuition, an astrology chart of some sort. And for any hard-core tropical readers, I'll also note that the

---

[†] *Ann Wigmore, who cured herself of gangrene and cancer at much earlier phases in her life, died on 2/16/94 at the age of 90.*

entities who inform my psychic associate refer to her as a "Gemini" even though she has a tropical Cancer Sun and Cancer rising. Sidereally they would both be in Gemini.

The Symbolism of Color

This chlorophyll issue also makes me want to add a quick comment on color as related to issues of life and death. Photosynthesis is itself a highly "occult" process where light produces useful oxygen in green plants for ultimate use by nearly all living things. Quite clearly, we all live through the consumption of light. Although Mercury's gem is green (emerald) and Jupiter's gem is yellow (sapphire), for knowledge and wisdom respectively, Jupiter has broad rulership over the trees and grasses of the natural world.

The opposite of green is red, and nobody disputes red's association with Mars. Are we then surprised to find that the molecular structures of hemin (part of hemoglobin) and chlorophyll are nearly *identical* except that chlorophyll has "the relaxer" magnesium as the central atom and hemin has (Mars–ruled) iron? [At this point, I will leave the reader to contemplate the question of why there are green plants, insects, reptiles, amphibians and fish, but not a single green mammal — except for green polar bears who actually aren't green but merely have algae growing inside their hollow hairs!]

Highly pressurized arterial blood is bright red — although oddly our bloodstream appears green through the skin (actually it's just unoxygenated). Despite the fact that red "opposes" green (arguing yet again for Mars being a killer) the signs ruled by Mars and Jupiter are inherently trine to each other (AR/SA, SC/PI). So this suggests that vascular Mars is basically anabolic until it reverses polarity. In support of this thought, Chinese astrology specifically states that the "wood planet" Jupiter governs birth and death, while the fire planet Mars governs growth and development. Venus they assign specifically to harvests which is not quite the same as growth and development.

A Case of Disappearance

Let's now move on to a final "detective" case, again involving my psychic associate, that puts yet another perspective on karmic deaths. It also teaches an important lesson on the interplay between the Dasa and Bhukti planets. Someone came to me on 25 July 1993 to ask whether the son of one of his employees was dead or not. The son had just disappeared very late on 15 July 1993. See chart # 13 for the chart of the son (b. 27–

11th Pisces Saturn RT- Sun	12th Aries Rahu Rx -- Venus ≈-	1st Taurus Ascendant	2nd Gemini
10th Aquarius Mercury T+	RAHU Jupiter beginning on 04/21/1971 RAHU Saturn beginning on 09/15/1973 RAHU Mercury beginning on 07/21/1976 RAHU Ketu beginning on 02/09/1979 RAHU Venus beginning on 02/27/1980 RAHU Sun beginning on 02/27/1983 RAHU Moon beginning on 01/21/1984		3rd Cancer Jupiter Ee
9th Capricorn	RAHU Mars beginning on 07/21/1985 JUPITER Jupiter beginning on 08/09/1986 JUPITER Saturn beginning on 09/27/1988 JUPITER Mercury beginning on 04/09/1991 JUPITER Ketu beginning on 07/15/1993 JUPITER Venus beginning on 06/21/1994		4th Leo ⌘ ♇
8th Sagittarius	7th Scorpio ♆	6th Libra Moon - Mars Rx ≈- Ketu Rx	5th Virgo

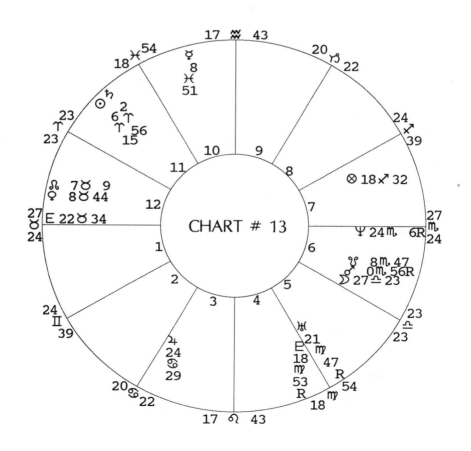

CHART # 13

March–1967 @ 9:00 AM CST in San Salvador, El Salvador 13N42 & 89W12).

Natally what you see is that the ruler of the 1st (Venus) is in a mutual reception with the ruler of the 7th (Mars). This Venus, which also rules the 6th, is in the 12th, conjunct the mNN within 3 minutes. Further, it opposes Mars, which also rules the 12th, in the same house with the SN. So the rulers of 1,6,7 and 12 are totally locked up with the nodal axis by both conjunction and reception. On the *exact* date he disappeared, he had moved into a new Bhukti (the SN), and the SN specifically rules invisibility and disappearance. When the nodes set it up, and the nodes set it off, it's "karma."

Here is part of what I told the inquirer:

1. This young man has a serious temper since the N. Moon is only 3 applying degrees from Mars (at the exact same declination), and the ruler of the 1st is in a mutual reception with Mars. But the temper works against him since both planets (Moon & Mars) are in Libra and assault their dispositor (Venus), ruler of the 1st in the 12th.

2. He has an utterly classic death indicator pattern which is composed of the following elements:

> A. Most significantly, the last prior T. eclipse was at 13-SA-55 (across his 1st & 7th). On the date of disappearance his P2 IC had arrived to square this point at 13-VI-33, while T. Mars (13-VI) was exactly conjunct this P2 IC. Only seconds of birth time error would have the P2 IC square the prior eclipse point TTM.

> B. As mentioned, this occurred on the exact date of entry into his Ketu Bhukti. This animated his Moon/Mars conjunction with Mars ruling the maraka 7th.

> C. A relational shock occurred because his P2 horizon (Asc/Desc) was now exactly square to N. Uranus. Again, only seconds of birth time error would have made this exact TTM. P3 Pluto was also conjunct N. Uranus within 1/4 of a degree thus also square the P2 horizon. Note, by the way, that N. Uranus is exactly octile the nodal axis.

> D. P2 Saturn was now only 7 applying minutes from being conjunct the Sun (ruler of the 4th).

E. When the Ketu Bhukti animated the ruler of the 7th (Mars) it also animated Neptune which natally is at the cusp of the 7th and only 3 degrees from the Desc. T. Pluto had actually hit N. and P3 Neptune months before. But it had never hit the Desc and was now backing away from Neptune.

My estimation was that months ago he may have become obsessed with a woman who seemed more glamorous than she was (point E), and that somehow his temper may have gotten him in hot water with someone else (point B). He was heavily burdened because of point D (certainly his father soon would be!). Offhand, it was hard to say whether the relationship shock (point C) was from a purely Mars person (likely a male) or just had to do with a Mars-ruled female.

Although everything tended to point to death, I couldn't totally rule out the possibility of escapism instead of death, because the one thing I haven't mentioned yet is that he had been in a Jupiter Dasa since 8/86. Jupiter had a lot of strength because it was very slow at birth and also exalted. Indeed, it was only four applying degrees from its best degree. It was even in its own nakshatra.

This excellent Jupiter was perfectly trine to N. Neptune in the 7th that had been hit by Pluto. It's true that Jupiter rules his 8th, but with such an excellent Jupiter casting such a perfect trine, I would have expected this to limit any problems through association with Neptune and the rulership.

As it turned out, the daughter of the inquirer had gone to my psychic associate before he approached me, but I didn't know it. She said there had been a jealousy problem involving a woman, that he had indeed been killed, and it was related to his temper. She described the killer and said that the currently hidden body would eventually wash (Neptune) into the open. She thought he may have been killed by accident (note Uranus being currently activated, and not Pluto).

The alleged female is currently unknown to the family (Neptune). She probably did really like him because of the strong effect of his Jupiter to his 7th, and that incited the other male (Mars) from the 7th. Note also that T. Venus (10-GE) was exactly conjunct P3 Venus (ruler of the 1st in the 1st), and this suggests that the woman may have been with him when he was killed.

Since I know how good the psychic is, I told the inquirer I had no problem deferring to her conclusion, especially since the vast bulk of astrological evidence supported it. But it did make a powerful statement about the one point of resistance on my part, i.e., a powerful Jupiter Dasa apparently could not protect against such a powerfully configured karmic Bhukti period especially when both the progression and transit patterns also support the tragic power of the Bhukti.

It's obnoxious to form a general theory out of one case, but it will probably be years before I get to see even one other chart with a remotely similar pattern. The reader may simply take note of the various issues and apply them to any subsequent considerations. By the way: several weeks after he disappeared, his body was found in a swampy area, and he had been decapitated. So my psychic friend was a bit wrong also (about the death being an accident).

The objective of this last case in particular is to sensitize the reader to the meaning of, and alternative possibilities contained within, some of the obscure "streams" of logical linkage associated with the two Dasa and Bhukti planets. When we get into the latter half of the book, the many demonstration cases will firm up your sense of any "karma" implied in various types of deaths.

DEATH ESCAPED

Many cases present themselves that look like they might result in a death but, in the end, they do not. Clearly we need to be able to tell the difference. We will find that the distinguishing factor is not any allegedly protecting trines (as some like to argue, and which are, in fact, present in most death charts), but rather due to the foreground presentation of a benefic within a very hard and angular harmonic, or of an immediately upcoming progressed station of a benefic, and the like.

My key point is that the supportive factor has to have as much countervailing "presentation strength" as the factors which brought about the stress event in the first place, and trines do not do that. I'll start out with the very unusual case of a woman who walked away from a massive car accident on one of the widest and busiest highways (I–95) near the Washington, D.C. Beltway in Arlington, VA on 6/3/92 at 4:35 pm EDT.

CASE 1 (Massive Car Accident)

She was exiting off a ramp when 1) a car made a right turn into her car sending her spinning into the highway where 2) another car struck her and sent her spinning again into 3) a big metrobus which she bounced off of onto on a grassy strip. Both cars ran from the accident and were never identified as traffic snarled behind the accident. She was uninjured, and the car was repaired. As a result of the accident, I rectified her birth data to be 40 seconds earlier than what her records showed (7:30) – b. 30–Nov–1950 @ 7:29:20 PM EST at 43N06 & 079W03 (see chart # 14).

What is stunning here is that *four* planets were *stationary* by progression which, in my experience, is completely unprecedented. Natally, Mercury rules her Asc and exactly squares her mean nodes. By P2 (1/11/51), Mercury and Saturn were *both* stationary *and* exactly square to each other. Thus the stationary ruler of the 1st (Mercury) came to a halt in more ways than one. Note also that her P2 Asc was conjunct P2 Pluto within a minute of arc, and in her chart relocated to the accident, the P2 Asc/Pluto conjunct did not even have this single minute of arc deviation (both were at 19–LE–18).

By P3, two *more* planets (Mars and Saturn) were essentially stationary (see 6/8/52). Mars would naturally have a lot to do with a potential strike

10th Pisces Rahu Rx +	11th Aries	12th Taurus	1st Gemini Ascendant ♓
9th Aquarius Jupiter −	SUN Moon beginning on 10/06/1983 SUN Mars beginning on 04/06/1984 SUN Rahu beginning on 08/12/1984 SUN Jupiter beginning on 07/06/1985 SUN Saturn beginning on 04/24/1986 SUN Mercury beginning on 04/06/1987 SUN Ketu beginning on 02/12/1988	2nd Cancer Moon O ♇	
8th Capricorn	SUN Venus beginning on 06/18/1988 MOON Moon beginning on 06/18/1989 MOON Mars beginning on 04/18/1990 MOON Rahu beginning on 11/18/1990 MOON Jupiter beginning on 05/18/1992 MOON Saturn beginning on 09/18/1993	3rd Leo	
7th Sagittarius Mercury e+ Mars ++	6th Scorpio Sun ++ Venus T+	5th Libra	4th Virgo Ketu Rx E Saturn T++ ♆

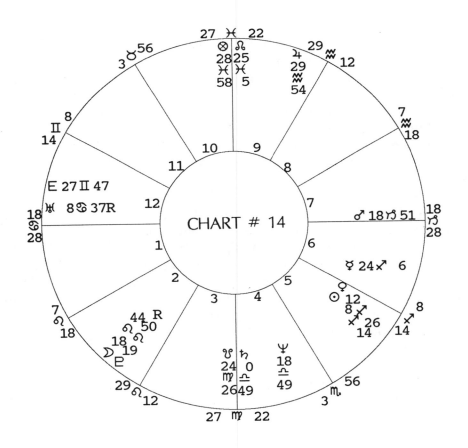

CHART # 14

by someone else since, natally, it is deeply angular being exactly conjunct her Desc. The relevance of stationary Saturn is that, relocating the chart to the accident, the P3 MC was also conjunct her stationary P3 Saturn (at 8-LI-12) TTM.

Transits at the accident offer even further confirmation of the 40 second rectification. Alcoholic Neptune was conjunct her N. Desc — again TTM (18-CP-58) and, in her relocated chart, crazy Uranus was exactly conjunct her Desc — again TTM (17-CP-18). These are four angle hits exactly to the minute! The fact that she was hit by two cars shows in the transits and arguably in both progressions.

The question clearly arises as to why she wasn't killed. Some key reasons are that she was in a Jupiter Bhukti which protected her 1st — see aspect rules already discussed in the Hindu chapter. In addition, her P3 Venus (strong in Taurus in the 12th) was exactly — within 1 minute — opposing N. Venus in the 6th (along with the P3 Moon and Asc within a degree or two), thus setting up a strong polarity vibration of Venus protection. She made the comment to me that she felt there were angels in the car with her. Researchers can note a number of other lesser reasons.

A third key reason was the absence of what you will eventually realize are the standard transiting eclipse patterns prior to the accident. Yet, oddly enough, there were two *very* significant eclipses that occurred several weeks *after* the accident. One was exactly on her Mercury (again, square her Nodes and ruling her Asc), and the other was exactly on her N. Uranus. Had these eclipses occurred prior to the accident, the result would have been entirely different.

Parenthetically, and continuing along this line, her P3 planets did not technically achieve complete station until several "ephemeris" days (months) after the accident. Thus her chart remained very energized. I now regarded this as a potentially very positive period as she had been in a Moon Dasa since 7/89 with the Moon strong in Cancer conjunct Pluto in the 2nd, and Jupiter (her Bhukti since June) was very happy in the 9th, the house of luck.

I told her I had indeed seen *big* lottery wins with similar patterns, including progressed Saturn stations (see, for example, P2 Saturn for Kathleen McLaughlin, born 2/17/57 at 6:35 AM EST in Boston who won $27 million on 12/13/91), since some of these big wins often followed closely upon periods of near personal catastrophe such as extended unemployment, imminent house foreclosures and the like. I recommended that she play the lottery weekly as a potential outlet for these residual post-accident patterns. Alas, she didn't win.

CASE 2 (Trade Center Bombing Victim)

This is a woman whom I had agreed to pick up at a Washington DC subway station on the evening of 26-Feb-1993. As it turned out, she works on the 65th floor of the World Trade Center building in Manhattan, and that was the same day the building was bombed (at 12:17 PM EST), and a number of people were killed. The question at hand is why she wasn't one of them. See chart # 15 (b. 1-Feb-1967 @ 8:13 AM EST in Massillon, Ohio 40N47 & 81W31). This chart will also be useful to emphasize a point that hasn't yet received enough attention in this book. And that is when there are serious external physical events to the body, the relocated angles are clearly informative.

This person had moved into a Saturn Dasa the last week of 1991, and was not yet into an offsetting Bhukti. Her BC TOB gives a birth location Asc of 23-AQ-15, so as you might expect, considering her Dasa, T. Saturn was at 22-AQ-58 at the bombing (if she was born 45 seconds earlier, it would have been exact). This was also right on her N. Mercury of 22-AQ-13 (this natal affiliation of Mercury with her Asc is confirmed by the fact that one of her hobbies is doing stand-up comedy routines at a local NY club).

And, indeed, T. Mercury in her 1st opposed her N. Uranus in the 7th with only 10 minutes of orb. Her P3 MC had also come into exact square to these three factors at 22-SC-28. Note also that T. Pluto had gone stationary that day in her 10th house (25-SC) while P2 Neptune had almost no velocity at the cusp of her 10th.

Her relocated chart has an Asc of 05-PI-06, and at the bombing her P3 Mars was at 05-PI-12. So what was the saving grace? First, that her P3 Venus (17-SA-02) was exactly conjunct her relocated MC (less than a degree away from the prior lunar eclipse), and second that her P3 Jupiter (04-VI-52) was exactly conjunct her relocated Desc (she said everyone behaved beautifully). These two fully angular placements greatly offset the two exactly angular events at the Asc.

Now it did end up being the case that she had to walk down 65 flights of a completely dark, packed and smoky stairwell with her travel bag, and

2nd Pisces Saturn -	3rd Aries Rahu Rx S--	4th Taurus	5th Gemini
1st Aquarius Ascendant e Venus T++	RAHU Moon beginning on 06/10/1973 RAHU Mars beginning on 12/10/1974 JUPITER Jupiter beginning on 12/28/1975 JUPITER Saturn beginning on 02/16/1978 JUPITER Mercury beginning on 08/28/1980 JUPITER Ketu beginning on 12/04/1982 JUPITER Venus beginning on 11/10/1983	6th Cancer Jupiter Rx E	
12th Capricorn Sun Mercury Te+	JUPITER Sun beginning on 07/10/1986 JUPITER Moon beginning on 04/28/1987 JUPITER Mars beginning on 08/28/1988 JUPITER Rahu beginning on 08/04/1989 SATURN Saturn beginning on 12/28/1991 SATURN Mercury beginning on 01/01/1995	7th Leo	♇
11th Sagittarius	10th Scorpio ♆	9th Libra Mars - Moon - Ketu Rx S	8th Virgo ♅

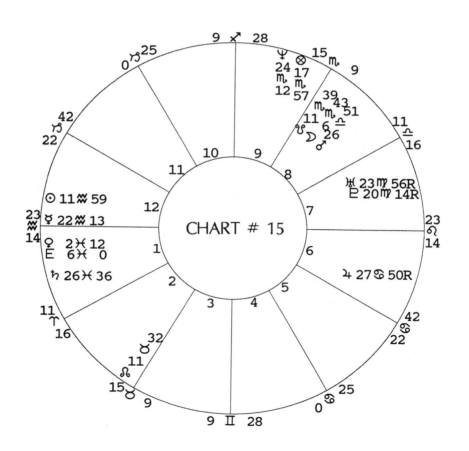

CHART # 15

that the trains were not running in the basement of her building, so she had to walk to the next train station. She then had to stand on the train for several hours, and so forth. But physical burden is to be expected with T. Saturn right on the Asc.

As an additional comment on her Jupiter, I should note that it is located at the single most exalted degree within the Hindu system of the entire zodiac (sidereally that is 5–CA). In this book I've made occasional reference to a strong psychic I use for referral under certain circumstances. It was amusing to me that when I sent one of my clients to her, the psychic became very excited when my client merely mentioned her friend (the woman at the WTC building) whom the psychic would never meet.

The psychic insisted that the WTC woman had been a Pharaoh in a prior life, and this was exciting to her because this was only the second person in her psychic "career" who had ever been "famous" in a prior life. This intrigued me as it would match quite well with the concept of an "inherited" Jupiter at its most exalted degree, although "The Pharaoh" herself, as we now refer to her, didn't take it very seriously. She will probably just roll the entire bombing adventure into her stand–up comedy routine — although I personally think "A Pharaoh Named Leslie" merits its own routine.

CASE 3 (Heart Attack)

Here is yet a third variation on the notion of protection factors. As I was working on this chapter a neighbor of mine had a heart attack on April 19, 1993 — see chart # 16 (b. 24–Feb–1940 @ 1:22 PM CST in Cape Girardeau, MO 37N19 & 89W32). People have heart attacks all the time; some live and some don't. In this particular case, despite being a very large fellow, he recovered quite rapidly and with apparent ease. Let's briefly look at some relevant natal factors and some associated precipitating factors.

Perhaps the first thing to point out is that his wife, whose chart is not shown, was in a one-year Saturn Bhukti when he had the attack, and natally Saturn is stationary in her own 1st. Although she herself suffers from several severe chronic illnesses, this placement will also cast an especially strong Saturnian pressure directed across the chart at her 7th during its period. Her husband is one of the most respected mechanical engineers in the D.C. area. Consequently, despite a major commercial property recession in Washington during this period, he had been regularly working at least 70 hour weeks for the past year.

10th Pisces Jupiter O Venus ET Ketu Rx –	11th Aries Saturn Tf Mars M ♓	12th Taurus	1st Gemini Ascendant
9th Aquarius Sun Mercury e+	RAHU Sun beginning on 04/27/1975 RAHU Moon beginning on 03/21/1976 RAHU Mars beginning on 09/21/1977 JUPITER Jupiter beginning on 10/09/1978 JUPITER Saturn beginning on 11/27/1980 JUPITER Mercury beginning on 06/09/1983 JUPITER Ketu beginning on 09/15/1985		2nd Cancer ♇
8th Capricorn	JUPITER Venus beginning on 08/21/1986 JUPITER Sun beginning on 04/21/1989 JUPITER Moon beginning on 02/09/1990 JUPITER Mars beginning on 06/09/1991 JUPITER Rahu beginning on 05/15/1992 SATURN Saturn beginning on 10/09/1994		3rd Leo
7th Sagittarius	6th Scorpio	5th Libra	4th Virgo Moon e Rahu Rx E ♆

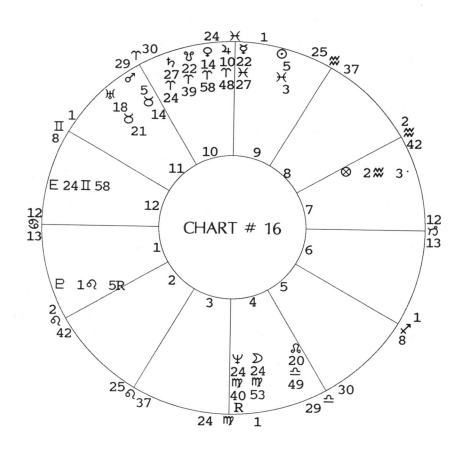

He is a self-employed consultant who works out of his home. You may notice the Moon/Neptune conjunction on his IC (all at the same degree), and indeed that probably will be a factor in his ultimate death. I asked him to tell me about his mother. He said that he and his brother used to go to bed every night hoping that she wouldn't dream about them because when she said she dreamed about someone, that person soon died!

When I asked him to tell me about his original home he said it was built on a type of bog near the river so that it floated, and in his current home (which has a swimming pool) he has a wife who insists she has psychic powers. Actually, a very interesting consequence of this configuration in Virgo is that it gives him a photographic memory for all the complex industrial drawings he has created. A former CIA Director had the same Moon/Neptune conjunct in Virgo, and he also had a photographic memory (except apparently when it became inconvenient).

So this point functions very oddly, and one of the things we see is that his P3 Asc was only about half a degree beyond an exact square to this point. While this could argue for about a 2 minute rectification, it was the case that his family had been counselling him for several prior weeks to slow down since his color was changing as he was obviously weakening (each week of P3 angle error usually corresponds to about one minute of birth time error). Based upon that, his given TOB is acceptable. A few other points:

> ➤ T. Uranus and Neptune were both almost stationary and square to his 4/10 nodal axis while he was in a nodal Bhukti.
> ➤ The P3 ruler of his 6th was also exactly square (TTM) to the P3 ruler of his 12th (Mars and Venus respectively).
> ➤ The T. Sun, P2 Sun and N. Saturn were all conjunct at 27-AR. Saturn is fallen in Aries, and the Sun rules the heart.
> ➤ His P3 Moon was exactly tri-octile (135 degrees) to N. Mars.

But the final timer was the fact that his P3 Uranus had gone fully stationary in his 12th (fully aspecting his 6th), and P3 Mercury, ruler of his 1st, was now exactly square this P3 Uranus station (keep in mind that T. Uranus was also stationary square to his nodes). So why wasn't he killed? Because 1) Uranus is not a killer, 2) no T. Saturn or Pluto problems, 3) no involvement of progressed angles, 4) no recent eclipse hits, nor most of the other classic items typically seen at death.

But even more to the point was the fact that there was a P3 Jupiter station (2/5/42) less than two days after the current P3 Uranus station, and he was still in his Jupiter Dasa. Jupiter is in its own sign in his natal chart (and also in his navamsha), and it is also in the same house with an exalted Venus. Since it has positive status and functions quite well, his first month of recuperation was fully protected by progressing into this Jupiter station during a Jupiter Dasa.

As a major side benefit he re-evaluated his compulsive work habits and soon discovered that by intelligently turning down certain types of projects his already substantial income actually went up even as he reduced his hours back from 70 to 40 per week.

CASE 4 (Heart Attack Comparison)

Now, for purposes of comparison, review the following case of a fatal heart attack (including stroke) that occurred about a month before the person died. You will see that, by comparison, there were no relieving considerations coming along to lift up the body after the attack. In fact, the factors tightened. This is the chart of a respected astrological author who died at age 86 on 6/11/93. His birth data, as supplied to a public astrological journal, is: 06–June–1906 @ 1:00 AM EST at 43N15 & 79W51 (see chart # 17). By the way, I think this TOB is short by about 4 minutes, but I left it alone to illustrate later why I think this is so.

Here we have a case of excellent longevity for a number of reasons. For example, Saturn is in its own sign very near the Asc. Jupiter is square the horizon (environmental support), and is also the midpoint of a 5–planet stellium spanning 15 degrees. The ruler of the 8th (Mercury) is in the same house with Jupiter and is in a mutual reception with a benefic (Venus) as a rajayoga planet linking the benefic 5th and 9th.

At death he was in a Rahu Dasa and Sun Bhukti. It has been noted that the Sun does not function as a maraka, but in his chart we see that Saturn is perfectly square to the Sun within 4 minutes, and Saturn rules the maraka 2nd. So the Sun, while not an active maraka, draws the energy of Saturn and hence becomes a passive maraka. In fact, T. Saturn indeed proves its status relative to the Sun because it had gone stationary only the day before he died (if he had been born 4 minutes later, his P3 MC(IC) would be conjunct it exactly at the death). The last T. solar eclipse had been at 00–GE–31, and T. Saturn had stopped in his 1st exactly square to the immediately prior eclipse point at 00–PI–20. By the way, his P3 Saturn at this point also had very low velocity.

2nd Pisces	3rd Aries	4th Taurus	5th Gemini
		Mercury T≈++ Sun Jupiter ♇	Mars R Venus RT≈++ ♆

1st Aquarius Saturn M Ascendant	MARS Mercury beginning on 01/03/1975 MARS Ketu beginning on 12/30/1975 MARS Venus beginning on 05/27/1976 MARS Sun beginning on 07/27/1977 MARS Moon beginning on 12/03/1977 RAHU Rahu beginning on 07/03/1978 RAHU Jupiter beginning on 03/15/1981	6th Cancer Rahu Rx --
12th Capricorn Ketu Rx ++	RAHU Saturn beginning on 08/09/1983 RAHU Mercury beginning on 06/15/1986 RAHU Ketu beginning on 01/03/1989 RAHU Venus beginning on 01/21/1990 RAHU Sun beginning on 01/21/1993 RAHU Moon beginning on 12/15/1993	7th Leo

11th Sagittarius ♓	10th Scorpio Moon f	9th Libra	8th Virgo

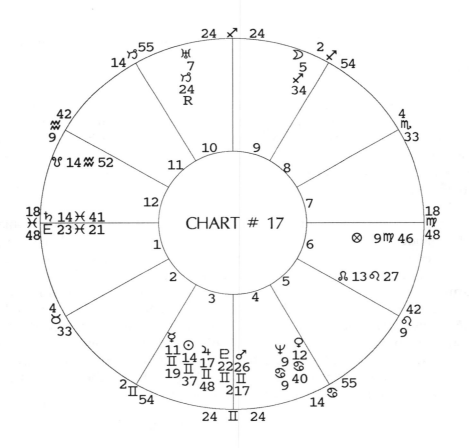

CHART # 17

Let's look at the nodal axis Dasa and see how it interplays with the Bhukti Sun and eclipses. The last T. lunar eclipse a week before he died was at 13-SA-55. Not only was this axis directly coincident with his N. Sun of 14-GE-37 (and therefore square N. Saturn), but his P3 tNN was also on his N. Sun at 14-GE-55. Further, his P3 Sun had reached 19-LE-8, and this put it on one of his two PNE's of 19-LE-40 (the Sun was only at 18 degrees at the heart attack as further evidence of a subsequent lack of relief). For the record, note also that the 3rd prior T. eclipse was at 18-GE-10 which had it squaring his horizon.

By the way, while T. Mars was square to T. Pluto (at the cusps of his sidereal 7th and 10th respectively), his P3 Pluto (26-GE-31) was now also conjunct N. Mars (26-GE-17) within 14 minutes. A second argument for adding 4 minutes to his birth time is the fact that his P3 Asc had only reached to 25-GE-27 when he died — about a degree short of this Mars/Pluto point, just as his P3 MC was also about a degree short of the T. Saturn station and prior eclipse point.

These four scenarios are sufficient to illustrate my three key points:

On the negative side, a certain "full bodied" pattern of a certain type must be present before even a very harsh set of transits and progressions will result in death. This is why some people will "justifiably" say, after a terrible but non-fatal event, that they would rather be dead. Sometimes a death pattern can technically be less brutal than a non-fatal pattern — even if it does result in death!

On the positive side, if the event pattern contains one or more benefics that have moved into a very strong position (esp. via conjunction or opposition), it will help protect the chart.

For events that merely set up the question of whether death will subsequently result, one needs to look at the "after pattern" and how it fits into the symbolic flow. After surgeries, does the pattern move on — or retrograde? Are benefics about to station — or malefics? And so forth.

Now we move into the second half of the book where over 55 cases will be used to reinforce the theory that has been refined to this point.

EXPECTED DEATH IN ONE'S OWN CHART

This chapter will highlight some cases where death was not unexpected and was often self-aware. It will be looking at this from the point of view of the chartholder him or herself. In the theoretical section on longevity, I noted some complex factors that Hindu astrology suggests would contribute to only a brief period of life. Let's begin with a somewhat gritty case that is probably more common around the world than we would wish to believe.

CASE 1 (Death of an Infant)

A couple of years back, the astrology magazine *Considerations* (Vol. 6 # 3) ran the following brief commentary in their Data section:

> *In New York City it is not unusual for newborn babies, some still alive, to be discarded like mistakes into trash cans and garbage bags, down refuge chutes and into dumpsters. Usually they die anonymously. Only rarely do they command the public's attention. Their departure from life is not usually announced in a note.*
>
> *Shortly after 9:30 PM on Monday, 29th April 1991, in the impoverished Bushwick section of Brooklyn, a policeman found a dead infant in a yellow plastic bag next to a garbage can. The baby was neatly wrapped in a white blanket, she had been powdered and wore brand new clothes, a diaper, a T-shirt and pajamas. Around the blanket was tied a white ribbon. A neatly printed note was pinned to the blanket:*
>
> *"Please Take care of My girl. She was born April 26, 1991 at 12:42 pm. Her name is April Olivia. I love her very much.*
>
> *"Thank You.*
>
> *"She Died at 10:30 am on April 29, 1991.*
>
> *"Sorry."*

In many ways this baby's main chart (see chart # 18) is really quite good: the Sun is exalted in the 10th, Venus is in its own sign in the 11th, Mars has rajayoga status in the 12th, Jupiter is exalted in the 1st while Saturn is in its own sign in the 7th. Had this baby survived it could have had a life to be reckoned with. The fact that the baby was treated so considerately in death (obviously from a relative point of view) attests to some of these strengths (as perhaps did the worldwide publicity that was received).

You will recall my earlier comment that Hindu astrologers tend to see infant mortality more as a working out of the karma of the parents; therefore the focus is more in the parents' charts than in that of the infant. Here we do not have the mother's chart. Yet some of the mother's stress can be seen in the fact that the baby's Moon (actually ruler of the 1st) is receiving a full aspect from a stationary fallen planet (Mercury) that in turn is ruler of the 12th (which itself contains Mars and the south node). Pluto is also in the 4th.

Looking at it another way, the two houses of poorvapunya ("what you have coming to you" as shown by the 5th) and luck (the 9th) are very weak. The ruler of the 5th is in the 12th with the south node, and the 9th containing a fallen planet whose deficiency is "strengthened" by being stationary and aspected by Saturn. In the navamsha, the 5th contains a fallen Saturn, and the ruler of the 9th is in the 8th. As a side note, although the 5th and the 9th did not provide any benefits to the chart, had the baby lived these houses would have received benefit from Jupiter in the 1st — especially the Pisces 9th. Yet another way of saying this is that the child's father was particularly debilitated, yet would have received much benefit from the child. That may somehow even be true as a result of the child's death.

Let's look at it from the point of view of its Dasa and Bhukti planets which are the Moon and Saturn respectively. The Moon is the ruler of the 1st. It receives a full aspect from the stationary fallen ruler of the 12th. Further, the Moon is aspected by Mars from the 12th. In the navamsha, the 6th house Moon is in a mutual reception with an 8th house planet.

Saturn is powerful in its own sign in the maraka 7th. Given this strength, and since it is the currently active Bhukti planet, it overpowers Jupiter in the 1st (which also is damaged somewhat by ruling the 6th), and it also overpowers the quite fallen Mercury in the 9th. In the navamsha, Saturn itself is fallen in the 5th, and is opposing the ruler of the 1st. As a curiosity, note that the baby's Saturn is within 6 minutes of being exactly con-

9th Pisces Mercury Rx Sf	10th Aries Sun E	11th Taurus Venus O	12th Gemini Mars RT Ketu Rx Ee
8th Aquarius	RASI CHART for Chart # 18 Born in Moon Dasa & Saturn Bhukti		1st Cancer Jupiter ET Ascendant
7th Capricorn Saturn O			2nd Leo
6th Sagittarius Rahu Rx e−	5th Scorpio	4th Libra	3rd Virgo Moon

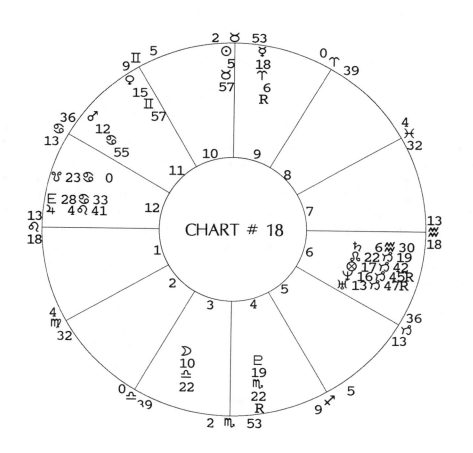

CHART # 18

junct the tSN of any of the commonly discussed U.S. charts (see 7/4/ 1776) which perhaps made her a media symbol for some failure in U.S. social policy.

Some other factors of significant note are that:

> ➤ The baby had a pre-natal eclipse in the month after conception on 8/6/90 at 13-AQ — which ultimately turned out to be exactly on her N. Asc/Desc axis. This is highly karmic.

> ➤ Her 6/12 true nodes are at the exact same declination — to the minute — as her natal Neptune (21S35), while Neptune still had almost no velocity from a prior station within the baby's natal 6th.

> ➤ A very slow Uranus was also exactly conjunct the tropical 6th house cusp in exact quincunx by degree to the Asc.

> ➤ N. Mercury actually went fully stationary two days after the baby's birth; the baby didn't quite live three days. Just under three degrees is also the arc of the difference between the child's Sun and Midheaven. The Sun is in almost a perfect T-square to Jupiter and Saturn, with Saturn at the highest degree.

CASES 2 & 3 (Death of Two Homeless Men)

In April 1993 Lois Rodden reprinted some timed birth data along with the dates of death for two homeless men that was supplied by researcher Frances McEvoy. I thought this might be interesting to review since, first of all, they constitute a type of random selection, and secondly because they might be interesting from the point of view of the IC and 4th house ruler (which may be different in the full house system) since both have to do with the home and with "the end of the matter." Additionally, by the time someone becomes chronically homeless, they often start to live on the edge where there is almost no buffer to ride out a sustained run of even average misfortune.

The first is Joseph Bulens b. 2-Jan-1943 @ 4:20 PM EWT in Boston, MA 42N21 & 071W4 (see chart # 19). By way of brief background, Mr. Bulens was the eldest of five children, at one point was married (unhappily) and had four daughters of whom he was proud. As the marriage failed, his drinking increased and he began living on the streets. He panhandled to buy alcohol, ate from trash cans and slept in cardboard boxes. He was

10th Pisces	11th Aries Saturn Rx T≈	12th Taurus	1st Gemini Ascendant Jupiter Rx e--
			♓
9th Aquarius Ketu Rx ++	MERCURY Mars beginning on 10/30/1977 MERCURY Rahu beginning on 10/27/1978 MERCURY Jupiter beginning on 05/15/1981 MERCURY Saturn beginning on 08/21/1983 KETU Ketu beginning on 04/30/1986 KETU Venus beginning on 09/27/1986 KETU Sun beginning on 11/27/1987		2nd Cancer
	KETU Moon beginning on 04/03/1988 KETU Mars beginning on 11/03/1988 KETU Rahu beginning on 03/30/1989		♇
8th Capricorn Venus RTe≈ Mercury R-	KETU Jupiter beginning on 04/18/1990 KETU Saturn beginning on 03/24/1991 KETU Mercury beginning on 05/03/1992		3rd Leo Rahu Rx --
7th Sagittarius Sun	6th Scorpio Mars 0	5th Libra Moon +	4th Virgo
			♆

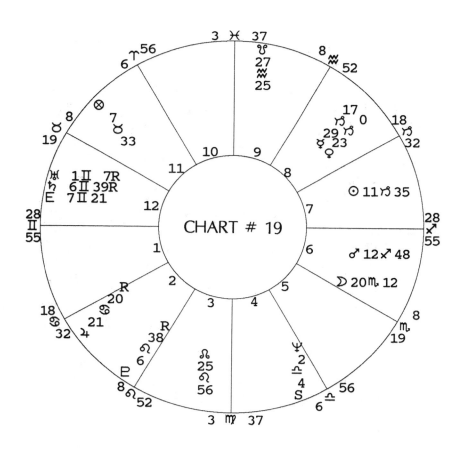

found dead on 4/27/92 — almost the exact day of a Bhukti shift as will be discussed below (again, this is using my ayanamsha of 5 minutes and 10 seconds off of Lahiri). There could be some birth time error.

Natally it is perhaps most salient to note that he was born when Neptune was basically stationary and the only planet in his 4th house. In addition to the potential lack of a firm psychological foundation and hence potential homelessness, we would also expect to see some Neptune weakness "at the end of the matter." And there was: this time T. Neptune, again with very low velocity, had been fully stationary at 18-CP (along with Uranus) only the week before he died. This station was not only directly on his 8th house Placidus cusp; it was also the exact same position of his P2 Mars on the day of his death.

There were a number of severe Saturn problems. Natally Saturn (in the 12th) was in a mutual reception with Venus (in the 8th), and this was true not only in the main chart — it was again the case in the navamsha chart. Statistically, this is quite unlikely. Natally, the ruler of the 1st (Mercury) is in the 8th conjunct this very unhappy Venus. It's also critical to note that P3 Saturn, ruler of the 8th, was in the 1st (in Gemini) exactly stationary the month of his death (the P3 date was 10/23/44).

So there was at this time yet another dark mutual reception, this time between the ruler of the 1st (Mercury in CP) and the stationary progressed ruler of the 8th (Saturn in GE). This P3 stationary Saturn was also applying to an opposition to the N. Sun within less than a degree. I should also note that he was in a Ketu (SN) Dasa during this time, and Ketu itself is disposed of by Saturn. So the chart continues to loop back upon itself.

Speaking further of Saturn, Mr. Bulens actually died on the last day of a Saturn Bhukti period that ran from 3/17/91 to 4/26/92. We can see that his last year was very difficult. For example, his P2 Asc had been exactly conjunct N. Pluto the prior year, T. Pluto had been conjunct his N. Moon (and was applying back again within a degree), and there had been a P2 lunar eclipse at 0-VI-43 the prior year. This was 3 degrees off his IC, admittedly an unacceptably wide orb for my tastes, but it reflected another total lunar eclipse that occurred during the pre-natal period at 2-PI-17 which was only one degree from the MC/IC axis.

These eclipse orbs might begin to suggest an argument for a slight adjustment in the birth time, but there are many reasons not to do this. Among them are the fact that the actual last T. lunar eclipse before death was at

29-GE-03 which was only 8 minutes from his given Asc of 28-GE-55 [parenthetically, another highly relevant aspect, also with an applying 8 minute orb, was the secondary progression of the ruler of the 1st (Mercury) so that it was exactly opposite P2 Pluto. And, concluding the Pluto effect, the P3 MC was exactly tri-octile Pluto with a 3 minute orb, while P3 Mars was exactly square Pluto with a 3 minute orb].

To promote clarity and focus, I have generally tried to stay away from derived points such as the Part of (Mis)fortune (Asc + Sun - Moon). As calculated ratios, these should just mimic that which can be seen more fundamentally elsewhere. But I will note that points such as these, if correctly calculated, are very typically activated. For example, in this case, the P3 Part of (Mis)fortune was at 21-TA-56 while T. Pluto was exactly opposing at 21-SC-58, and the P2 Part of (Mis)fortune was at 17-AQ-39 exactly conjunct T. Saturn at 17-AQ-43.

The second homeless case is that of Joseph Eaton who was also born in Boston on 8/5/50 at 00:57 AM EDT (see chart # 20). He started out life as the son of a financially strong family. He began going downhill at around age 13, and he also became aware of his growing homosexuality. He began drinking and drifting, and ended up in San Francisco in 1981. His homosexual partner died of AIDS in November of 1987. Eaton also had AIDS, and he eventually died on the street 12/02/88 at age 38.

Using Hindu signs and houses, homosexuality or bisexuality, whether male or female, is tied to a more consistently limited number of factors, often including, for example, a strong link between Mars and the 7th (most commonly Mars is in it) and typically with some clear tieback to the 1st. A Venus or Mars ruled sign is often rising and is often in a mutual reception with the ruler of the 7th. In Eaton's case Mars rules his 7th (and 12th), and is in the 6th opposing his Moon. The navamsha confirms this with both Saturn and Mars in Scorpio in the 7th. In both charts, Mars aspects a Venus-ruled Taurus 1st house.

The special significance of this oppressive combination is that he met his partner during a Saturn Bhukti (1982) thus both animating and aspecting Mars, and he moved into his Mars Dasa and Bhukti in February of 1987. He was still in this unrelieved Dasa when his partner died. Mars, as ruler of the Scorpio 7th in both charts, is also therefore a very powerful maraka. Note two related facts: 1) the ruler of his 1st is in the other maraka house (the 2nd), and 2) the ruler of the 7th is in the 6th, while in turn the ruler of the 6th is in the 2nd, i.e., both maraka rulers involve the 6th.

11th Pisces Rahu +	12th Aries Moon −	1st Taurus Ascendant	2nd Gemini Venus ++ ♓
10th Aquarius Jupiter Rx −	MOON Moon beginning on 02/19/1977 MOON Mars beginning on 12/19/1977 MOON Rahu beginning on 07/19/1978 MOON Jupiter beginning on 01/19/1980 MOON Saturn beginning on 05/19/1981 MOON Mercury beginning on 12/19/1982 MOON Ketu beginning on 05/19/1984	3rd Cancer Sun ++ ♇	
9th Capricorn	MOON Venus beginning on 12/19/1984 MOON Sun beginning on 08/19/1986 MARS Mars beginning on 02/19/1987 MARS Rahu beginning on 07/16/1987 MARS Jupiter beginning on 08/04/1988 MARS Saturn beginning on 07/10/1989	4th Leo Mercury T++ Saturn RT	
8th Sagittarius	7th Scorpio	6th Libra Mars −	5th Virgo Ketu E ♆

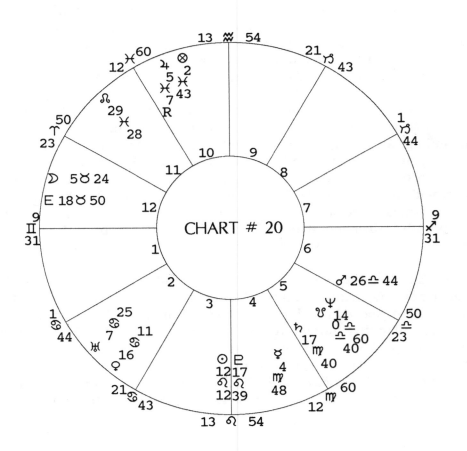

CHART # 20

What perhaps most distinctively fascinated me about this case was an immediately prior twin set of technically-unrelated eclipses that happened to hit on the exact same sign, degree and almost minute. There was a P2 eclipse at 18-VI-48 (see 9/12/50) while the last T. solar eclipse before his death was at 18-VI-40. The "double whammy" of these technically unrelated eclipses were within a degree of his N. Saturn.

While Saturn is the natural karaka of death, he was in a Jupiter Bhukti. So what was the issue here? It turns out that the last T. lunar eclipse before death was conjunct his N. Jupiter (ruler of his 8th) within half a degree. N. Jupiter in turn was opposing N. Mercury within 19 minutes, so Mercury was also linked by association to the eclipse. In addition, Mercury is a maraka as ruler of the 2nd. Further Mercury confirmation is that his P2 mSN was conjunct P2 maraka Mercury with only one minute of orb (and, if we want to mix progression systems, the P2 ruler of 1st was conjunct the P3 mSN within half a degree). Finally, and again in support of intermediate Placidus house cusps, T. Uranus and Neptune were conjunct his 8th house cusp of this system.

CASE 4 (Death From Cancer)

I've mentioned earlier about Saturn being the karaka or natural planetary indicator for death. In this case of a former "important person" within one of the major political parties who died on 8/3/91 (see chart # 21 b. 20-Dec-1927 @ 7:30 AM CST per BC @ 36N24 & 97W53) we will be able to observe its central operating predominance. I had been able to impress some doubters with a series of well-timed health-related forecasts about this person over a year ahead of time. But I must say that my conclusion was supplemented to a certain extent by an opportunity to observe him on an almost daily basis and therefore to factor in a spiritual perception that I won't go into, except to say that I feel I somewhat observed his soul's discouragement with life.

Concerning his death, a key initial observation is that P3 Saturn was within only two applying "days" of being totally stationary Rx in his 1st house (4/19/30 vs. 4/21/30). Therefore this maraka essentially had no velocity. While this is the image of 1st house activity grinding to a halt, it doesn't necessarily kill you. However, within the context of other factors to be noted, this P3 Saturn (11-CP-53) was stopping only 9 minutes from his natal East Point (11-CP-44), and his relocated Asc (12-CP-38) was also well within orb.

4th Pisces Jupiter ○ ♓︎	5th Aries	6th Taurus Rahu	7th Gemini ♇
3rd Aquarius	KETU Moon beginning on 06/19/1976 KETU Mars beginning on 01/19/1977 KETU Rahu beginning on 06/16/1977 KETU Jupiter beginning on 07/04/1978 KETU Saturn beginning on 06/10/1979 KETU Mercury beginning on 07/19/1980 VENUS Venus beginning on 07/16/1981		8th Cancer
2nd Capricorn	VENUS Sun beginning on 11/16/1984 VENUS Moon beginning on 11/16/1985 VENUS Mars beginning on 07/16/1987 VENUS Rahu beginning on 09/16/1988 VENUS Jupiter beginning on 09/16/1991 VENUS Saturn beginning on 05/16/1994		9th Leo ♆
1st Sagittarius Ascendant e Sun T++	12th Scorpio Mars OT Saturn -- Mercury - Ketu --	11th Libra Venus M Moon -	10th Virgo

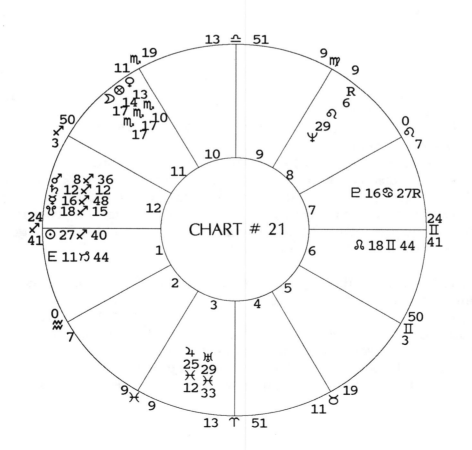

CHART # 21

T. Neptune (11-CP-53) had been exactly on this P3 Saturn point about a year earlier when he went in for cancer surgery on 10/10/90. From this I correctly advised that he would have to go back for corrective surgery within a few months due to the fact that T. Uranus would be the third factor to exactly hit this same point, and that the most severe consequences would ensue in late July of 1991 for the same reason — plus the fact that Pluto would also be stationing on his N. Moon in late July (it was still essentially stationary at his death). It can also be noted that P3 Uranus was at 12-AR-19 which was square to this stationary Saturn and only a degree from his IC.

He had been in a Venus Dasa since 1981, and P3 Venus was now conjunct P3 Mercury. Mercury is one of his most besieged natal factors being closely located between Saturn and the SN in the 12th house (both in the signs of "great enemies"), and it also invoked a powerful 12th house Mars in Scorpio that is frustrated being in the 12th with Saturn. Mercury therefore suffered much, and Venus was now picking this up by progressed association. Natally, Venus was with the Moon and, as noted above, Pluto was now stationing on his Moon.

At death, he was in the last month of a three year Rahu Bhukti. Since this node is in the 6th, it invoked the very unattractive natal congestion in the 12th that was noted above. By P3 the NN was now at 2-TA-50. At his death T. Saturn was exactly square at 2-AQ-56 and indeed, the last T. full Moon before his death was an eclipse at 3-AQ-16. This is all part of the link back into the nodal Bhukti that was currently active (by the way, the last full moon before he was born was also an eclipse). Two final Saturn points can be noted at death: his P2 Moon (12-PI) was square N. Saturn, and T. Mars (12-VI) was also square N. Saturn — overall a hard T-Square.

CASE 5 (Arthur Ashe — AIDS/Pneumonia)

Arthur Ashe was the well-known tennis player who died in New York city at age 49 on 2/6/93 of pneumonia, a complication of AIDS that had been further brought on by a tainted blood transfusion received some years earlier. His data is 10-July-1943 @ 12:55 PM EWT in Richmond, VA 37N33 & 77W28 (see chart # 22).

This was quite a "soft" death compared, for example, to the one above. For example — and this is very rare — neither Uranus, Neptune nor Pluto had any involvement at all, although Uranus and Neptune would seem to have been involved at the time he became aware of the problem since

7th Pisces	8th Aries Mars M	9th Taurus Saturn T++ ⌘	10th Gemini Mercury O Sun –
6th Aquarius 5th Capricorn Ketu Rx S	JUPITER Mercury beginning on 06/05/1972 JUPITER Ketu beginning on 09/11/1974 JUPITER Venus beginning on 08/17/1975 JUPITER Sun beginning on 04/17/1978 JUPITER Moon beginning on 02/05/1979 JUPITER Mars beginning on 06/05/1980 JUPITER Rahu beginning on 05/11/1981 SATURN Saturn beginning on 10/05/1983 SATURN Mercury beginning on 10/08/1986 SATURN Ketu beginning on 06/17/1989 SATURN Venus beginning on 07/26/1990 SATURN Sun beginning on 09/26/1993 SATURN Moon beginning on 09/08/1994		11th Cancer Jupiter E Rahu Rx S ♇ 12th Leo Venus T
4th Sagittarius	3rd Scorpio	2nd Libra	1st Virgo Ascendant Moon ++ ♆

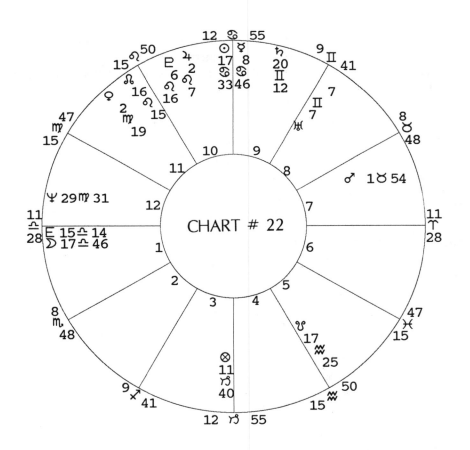

they had transited his IC in 1990 and 1991. We might expect that self-aware deaths would not represent the symbolic features of shock and so forth such as would necessarily be seen in an automobile accident, for example.

Ashe had a generally excellent life force with Mars in Aries in the 8th house. His fame is seen in the fact that the ruler of both his 1st and 10th is in fact in the 10th along with his Sun. From ages 6-40 he was in his NN and Jupiter Dasas with Jupiter being exalted in his 11th, so life went fine until that time. Further, Jupiter was only 4 degrees from its most exalted degree, and it gained even more power from its association with Pluto.

Let's look at what was the most immediate cause of death. Mercury rules his chart, and you will recall that he died of pneumonia (Mercury ruling the lungs). The last total solar eclipse before his death was at 8-CA-57 about seven months earlier. This was exactly conjunct his Mercury within 11 minutes of orb. From this one may have expected severe problems seven months later on 2/15/93 when T. Mars would go totally stationary on this sensitized ruling point at 8-CA-41. Instead he died about a week earlier as Mars was Rx and slowing at 9-CA-10. Let's now look at the supporting considerations:

➤ He had a PNE at 0-VI-43. At death, his P2 MC was exactly conjunct this at 0-VI-26.

➤ He was in a Saturn Dasa, and T. Saturn was at 20-AQ-34. At death his P2 Asc was at 20-SC-34, i.e., perfectly square T. Saturn TTM. By the way, in his navamsha chart-ruler Mercury was in a mutual reception with Saturn.

➤ His N. tNN was at 16-LE, and this was reinforced by a PNE at 15-AQ. At death, his P3 Asc had arrived at 16-LE.

➤ His P3 mSN was at 12-CP; this was conjunct his IC.

➤ P3 Pluto was at 7-LE-57. With only a 5' orb this was square his P3 MC/IC axis. This MC of 8-TA-5 was conjunct the Placidus 8th cusp (and therefore the P3 IC was conjunct the Placidus maraka 2nd).

➤ He was in a Venus Bhukti, and Venus was ruler of his maraka 2nd. Venus was located in his 12th and natally square Uranus — but with a 5 degree orb (the prior cancer case noted just above was also in a Venus Bhukti with Venus also in his 12th and also receiving stress from Uranus). P3 maraka Venus had arrived in his maraka 7th at 17-AR. From here it functioned as a soft malefic by perfectly opposing his Moon in the 1st (17-LI) and perfectly squaring his Sun in the 10th (17-CA).

To my mind, it would have been quite a challenge to forecast this death in general. But once the parameters of death had become quite well defined, it shouldn't have been too hard to isolate down to the month using the progressed angles in the context of various nodal axes. And then the final eclipse followed by the Mars station would narrow it down quite a bit more.

CASE 6 (Willy Brandt — Intestinal Cancer)

That same total solar eclipse as above (at 8-CA-57 at the end of June 1992) reminded me of the death of Willy Brandt, a popular former Chancellor of what was then West Germany, because his Asc is 9-AR-5, and he died on 10/8/92 at age 78 of intestinal cancer only three months after this eclipse which exactly squared his Asc. His data is: 18-Dec-1913 @ 12:45 PM (-1ST) in Lubeck, Germany 53N52 & 10E40 (see chart # 23).

This is clearly the chart of a popular leader since the 1st and 10th are ruled by Jupiter, and Jupiter is in its own sign in the 10th with the Sun. In fact, Jupiter is also in Sagittarius in his navamsha (as already noted, a double positive condition referred to as "vargottama"). This strong Jupiter further demonstrated itself in the fact that he also won the Nobel Peace Prize. Jupiter is also an atmakaraka (soul indicator) since it is the planet at the highest degree (over 29).

Having made the point about the eclipse above, let me say that I actually think his birth time is short by about 3-4 minutes for two main reasons. First, at death his P3 MC was at 20-SC-26, but T. Pluto was at 21-SC-25. Second, his P2 Asc was at 24-CA, but P2 Neptune was at 25-CA. Adding 3-4 minutes to his birth time would make both aspects exact (as you have the right to expect). It would also have T. Mars right on his P3 Desc. For a cancer death, the Neptune observation is of special significance as noted further below.

Brandt was in a Jupiter Dasa and Mars bhukti. Mars exactly opposes Jupiter. Since Jupiter is stronger, this is not all bad; it had the lifelong effect of motivating high external achievement that I have seen in the charts of

1st Pisces Ascendant	2nd Aries	3rd Taurus Saturn Rx	4th Gemini Mars Rx　　　Te≈--
			♇
12th Aquarius Rahu Rx　　++	RAHU　　Venus　beginning on 11/29/1972 RAHU　　Sun　beginning on 11/29/1975 RAHU　　Moon　beginning on 10/23/1976 RAHU　　Mars　beginning on 04/23/1978 JUPITER Jupiter beginning on 05/11/1979 JUPITER Saturn beginning on 06/29/1981 JUPITER Mercury beginning on 01/11/1984		5th Cancer
11th Capricorn	JUPITER Ketu　beginning on 04/17/1986 JUPITER Venus beginning on 03/23/1987 JUPITER Sun　beginning on 11/23/1989 JUPITER Moon beginning on 09/11/1990 JUPITER Mars beginning on 01/11/1992 JUPITER Rahu beginning on 12/17/1992		6th Leo Moon　　　　T Ketu Rx　　--
			♆
10th Sagittarius Sun Jupiter　　Me	9th Scorpio Mercury　　≈- Venus　　　-	8th Libra	7th Virgo

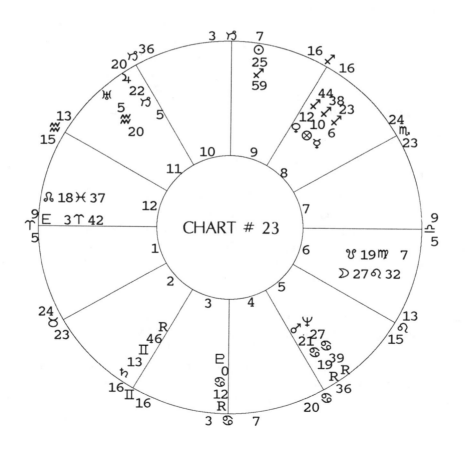

CHART # 23

other famous men (and don't forget that such a Jupiter also has great power to help Mars). However, since even the best chart has to die of something, the equation changes a bit when one is 78 years old. Now we regard Jupiter more as ruler of the 1st than ruler of the 10th. And we regard Mars more as a plain malefic and maraka (ruler of the 2nd) that seeks to assault the ruler of the 1st. This is especially so once knowledge of cancer has been established.

Neptune often plays into a cancer equation (cellular disorder). We see here that when the Mars Bhukti became animated, it is only 6 degrees from N. Neptune. And a really strong clue to this death is the fact that his P3 Neptune had come to a full station on this month (see 11/6/16). And that is why I would like to have seen his P2 MC exactly conjunct P2 Neptune instead of being a degree short. Those astrologers who use modern rulerships may be intrigued by the image of Neptune, as ruler of the 1st, coming to a complete halt.

As some supporting elements, note also that P2 Mercury (maraka ruler of his 7th) had arrived at 22-PI, and there had been a PNE exactly on this point. Also P2 Jupiter, ruler of his 1st, was now at 10-AQ, and T. Saturn was Rx and almost stationary at 11-AQ; this is a further indicator of the body coming to a halt in the context of everything else. A positive note for this death is that he died at his home in Unkel, Germany, and the relocated angles would have T. Jupiter exactly upon his revised Desc of 29-VI (in fact, all angles become 29). This is really quite fine for Pisces-rising.

CASE 7 (H.R. Haldeman — Cancer)

H. R. Haldeman was Richard Nixon's former Chief of Staff and was variously referred to as "The Iron Chancellor," a "robot type," precise, efficient, conservative and the object of a lot of "Nazi" jokes due to his blind loyalty, and the imperial terror, that he inspired among the White House staff. He died of cancer on 11/12/93. His birth data is 27-Oct-1926 @ 3:30 AM PST in Los Angeles, CA 34N4 & 118W15 (see chart # 24).

Like Hillary Clinton, Haldeman not only had his Sun at its single most fallen degree in the Hindu system (10-LI sidereally), but they both have Venus in the same house (with the deeply fallen Sun) in its own sign of Libra. So it's odd they both ended up being the primary assistants to a U.S. President (I've seen the exact same thing in the charts of secretaries to very powerful businessmen). Hillary's placement is much better, how-

7th Pisces	8th Aries Mars Rx M	9th Taurus	10th Gemini Rahu D E Moon e
♓			♇
6th Aquarius	KETU Saturn beginning on 03/16/1972 KETU Mercury beginning on 04/25/1973 VENUS Venus beginning on 04/22/1974 VENUS Sun beginning on 08/22/1977 VENUS Moon beginning on 08/22/1978 VENUS Mars beginning on 04/22/1980 VENUS Rahu beginning on 06/22/1981	11th Cancer	
5th Capricorn Jupiter f	VENUS Jupiter beginning on 06/22/1984 VENUS Saturn beginning on 02/22/1987 VENUS Mercury beginning on 04/22/1990 VENUS Ketu beginning on 02/22/1993 SUN Sun beginning on 04/22/1994 SUN Moon beginning on 08/10/1994	12th Leo	♆
4th Sagittarius Ketu D +	3rd Scorpio Mercury – Saturn T--	2nd Libra Venus MT Sun f	1st Virgo Ascendant

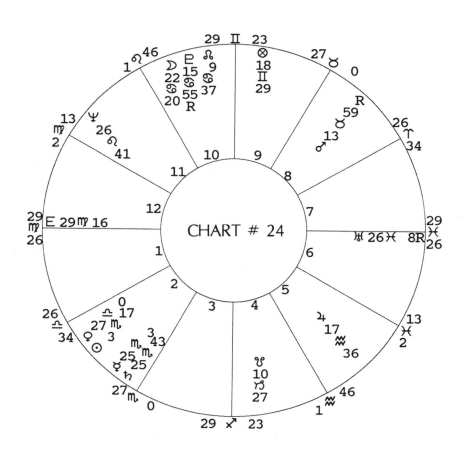

CHART # 24

ever, since Mercury is also in the same house (which in her case is the 5th), and a Mercury/Venus combination creates a rajayoga for her alleged Gemini-rising.

Haldeman is another case of a self-aware cancer death, but one wouldn't expect someone like him to let go easily because, among other things, we see natally that Mercury, ruler of his 1st, is exactly conjunct Saturn. At his death, this Saturn had dropped by P3 to within 1 applying degree of his IC and then went completely stationary (see 4/10/29).

The distress of the 1st house ruler is further distributed into the progressions. P2 Mercury was at 26-SA-10 thus perfectly square N. Uranus at 26-PI-8. This was rendered much more karmic by the fact that he had experienced a P2 eclipse during his lifetime (12/19/26), and that was at 26-GE-35. This further sensitized, and strongly "wired up," the point at which the ruler of the 1st ultimately arrived. P3 Mercury (12-AR-58) was further stressed by being exactly square to P3 Mars (13-CA-18), and his P2 Asc was also square to P2 Neptune (if he had been born about 2 minutes earlier it would be exact).

At his death in 1993, Haldeman was in the last few months of a 20-year Venus Dasa that had actually begun about four months before Richard Nixon resigned in 1974. This was around the month that Haldeman received a criminal indictment and around the time that Nixon jettisoned him from the White House. So Venus began with one "death" and ended with another. Venus is perfectly okay by itself, but it invokes a totally fallen Sun which rules his 12th. It also invokes his strong Mars in Aries from the 8th (which by itself contributed to his strong metabolism) but was not well-received by the maraka 2nd holding such a deeply fallen Sun.

He was in a Ketu Bhukti, and this house shares maraka, and fallen, Jupiter as its ruler. Consequently, at his death, we see P2 Jupiter was opposing N. Neptune in the 12th within 5 applying minutes. In addition, this 4th house node was being opposed by Pluto in the 10th, and this Pluto had been karmically sensitized by a PNE. Consequently, at his death T. Pluto was at 25-SC, exactly conjunct his 1st house ruler, Mercury, and its life-long twin companion, Saturn.

CASE 8 (Petra Kelly — Murder?)

In the above cases of Ashe and Brandt, I made the point about the eclipse at 8-CA-57 to the ruler of the Asc and to the Asc itself respectively. Let me now hammer that point home with an example of yet another national figure, who in this case died violently, but it was never established quite how or by whom (it seemed like a murder/suicide, but she had a lot of enemies). For that reason, I didn't include it in the chapter on unexpected deaths. Instead I will use it here to reinforce my point on eclipses.

This is Petra Kelly whose body was found with that of her long-time lover on 10/19/92. Kelly was a key founder of the Green political party in Germany, and was very influential in the "Green" or ecological movement that has since affected politics around the world. Her data is: 29-Nov-1947 @ 18:30 PM (-1ST) in Gunzburg, Germany 48N27 & 10E16 (see chart # 25). This gives 8-CA-38 rising, and again, the last T. eclipse before her death was that same one, now for the 3rd time, at 8-CA-57. Are you starting to see a pattern here?

This was my simple point, but before leaving this case I may as well note the following half dozen classic supporting considerations:

➤ She was in Saturn Dasa and Venus Bhukti. Karaka Saturn is also a maraka since it is in the 2nd (while T. Saturn was strong in its own sign in the 8th). And Venus functions as a maraka since it is in the 7th (along with T. Uranus and Neptune). Some proof of this is that her P3 Asc was also conjunct Venus at death.

➤ The Moon also happens to be the ruler of the maraka 2nd, and it is exactly conjunct Uranus in her 1st.

➤ Let's look at her four PNE's:

  • One day before birth there was a PNE 1 degree from her N. Sun — which itself is in a mutual reception with Mars — and her Sun is closely conjunct Jupiter, ruler of the maraka 7th.

  • 17 days before birth there was a PNE at 19-SC; this was less than a degree from Mercury, the ruler of her 1st.

  • Another PNE was at 12-SA thus right along her East Point.

  • The last was at 28-TA thus 8 minutes off her Placidus 12th cusp.

➤ Her P2 Desc was at 11-AQ, and T. Saturn was essentially stationary

10th Pisces	11th Aries Rahu Rx e	12th Taurus	1st Gemini Moon Ascendant ♓
9th Aquarius	JUPITER Saturn beginning on 06/18/1970 JUPITER Mercury beginning on 12/30/1972 JUPITER Ketu beginning on 04/06/1975 JUPITER Venus beginning on 03/12/1976 JUPITER Sun beginning on 11/12/1978 JUPITER Moon beginning on 08/30/1979 JUPITER Mars beginning on 12/30/1980		2nd Cancer Saturn Te ♇
8th Capricorn	JUPITER Rahu beginning on 12/06/1981 SATURN Saturn beginning on 04/30/1984 SATURN Mercury beginning on 05/03/1987 SATURN Ketu beginning on 01/12/1990 SATURN Venus beginning on 02/21/1991 SATURN Sun beginning on 04/21/1994		3rd Leo Mars ≈++
7th Sagittarius Venus T+	6th Scorpio Ketu Rx e Sun ≈++ Jupiter ++	5th Libra Mercury ++	4th Virgo ♆

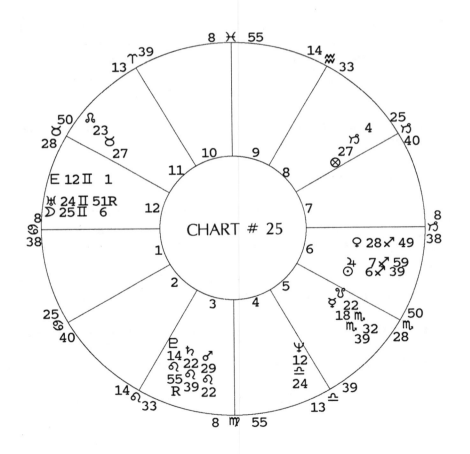

at 11-AQ.

➤ N. Saturn is exactly square her N. Nodes at sidereal sign cusps. At death, T. Pluto was conjunct her SN and hence square N. Saturn. She died at age 45, and it was 45 degrees from her Saturn to her recently eclipsed Asc.

➤ Along this same line, her P2 Neptune in her 4th had also gone completely stationary 45 lines into the ephemeris (see 1/13/48) hence the inability to clarify her death. As you will observe in the final chapter of this book, Neptune seems to be quite predominant in both successful and unsuccessful assassinations.

EXPECTED DEATHS OF OTHERS
IN YOUR CHART

As you proceed through life, you start to notice that people around you tend to die more frequently than you do. Consequently, with some experience, one of the more useful aspects of this topic is the ability to anticipate, with reasonable accuracy, the deaths of close family simply by monitoring your own chart (ideally in conjunction with theirs). This is most especially valid when the death would be greatly felt, and is more or less expected within some kind of defined time parameter.

As usual, my approach here is not one of presenting sweeping rules and generalizations. Rather I am interested in strengthening within you an incremental ability to appreciate how a matrix of considerations coalesce into a uniquely informative message. To further support this, we will look at some random cases of expected deaths for fathers, mothers, spouse and children.

CASE 1 (Death of Elderly Father)

This case (see chart # 26 b. 11-Jan-1931 @ 4:35 PM EST 39N57 & 75W10) presents the chart of a someone who is over 60 years old, yet both of his parents were still alive. He continued to maintain an active business, play sports and so forth. Obviously good genetics were at work here. In the course of a discussion in the Spring of 1992, a veiled inquiry was made with respect to the longevity of his parents who seemingly were beginning to falter physically.

When you look at his partial Dasa listing, you see he was moving into a new Bhukti period of Mars on 7/28/92. His Mars is fallen natally in the maraka 2nd. You will recall that the rule on Mars is that it aspects the 4th, 7th & 8th from itself. From this position, a defective Mars will therefore assault the 9th which is the Hindu house of the father (note: in the West the father is represented by the 10th house, but South India emphasizes the role of the father as a source of moral guidance, and logically this is further supported by the fact that the 1st is the 5th from the 9th). Under the circumstances, we would normally focus in on this period for finer review through the P3 listing. There would be no point in looking at any potential date before 7/27.

10th Pisces Rahu Dx ♓ +	11th Aries	12th Taurus	1st Gemini Jupiter Rx ≈-- Ascendant ♇
9th Aquarius	SATURN Ketu beginning on 10/10/1970 SATURN Venus beginning on 11/19/1971 SATURN Sun beginning on 01/19/1975 SATURN Moon beginning on 01/01/1976 SATURN Mars beginning on 08/01/1977 SATURN Rahu beginning on 09/10/1978 SATURN Jupiter beginning on 07/16/1981		2nd Cancer Mars Rx f
8th Capricorn	MERCURY Mercury beginning on 01/28/1984 MERCURY Ketu beginning on 06/25/1986 MERCURY Venus beginning on 06/22/1987 MERCURY Sun beginning on 04/22/1990 MERCURY Moon beginning on 02/28/1991 MERCURY Mars beginning on 07/28/1992		3rd Leo Ψ
7th Sagittarius Mercury Rx ≈- Saturn T- Sun	6th Scorpio Venus T-	5th Libra Moon +	4th Virgo Ketu Dx E

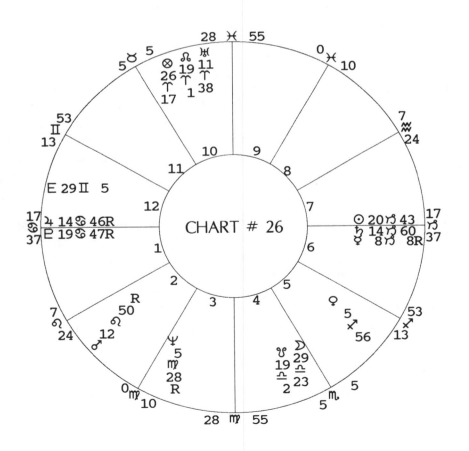

However, the P3 printout (not shown) showed an unusually strong competing consideration that preceded the beginning of the Bhukti period by about six weeks. That is the fact that P3 Mars was going totally stationary on 6/16/92. I never gave him this date but, in fact, he did call me exactly on that date to validate a very high level of stress, and this was something he had never done before or since. His father actually died six days later on 6/22/92.

This five week discrepancy (between a P3 planetary station and its Bhukti) would normally raise some doubt in my mind about the accuracy of his TOB because the discrepancy could be fully resolved by pushing up his TOB by 14 minutes to 4:49 PM. This would have the tertiary Mars station *exactly* coincide with entrance into the Mars Bhukti on 6/16 (and his father dying a week later). And "for the record," a birth time of 4:50 PM would have his father die *exactly* on the day of the beginning of the Mars Bhukti.

Using my ayanamsha, I have seen quite a number of significant Mars happenings on the *exact* date of entrance into a Mars Bhukti (such as a client hijacked in a plane, another client hospitalized after an assault by three thugs, and yet another person stung by 11 bees). But 14 minutes would be quite a large amount of recorded birth error and, in any case, such errors are typically in the other direction.

I was also discomforted by the fact that although there were plenty of factors supporting death (such as his P3 mSN conjunct N. Neptune within 4 minutes, and so forth) there was no exact hit from or to the progressed angles exactly on 6/22. However, I received some consolation from the fact that when the chart with the given time was progressed sidereally (i.e., expunging precessional considerations) then the P3 Asc was square N. Pluto on the exact date of his father's death.

The following question must also be answered: using the given TOB, *was* there a significant happening at the Mars Bhukti shift? And the answer is "yes." Note that Mars now also assaults the house of children (5th). Exactly on 7/27 he was visited by a suitor of his attractive daughter, and the suitor basically told the father that the he intended to marry her.

It turned out that the Sun of the daughter's fiance is exactly conjunct her father's Mars (remember: his new Bhukti). So they both found themselves in that odd classical competition. This visit was also traumatic since religious differences with the suitor were a source of inner conflict for the father (natally angular Jupiter/Saturn/Pluto). The upshot was an immediate deterioration between him and his daughter. A separation also occurred between him and his adult son within about a month. Of course, these problems only lasted through the end of the Bhukti period.

So, in the end, there is sufficient argument to accept the very rare fact that what "should" have occurred during the Mars Bhukti period did, in fact, occur a few weeks prior to it due to the strength of a somewhat earlier P3 Mars station. I have briefly highlighted some of my thinking on this matter because I would very much like to condition the reader to expect angular events to happen *exactly* on certain dates and further, to expect a tightly-linked coincidence between what goes on in the Dasa/Bhukti system and the tertiary progression system ("Houck's Law"). This case is presented as an exception to the rule just to highlight what is actually, in fact, a very consistent rule.

CASE 2 (Death of Mother — Leukemia)

The following case is superficially more challenging since it involves the generally expected death of a client's mother (from leukemia) during the Dasa/Bhukti of a normally benefic planet (Venus). This case is so odd it verges upon amusing (assuming you like Saturn/Pluto humor). See chart # 27 (b. 15-July-1949 @ 3:01 PM PST per BC in San Francisco, CA 37N47 122W25). His mother died at around 2 PM PST on 4/14/93 — but that was just a small piece of quite a pathological day.

Earlier that same morning he found out from his accountant that he would have to write a check that day to the Internal Revenue Service in the amount of $13,500 (in fact, he had been expecting a refund). Coming home from the hospital he got a speeding ticket. Upon arriving home, he surprised several burglars who had stolen about $40,000 worth of objects; he was unable to catch them as they fled. The police told him that the thieves were likely to be back soon for the other items they had to abandon. So, as he was sitting there talking to me, he had a cat in his lap and a gun in his hand.

Lawyers arrived later that day so he could sign Quit Claim Deeds on several hundred thousand dollars worth of property. Essentially he was foreclosing on himself due to various difficulties. In part, these were related to a tangle of increasingly shady real estate deals involving a partner who was somehow involved with organized crime and who had been signing my client's name to various real estate documents. To this point, my

5th Pisces	6th Aries	7th Taurus	8th Gemini
Moon T+ Rahu Rx +			Mars -- Mercury o ♓

| 4th Aquarius | MERCURY Saturn beginning on 04/27/1980
 KETU Ketu beginning on 01/06/1983
 KETU Venus beginning on 06/03/1983
 KETU Sun beginning on 08/03/1984
 KETU Moon beginning on 12/09/1984
 KETU Mars beginning on 07/09/1985
 KETU Rahu beginning on 12/06/1985
 KETU Jupiter beginning on 12/24/1986
 KETU Saturn beginning on 11/30/1987
 KETU Mercury beginning on 01/09/1989
 VENUS Venus beginning on 01/06/1990
 VENUS Sun beginning on 05/06/1993
 VENUS Moon beginning on 05/06/1994 | 9th Cancer
 Sun   e
 Venus   --

 ♇ |

3rd Capricorn			10th Leo
Jupiter Rx Tf			Saturn

| 2nd Sagittarius | 1st Scorpio
 Ascendant   e | 12th Libra | 11th Virgo
 Ketu Rx   E

 ♆ |

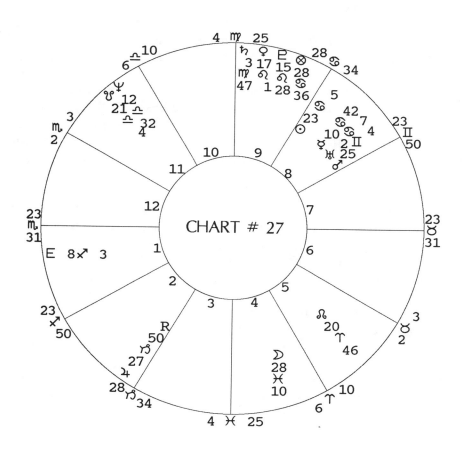

client had spent over $40,000 in legal fees related to four ongoing lawsuits involving real estate. He was now taking medication for stress, and the next day was admitted to the hospital with a raging urinary tract infection (as a quirky aside, I know another male whose mother became terminally ill while he was battling a raging urinary tract infection!).

The generally expected death of his mother can be most quickly seen in four observations: 1) his P3 Moon was conjunct P3 Pluto within 7 minutes, 2) T. Pluto was also applying (at slightly more than one degree) to being conjunct his N. Asc, 3) P2 Pluto was only 15 minutes from being conjunct N. Venus, and 4) the P3 IC was conjunct N. Neptune within nine minutes (perhaps suggesting a few seconds of birth time error). As I have noted before, progressed involvement of the IC (or SN — see case above) with Neptune seems to be one of the clearer indicators of a family-related death if other things confirm. Anyway, the three Pluto considerations lead directly back to a Venus Dasa discussion.

Other than the fact that P3 Venus was within only 14 minutes of being square to natal Mars, how can it be that Venus brought such a volume of tragedy? In my opinion, this is another instance where the failure of the Hindu system to use the outer planets masks critical information. Natally you will note that my client has Venus conjunct Pluto within less than two degrees. Western astrologers have long recognized that tight hard aspects between Venus and Pluto (especially with confirming declination) often lead to severe Venus-related tragedies including the real or symbolic deaths of those they love. [However, this is by no means necessarily so depending upon the extended status of Venus. If Venus is otherwise exceptional, Pluto may just give great depth to Venus' excellent qualities.]

For males, less severe indicators are partners who abruptly leave them, partners who must have emergency hysterectomies, and the like. I'll also mention here that one of my client's fondest memories from his youth involved having sex on a spontaneous basis in the back of a dumpster in an alley with an extremely recent acquaintance (the most carnal variation on Venus/Pluto stress). If this pattern is in the chart of a female, it may have her abruptly and totally severing romances or having drastic surgeries involving Venus-related zones of the body assuming, of course, that other chart factors support and confirm.

His Venus is in the sign of a "great enemy," and so Venus is expected to somewhat malperform ("detriment" is a somewhat similar Western concept, but Westerners do not consider Venus to be detrimentally placed in Cancer). More powerful in Hindu astrology is the fact that when a planet "goes on stage" as the Dasa or Bhukti planet, it will typically activate the essential qualities of any planet very nearby or in tight hard aspect.

Since ancient Hindu astrologers didn't recognize Pluto, they would not project its activation even by the rules of their own excellent system. This would consequently force them into a much more convoluted rationalization of the effect of a pattern that is otherwise much more benign (i.e., without the presence of Pluto).

Venus also relates to his father since it is in the 9th, so I asked in passing about him. It turned out that, over the past year, his father had lost over 60 pounds caring for his wife at home, his hair had gone from black to grey, and he was now stooped over. And just like my client, he also had a car problem (an accident) on the way back from the hospital! This is somewhat confirmed by the fact that P2 Mars in my client's chart was also conjunct his N. Sun (father) in the 9th. T. Uranus and Neptune were also conjunct and going stationary in his 3rd (transport) and therefore also opposing his Sun.

Three closing notes on this case are that first, his P2 Mars was octile P2 Saturn (ruler of the 4th) with perfect orb, while P3 Mercury (messenger of the 8th) was exactly opposing natal Venus (the Dasa/Bhukti planet) with a 2-minute applying orb. Second, the 8th house message of Mercury was further seen in the fact that T. Mercury was conjunct his N. Moon (mother). Finally, as owner of a biotechnology company his career continues to boom, and this is partially due to the fact that his P2 Sun and Saturn were both now conjunct his Leo MC. This powerful strength at the exact top of his chart pushes down very hard on the bottom of the chart where Saturn is "welcome," but the Sun is not.

CASE 3 (Death of Another Mother — Cancer)

Here the mother was again known to be mortally ill. Her ultimate death on 5/17/92 was felt as a great loss by her grown son. His data is 30-Sept-1959 @ 12:25 PM in Zone -5.5 6N41 & 80E24 (see chart # 28). Unfortunately, but by random coincidence, it shares a quality with the chart just discussed in that Pluto is once again only 2 degrees from the Dasa planet. On the other hand, this can serve to reinforce some of my points.

This person was in a Moon Dasa and Ketu Bhukti. This has a double

4th Pisces Ketu S–	5th Aries	6th Taurus	7th Gemini
3rd Aquarius	SUN Saturn beginning on 07/22/1981 SUN Mercury beginning on 07/04/1982 SUN Ketu beginning on 05/10/1983 SUN Venus beginning on 09/16/1983 MOON Moon beginning on 09/16/1984 MOON Mars beginning on 07/16/1985 MOON Rahu beginning on 02/16/1986	8th Cancer ♓
2nd Capricorn	MOON Jupiter beginning on 08/16/1987 MOON Saturn beginning on 12/16/1988 MOON Mercury beginning on 07/16/1990 MOON Ketu beginning on 12/16/1991 MOON Venus beginning on 07/16/1992 MOON Sun beginning on 03/16/1994	9th Leo Venus Moon ++ ♇
1st Sagittarius Saturn + Ascendant	12th Scorpio Jupiter ++	11th Libra ♆	10th Virgo Rahu SE Sun T– Mars T-- Mercury E

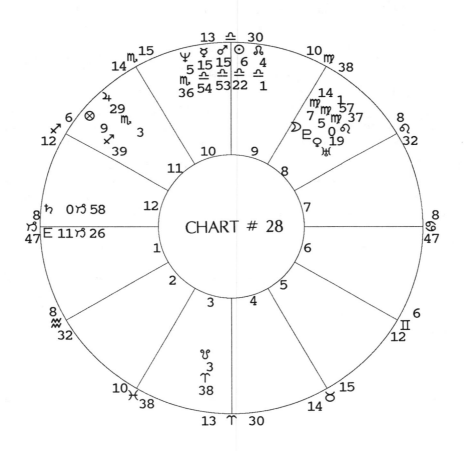

reference to his mother since the Moon is the general karaka for the mother, and the SN is in his 4th. As already noted, we see that the natal Moon is only 2 degrees from Pluto (and only 4 from Venus). This is a very religious person who, to the age of 32, was still by choice leading a monastic life (Gandhi, you may recall, ultimately did the same thing with his natal Venus/Pluto). Let's see why 5/92 was a death-invoking month for his mother.

There are two immediate lunar factors. First, the month she died Pluto had crossed over and gone fully stationary by P3 (see 12/9/60) on the other side of his Moon at 08-VI-08. Meanwhile T. Jupiter, as ruler of both the 1st and 4th (him and his mother), was exactly conjunct his N. Pluto TTM on that day. Second, the day before she died there was a full Moon at 26-SC while his P3 Moon was at 26-LE and P3 Uranus was at 25-LE-46.

He was in a Ketu Bhukti, so we should expect actions through eclipses and nodal activity. This is clearly so. First, his natal IC is 13-AR-30, and the last T. eclipse before her death exactly squared this at 13-CP-51. Second, the last PNE about two weeks before his birth was at 23-PI-24. At the death of his mother, his P3 Asc was conjunct this at 23-PI-16 (note that because of these two eclipse events he not long after also quit his job and moved to a new city). Third, the T. tNN was conjunct his N. Saturn TTM (there is a further hidden link between these two in that his N. Saturn is in a nakshatra of Ketu while his Ketu is in a nakshatra of Saturn).

Early in his life he had moved almost exactly halfway around the world to 39N10 and 77W16. I find it very stressful to get clients who have done this, because typically the angles of both charts do function thus doubling the amount of attention that must be paid. The above paragraph noted the key eclipse effects to the fundamental natal chart. And the relocated chart confirms it. For example, his relocated P3 Asc was at 15-LI-51. This was perfectly conjunct N. Mars at 15-LI-53 and N. Mercury at 15-LI-54 (whose maraka quality is fully confirmed by its association with Mars). Actually, being in the 4th house Ketu Bhukti invoked the powerful energies of his Sun, Mercury and Mars residing in the opposing house.

His relocated P3 IC was at 18-CP-12 thus putting it just a little beyond what I would consider a satisfactory conjunction with P3 Saturn at 17-CP-02. But this separating orb of slightly over 1 degree was effectively pulled back together and animated by the Rx transits of Uranus and Neptune that were applying at 17-CP-45 and 18-CP-46 respectively (this is a variation on the concept of "translation of light" where a transiting planet symbolically links together two planets that would not otherwise seem to be linked). You may wish to further note that his relocated IC is at 07-SC-06, and this is only 20 minutes from his applying P2 Neptune at 06-SC-46 which you should now recognize as a family death theme.

I want to close this case by again noting that, from an unconvoluted point of view, this chart has a good Moon since it is 1) in the 9th house 2) with Venus 3) in the sign of a great friend, 4) unaspected by a malefic and 5) in his navamsha the Moon is with Jupiter. Yes it rules his 8th, but his mother lived to a respectable age, and in any case, Hindu astrology does not seem to be concerned about the Moon ruling the 8th. Perhaps this is because of the occult links between the Moon and Saturn, and the fact that Saturn is the karaka for 8th house matters.

That death would occur during a Moon Dasa *again* makes a statement about the "hidden" planet that goes unacknowledged by the Hindu system — Pluto. Such a recognition by Hindu astrologers would help disarm the apparent Hindu paradox which asserts that the Moon cannot be a maraka — even when death obviously often occurs during its periods.

CASE 4 (Death of Father from Hepatitis)

As I was scouting more cases for this chapter I remembered that the father of one of our family friends had died on 2/16/80 when she was only 25 years old. This was a lingering death subsequent to a coma, and this had been brought about by a case of hepatitis he had contracted many years earlier. Her given data is: 1-Jan-1955 @ 11:20 AM EST in Ashland, PA 40N47 & 76W21 (see chart # 29).

His death occurred during her Ketu Dasa and Saturn Bhukti. The Sun is the general karaka for the father, and we see that natally it is involved with the nodal axis. Therefore during her nodal Dasa we would expect further precise action involving either eclipses or the nodes, and this was certainly true as will be demonstrated below. But let's look next at the natal status of the Bhukti factor (Saturn).

The 9th house rules the father, and Venus, ruler of her 8th (and therefore his 12th), is in this house. Venus is under further significant natal stress since it is perfectly square to Pluto (although this stress is somewhat relieved since Venus is also perfectly trine to Jupiter, but Jupiter is with Uranus thus adding back in a factor of unpredictability). Is there a fur-

1st Pisces Ascendant Moon T≈–	2nd Aries	3rd Taurus	4th Gemini Ketu Dx E
12th Aquarius Mars T–	KETU Ketu beginning on 03/20/1974 KETU Venus beginning on 08/17/1974 KETU Sun beginning on 10/17/1975 KETU Moon beginning on 02/23/1976 KETU Mars beginning on 09/23/1976 KETU Rahu beginning on 02/20/1977 KETU Jupiter beginning on 03/08/1978		5th Cancer Jupiter Rx E≈ ♓
11th Capricorn	KETU Saturn beginning on 02/14/1979 KETU Mercury beginning on 03/23/1980 VENUS Venus beginning on 03/20/1981 VENUS Sun beginning on 07/20/1984 VENUS Moon beginning on 07/20/1985 VENUS Mars beginning on 03/20/1987		6th Leo ♇
10th Sagittarius Rahu Dx – Sun Mercury –	9th Scorpio Venus +	8th Libra Saturn E ♆	7th Virgo

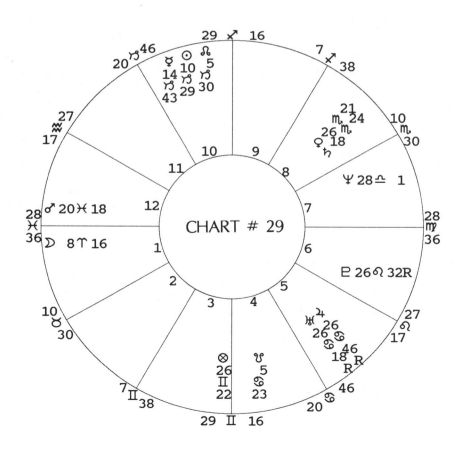

CHART # 29

ther link of her Venus to the Saturn Bhukti factor? Yes. In her 8th (ruled by Venus) we see an exalted Saturn. Although these two factors are in separate houses, they are only 8 degrees apart, and they are further linked by the fact that both are at the exact same declination. Let's now see how these linkages work out through progression and transit.

➤ We saw that natal Pluto is square Venus. Her P3 date for this death was 12/3/55. Well, on 12/1/55 P3 Pluto went completely stationary, so essentially it was still totally stationary thus ripening the "promise" of the aspect.

➤ Venus was pushed further over the brink by the fact that P3 (Bhukti factor) Saturn had, in fact, progressed the 8 degrees between it and Venus to now be conjunct Venus.

➤ T. Uranus, at 25-SC-30 provided impetus energy by being exactly conjunct Venus (and hence square Pluto).

➤ However, the final true impetus is that there was a transiting total solar eclipse exactly on this date (2/16/80) at 26-AQ-50 thus perfectly squaring Venus and perfectly opposing Pluto (which, as has already been noted, had gone fully stationary by P3). Since she was in a nodal dasa, this eclipse was the one that "extinguished her Sun." You might further notice during this Bhukti that strong Saturn from the 8th aspects her Sun in the 10th during its run.

➤ This exact and perfectly-timed eclipse was the primary agent of the dasa nodal factor. The secondary agent is that the T. SN was at 29-AQ, and this was perfectly square her P3 IC of 29-TA. For that matter, her P2 IC was at 24-CA-51, and this was conjunct her P2 Uranus at 25-CA-13. A minute or two of birth error would make this exact.

➤ For further precision here are Mars timers at 3 levels:

• P2 Mars was conjunct her N. Moon within 3 minutes (8-AR),
• P3 Mars (2-SC) was square P3 Uranus (2-LE), and
• T. Mars was conjunct her P3 Asc (both at 8-AQ).

CASE 5 (Mother With 2 Boys Who Died of AIDS)

This is the case of a mother who had four children, two males and two females. The two males were both homosexual, and both died of AIDS. Her data is 30-March-1938 @ 4:02 PM EST in New Brunswick, NJ 40N30 & 74W27 (see chart # 30). The first boy died on 10/6/87 with only about a week's notice that he had AIDS and was terminally ill. The second boy died on 11/26/91 with about 10 years of notice that he had AIDS.

Let's ask some of the classic questions:

Q: Does this chart suffer any inherent natal defects suggesting a possible focus upon the death of children? Yes, and here are four of them:

➤ The ruler of the 5th is the same as the ruler of the 8th (Jupiter). Jupiter is fallen in the 6th, and in a mutual reception with Saturn in the 8th (however, note that Jupiter, in the last degree of a sign, is less than 1 applying minute from the cusp of the sidereal 7th thus making it difficult to decide whether to play it as a fallen Jupiter in the 6th or as a maraka in the 7th). In this reception, Saturn is both the karaka and a maraka (rules the 7th).

[In this particular case, Westerners could argue that their chart also gives an accurate message with the ruler of the 5th (now Saturn) exactly conjunct the 8th house cusp. Notice however that, in the sidereal chart, the ruler of the 1st is actually the Sun, and the Sun is also exactly conjunct this Saturn thus tying the mother into the issue of death. She would be ruled by Mercury in the Western chart, and Mercury is widely disconnected from Saturn on the Western 8th house cusp.]

➤ She had a PNE at 10-SA-23, and this was exactly conjunct her IC suggesting death-related issues in this life.

➤ N. Mercury is a potential maraka since it rules the 2nd. To my way of thinking, it becomes a certain maraka when we see that it is exactly square Pluto. This likelihood is elevated by its residence in the same house with a strong Mars (in Aries) that is itself conjunct Uranus.

➤ By the ashtakavarga weighing system, her 8th is not only extremely weak; it is the weakest of all 12 houses. Yet it is heavily burdened with three planets including the exact Sun/Saturn conjunction.

8th Pisces	9th Aries	10th Taurus	11th Gemini
Moon +	Venus e-	Ketu Rx ++	
Saturn ≈+	Mercury -		
Sun ++	Mars MT		
	♓		

7th Aquarius			12th Cancer
	KETU Mars beginning on 03/27/1974		
	KETU Rahu beginning on 08/24/1974		♇
	KETU Jupiter beginning on 09/12/1975		
	KETU Saturn beginning on 08/18/1976		
	KETU Mercury beginning on 09/27/1977		
	VENUS Venus beginning on 09/24/1978		
	VENUS Sun beginning on 01/24/1982		

6th Capricorn	VENUS Moon beginning on 01/24/1983	1st Leo
Jupiter Tfe≈	VENUS Mars beginning on 09/24/1984	Ascendant
	VENUS Rahu beginning on 11/24/1985	
	VENUS Jupiter beginning on 11/24/1988	
	VENUS Saturn beginning on 07/24/1991	♆
	VENUS Mercury beginning on 09/24/1994	

5th Sagittarius	4th Scorpio	3rd Libra	2nd Virgo
	Rahu Rx --		

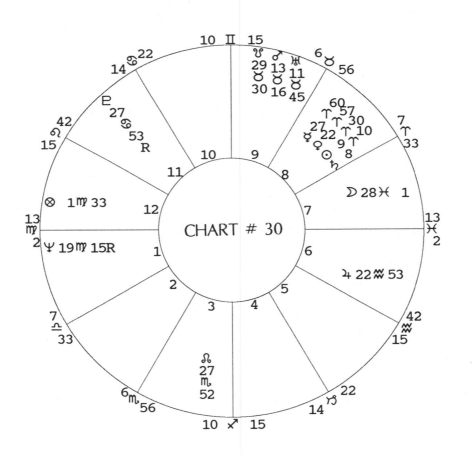

Q: She was in a Venus dasa for both deaths. What is the status of Venus?

➤ The ayanamsha for her year of birth was 22 degrees and 54 minutes. Excluding sign considerations, this was almost the exact degree and minute of both Venus and Jupiter in her chart thus putting them both exactly at zero. She then had a P2 eclipse before these deaths at 22-SC-54 — exactly quincunx Venus at yet another perfect zero, and this time exactly upon her sidereal 4th house cusp. Venus is also very stressed by being in the same house with a strong Mars (in Aries) that is very near Uranus.

➤ At the first death, which was the shocking one, Venus by P2 was at 23-GE-38. This was then opposed by T. Uranus at 23-SA-14. The P2 Moon (23-CP-01) was square N. Venus within 4 minutes. At the 2nd death, Venus and the Moon were reversed. Here P2 Venus (28-GE-38) was exactly square the N. Moon at 28-PI-01. The relevance of the Moon is that it is natally in the 8th with the Sun/Saturn conjunction discussed above.

Q: The 1st boy died during a Rahu Bhukti. Therefore, what about the nodes and eclipses? The answer is that there are at least half a dozen exact hits to validate the Bhukti:

➤ The N. NN is in her 4th. We have already seen how there was a PNE exactly on her IC, and a P2 eclipse TTM on her sidereal 4th cusp, thus creating a critical sensitivity.

➤ There was a T. lunar eclipse (in EST) on 10/6/87, i.e., the exact date her son died. This was at 13-AR, and was conjunct her P2 Saturn of 13-AR.

➤ There was a total solar eclipse 3/87 at 8-AR, and her N. Saturn is at 8-AR (conj the ruler of the 1st in the 8th).

➤ Her P2 Sun was at 27-TA-45; this was exactly conjunct her N. tSN of 27-TA-52.

➤ The last T. solar eclipse (2 weeks before he died) was at 29-VI in her maraka 2nd. At death, T. Mars had arrived at 29-VI.

➤ The P3 SN is exactly conjunct P3 maraka Saturn (both at 24-AR), and this was exactly square P3 maraka Mercury (24-CP).

For this first death, let it also be noted that the P3 Moon was exactly square her 1st house Neptune, and her P2 MC was exactly conjunct P2 Pluto at 28-CA.

Q: The 2nd boy died in a Saturn Bhukti. Was it in a deadly configuration?

➤ Yes. T. Saturn was at 2-AQ-21, her P2 IC was at 2-AQ-29, and the last T. eclipse was at 3-AQ-16.

Q: Since this death was expected, was there a Uranus effect, and what other clues were there to this death?

➤ As should be expected, there was no Uranus effect by transit or progression. But other factors are that:

- The disturbed P2 Moon from the 8th (now at 13-PI-26) was exactly conjunct the Desc.

- Maraka Mercury (exactly square to Pluto natally) was now exactly conjunct the P2 Desc (27-AR-32).

- The Placidus 5th house of children is at 14-CP-22. T. Neptune was at 14-CP-58.

- T. Jupiter at 12-VI-50, as the natural karaka for children, and with its characteristics noted above and as ruler of the 5th and the 8th, was exactly conjunct the mother's Asc at the death thus validating its malefic status.

It is interesting that the mother's navamsha has Libra-rising with Mars in the 1st in a mutual reception with Venus in Aries in the 7th. In my passing remarks on homosexuality (when discussing one of the homeless men in the prior chapter) I noted that this is a typical sign-and-planet configuration that often supports either homosexuality or bisexuality both in theory and by my observation (among other reasons because of the further linkages to the 2nd and 8th). This may have something to do with the presentation of the issue in her life.

CASE 6 (Death of a Spouse — Pat Nixon)

This is a public figure case concerning Pat Nixon (wife of former U.S. President Richard Nixon) who died of lung cancer on 6/22/93. There was rarely any doubt they had a close and mutually-supportive relationship, and their closeness is reinforced by the presence of many of the classically-expected considerations under such a circumstance. For Richard Nixon see chart # 31 (b. 09-Jan-1913 @ 9:35 PM PST in Yorba Linda, CA 33N53 & 117W49).

At age 80, Mr. Nixon had moved into a Saturn Bhukti on 9/13/92 that would last a little over a year, and he had been in a Ketu Dasa since late 1987 (the SN being located in the maraka 2nd in the main rasi chart and in his maraka 7th in the navamsha). We should expect a strong presentation of these two factors at death, and it will be shown that this was the case. Natally, Saturn is in his 10th. From there it not only aspects his 7th which contains Venus; they both are locked together in a mutual reception since Saturn rules his 7th and Venus his 10th. So his wife bore a great responsibility by being bound so tightly to his career.

Here are the four significant and exact Saturn factors as of 6/22/93 that delivered the message of his Saturn Bhukti:

➤ P2 Saturn was at 00-GE-29. On 5/21/93, exactly a month before his wife's death, and recalling Saturn's mutual reception with Venus in the 7th, there was a final eclipse at 00-GE-31.

➤ T. Saturn had stationed within his 7th on 6/10/93 at 00-PI-19; this was in exact square to the prior eclipse exactly on P2 Saturn. T. Saturn was still at that degree at death (and 00-PI-48 was also his P3 Part of (Mis)fortune).

➤ Natally, Mr. Nixon has his Saturn at 27-TA-29. At his wife's death, his P2 Desc was at 27-TA-20 (less than a minute of birth error would have made this exact).

➤ His P3 Asc was conjunct P3 Mars TTM (29-LE-10), and this was perfectly octile to P3 Saturn (14-CA-10). Note, by the way, that this P3 Asc/Mars conjunction at 29-LE was also only one applying degree from opposing T. Saturn, and T. Mars, also at 29-LE, was exactly conjunct both of them.

8th Pisces Rahu Rx +	9th Aries	10th Taurus Saturn Rx ≈++	11th Gemini
7th Aquarius Venus ≈++	MERCURY Saturn beginning on 02/10/1985 KETU Ketu beginning on 10/19/1987 KETU Venus beginning on 03/16/1988 KETU Sun beginning on 05/16/1989 KETU Moon beginning on 09/22/1989 KETU Mars beginning on 04/22/1990	♇ (11th Gemini cont.)	12th Cancer
6th Capricorn Moon −	KETU Rahu beginning on 09/19/1990 KETU Jupiter beginning on 10/07/1991 KETU Saturn beginning on 09/13/1992 KETU Mercury beginning on 10/22/1993 VENUS Venus beginning on 10/19/1994	1st Leo Ascendant ♅ (♆)	
5th Sagittarius Mars RT Mercury − Jupiter MRT Sun	4th Scorpio	3rd Libra	2nd Virgo Ketu Rx E

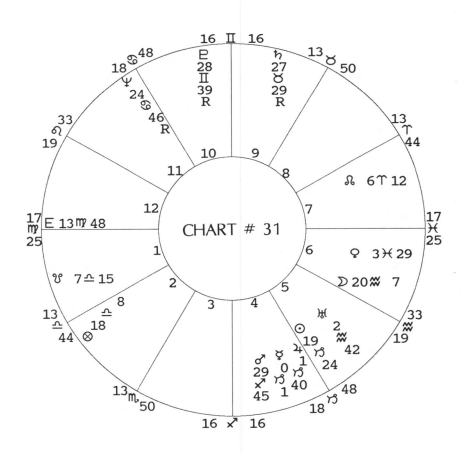

CHART # 31

The Pluto factors are shown in the fact that his P3 Sun (28-SA-44) was exactly opposite N. Pluto (5 minute orb) while his P3 Pluto was exactly conjunct the last full Moon before his birth (02-CA-02). His P3 Moon was exactly between N. and P3 Pluto.

Under the circumstances, we might also expect a Neptune factor, and there were two. First, P3 Neptune was exactly tri-octile to his Desc (wife). Second, T. Neptune was exactly conjunct his Sun (having already crossed it once, and now returning). T. Uranus was also heading back with an applying orb to his N. Sun of well under 2 degrees. As has been said, Uranus never kills, but it does supply the shock.

Death of President Nixon Himself

We already have the chart here, so let me further digress for a few paragraphs with some comparative comments on the death of former President Nixon himself. Almost a year after his wife's death, Mr. Nixon had a massive stroke on 4/18/94 and died on the evening of 4/22/94. He was still in his Ketu Dasa, but had now moved into a Mercury Bhukti. Mercury is ruler of his maraka 2nd. Natally, it is only 1/4 of a degree away from Mars. This natal configuration is common for a stroke (I have it in my own chart).

However, Jupiter is also less than two degrees away from Mercury and strong it its own sign. Why did it not offer protection from the Mars problem? Well, for 81 years it did. But the unseen factor this time was the fact that when he was in this Mercury Bhukti, P3 Mars had gone fully stationary this particular month. The "invoked Mars" effect was therefore too intense.

In addition, there were other supporting factors. His N. Saturn is at 27-TA-29. It is the ruler of his maraka 7th (as well as being the karaka of death). At the stroke, T. Pluto was opposing this Saturn TTM at 27-SC-29. Also rolled into the complex was his P2 Asc at 27-SC-57 (at death). T. Saturn was actually in his 7th, strong in its own sign as it aspected his 1st.

Remember that he was still in a nodal Dasa, so there had to have been an eclipse effect. And there was. The last T. eclipse before his death was 7-GE-3. At the stroke, his P3 MC was at 6-GE-49, and at his death, his P3 MC was at 6-GE-58 — only 5 minutes from the eclipse. Traditional Western readers may also wish to note that his P3 Uranus was conjunct the cusp of the placidus 2nd cusp TTM.

Final Case Comment

I'll close out this chapter with a brief comment on the chart of a friend of mine whose mother died of cancer while this book was being finalized. His data is 26-April-1963 at 4:44 AM EST in Detroit, MI 42N20 & 83W03 (chart not shown). This chart is worth commenting on because it demonstrates how a Jupiter factor could cause a misdirection of perception.

Natally, he has Jupiter and Venus in Pisces in the 1st (rulership and exaltation respectively). He was in the last few weeks of a Jupiter Dasa and Bhukti when his mother died on 3/11/94. Why didn't this death hold off until the next month when not only would he have been in a Saturn Bhukti, but P3 Saturn would also have been totally stationary (per "Houck's Law")?

His N. Saturn is at 21-AQ-57. It had been permanently sensitized by a PNE at 22-AQ-30. The last T. solar eclipse before this death was at 21-SC-32, thus exactly square to this sensitized Saturn. And, without going into a lot of other considerations, his P3 MC had arrived at 21-AQ thus exactly conjunct this entire complex. But why at the end of the Jupiter period? Because if you had been monitoring T. Jupiter, it was exactly conjunct (almost TTM) N. Neptune which is in his 8th (and which itself is perfectly square to a fallen N. Mars).

There were other factors, of course. Examples are: his nearly stationary P3 Saturn was exactly square P3 Mercury (ruler of his 4th, the mother), P3 Pluto was square his N. Moon (mother) TTM, and his P3 mSN was square N. Venus TTM. But remember that this was not his death but the death of someone else (and a relatively easy one at that). When discussing someone else's death, as was mentioned early on when discussing the uses of the 8th house in a more theoretical way, 8th house factors can be more informative than traditional marakas when other factors clearly support. And, in this case, the Jupiter/Neptune factor provides some simple proof of that.

UNEXPECTED DEATH IN ONE'S OWN CHART

This chapter will look at six random examples to illustrate how an unexpected death, such as by drowning, auto or plane accident, stroke or fall from a high place might be configured in the chart of the person it represents. Of course, if you could see it in your own chart, one could argue that, by definition, it would not be unexpected. I will leave that issue for the philosophers to unravel.

It would have been interesting to look at people hit by lightning and the like (some people have actually been hit multiple times), but that would increase the ever present risk of drifting a bit too much towards the obscure at the expense of the more typical. My own initial expectation was for a natal chart with highly tensioned and/or sharply angular features along with, at some point, a strong presentation of Uranus.

CASE 1 (Billy Martin Driven Off a 300-Foot Cliff)

The first to be looked at is that of Billy Martin, a former manager of the N.Y. Yankees baseball team, and it certainly confirms the hypothesis that Uranus would be strongly presented (see chart # 32 b. 16-May-1928 @ 3:44 PM PST in Berkeley, CA 37N52 & 122W16). He died of a broken neck on 12/25/89 when an intoxicated bar owner drove him off a 300-foot cliff.

Some brief natal comments: Mr. Martin was considered very highly strung. He was notorious for burning out his players and was constantly striking people. As part of his "maniac" image, he once completely destroyed his own office and broke several fingers in the process. One of his own players broke Mr. Martin's arm. He was widely considered a "walking psychodrama" who "never knew himself."

Much of this can be inferred from the highly angular Pluto, Mars with Uranus and the emotional Moon in the 7th (erratic violence to and from others plus "burning out" others), Mercury (ruler of 1 and 10) is exactly conjunct the mNN (potential mental disconnect or unhingement), with Neptune in the 12th exactly square the Sun (heavy drinking with a self-knowledge problem). Saturn in the 3rd with the SN (located in Saturn's own nakshatra) didn't help.

We might expect his death to be involved with the animation of all of

7th Pisces	8th Aries	9th Taurus	10th Gemini
Mars ≈++ Moon + ♓	Jupiter ≈++ Venus T+	Sun Rahu Rx ++ Mercury ++	♇

6th Aquarius	MARS Mars beginning on 05/23/1975 MARS Rahu beginning on 10/20/1975 MARS Jupiter beginning on 11/08/1976 MARS Saturn beginning on 10/14/1977 MARS Mercury beginning on 11/23/1978 MARS Ketu beginning on 11/20/1979 MARS Venus beginning on 04/17/1980	11th Cancer
5th Capricorn	MARS Sun beginning on 06/17/1981 MARS Moon beginning on 10/23/1981 RAHU Rahu beginning on 05/23/1982 RAHU Jupiter beginning on 02/05/1985 RAHU Saturn beginning on 06/29/1987 RAHU Mercury beginning on 05/05/1990	**12th Leo** ♆

4th Sagittarius	3rd Scorpio Ketu Rx -- Saturn Rx T--	2nd Libra	1st Virgo Ascendant

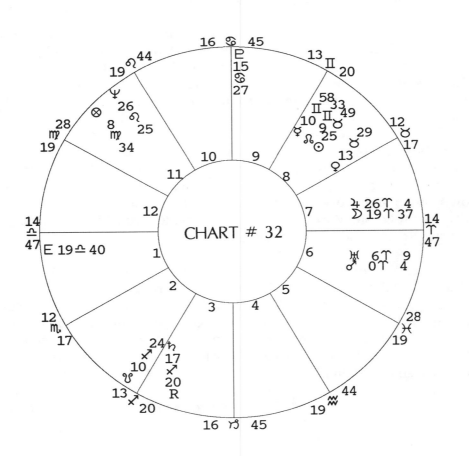

CHART # 32

these factors and, in fact, that's true. The first thing that jumps out is the fact that, at death, his P3 IC (15-AR-51) is exactly conjunct P3 Uranus (15-AR-4) on the natal horizon, and this forms a perfectly hard square to the N. Pluto/MC. Indeed there might be some argument for backing up his TOB by a minute or two to make this pattern even more perfectly angular.

Two months before his death there was an eclipse at 24-AQ. At death his P3 Sun hit 24-LE which was the south end of the prior eclipse, and this animated the Sun/Neptune square. Why was he killed by someone else? A sidereal mutual reception was part of the setup. The ruler of the 7th (Jupiter) is in the 8th, and the ruler of the 8th (Mars) is in the 7th (and conjunct Uranus). Jupiter, with its status as a maraka, is itself conjunct the other maraka (Venus, ruler of the 2nd), and both are in the 8th.

Let's look at Dasa/Bhukti factors. Mr. Martin moved into his Rahu Dasa in 1982, and he was in a Saturn Bhukti as of 1987. At death, these two factors were exactly activated in at least three ways:

➤ The P3 Moon (9-GE), functioning as a timer, was conjunct the N. tNN (indeed, the P3 Moon of the owner of the NY Yankees, George Steinbrenner, who had fired and rehired Billy Martin numerous times, was also exactly conjunct Mr. Martin's nodal axis at the other end).

➤ The mNN activates N. Mercury since it is exactly conjunct it. Mercury, ruler of the 1st and the 10th, had moved to 05-CA by P2. Note that P3 Saturn was now at 05-CP exactly opposing it, and T. Uranus was also at 05-CP (further opposing T. Jupiter at 05-CA). Natally, Mercury and Saturn are widely opposed (3rd and 9th houses) although the nodal axis pulled them together karmically. Now they achieved true opposition and were further animated by the exactly conjunction exaggeration of a Jupiter/Uranus opposition (Jupiter ruler of the maraka 7th; Uranus in the 7th).

➤ T. Saturn was at 14-CP-50 thus exactly square to the natal horizon and pulling together multiple factors into a perfectly formed grand cross involving the angles. Other cases in the book show that Saturn at the IC can often be a death indicator, but this would most especially be so when A) it is currently a Dasa or Bhukti planet, B) the rest of the pattern confirms, and C) it happens to also square the Asc. Some readers may also be interested in the fact that the P2 East Point was also exactly conjunct N. Saturn.

CASE 2 (Conor Clapton, Eric Clapton's son, falls over 500 feet)

Having just confirmed a clear Uranus factor in a large unexpected fall, let's look at another. The 4 & 1/2 year old son of famous British musician Eric Clapton was killed shortly after 11 AM when he fell through a window left open by a housekeeper on the 53rd floor of a NYC apartment on 03/20/91. His data is 21-Aug-1986 @ 6:20 AM GDT in London, England 51N18 & 00W10 (see chart # 33). For this event, note that we looked at his father's chart in the rectification chapter, and we will look at his mother's chart in the following chapter.

Before I highlight the Uranus factors, I'll note that Conor was in a Jupiter Dasa and Venus Bhukti. Natally, both planets were in maraka houses — Jupiter in the 7th and Venus in the 2nd. Venus was fallen — in fact, within 6 applying degrees of what Hindu astrology would identify as its single most fallen degree (27-VI sidereally).

Along this same line, Uranus had almost no velocity when Conor was born and, in fact, went fully stationary direct 6 days after birth. So again, P2 Uranus was basically stationary the year of his death paving the way for some extreme shock. Is there a hard link from Uranus to the Dasa planet (Jupiter) so that the Dasa planet could set it off? Yes. Natally, Uranus is closely square to Jupiter (2 degree applying orb).

Is there a hard link from Uranus to the fallen Bhukti planet (Venus)? Yes. N. Venus was at 13-LI-48 and T. Uranus was exactly square at 13-CP-26 (to ultimately station at 13-CP-48 — square N. Venus TTM). Note also that Eric Clapton's own N. NN is at 13-CP-59 and is thus tightly caught up in this same fated condition. Indeed, to put the nail in the coffin, so to speak, Mr. Clapton's first PNE after his own conception was at 13-CP-58.

Pluto hit Conor's Bhukti planet also: T. Pluto was Rx at 20-SC-11 conjunct P3 Venus at 19-SC-44. There is more Pluto: natally it's at 04-SC, and 04-SC was exactly the last eclipse before his birth, suggesting possible into-the-abyss karma (when everything else confirms). This formation was animated when the T. Dasa planet (Jupiter) was square at 04-LE and opposed by T. Saturn at 04-AQ. P3 Pluto was also exactly square to P3 Mars (10 minute orb) — which in turn was exactly conjunct the P3 anti-Vertex for those who monitor that.

8th Pisces Rahu Rx e+	9th Aries	10th Taurus	11th Gemini
7th Aquarius Moon + Jupiter Rx T+	JUPITER Mercury beginning on 11/07/1987 JUPITER Ketu beginning on 02/13/1990 JUPITER Venus beginning on 01/19/1991 JUPITER Sun beginning on 09/19/1993		12th Cancer Mercury --
6th Capricorn	JUPITER Moon beginning on 07/07/1994 JUPITER Mars beginning on 11/07/1995 JUPITER Rahu beginning on 10/13/1996 SATURN Saturn beginning on 03/07/1999		1st Leo Sun Ascendant M
5th Sagittarius Mars T++ ♆	4th Scorpio Saturn ♅	3rd Libra ♇	2nd Virgo Venus f Ketu Rx Ee

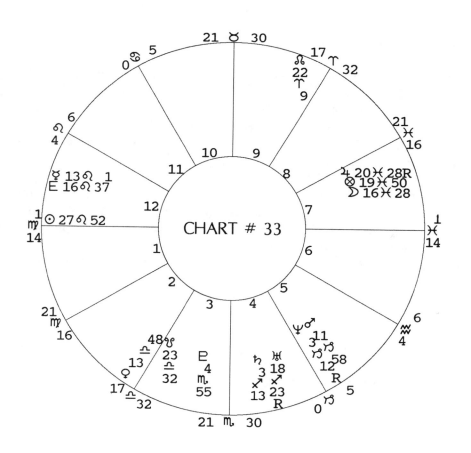

CHART # 33

A few other timers:

➤ His N. Mercury (ruler of his New York Asc) was at 13-LE while his relocated P3 Asc had just arrived at 13-LE. Note: his last new Moon before birth was at 13-LE.

➤ There was a P3 eclipse at 24-AR-07 four days/months prior to his death, and this was on his N. mean node of 23-AR-32. This was also exactly square his father's final PNE at 23-CP-41. Here I will note another curiosity: Conor's SN had progressed (by P3) to the exact final degree where Hindu astrology would consider the current Bhukti planet (Venus) to be most severely fallen (27-VI sidereally).

➤ Excluding all the above considerations, you also have to wonder: how could someone almost 5 years old wander out a window at that height? T. Neptune was at 16-CP-30 while his P3 Asc was exactly square it at 16-LI-14. At the same moment, his P3 Asc was exactly octile his N. Asc TTM thus doubling the Neptune harmonic.

CASE 3 (Severe Stroke of Famous Astrologer)

This is the chart of an astrologer who made an excellent technical and leadership contribution to the astrological world. He died of a severe stroke on 9/19/92 at 9:05 PM EDT in NYC after a related illness of only a few days (see chart # 34 b. 26-July-1923 @ 9:18:43 AM CST at 41N16 & 95W56). This TOB is according to him, and I do not know to what extent it may have been rectified.

An initial glance at his chart might quickly suggest the possibility of about a 4-minute birth error since P2 Mars is one degree beyond his Asc, and P2 Venus, ruling his active Bhukti period, is one degree beyond a conjunction to his Placidus 2nd house cusp. However, as we will see, the solar and lunar return charts argue against this, and we must assume that this individual, given the intricate technical way in which he practiced his craft, would have been able to correctly confirm his own TOB.

A stroke will typically imply Uranus and Mercury difficulties for general neural disorder. Many argue that Saturn is often involved, either due to the paralysis, or just due to the general symbolism of immobile constriction. Neptune is also an expected factor due to the neurasthenia and disorientation.

8th Pisces	9th Aries	10th Taurus	11th Gemini Venus ++ ♇
7th Aquarius Ketu Rx ♓	JUPITER Ketu beginning on 05/21/1976 JUPITER Venus beginning on 04/27/1977 JUPITER Sun beginning on 12/27/1979 JUPITER Moon beginning on 10/15/1980 JUPITER Mars beginning on 02/15/1982 JUPITER Rahu beginning on 01/21/1983		12th Cancer Sun Mars Tf Mercury -- ♆
6th Capricorn	SATURN Saturn beginning on 06/15/1985 SATURN Mercury beginning on 06/18/1988 SATURN Ketu beginning on 02/27/1991 SATURN Venus beginning on 04/06/1992 SATURN Sun beginning on 06/06/1995		1st Leo Rahu Rx Ascendant
5th Sagittarius Moon +	4th Scorpio	3rd Libra Jupiter T--	2nd Virgo Saturn ++

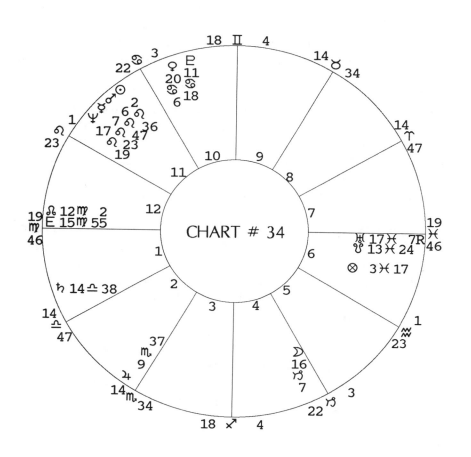

CHART # 34

Natally, like Richard Nixon, his Mercury is conjunct vascular Mars within one degree (and the Sun within 5 degrees). Uranus is 2+ degrees from being exactly angular at the Desc (it is also exactly quincunx Neptune). Tropically, Saturn is exactly conjunct the Placidus 2nd cusp, and sidereally, it is also in the maraka 2nd, ruling the 6th (health) and the 7th (the other maraka). From the 2nd, it aspects the 8th (vitality) and Venus in the 11th (thus also activating Pluto).

He had moved into a Saturn Dasa in June 1985 and a Venus Bhukti in March 1992. In his navamsha, Saturn further ruled his 2nd and was in Cancer in the 8th. Westerners consider this a "detrimental" sign placement. At death, T. Saturn was in the maraka 2nd in the navamsha, and in the main (rasi) chart, Saturn was strong, transiting the 6th in Capricorn, thus fully aspecting the 12th which contained his chart ruler (the Sun), a fallen Mars in Cancer, an arguably combust Mercury plus Neptune. Those three inner planets were also located in a Saturn-owned nakshatra.

With Saturn now "Dasa activated," note that at death T. Uranus was exactly "stationary" square to N. maraka Saturn, and this was at the same moment that his P2 Uranus was quincunx N. Saturn TTM. As you know, I agree with the observation that Uranus has no capacity to kill. Yet it does seem to be involved in sharp and/or unexpected disorders of many kinds, and these often lead to death.

Relevant here about Uranus is A) its natal near angularity, B) that P2 Uranus was conjunct the IC of the relocated chart (often considered a death point), C) that P3 Uranus was exactly conjunct the sidereal 8th cusp, and D) that both T. & P2 Uranus was exactly hard aspecting a maraka ruler located in a maraka house during its Dasa period. Note also that the horizon of the chart is also the midpoint of N. and P3 Uranus.

For variation, and because this chart had been rectified by a technically respectable astrologer, we can look with confidence at the return charts. The tropical unrelocated solar (TSR) and lunar (TLR) returns did a fine job of acquitting themselves. The TSR had the ruler of the 1st (Mercury) exactly conjunct the IC TTM (16-LE-21), and this was exactly opposing Saturn at the MC (16-AQ-06).

This perfect angularity along the meridian, and with these particular planets, strongly implied death where many of the other factors may just have implied illness or disorder. Accidents for example, being environmental, are more typically found along the horizon instead of the meridian. The final TLR had 26-SC rising. Note that P3 Saturn was at 25-SC, and the P2 MC was at 25-LE. This has Mars ruling the TLR chart, and it is exactly conjunct the mean lunar SN at the cusp of the Placidus 8th.

In the TLR the Moon was also conjunct Neptune in the maraka 2nd within 11 applying minutes. T. Neptune at the event had almost no apparent velocity at 16-CP-12 conjunct his N. moon at 16-CP-07. This was opposing his P2 Moon at 16-CA-02 (his Venus/Pluto midpoint). The further grace of this pattern was found in the fact that, when his P3 Asc arrived at 07-TA, it found itself in a perfect T-Square to his N. Mercury/Mars (07-LE) opposing a P3 Mercury/Jupiter conjunction at 07-AQ. A tight T. Sun/ Mercury/ Jupiter conjunction had just entered his sidereal 2nd only days before his death.

Three final miscellaneous notes:

➤ His P3 IC was exactly square the last P2 full Moon.

➤ The importance of Uranus to this chart (natally at 17-PI-07) is further highlighted by the fact that it is square the meridian within one degree and, at age 46, was perfectly eclipsed by P2 (9/10/23) at 17-VI-06 (any planet eclipsed by progression is always rendered permanently critical).

➤ A P2 final quarter Moon had just occurred in his chart the year of his death at 08-CA-59. The last T. eclipse before his death was at 08-CA-57 (you may remember this exact eclipse from two chapters back that was a repeated theme when discussing expected deaths in one's own chart).

CASE 4 (John Tower's Plane Crash)

John Tower was the former powerful chairman of the Senate Armed Services Committee and four-term Senator from Texas who went through a bruising nomination battle for Secretary of Defense under former President Bush. He lost the nomination under an onslaught of increasingly bizarre womanizing accusations during a P2 Uranus station when T. Pluto was right on his Venus/Saturn conjunction and T. Neptune was right on his Asc. He subsequently had both a malignant rectal polyp and cancerous prostate gland removed.

He was killed with his daughter in a plane crash on 4/5/91 near Brunswick,

Georgia as his plane approached Flynco Jetport. His birth data is 29-Sept-1925 @ 1:35 PM CST in Houston, TX 29N46 & 95W22 (see chart # 35). This was during a Ketu Dasa and Venus Bhukti. If you want to see quite a good horoscope for a career at the top of government, this is one.

The ruler of the 5th and the ruler of the 9th are both nearly conjunct in the 10th. Although technically malefics (Mars and the Sun), in fact these two perform excellently in the 10th. Further, Mercury is also in the 10th, in its own sign, and exactly conjunct the ruler of the 5th. Venus is in its own sign in the 11th, and is conjunct Saturn in its single highest degree of exaltation when converted to the Hindu system (such would be especially excellent for a businessman, but note that Saturn is the stronger of the two). Earlier in this text I discussed why Venus and Saturn are "great friends."

Jupiter is conjunct the Asc in its own sign and gets power from the full aspect of Pluto that is nearly angular. This is a variation on the Saddam Hussein chart where Jupiter is at its single most fallen degree — 5-CP sidereally — getting power from Pluto which is exactly opposite it sitting on Jupiter's most exalted degree of 5-CA sidereally.

Compare all this to Tower's relatively insipid and misdirected Western chart. My much earlier discussion of the Casper Weinberger sidereal chart, concerning a very well-regarded individual who held multiple cabinet positions in multiple administrations, made exactly the same point at the end of the chapter that introduced basic Hindu astrology concepts.

With this case, I would like to introduce a variation on the concept of relocation which is the idea of geographic danger points. In my later chapter on assassination I confirm the generally well known astrological fact that for John F. Kennedy, Dallas was one of those places.

Many readers may already be familiar with the concept of "Astro-cartography" as originally popularized by Jim Lewis and now available in several screen-addressable PC packages. That is a custom map with various curved and vertical lines on it. It is keyed to the idea that, at the time you were born, you *could* have been born, at least in theory, at any place on earth.

What these specialized maps do is highlight every place on earth where you would have had each planet on each of the four angles of your chart if you had been born in that location. Most astrologers accept that if you

4th Pisces	5th Aries	6th Taurus	7th Gemini
♓			♇
3rd Aquarius Moon –	MERCURY Mercury beginning on 10/23/1972 MERCURY Ketu beginning on 03/20/1975 MERCURY Venus beginning on 03/17/1976 MERCURY Sun beginning on 01/17/1979 MERCURY Moon beginning on 11/23/1979 MERCURY Mars beginning on 04/23/1981 MERCURY Rahu beginning on 04/20/1982	8th Cancer Rahu Rx ––	
2nd Capricorn Ketu Rx ++	MERCURY Jupiter beginning on 11/08/1984 MERCURY Saturn beginning on 02/14/1987 KETU Ketu beginning on 10/23/1989 KETU Venus beginning on 03/20/1990 KETU Sun beginning on 05/20/1991 KETU Moon beginning on 09/26/1991	9th Leo	♅
1st Sagittarius Ascendant Jupiter M	12th Scorpio	11th Libra Saturn E Venus M	10th Virgo Mercury E Mars T–– Sun T–

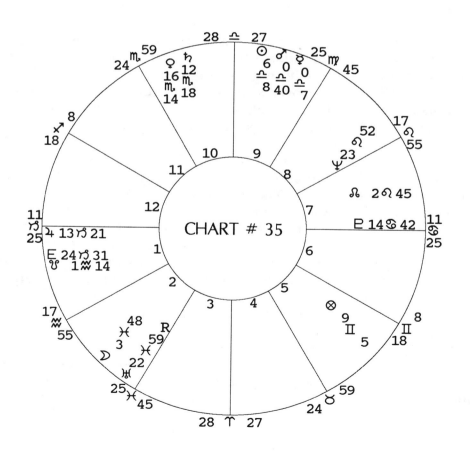

were to move onto one of those lines, the quality of that planet would begin to become much more dominant in your life. This would be for better or worse depending on the nature of the planet, the phase your chart is in, the way that planet is natally configured by sign and aspect, and so forth.

Occasionally one of the curved lines will cross one of the vertical lines. Again, for better or worse, this is a particularly intense location since, at that place, one planet will be directly on the new "horizon," and another will be directly on the new meridian. This is sometimes referred to as a "mundane square" since, even though the planets may not be separated technically by 90 degrees of longitude, the combined effect is typically at least as intense, since double angularity is always very personal. All of which leads us back to John Tower who was, as noted earlier, killed very near an airport very near Brunswick, GA.

When you move John Tower's chart to Brunswick, you find that his N. Saturn is now directly conjunct the new MC. Since it is at its single most exalted degree (20-LI sidereally), this means that the single weakest degree for Saturn is on the new IC (which you should have already begun to realize has something to do with death). Recall that he was in a Venus Bhukti, so Venus was invoking Saturn from only 4 degrees away. Also, Saturn is at 12-SC-18, and this was "square sensitized" by a PNE at 11-AQ-34. Also: P2 Saturn had moved to 19-SC-53. So guess where T. Pluto was – perfectly conjunct TTM at 19-SC-53. And this point was pre-sensitized by yet another perfectly square PNE from the other direction at 19-LE-39.

At Brunswick, Tower's Asc was 24-CP-50. About a minute of birth error, or a few miles of relocation correction, would have it at 25-CP. The relevance of this is that the last T. solar eclipse before he died was at 25-CP-20 – directly on the new location. And where do you think his P3 Mars was at? Right on this new eclipse-sensitized Asc at 25-CP-44. So, with the IC at Saturn's weakest degree and Saturn being activated, he flew to an eclipse sensitized location that had his progressed Mars right on it (with progressed Mars itself strong in exaltation). Some might like to argue that he wouldn't have died at any other location, while others would argue that it was inevitable that he would, in fact, fly to this location.

By the way, his P2 tSN was only a degree away from all this (at 26-CP-13). On the other side of the relocated chart, his P2 Moon was exactly conjunct the north end of the progressed node at 26-CA-25, and this is probably what drew his daughter into the action. This Moon was also progressing into another PNE of 27-CA-37. As a final comment on his Ketu Dasa, his N. tSN was at 02-AQ-45, and T. Saturn was exactly conjunct it at 02-AQ-40 (Saturn being Bhukti-activated via Venus).

Going back to his original non-relocated chart, we see that Jupiter rules this chart, and it is 2 degrees from the Asc at 13-CP-21. In keeping with the theme of unexpected and hence shocking deaths, note that T. Uranus was conjunct the Asc ruler at 13-CP-00 (and P3 Uranus had been opposing his N. Mars for quite a long time). Speaking of Jupiter, plane crashes seem like the way to go since here the P2 Asc of 6-AR-17 was conjunct P3 Jupiter at 6-AR-12. These both fully aspected the Sun at 6-LI-8.

A minor closing fact that may be of interest to Placidus fans is the fact that his P3 Saturn was now on his N. 12th cusp TTM while his P3 MC was at the cusp of the 3rd. This could possibly support an assertion about some sorrow associated with transportation, and it has the feel of a "minor mutable mundane square" of its own.

CASE 5 (Peace Corps Volunteer Driven Off 450-Foot Cliff)

I thought I'd do this as a follow-on to the John Tower event. The point to be reviewed is that, in the above case, he was killed with his daughter while his progressed Moon was exactly conjunct his progressed Node on the west side of his chart. In this case, a woman was killed with another woman (both of whom were in the back seat) while the two men in the front seat, including the driver who missed a mountain curve, were not killed.

In this case the P3 Moon (exactly square to T. Uranus) was only 2 degrees from the P3 Node on the west side of the chart, while her P2 Moon was exactly conjunct her P2 Desc and only 3 degrees from her P2 Node on the west side of the chart. As noted earlier, Billy Martin, who was also driven off a cliff by someone else (but not a female), also had critical activation on the western side of his chart (but not involving the Moon). The symbolic point should be self-explanatory.

I became aware of this case in the July 1989 issue of the *Mercury Hour*. A Peace Corps volunteer was in the news for the above fatal accident which occurred on 12/16/88 near Belfast, South Africa (25S43 & 30E03) as they were driving to a vacation in Zimbabwe. Astrologer Don Borkowski wrote in to say that he happened to have her birth data from 15 years earlier. He wrote that, according to her, Juanita Quiton was born 11-May-1949 @ 3:00 PM PDT in Portland, OR 45N31 & 122W41 (see chart # 36).

8th Pisces	9th Aries Rahu Rx -- Mars MT Sun E	10th Taurus Venus 0 Mercury	11th Gemini ♓
7th Aquarius 6th Capricorn Jupiter Tf	SATURN Saturn beginning on 04/16/1966 SATURN Mercury beginning on 04/19/1969 SATURN Ketu beginning on 12/28/1971 SATURN Venus beginning on 02/07/1973 SATURN Sun beginning on 04/07/1976 SATURN Moon beginning on 03/19/1977 SATURN Mars beginning on 10/19/1978 SATURN Rahu beginning on 11/28/1979 SATURN Jupiter beginning on 10/04/1982 MERCURY Mercury beginning on 04/16/1985 MERCURY Ketu beginning on 09/13/1987 MERCURY Venus beginning on 09/10/1988 MERCURY Sun beginning on 07/10/1991	12th Cancer ♇ 1st Leo Saturn -- Ascendant
5th Sagittarius	4th Scorpio	3rd Libra Ketu Rx Moon -	2nd Virgo ♆

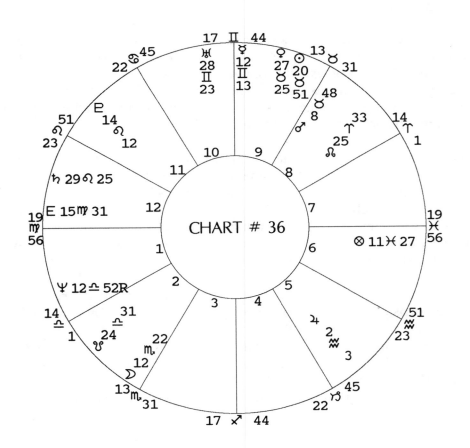

This chart makes most of the usual points. The last eclipse before death was 18-VI-40. This is slightly more than 1 degree under her Asc of 19-VI-56 and slightly less than 1 degree over the square to her IC of 17-SA-44. In effect, the eclipse hit only 10 minutes off the midpoint of all four angles which is 18 degrees and 50 minutes of the tropical mutables. P3 Mars contributed to the activation since it was at the bottom of the chart at 19-SA-37 thus square to the eclipse-sensitized Asc.

We know that Mars absolutely portends trouble because N. Mars at 8-TA-48 had been exactly hit by not one, but two, solar PNE's: one at 7-TA-42 and the other at 8-SC-44. And indeed, at death T. Mars at 12-AR-52 opposed N. Neptune in the maraka 2nd TTM at 12-LI-52. Further, Mars is caught up in a fairly harsh T-Square since natally it opposes the Moon while Pluto squares the Moon. Just as with Senator Tower above, here we again see the relevance of the Placidus 3/9 transport cusps since N. Pluto squares them, and the N. Moon is only one degree from being conjunct the 3rd. This was further activated by the fact that T. Pluto, proceeding from the natal T-Square noted above, had just conjunct the N. Moon and was now square N. Pluto within 6 minutes.

A couple of additional Uranus factors are that P3 Uranus at 9-CA-28 was being opposed by T. Neptune at 9-CP-20 while the P2 Sun, ruler of her 1st, was conjunct N. Uranus. A strong Jupiter factor showed once again since her P3 IC was within a degree of being square to P3 Jupiter, and P3 Jupiter would be fully stationary the following month — a seemingly excellent development from a transitional point of view. This P3 Jupiter was also exactly square to the N. Bhukti Venus (and thus the P3 IC was almost conjunct Venus — arguing perhaps for a later birth time of maybe 2 minutes). But this Venus discussion raises the question of where was the "typically to be expected" Saturn effect?

She was in a Mercury Dasa (ruler of the maraka 2nd) and Venus Bhukti (ruler of the transport 3rd). Natally, Venus is only 2 applying degrees from being square to Saturn. In her navamsha, Saturn is in a mutual reception with Venus. With this double connection, Saturn (ruler of the maraka 7th) is activated when Venus is highlighted. Here we now see both of them simultaneously caught up with the nodes since P3 Venus was conjunct her N. SN while P3 Saturn was conjunct her P3 SN. Adding to the nodal complex is the fact that her P2 IC was also exactly square to the N. nodes.

As can be done when only talking about one case, Borkowski made a number of extended points regarding converse progressions, solar arc directions, the calculation of a diurnal to estimate the time of the accident, the last prior lunation right on her IC, important midpoints, return charts, heliocentric factors, and the like. This book has more narrowly focused objectives but, as I noted in the Introduction, there are many other fertile areas for investigation. In support of the concept of relocation noted above, he did observe that her relocated chart now had her original (eclipse-sensitized) Asc directly on the relocated 8th house Placidus cusp.

CASE 6 (Drowning Death of TV Personality)

This final example concerns Jessica Savitch who was the first female TV anchor to appear regularly on a TV network (NBC). She drowned at age 36 in an auto accident on 10/23/83 (note: several other research resources said 10/24, but it won't matter for our purposes). Her car, driven by her fiance, overturned into the Delaware Canal outside a restaurant near New Hope, PA as an apparent result of disorientation (this had happened to another restaurant patron many years earlier). Her birth data as presented by her agent from a BC is 1-Feb-1947 @ 11:51 AM EST in Wilmington, DE 39N45 & 75W33 (see chart # 37).

This is a rather complex case due to the dispute over her birth data. The *AFA Journal* has quoted a birth time 4 minutes later, and *The Washington Post*, *The New York Times* and *Facts On File* said she died at age 35. The *Post* also said she was born in Kennett Square, PA. Nevertheless, the agent's data seems the most reputable. It also presents a chart that seems to match well to her life (including her navamsha). Despite all this confusion, I would especially like to pursue the case if only to highlight how to weave through some of the issues that the confusion raises.

Natally, as might be expected considering her ascendancy within the highly competitive world of broadcasting, we see here a very powerful and animated chart. For example, the N. Sun is perfectly opposed by Pluto. But what strikes the viewer even more immediately is that Mars and Saturn not only exactly oppose each other; they are also both exactly angular. It is immediately apparent, however, that the top of the chart is much more powerful than the bottom because Mars is exalted at the top and both the 10th and the MC (actually in the 9th) receive Saturn's energy well due to their Saturnian signs.

Conversely, however, that means that the IC in the 3rd is battered by its

11th Pisces	12th Aries	1st Taurus Ascendant Rahu Rx Moon M ♓	2nd Gemini
10th Aquarius	RAHU Venus beginning on 02/18/1965 RAHU Sun beginning on 02/18/1968 RAHU Moon beginning on 01/12/1969 RAHU Mars beginning on 07/12/1970 JUPITER Jupiter beginning on 07/30/1971 JUPITER Saturn beginning on 09/18/1973 JUPITER Mercury beginning on 03/30/1976	3rd Cancer Saturn Rx RT ♇

9th Capricorn
  Mars   E
  Sun   --
  Mercury   T-
	JUPITER Ketu beginning on 07/06/1978
	JUPITER Venus beginning on 06/12/1979
	JUPITER Sun beginning on 02/12/1982
	JUPITER Moon beginning on 11/30/1982
	JUPITER Mars beginning on 03/30/1984
	JUPITER Rahu beginning on 03/06/1985
		4th Leo

8th Sagittarius
  Venus   +
	7th Scorpio
	  Jupiter ++
	  Ketu Rx
		6th Libra	5th Virgo
			
			♆

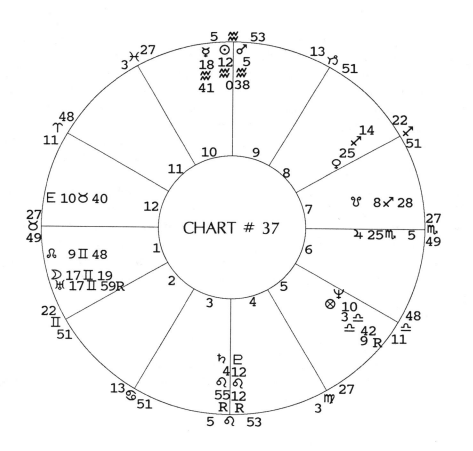

CHART # 37

exact conjunction with a weakened Saturn (with Pluto nearby) and is further oppressed by the "bearing down," as it were, of an exalted Mars from above. Excluding other considerations, this type of pattern will invariably produce powerful career energy at the expense of other inner dimensions. However, the perfect angularity brings a much greater concentration to this consideration including the chronic possibility of death related to transport, the death of one of her siblings (or, using Western thinking, the parent most internalized), and other similar symbolic possibilities.

[After I completed this chapter I felt compelled to go to the library and read her full obituary on microfilm from *The Washington Post* of 10/25/83. I then discovered that her father died when she was 12 years old and, indeed, this was during a Saturn Bhukti (which would not have been true if she was born in 1948). Also, she came home on 8/2/81 to find that her 2nd husband had hanged himself in their basement. So I add this paragraph in support of my last sentence in the above paragraph.]

To say that this person has a karmic life is to understate indeed, for we see how charts behave when energetic planets merely progress, one by one, to the angles. Jupiter, in fact, was a 3rd completely angular factor (at the Desc) by P2 once she hit her 30's, thus contributing further to her support from others (you may also notice that Venus, ruler of her 1st, was now within 7 minutes of her MC by P2 thus further pushing her to the pinnacle of her external aspirations — even as it was now experiencing the natally powerful Mars and drawing in the meridian-linked Saturn). [In support of these two planetary placements, notice that her 2nd husband killed himself during a Jupiter Dasa and Venus Bhukti.]

Jupiter was her Dasa planet. At her death it was conjunct Venus, the ruler of the 1st, within 4 minutes (thus arguing again for accidents being a pleasant way to go). The impelling energy behind this otherwise pleasant linkage was the fact that P3 Uranus exactly opposed it (and thus also the natal ruler of the 1st). As you will see, Uranus made its contribution in another key way, and to me this again demonstrates how Hindu astrology unnecessarily labors under a perceptual deficiency by failing to use the outer planets.

Savitch was in a Moon Bhukti, and it is definitely over-reaching to attempt to argue that, by their own rules, this waxing and exalted 1st house Moon, while ruler of the transport house, is either a maraka or even under particular stress. As you know, the Moon can supposedly never be a maraka, and anyway this one is just too good. Being in the same house with the NN is simply not enough, especially considering that neither node is the Dasa — although, of course, we will see plenty of the usual and exact nodal activity.

But Westerners would see her Moon in an entirely different way because what we see is that the Moon is already exactly conjunct Uranus natally (even as they both continue to mutually apply). Now, unlike our Eastern associates, Westerners can easily see the latent instability of the 1st house Moon Bhukti which went into effect the year before. Knowing that, let's take a further look at what is happening to the (Bhukti) Moon at her death.

The P2 Moon is at 0-SC-12 while T. Pluto is conjunct it at 29-LI-28 (actually they had been running along in near tandem for quite a while). The 17-GE N. Moon/Uranus conjunction was sensitized by a PNE at 16-GE-3 (this PNE point was also conjunct at her death with the P3 Sun at 15-GE-47). The last T. solar eclipse was at 19-GE-43. As you know, this 2 degree orb is way too wide for my taste, but perhaps the P3 Sun and the PNE to the Moon/Uranus helped to pull it all together.

Continuing the nodal observations, we see that the true P2 SN was at 5-SA-36, and P2 Mars (ruler of the maraka 7th) was applying into the square of it at 4-PI-31. The same thing was happening in the tertiaries as P3 Mars at 8-VI-20 was perfectly square to the N. mSN of 08-SA-28 while T. Uranus was nearly conjunct it at 7-SA-2. As a further touch, the P3 IC of 9-SA-40 was now also conjunct the N. tSN of 9-SA-48. Final "cross systems" confirmation is shown in the fact that her P3 Asc of 12-VI-25 was conjunct her P2 IC of 12-VI-53.

Support for death by drowning is found in the fact that P3 Venus, Rx ruler of the 1st, was applying at 10-CA-54 into a perfect square to N. Neptune at 10-LI-42. Venus was also at a very low velocity having gone Rx by P3 only 3 days/months earlier. Note that if this had not happened, it would have continued its exit from the square. Instead it turned around to apply back into the perfect square once again, and other factors took advantage of this situation. You will also recall the status of P2 Venus discussed above.

Venus was not the only slow planet by P3. Mercury, ruler of the maraka 2nd, was also about to go Rx by P3 in 5 day/months. And, at 6-CA-23, what was it stopping on? Another PNE at 6-CA-49 in the 2nd (note: it would have stopped at 7-CA-16). It is also the case that N. Mercury at 18-AQ-41 was being opposed by P3 karaka Saturn at 17-LE-55, while T. Saturn at 6-SC-14 was also square the N. IC of 5-LE-53. As a closing note on the 2nd house, Placidus fans may appreciate noting that there had been yet another PNE at 23-SA-05 directly on the 8th cusp of 22-SA-51.

With the reader having read this entire argument, plus the chapter on rectification, I now suggest an exercise. Continue to consider the possibility that Savitch was indeed born in 1948. Go through the same set of considerations and see if you can re-persuade yourself that she was indeed born in 1947. Along the way, expect a lot of little tricks and quirks to aggravate you. If someone had her BC in hand, and you had to bet a lot of money on it, would you still choose 1947?

In closing, readers may wish to compare this highly angular case to the chart of formerly well-known astrologer Marcia Moore. Natally, the ruler of her 1st was in the 12th conjunct Pluto (similar to the chart of sports celebrity O.J. Simpson, whose ex-wife was murdered, which has the ruler of his 7th in his 12th conjunct Pluto). At her death, her body was found decapitated. Natally, she had Uranus exactly angular at her MH, and N. Mars was only 2 degrees from this Uranus (the chart of Karen Carpenter, discussed later, also had N. Uranus exactly angular). Marcia Moore was born on 22-May-1928 @ 9:00 AM EDT in Cambridge, MA 42N22 & 71W06 (chart not shown)[†].

[†] *Ms. Moore's TOB is given in some modern books as 9:00 AM EDT, but in her own book it is shown as 9:10 AM. The error was apparently on Marcia's part. In her book of several decades back, her chart was calculated by hand. She displayed an Asc of 25-CA and a MH of almost 7-AR. These are the same angles produced by computer programs that use 9:00. I assume that Ms. Moore believed her angles were correct. Somewhere along the line there must have been either a defective hand calculation or an incorrectly recorded TOB. But the end result, i.e., the angles, are the same. Therefore I consider that there is no disputed issue.*

UNEXPECTED DEATHS OF OTHERS
IN YOUR CHART

This section will look at the issue of seeing the unexpected death of others in your own chart. This review will emphasize family charts such as spouse, siblings and children. Again, there is no particular selection pattern to these cases. They just somewhat randomly came to my attention during my relatively recent decision to assemble this concept. The pattern reveals itself to the attentive through induction and repetition.

Let's start out by looking at the death of two unrelated brothers: one who was shot and one who died in an auto accident. In both Eastern and Western systems the 3rd rules siblings, although in the Hindu system the 11th is usually said to rule the eldest brother (and sometimes sister, according to some authorities).

CASE 1 (Brother Killed By Gunshot)

In the past I had the opportunity to do some astrological work for someone who was a presidential candidate outside the U.S. I was given full data for the candidate, his wife and his campaign manager, plus some information on the person he was running against. As I always do, I required a list of qualified non-symbolic life events that were out of their control in order to validate their times of birth.

After several passes at getting them to understand what I needed, it turned out that in their past, the candidate had himself been shot, the campaign manager's son had been shot, and the only brother of the candidate's wife had been shot (all for political reasons)! Since only the wife's brother was actually killed, and her time of birth easily validated itself, I'll use that for the illustration.

His wife was born at 11-Dec-1938 @ 3:55 AM CST at 13N42 & 89W12 (see chart # 38). I was able to easily get the attention of their office by immediately asserting that she must have been a stunning attractive female who won beauty contests when she was about 18-21 years of age and then again at age 23. As it turned out, she was the top beauty queen in her original country of birth during that period! Here is the collection of key natal factors: the tNN is exactly conjunct her Asc while Venus is only 2 degrees away and is almost totally stationary in its own 1st house

6th Pisces Saturn Rx SRT≈+	7th Aries Ketu Rx --	8th Taurus	9th Gemini
		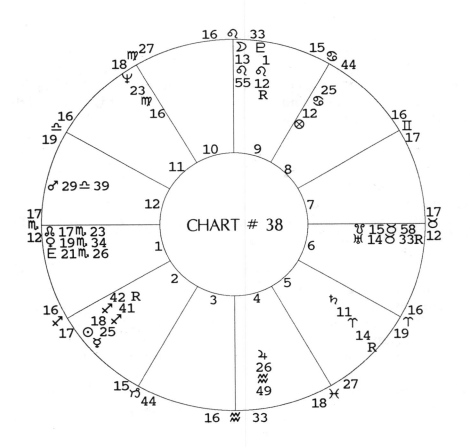 ♅	
5th Aquarius Jupiter ≈+	SUN Moon beginning on 09/29/1977 SUN Mars beginning on 03/29/1978 SUN Rahu beginning on 08/05/1978 SUN Jupiter beginning on 06/29/1979 SUN Saturn beginning on 04/17/1980 SUN Mercury beginning on 03/29/1981 SUN Ketu beginning on 02/05/1982 SUN Venus beginning on 06/11/1982 MOON Moon beginning on 06/11/1983 MOON Mars beginning on 04/11/1984 MOON Rahu beginning on 11/11/1984 MOON Jupiter beginning on 05/11/1986 MOON Saturn beginning on 09/11/1987	10th Cancer Moon 0 ♇	
4th Capricorn			11th Leo
3rd Sagittarius Mercury Rx T+	2nd Scorpio Sun ++	1st Libra Mars - Ascendant Rahu Rx Venus D M	12th Virgo ♆

sign of Libra. The Asc, Venus and the Node are also all conjunct within slightly over one total degree of declination. Jupiter aspected the 1st house, and the Moon was also in its own sign in the 10th house.

The navamsha totally confirmed because she *again* had Venus in its own sign (Taurus) in the 1st along with the north node, with Jupiter aspecting the 1st from the 7th. This is a stunning collection of factors for beauty combined with public popularity. As far as the timing went, she was in a Venus Dasa and Bhukti from age 18-21 and then in a Venus Dasa / Moon Bhukti at age 23. So this is when she was actually winning the contests.

Nevertheless, with the nodal axis along the horizon and Uranus at the south end near the Desc, we see here the reality of a karmic life (especially in relationships), and this thought is supplemented by a nearly stationary Saturn in the 6th. As a result of this nodal emphasis I would expect profound confirmation through the pre-natal eclipse patterns, and you will soon see that this was so.

Her brother was killed on 9/5/86. This was during her Moon Dasa and Jupiter Bhukti, both natural benefics. In the main rasi chart we see that Jupiter was in a mutual reception with her nearly stationary Saturn. You will often find that a mutual reception between "good" and "bad" factors will cause a "flip" in their normally expected performance during their respective periods (this is also usually true when they stand in exact "opposition" or conjunction without regard to a mutual reception). Note also that her nearly stationary Saturn aspects her 3rd (siblings), her 8th (the concept of death and whose ruler is in the 1st with Mars), and the 12th ("secret sorrows" whose ruler is in the 3rd of siblings).

Jupiter in the navamsha confirms its defective natal status in the rasi chart. In the navamsha, Jupiter is in a mutual reception with Mars in the 8th, with Mars in turn conjunct an almost stationary Saturn in the 8th. Jupiter is also with the SN.

By transit, Uranus was exactly conjunct her Sun. The P2 Uranus/SN conjunction had tightened up to within less than half a degree with the P2 Asc very tightly tri-octile to it. P2 Uranus was also now only 4 minutes from being conjunct her public N. Moon (recall she was in a Moon Dasa). In the month before she was born, there were two eclipses: one at 29-SC and the other at 14-TA. Well 14-TA is exactly her natal Uranus, and 29-SC is exactly her P2 Mars. At death, T. Mars was exactly conjunct her Placidus 3rd house cusp (siblings).

P3 data is even more informative. She was in a Moon Dasa, and the P3 Asc was conjunct the Moon within 8 minutes (about 10 seconds of birth rectification would make it exact). In turn, the P3 Moon was conjunct her natal 3rd house Mercury within 5 minutes. The true P3 SN was conjunct N. Saturn within 3 minutes. P3 Venus (ruler of 1 and 8) was conjunct Pluto within less than half a degree.

But perhaps even more interesting was the clustering around the Desc. Her P3 MC (IC) was conjunct Uranus TTM, and you will recall that this was also an exact pre-natal eclipse point. P3 Saturn was also only 6 minutes from this conj. And P3 Jupiter was only a degree away from all this, and 20 minutes from the N. mSN. This is an altogether appropriate and precise set of timing indicators.

I've mentioned earlier that, to reduce the clutter, I wouldn't talk about the Part of (Mis)fortune, but as a major ratio factor, it does show up a lot. Here again we see the P3 Part only 2 minutes from yet another PNE at 22-SC while, in the P2 chart, it's only 5 minutes from opposing P2 Neptune (note: T. Neptune was itself verging upon station at the murder).

CASE 2 (Brother's Auto Death)

For another glance at the death of brothers, I'll mention my wife's chart. She was born on 15-Feb-1947 @ 2:40 AM EST (possibly 2:39) in Endicott, NY 42N06 & 76W04 (chart not shown). Her younger brother died 11/05/72 while driving a Corvette over 100 mph on a pitch dark winding country road with a speed limit of 25 mph. She has a powerful Mars in Capricorn in the 3rd, with Saturn and Pluto in the opposing 9th. So her brother was indeed a physically strong but frustrated and angry individual.

I won't bother to show her chart since I'll only be discussing it in the context of one planet – Jupiter. When her brother was killed, her P3 Asc was conjunct N. Jupiter while her P2 Jupiter was nearly stationary (although I also note that her P3 Saturn was square her P3 true nodes TTM). On the day her favorite grandmother died (5/17/73) there was a full Moon exactly on her N. Jupiter. When her other grandmother died (08/17/77), that day marked the exact beginning of her Jupiter Bhukti. When her mother died (3/11/84), Mars was only one degree from natal Jupiter (at last – a "real" malefic).

Her Jupiter is relatively good in her N. 1st house (Scorpio-rising), and thus contributes to the illusion of Sag-rising. But I'm trying to make a point about the malperformance of natural benefics. Her Jupiter, as ruler of the 2nd is a maraka, and it is damaged by its association in her 1st house with the nodal axis and a fallen Moon. This weakened Jupiter is further stressed and animated by a full aspect from an almost angular Uranus on the Desc — all of which, by the way, make a statement about her mother (fallen Moon) who was institutionalized late in life.

CASE 3 (Conor Clapton's Mother — Whose Son Fell To His Death)

In the prior chapter on unexpected deaths in one's own chart, I wrote about Conor Clapton. He was the young child who fell to his death from a 53 story residence on 3/20/91. In a chapter before that on rectification via death, I discussed this event from the point of view of his famous musical father Eric Clapton. Now I will look at it from the point of view of the child's mother, Italian actress Lory Del Santo (see chart # 39 b. 28-Sept-1958 @ 01:20 AM Zone -1 in Povegliano Veneto, Italy 45N20 & 10E54).

At this point, we can almost start doing this as a drill. Let's ask what we have come to recognize as some of the classic questions:

➤ What were the Dasa/Bhukti planets? She was in both a Venus Dasa and Venus Bhukti (from 11/88 to 3/92).

➤ What is the status of Venus?

- N. Venus, at 29-LE, is in the maraka 2nd along with Pluto and only 15 applying minutes from being fallen.

- N. Venus is at 22-VI-55; P2 Saturn was square it at 22-GE-31.

- P2 Venus was at 3-SC-31. It was therefore conjunct N. Neptune at 3-SC-25. Three years before, this point was sensitized by a P2 eclipse at 3-TA-43 (on 10/27/58). T. Saturn T-squared at 4-AQ.

- P3 Venus was at 28-LI-15; she had a PNE at 28-AR-34.

➤ Was there any other relevant exact eclipse activity other than the one noted above? Yes, the last T. eclipse (9-LE-51) before the fall was less than one degree from being conjunct her Asc (8-LE-58).

➤ Were there any other potential karmic indicators? Yes, at least four:

9th Pisces
  Moon   –
  Ketu Rx   e–
	10th Aries	11th Taurus
		  Mars RT+
			12th Gemini

8th Aquarius	MERCURY Jupiter beginning on 12/03/1976 MERCURY Saturn beginning on 03/09/1979 KETU Ketu beginning on 11/18/1981 KETU Venus beginning on 04/15/1982 KETU Sun beginning on 06/15/1983 KETU Moon beginning on 10/21/1983 KETU Mars beginning on 05/21/1984	1st Cancer Ascendant
7th Capricorn	KETU Rahu beginning on 10/18/1984 KETU Jupiter beginning on 11/06/1985 KETU Saturn beginning on 10/12/1986 KETU Mercury beginning on 11/21/1987 VENUS Venus beginning on 11/18/1988 VENUS Sun beginning on 03/18/1992	2nd Leo Venus e

6th Sagittarius	5th Scorpio
	  Saturn ––
		4th Libra
		  Jupiter T
			3rd Virgo
			  Mercury E
			  Sun –
			  Rahu Rx Ee

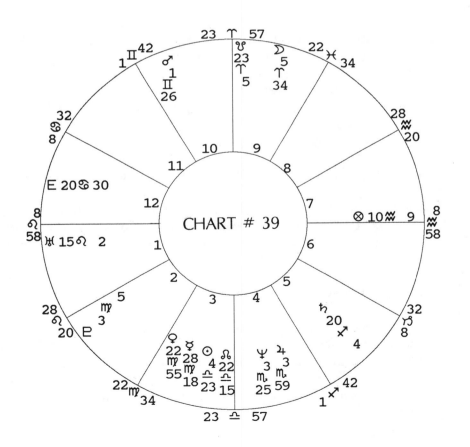

- The ruler of her 8th is Saturn, and Saturn is in the sign of a "great enemy" in the 5th of children. Ruler of 8th in 5th, especially if it is death-karaka Saturn, is often seen in the charts of people whose children die, often via abortion, when other factors confirm. In addition, this 5th house is fully aspected by Mars. [In the navamsha, Mars and Saturn are both in the 5th along with the SN. Saturn is in a mutual reception with Jupiter, but Jupiter cannot assist since it is defective by being in a fallen sign and exactly conjunct Neptune.]

- Her natal chart has the mean nodal axis exactly conjunct the IC, and this is further at a sidereal zero.

- N. Mars is exactly conjunct the Placidus 11th cusp thereby sensitizing the 5th cusp.

- She had an eclipse right before her own conception at 14-TA-55 which ultimately squared her N. Uranus in the 1st at 15-LE-02.

➤ Other than 2B & 2C noted above, what was the main immediate timer?

- P3 Mars was at 1-SA-42 which was the exact cusp (TTM) of the Placidus 5th, and exactly opposed to N. Mars. The P3 Moon formed an utterly perfect T-Square to this Mars/Mars opposition at 01-PI-42 (also note natal Pluto at 3-VI-5 which would be hit by the P3 Moon in 2-3 days at the funeral).

- Her P3 IC was at 2-CP-50 while her P2 Placidus 5th cusp was conjunct at 2-CP-15 (actually, all P3 angles were at 2 cardinal tropical degrees).

➤ Given the circumstances, any other Pluto stress? Yes:

- Her P2 Asc was one applying degree from P2 Pluto.

- P3 Pluto (12/6/59) was only two applying days from being fully stationary (12/8/59). So it was essentially stationary.

CASE 4 (Severely Defective Birth)

This is the case of a mother who was shocked by a baby born 1/13/88 with numerous major birth defects, who was consequently unable to thrive and died the same day. See chart # 40 (b. 19-Oct-1950 @ 8:12 AM EST 48N07 & 77W47). At age 38, she worried that somehow she "owed" this baby to her husband, and you will see multiple clues in the chart about that. Since this is a Canadian birth, you will also notice quite a distortion between the Eastern and Western charts (for example N. Jupiter, while only 2 degrees from the IC, is found in the 5th). Let's go through the same question and answer drill asking basically the same classic questions as we did above.

➤ What were the Dasa/Bhukti planets in effect? Two natural benefits: Jupiter was the Dasa (from 7/78) and Venus was the Bhukti (from 6/86).

➤ What was their natal status?

• Jupiter was almost stationary in the 5th house (she did have another perfectly fine child born much earlier in the Jupiter Dasa). We note, however, that Jupiter and its house is disposed by Saturn, and Saturn is in the 12th exactly conjunct the SN. Jupiter is also stressed because it is aspected by Mars, strong in its own sign, and this powerful Mars is also a double maraka since it rules both the 2nd and the 7th. We will therefore watch the behavior of Jupiter and Saturn.

• Venus shares rulership of the 1st and 8th. By Hindu designation, Venus is within less than one degree of its single most fallen degree in the entire zodiac (27-VI sidereally). In addition, it is less than 2 degrees from Neptune and is also found in the 12th house (along with Saturn, ruler of the 5th, conjunct the karmic SN).

• At the death, it is therefore very interesting to note that T. Venus (the defective Bhukti planet) was conjunct her N. Jupiter (the Dasa planet) TTM (27-AQ-38).

• In the navamsha, the 12th (and 6th) are again loaded with the same factors: Mars/Saturn/SN in AQ in 12 (Saturn being strongest) aspecting Mercury/NN/Venus/Neptune in the 6th. Here

6th Pisces Rahu +	**7th Aries**	**8th Taurus**	**9th Gemini** ♓
5th Aquarius Jupiter Rx S–	RAHU Saturn beginning on 08/30/1965 RAHU Mercury beginning on 07/06/1968 RAHU Ketu beginning on 01/24/1971 RAHU Venus beginning on 02/12/1972 RAHU Sun beginning on 02/12/1975 RAHU Moon beginning on 01/06/1976	**10th Cancer** ♇
4th Capricorn Moon –	RAHU Mars beginning on 07/06/1977 JUPITER Jupiter beginning on 07/24/1978 JUPITER Saturn beginning on 09/12/1980 JUPITER Mercury beginning on 03/24/1983 JUPITER Ketu beginning on 06/30/1985 JUPITER Venus beginning on 06/06/1986 JUPITER Sun beginning on 02/06/1989	**11th Leo**
3rd Sagittarius	**2nd Scorpio** Mars O	**1st Libra** Sun f Ascendant	**12th Virgo** Saturn RT Ketu E Mercury ET Venus f ♆

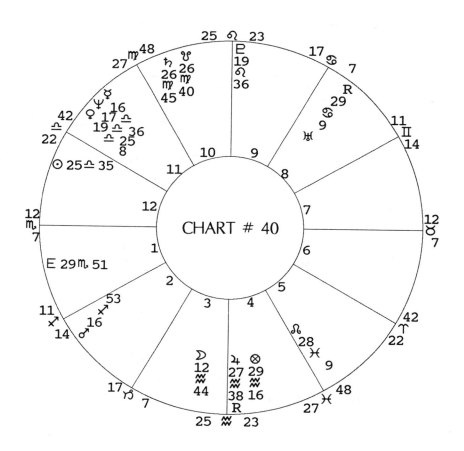

Venus is in a mutual reception with a fallen malefic in the 8th (the same malefic is also fallen in her main chart).

➤ Was there significant eclipse activity? Yes, a lot:

- Her Placidus 5th cusp is 27-PI-48. She had a PNE at 27-PI-28. She was then born with the true nodal axis at 28-PI-09. At the death, T. Uranus was square this complex at 28-SA-24, and this was conjunct the last new Moon before the death at 28-SA-20.

- Her N. mSN was at 26-VI-40 conjunct N. Saturn at 26-VI-45 (a generally tragic indicator). The T. SN had cycled around to be conjunct this point again at 26-VI-29 while T. Saturn was square at 26-SA-55 thus fulfilling its promise.

- Her P3 Saturn (ruler of her 5th) was at 13-LI-54; the last T. eclipse before the death was at 13-AR-22.

- There was a P3 eclipse at 5-PI-43 (2/25/52), and this was four P3 days/months before the death; this was square the damaged P2 Venus at 5-SA-51.

- The last PNE before her birth was at 2-AR-31; at the death her P2 IC was at 2-AR-45.

➤ In addition to the last point above, what about the other angles?

- Her P3 IC was at 9-CA-28, and this was exactly conjunct (TTM) N. Uranus (9-CA-29) which was very powerful in her chart as it had almost no velocity having gone stationary 3 days before her own birth.

- Her P3 Asc was at 21-AR-17. This opposed P3 Neptune (21-LI-21) and was conjunct T. Jupiter (21-AR-13). Note that P2 Neptune was now less than half a degree from her N. Venus.

➤ What about other timers and the usually expected Pluto problems?

- Her natal Moon (12-AQ-44) is exactly tied into the horizon (12-SC-7) by 4th harmonic aspect. T. Pluto at 12-SC-17 was exactly conjunct her Asc and square this Saturn-ruled Moon at the death, and indeed would station at that degree one month later. P2 Pluto had also been stationary four years earlier; given the velocity of Pluto, it could still be considered fully stationary after only four days of progressed "motion."

- P2 Mercury was now conjunct double maraka N. Mars (both at 16-SA); the P2 Moon opposed this at 15-GE. The P3 Moon was conjunct the cusp of the P3 Placidus 5th.

CASE 5 (Young Wife's Heart Attack)

This is someone I had just met whose young wife had a heart attack and died on 12/18/87. He was born 9-July-1948 @ 1:00 AM EDT in Bronx, NY 40N51 & 73W54. For the record, I have pushed back his recorded TOB by 45 seconds to 00:59:15 (see chart # 41).

Let's do the drill once again but compress the questions:

➤ What were the Dasa/Bhukti planets? He was in a Moon Dasa and Rahu Bhukti.

➤ Did this chart show inherent natal stress to/from the wife? Yes.

- The ruler of the 1st (Mars) is perfectly square to the ruler of the 7th (Venus) and, for Aries-rising, Venus is a double maraka since it also rules the 2nd. Further, Venus is unstable because it is conjunct Uranus within 2 applying degrees. We will see later how it was set off by a large dose of exact transits and progressions.

- Regarding the Dasa planet (Moon), while it is strong by sign it is significantly besieged by being bracketed natally in the 4th between Pluto and less than 2 applying degrees from Saturn. It invoked these two factors during its period, and we will further see how it was subjected to significant PNE sensitization.

- Regarding his nodal Bhukti factor, the SN is in his 7th. We will also see how it was subject to significant sensitization and strikes.

- He has the Sun exactly conjunct the IC TTM, so they always

12th Pisces	1st Aries Ascendant Rahu Rx --	2nd Taurus	3rd Gemini Venus Rx Mercury o Sun T- ♓
11th Aquarius	SUN Sun beginning on 02/25/1980 SUN Moon beginning on 06/13/1980 SUN Mars beginning on 12/13/1980 SUN Rahu beginning on 04/19/1981 SUN Jupiter beginning on 03/13/1982 SUN Saturn beginning on 01/01/1983 SUN Mercury beginning on 12/13/1983		4th Cancer Moon o Saturn e-- ♇
10th Capricorn	SUN Ketu beginning on 10/19/1984 SUN Venus beginning on 02/25/1985 MOON Moon beginning on 02/25/1986 MOON Mars beginning on 12/25/1986 MOON Rahu beginning on 07/25/1987 MOON Jupiter beginning on 01/25/1989		5th Leo
9th Sagittarius	8th Scorpio Jupiter Rx Te++	7th Libra Ketu Rx	6th Virgo Mars ♆

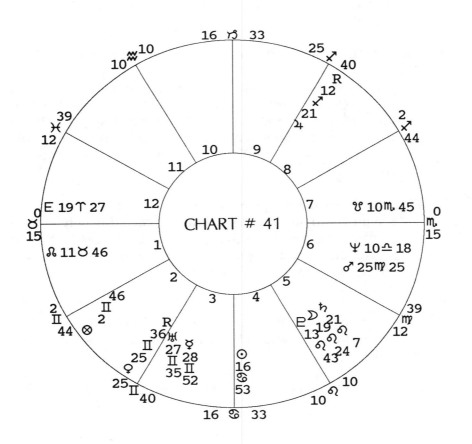

CHART # 41

progress together by solar arc. This compounds IC issues.

- In his navamsha, Jupiter rules his 7th, and it is in the same house with Saturn and the SN.

➤ List key eclipse issues:

- Natally, his besieged Dasa moon (19-LE-25) had been hit by not just one, but two, PNE's. One occurred about a month after his conception and was exactly square at 19-SC-36. The other was his final one before birth and was conjunct at 18-LE-22 (a little wide). At the death, P3 Pluto was in the midst of this at 18-LE-00.

- N. Mercury (28-GE-52) is with his N. Venus/Uranus conjunction. The last T. solar eclipse before the death was square it at 29-VI-34 while P3 Uranus was conjunct at 29-GE-32. At the funeral there was another eclipse at 28-SA-20, again right on Mercury. He mentioned that this event totally rearranged his thinking about life.

- His P3 tNN (Bhukti planet) was at 13-AR-54. The last T. lunar eclipse before his wife's death was at 13-AR-22.

- His N. tNN (Bhukti factor) was at 11-TA-46. Conjunct the south end in the 7th was T. Pluto at 11-SC-36.

➤ List the other key timers:

Fundamentally, there was a powerful T-square formation involving many factors at 25-26 degrees of the tropical mutables, thus setting off the latent implication of this particular Venus/Mars square.

- His P3 MC was at 26-GE conjunct his N. Venus/Uranus and square his N. Mars.

- This means that his P3 Sun/IC opposed and squared at 26-SA. Note that T. Uranus was conjunct this P3 IC at 26-SA (as was the T. Sun).

- P3 Mars had come around so that it was once again at its natal point — but one degree beyond at 26-VI-48. His P3 Asc was conjunct this Mars TTM (26-VI-47) and perfectly square to T. Uranus TTM at 26-SA-49 (the perfectibility of this formation contributed to my 45 second birth correction).

- Venus was in his 3rd, and a T. Mercury/Saturn conjunction was just entering his sidereal 9th house (tropically both were at 23+ of SA).

- It's also worth noting that the P2 Sun/IC was at 24-LE applying to P2 Saturn was at 25-LE.

CASE 6 (Miscarriage plus a Child's Suicide)

This case is that of a successful businesswoman I met at a party while working on this chapter. She had a miscarriage on 1/26/88, and her son (b. 5/3/77) apparently committed suicide at age 15 in his room on 3/29/92. I say "apparently" because there were no prior clues to this at all, and the bullet went directly into the front of his forehead at an angle directly perpendicular to his body which is not a typical angle for a gunshot-related suicide. She divorced her husband shortly thereafter. She has an older daughter born 2/15/75 with whom she has problems, but perhaps no worse than most. Her birth data is: 04-Jan-1955 @ 6:10 AM CST in Mexico City, MX 19N24 & 99W09. For the record, I have added 1 minute to her recorded TOB, i.e., I'm using 6:11 AM (see chart # 42).

As a natal signature we see the Moon is in the 5th house of children in a Mars-ruled sign (as, for that matter, is Venus, the planet of love, in her 12th square Pluto). And the 5th house Moon is perfectly opposed (within 9 minutes) by a N. Saturn strengthened through its exaltation status. Neptune is also in the same house opposing the Moon. The ruler of her 1st is an exalted Jupiter in the 8th which is exactly conjunct Uranus (on the positive side, this has brought her many 8th house adventures and quite a lot of money through speculative activities and real estate).

In the navamsha, Saturn in the 1st once again opposes the Moon in the maraka 7th. In addition, in the navamsha the Moon is fallen and conjunct Mercury (sharing rulership of the 5th with the 2nd) in a mutual reception with maraka Mars (as ruler of the 7th) in the maraka 2nd. This complex in the navamsha helps explain why she both gave birth to the suicidal son and had the miscarriage during Mercury Bhuktis. It may also be of interest to note that there was an eclipse only 4 days after her birth less than 2 degrees from her N. Mercury (although, again, this is a little wide

4th Pisces	5th Aries Moon +	6th Taurus	7th Gemini Ketu E
3rd Aquarius Mars Te–	MARS Saturn beginning on 05/22/1975 MARS Mercury beginning on 07/01/1976 MARS Ketu beginning on 06/28/1977 MARS Venus beginning on 11/25/1977 MARS Sun beginning on 01/25/1979 MARS Moon beginning on 06/01/1979 RAHU Rahu beginning on 01/01/1980	8th Cancer Jupiter Rx E
2nd Capricorn	RAHU Jupiter beginning on 09/13/1982 RAHU Saturn beginning on 02/07/1985 RAHU Mercury beginning on 12/13/1987 RAHU Ketu beginning on 07/01/1990 RAHU Venus beginning on 07/19/1991 RAHU Sun beginning on 07/19/1994	9th Leo ♓ ♇
1st Sagittarius Ascendant Rahu – Sun T Mercury –	12th Scorpio Venus +	11th Libra Saturn E Ψ	10th Virgo

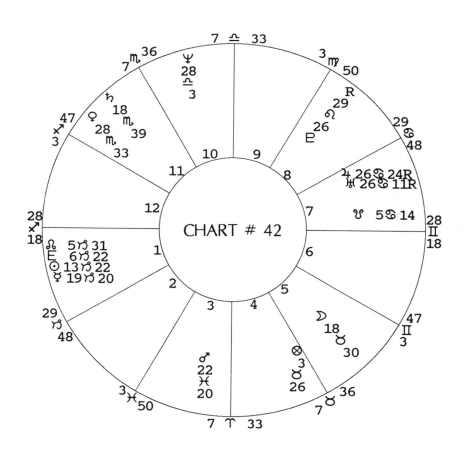

for my taste).

Let's give a two paragraph look at the miscarriage. She has 28-SA-18 rising. On the date of miscarriage, T. Saturn was at 28-SA-18 (i.e., conjunct
TTM), and T. Uranus was at 29-SA-04. These late mutable degrees caused
me to recall that I actually wrote an article in early 1988 fully dedicated to
documenting all the things that happened to people I knew with significant placements at 28 degrees of the tropical mutables. Because one
of the things that added to this was the odd fact that the last prior new
Moon (12/20/87) was at 28-SA-20 (and, in this woman's case, the immediately prior new Moon was exactly square N. Neptune and conjunct
her P3 Uranus and P2 Asc at 28-CA/CP respectively). Her P2 Moon was
also square her P2 IC within less than a degree.

I didn't realize until writing this paragraph that this event occurred only
a month after the wife's death for the person in the case discussed immediately above. So the very same eclipses should have hit exactly again,
and they did. This is especially to be expected since these stressful events
all occurred during her nodal Dasa. For example, the last T. lunar eclipse
was at 13-AR-22. This is exactly square (TTM) her N. Sun at 13-CP-22
which is in the 1st with the node.

The last T. solar eclipse was at 29-VI-22 which squares her Asc. For that
matter, the immediately prior 3rd eclipse was at 8-AR-18 which puts it
less than 1 degree from her Desc and exactly square to T. Neptune. I
could go on, such as the fact that her P3 Asc was conjunct N. Mars, but
hopefully you are getting the idea at this point.

Now let's now look at her son's suicide. Some powerful natal weaknesses
regarding children have already been noted in her chart. This death occurred during her Rahu Dasa and Venus Bhukti. Considering the Dasa,
let's focus in on the volume of exact nodal/eclipse activity involved with
this death starting with the last five T. eclipses during the prior year (listing backward from the most recent):

A.	13-CP-51	=	right on her N. Sun of 13-CP-22 in 1st
B.	29-GE-03	=	on her Desc within a degree (28-GE-18)
(note:	28-VI-24	=	last full Moon before the death — square horizon)
C.	03-AQ-16	=	conjunct her P2 Asc of 03-AQ-31
D.	18-CA-59	=	opposing N. Mercury of 19-CP-20 in 1st
E.	05-CP-00	=	N. mNN of 05-CP-14

> =   T. mNN of 04-CP-59 (karmic recycling)
> =   P3 Venus (Bhukti planet) at 04-CA-50
> =   square to P2 Moon at 05-LI-56

We also see some other exact angle timers: The P3 MC is conjunct P3 Mars TTM, and T. Saturn is exactly square the P2 MC.

In addition, special stress to N. Mercury from children (noted above in the navamsha comments) registers again in two ways. First, T. Neptune is conjunct N. Mercury in the main chart within 1/2 a degree, and conjunct T. Uranus by slightly more than a degree. To bring back the nodes for one last time, P3 Mercury was conjunct the P3 mSN within 8 minutes.

These cases, in the context of all the other examples and discussion in this book, should provide you with an excellent set of focus clues concerning how to determine whether and when a formerly unexpected death of someone else can nevertheless be anticipated from within your own chart. The mosaic is not simple-minded. Yet, at the same time, it is certainly not unclear to those readers with the mental energy to unwrap the symbolism.

SUICIDE

There is a tendency to think that suicide is a rare phenomenon, but that is somewhat untrue. For example, in the United States suicide is the second leading cause of death among children and adolescents. A lot of suicide may also go undocumented, and an example of this was suggested by sociologist David Phillips in the 1993 Winter issue of *Suicide and Life-Threatening Behavior*, the journal of the American Association of Suicidology. Phillips was investigating the relatively low official suicide rates of blacks and females which he felt was counter-intuitive.

In an earlier study of California death certificates, he set markers at the symbolically important ages of 30, 40, 50, 60 and so on. This study demonstrated more suicidal peaking around those ages. Now, when he looked at other causes of death, he found the same type of peaking in certain types of cases such as single-car crashes, drug overdoses and pedestrian deaths, yet he did not find similar peaking from natural causes or multi-car crashes.

A further examination by race and sex showed that the peaks were especially high among blacks and women. Of course, some people might suggest, for example, that living in a large American city demonstrates behavior which is inherently more suicidal than living elsewhere, but I think I won't get into that!

The extensive legal and media attention currently being given to the activities of Dr. Jack Kevorkian has also helped elevate this topic into the arena of public discussion. Suicide motivation seems to be of two types: A) those which are motivated by intractable physical pain or the near total collapse of physical systems, and B) those which are motivated by an unwillingness of the personality to submit to the demands of their soul.

The reason the former category of cases will not be discussed here is because, as noted by Dr. Ira Byock, current ethics chairman of the Academy of Hospice Physicians, there is no reason that these cases should ever occur at all. He asserts "unequivocally" that *all* cases of physical distress associated with death can be treated symptomatically, without exception, by a competent medical team. As he has written, "The requisite knowledge, medicines, techniques and technology all exist; they are simply not being applied." Dying need not equal suffering, and therefore dying need not be artificially stimulated.

He has further written that, "The surprising fact is that in the midst of their dying, many people are able to experience not merely comfort but an increased sense of well-being, which often includes a deep sense of connectedness to others and the world. This is not some religious tract or wistful, new-age thinking. It is the direct experience of clinicians who are privileged to care for the dying in modern hospice-like settings. These words will sound odd to many modern American ears. Stories of wondrous dyings have infrequently been told and do not lend themselves to sound bites or headlines."

But the latter category of cases is much more common, and these often include people referred to as suffering from, among other things, a quality of the spirit labeled "depression" or "the dark night of the soul." Depression is often thought to be chemically manageable, and in other cases some people do seem to be able to work their own way out of it, although not without a huge effort. Depression is also sometimes linked to a nutrient deficiency. It is therefore interesting that certain ascending systems of metaphysical thinking assign a specific spiritual quality to each of the chemical elements. So-called "aromatherapy" also conceptually links into this.

But, in fact, many suicides seem to be motivated by fear of necessary change brought on by transitional life events with which the person simply does not want to deal: the death of someone else, loss of job or fortune, performance failure against expectation, rejection in love, and so forth. If a competent astrologer can do only one useful thing, it is to help a distraught person center him or herself by, among other things, learning the exact date when such acutely stressful phenomena will positively be *over*.

In cases such as this, I hope that the reader would guide any potentially suicidal person to seek as much empathetic assistance as possible, since there is no tragedy that has not befallen many others. Consider guiding them to some of the classical spiritual books that discuss the topic of "the world of the dead." I'm personally thinking of Tibetan and Hindu books in particular where knowledge of this realm ("bardos" and "lokas" respectively) was derived not through alleged revelation or abstract philosophical speculation, but through observed experience after conscious physical induction of the full death condition itself. This is only farfetched to those who are ignorant of the scientific observations and evidence that already support this as a fact.

Clearly, spiritual pain is a quality of the soul and not the body or personality. Its function is to stimulate spiritual growth. This type of suffering does not become unreal or go away just because the body has been destroyed. Suicide only extends suffering since, now that the finite body is gone, there is no more brake on time, nor a way to effect a tangible result. Hinduism calls this condition "Hell" (where, speaking somewhat metaphorically, time slows down even more, and space becomes more dense) — but without the Christian additive of eternal damnation. From the Tibetan Buddhist perspective, I would particularly like to recommend a modern classic titled *The Tibetan Book of Living and Dying* by Sogyal Rinpoche.

It is specifically the case that here on the earth is the place and time to deal with the event cycles the soul has pre-programmed. The personality ego does not own the soul, but vice versa. And the soul will never kill itself. Consequently, the personality ego has no right to artificially terminate the soul's intended cycles and experiences. Ultimately, there are no other options except engagement. However, all this proscriptive commentary notwithstanding, it is a much higher value to make no judgement upon those who commit suicide. It is the most foolish arrogance to do otherwise, and in any case, all judgements polarize and hence artificially sustain a false separation.

Astrological Indicators of Suicide

When a highly-regarded astrological researcher killed himself in 1991, certain related circumstances hardened my resolve to further investigate this whole topic (see his case discussed first below). After collecting over 50 timed charts on "suicide by gunshot" from what was then called the Rodden/ISAR database, I subsequently lectured on this topic in early 1992. In the course of preparing for this lecture, one of the things I did was review a New York suicide study as discussed by Nona Gwynn Press in a 1978 issue of the *Journal of Geocosmic Research* (Vol 2 No 2).

This was a statistical study composed of 311 timed New York City suicides that occurred from 1969 to 1973 for people born after 1930. There was a similarly-sized and well-constructed control group and, as documented in the study, many knowledgeable efforts were made to assure statistical validity. The analysis was purely tropical, used placidus house cusps, the ten traditional plus eight Uranian planets and the four major asteroids.

Looking for a natal signature, topics investigated included: signs, houses, elements, qualities, rulership, interception, classic aspects plus other angular separation issues, close midpoints, specific degrees, and certain formations such as T-squares and grand trines. They also investigated other factors such as various assertions made by C.E.O. Carter about suicides, 8th harmonic planetary pictures, formulae/personal points for suicide or violent death as given by Witte-Niggermann, Gauquelin sectors, and a limited number of other geocentric factors distributed along the ecliptic.

In the end, this careful study concluded that, at least to that point, nothing of statistical significance presented itself relative to the controls. Without going into it, I think there is a major philosophical flaw in large number statistical approaches to the study of timed astrological events (as opposed to very-focused large-number natal studies). In practical terms, no chart can ever be the same and, even if it were possible, different souls would possess any hypothetically identical chart overlays (recall the simple issue of twins). To play on a common analogy, every death is a snowflake, but every snowflake is different (actually, every snowflake isn't different, but you get the idea...).

In monitored tests, astrologers have generally performed poorly trying to distinguish suicidal from non-suicidal natal charts, although they do a little better when the date of death is known. I think this may relate more to the general quality of people who label themselves astrologers, and also to the likely fact that they have not studied many suicidal charts (if they have studied any) to develop a conditioned feel for the critical considerations.

And, as you can see from the thrust of this book, factors traditionally reviewed may not be the stronger ones. Progressed positions and stations (emphasizing tertiary), eclipses on angles and on key progressed factors (especially during key Dasa/Bhukti periods), use of the sidereal zodiac (with a big emphasis upon planetary strength and weakness), attention to planets with maraka status, pre-natal eclipses and the like are, to my mind, more likely to lead to confident conclusions in this area.

By the way, a follow-up article by Ruth Hale Oliver in the same issue of The Journal mentioned above made a number of interesting observations that could impact upon any expectation of a suicide. Examples are:

Catholics have a relatively high rate of murder and low rate of suicide. Jewish people, Japanese and Scandinavians have the reverse.

 The affluent and educated tend more towards suicide than murder; less affluent tend towards the reverse.

 One large study across 86 cities found that murder and suicide rates varied inversely "as if there were a fixed amount of aggression in a given population."

[This resonates somewhat with a remark of well-known Hindu astrologer, James Braha, to the effect that, given the statistical inevitability of Mars and Saturn aspects upon the 5th house, the problem of natural infant mortality in poor countries may work out instead through abortion in more affluent countries, as if a certain fixed amount of aggression against childhood — essentially a "natural" statistical distribution of derangement to the 5th house, which seems perfectly likely — is destined to occur.]

 In her own studies on this matter, Oliver concluded that "a suicide-prone person will not take his life, or attempt to, unless he is under extraordinary progressed pressures... In addition there are some people who are not entirely suicide-prone at birth, but who come into such a period by progression... (and) not every ordinary person is capable of murder or suicide. Both the murderer and the suicide must have an overage of aggression in their charts, no matter how deeply repressed it may be..."

In the earlier chapter on longevity, I mentioned the Hindu belief that various places upon the earth also have karma. Perhaps Finland is a good example of that since it consistently has one of the world's highest suicide rates. It is a rich, modern, clean, efficient, homogeneous country with very little crime or other apparent social grounds for despair. The long dark winters, level of alcoholism, economic and political problems, and so forth can all be duplicated or exceeded in other countries with no comparable level of suicide.

But is it not intriguing that even in their most ancient national folk tales, the level of aggression is much higher than average, and many of the heroes of these folk stories committed suicide? It is also the case that the other countries (Hungary and Estonia) that compete with Finland for its dubious distinction share an ancient linguistic link (Finno–Ugric) even though they are apparently unrelated genetically. So the only apparent suicidal link at this time is through mythology and the making of symbols. This simply will not pass muster in this "modern" era, so "scientific" inquiry continues.

Let's now look at some individual cases.

CASE 1 (Suicide of Famous Researcher)

In the Summer of 1991, the alleged chart of a famous research scientist and prolific author, who committed suicide near 05/20/91, was reprinted in an issue of a newsletter published by a well–known astrological organization. This is when his body was discovered in his home; he may have died a day or two earlier. I had met this person about five times and therefore had somewhat of a feel for his general temperament.

Many people in the "top tier" of the world astrological community told me he shot himself, so I assume it is true. A less–connected tier speculated that he may have used some kind of drug because of an allegedly angular Neptune (this is implausible for reasons that follow). This suicide was further allegedly to be related to some relationship difficulties (he had recently remarried). I took one look at this chart and felt certain it was wrong (see wrong chart # 43A b. 13–Nov–1928 @ "11:20 PM GMT" in 2E20 and 48N52).

Even at a glance, how could anyone think this chart could commit suicide? And, considering the placement of the transiting outer planets, where was the build up in overpowering pressure to make a person of his famously unrelenting will and patience destroy himself? And why on that date?

This led to four quick hypotheses:

➤ A natal chart doesn't have to demonstrate a suicidal "signature," whatever that is, to commit suicide (i.e., the fundamental concept that something has to be "promised," or fundamentally latent, in the natal chart before it can actualize is *not* valid), or

➤ This well–known Western astrology organization did not know what a suicide chart even should, in theory, look like, or

➤ I don't know what I'm doing, or

➤ There is otherwise something wrong or missing. Or perhaps there

8th Pisces	9th Aries		10th Taurus	11th Gemini	
	Jupiter Rx	T++	Rahu S	Mars Dx	T--
♓					♇

7th Aquarius	SUN	Venus	beginning on 05/30/1979	12th Cancer	
	MOON	Moon	beginning on 05/30/1980		
	MOON	Mars	beginning on 03/30/1981		
	MOON	Rahu	beginning on 10/30/1981		
	MOON	Jupiter	beginning on 04/30/1983		
	MOON	Saturn	beginning on 08/30/1984		
	MOON	Mercury	beginning on 03/30/1986		
6th Capricorn	MOON	Ketu	beginning on 08/30/1987	1st Leo	
	MOON	Venus	beginning on 03/30/1988	Ascendant	
	MOON	Sun	beginning on 11/30/1989		
	MARS	Mars	beginning on 05/30/1990		
	MARS	Rahu	beginning on 10/27/1990		♆
	MARS	Jupiter	beginning on 11/15/1991		

5th Sagittarius	4th Scorpio		3rd Libra		2nd Virgo
Venus -	Ketu	S--	Mercury	++	
	Moon	f	Sun	fe	
	Saturn	--			

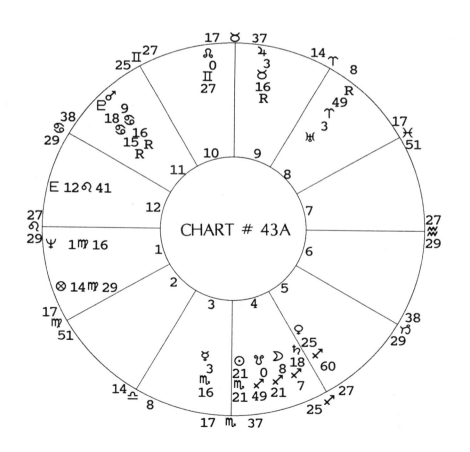

CHART # 43A

was a combination of the above.

Scraping around for some reasons why a Western astrologer might think this could be a suicidal chart, I observe that Mars in the Placidus 11th is closely quincunx the Moon and widely separating from Uranus in the Placidus 8th. In addition the Sun, as joint ruler of the Placidus 1st (personal environment) and the Placidus 12th (self-undoing), was somewhat angular near the IC. This is often referred to as an "end of the matter" point but this hardly has the supporting qualities to make it so. You can see that this is all quite wimpy stuff compared to the power and clarity of what you have hopefully digested to this point.

This scientist was a ranking tennis player, yet Neptune, which hardly promotes physical vitality, is only 4 degrees away from his alleged Asc, and his Mars was allegedly fallen (in tropical Cancer) although Mars does seemingly rule the Placidus 8th (which a Westerner would think has to do with death). Generally this overall pattern was entirely too deficient and unfocused to persuade me that such a mentally-tough person had a capacity for self-destruction. Although not an astrologer, he had been pounded decade after decade by the scientific, and pseudo-scientific, community (for his statistical work that established correlations between celestial and terrestrial patterns), and he unrelentingly returned to the fray.

In frustration, I called Lois Rodden who, as I have noted earlier, takes birth time accuracy very seriously. Lo and behold, she had a different time of birth for this person — 10:15 vs. 11:20 — and she was completely confident of her source (see corrected chart # 43B). This TOB pushed Neptune off the Asc and also makes his exact Jupiter/Mercury opposition nearly angular. This would make sense for someone who has published numerous books, since angularity promotes the externalization of symbols associated with the planet(s) involved (in this case, a high volume of writing).

It was also odd, as I see in so many tropical charts, that here we have a person who was an intense researcher, lecturer and prolific writer, yet he had no planets in air signs (said to rule communication in the West). In the West this deficiency is rationalized away as "over-compensation," but I consider this one of many unacceptable behaviors of Western astrology which allows believers to have it both ways.

When we set up the sidereal chart, a number of issues start to come into sharper focus.

9th Pisces	10th Aries Jupiter Rx T++	11th Taurus Rahu D	12th Gemini Mars Dx RT--
♓			♇
8th Aquarius	SUN Ketu beginning on 10/27/1979 SUN Venus beginning on 03/03/1980 MOON Moon beginning on 03/03/1981 MOON Mars beginning on 01/03/1982 MOON Rahu beginning on 08/03/1982 MOON Jupiter beginning on 02/03/1984 MOON Saturn beginning on 06/03/1985	1st Cancer Ascendant
7th Capricorn	MOON Mercury beginning on 01/03/1987 MOON Ketu beginning on 06/03/1988 MOON Venus beginning on 01/03/1989 MOON Sun beginning on 09/03/1990 MARS Mars beginning on 03/03/1991 MARS Rahu beginning on 07/30/1991	2nd Leo ♆
6th Sagittarius Venus -	5th Scorpio Ketu D -- Moon f Saturn --	4th Libra Mercury ++ Sun fe	3rd Virgo

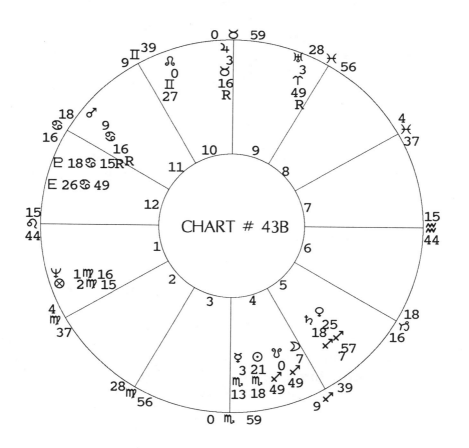

➤ Jupiter is now in Aries and Mercury is now in Libra. These signs are both "great friends" to these planets. And, by Hindu logic, both planets mutually aspect each other in a constructive fashion since such an opposition between two such benefits is typically good excluding other considerations (and note, by the way, that the Sun and Mars are also now in an air sign).

➤ With Mars now out of the non-suicidal 11th and into the self-undoing 12th we take an even closer look at associated natal issues. We note that when this person was born, Mars had almost no velocity and was essentially stationary. As I've noted before, Hindu theory states that any stationary or very slow-moving planet takes on tremendous strength, and this strength is for good or bad depending on its sign, house, relationships, Dasa/Bhukti periods, etc. Here a powerful Mars is in the 12th causing clear problems of "deployment."

➤ Mars is also in the sign of a "great enemy" (Gemini). In addition, the tight quincunx from stationary Mars to the Moon is much more important because the Moon now becomes the ruler of the 1st. Hindu astrology doesn't make reference to a quincunx per se (except as a full Mars aspect in one particular direction). But it does emphasize that it is bad for astrological factors to have a mutual relationship which partakes of 6th and 8th house symbolism.

➤ Recalling that Mars aspects the 4th, 7th and 8th houses from itself, stationary Mars now aspects his 7th. This creates kujadosa (a condition of difficulty as pertains to relationships), but the 7th is stronger than the 1st because Mars is exalted in Capricorn (his 7th) but fallen in Cancer (his 1st).

➤ Saturn rules both the 7th and the 8th, and is also in the sign of a "great enemy". The Moon, as ruler of his 1st, is now fallen in a martial sign (Scorpio) and bracketed ("besieged") between the distressed 7th house ruler and the SN. The fallen Moon is also located in a Saturn-owned nakshatra or lunar mansion.

➤ This is not the end of the Moon's suffering across the relationship axis, for when we glance at the supporting navamsha chart (not shown) the Moon *again* is fallen in Scorpio (this time as ruler of the 7th). And further, Mars, as the dispositor of Scorpio, is in a maraka (the 2nd), and is conjunct Saturn, ruler of the 1st.

➤ In the main chart, the two rulers of the 2nd and 7th are respectively Saturn, which is conjunct the ruler of the 1st, and a fallen Sun in Libra.

➤ In addition to alleged problems with love (5th) I was told that he was also having recent problems duplicating the results of his life's work (10th). Mars rules both the 5th and the 10th and is damaged and frustrated in the 12th. So much seems to point to Mars which, despite various Western attempts to rehabilitate it, has always been the classical "causal" killer of ancient astrology.

The next question is one of timing. Why did he kill himself between May 18-20 of 1991? Almost three months before his death, T. Pluto had been applying pressure to within one degree of his N. Sun, but by mid-May turned away and, at his death, had a separating orb of 3 degrees (an unacceptably wide orb, and separating besides). At his death, T. Pluto was at 18-SC-45, so I didn't give this factor much regard.

But note here that only the day before he was born, there was a solar eclipse at 19-SC-46, and Pluto *did* recently hit this point. [Also note that he had a PNE within 1/2 a degree of his Venus, and the first full Moon (14 days) after his birth was a total lunar eclipse. So, like Elvis Presley, his birth was bracketed by eclipses.] But, so what? People get Pluto transits all the time and live to tell about it. What was so different about this one?

The answer is found in his Dasa/Bhukti listing where only two months before his death he had moved into his Mars Dasa. This focusing of an intense spotlight on this stationary 12th house Mars set off all the factors and linkages noted in the natal analysis above.

On the date of death, P2 Uranus was also exactly conjunct the P2 maraka Desc (thus, by the way, further reinforcing the validity of the revised TOB), and the P2 mean node was exactly conjunct the P2 Placidus 12th cusp. The P2 Moon was in his 8th. On the date of death, his P3 Venus (natally opposed by his stationary Mars) was exactly octile the ruler of the 1st (the Moon).

There were many supporting transits. For example:

➤ Saturn, karaka of death and also ruler of his 7th and 8th, was now, in fact, stationary in his 7th.

➤ Mars had just entered his 12th a day or two earlier (and was now exactly conjunct his East Point).

➤ Venus was exactly conjunct the stationary Mars in the 12th.

➤ The Sun was exactly conjunct his first PNE at 28–TA.

➤ The last two eclipses before his death were at his Venus degree (25) and his Mars degree (9), and some older books think this sets up a significant resonance even though the signs are not the same.

CASE 2 (Deranged Metabolic Suicide — 900 lb. Man)

While offbeat, I thought it might be interesting to take a look at the issue of death from a suicidal eating disorder because such a focus further reinforces key points regarding the fundamental Hindu proposition that "good" planets such as Venus, Jupiter or a bright Moon can go "bad" from a functional point of view.

These three planets are probably considered "good" in the first place because they support anabolism. In nature, there is nothing inherently "bad" about catabolism (cat kills bird). It is the illusion of loss through decay and death that is regarded as bad (your cat killed *my* bird). Yet if Mars were not to "tear down," Saturn to "grind down," Neptune to "dissolve," the Sun to "burn up" and the like, the world would rapidly be overrun from the many toxic byproducts caused by too much of a "good" thing (such an aggression-free world reminds me of the saccharine state of being often promoted by female kindergarten teachers and many metaphysical practitioners).

This is also true with regard to our own biological ecology. In discussing this book with a friend of mine, he mentioned hearing death referred to as a "cosmic colonic" or "radical fast," which plays on the same idea. The following sample case demonstrates how such a deadly condition might present itself.

The chart of the "fattest man in the world" (b. 29–March–1896 @ 5:30 AM MST in Florence, AZ 33N02 & 111W23) was identified by Dr. H. L. Cornell on page 239 of his *Encyclopedia of Medical Astrology*. This man weighed 900 pounds when he died at age 30 on 5/27/26, and he gained

150 of that in the last 10 days of his life.

[Parenthetically, this chart was reprinted by another tropical astrologer who wanted to highlight the absence of earth signs in the tropical chart, plus the heavy water emphasis with almost no countervailing fire. The objective was to characterize this as a low–burn saturation/accumulation metabolism with a highly compensatory craving for the earth element. But from the point of view of the Hindu chart, the 900–pound man does not at all lack earth placements, although he still remains very low on fire.

This dichotomy becomes even more puzzling to me upon noting, via lectures and text, that this astrologer does element diagnosis from the tropical zodiac, yet proposes excellent remedies heavily based upon Indian ayurveda which is itself grounded in the sidereal zodiac. For readers interested in ayurveda, I'd like to express my personal opinion that the analytic dimension should always overlap the prescriptive dimension.]

But getting back to factors more specific to death timing, as opposed to underlying medical pathology, let me note that I do not accept the given birth time of 5:30. I have therefore rectified it to 8 minutes earlier (5:22), and this may be one of the greatest birth time adjustments proposed in this book (when not discussing rectification per se). As usual, the reader is welcome to disagree. My rationale is that not only does this put T. Mars at death exactly on the N. Asc (17–PI) and almost TTM; it is further confirmed by the fact that it also puts the P3 IC exactly TTM on N. Jupiter (see chart # 44). When *two* angles hit exactly like that, and on the appropriate symbolism, it clearly merits consideration.

As I will discuss shortly, Jupiter is very key to the basic dysfunction in this chart (in fact, Cornell emphasized this when discussing the topic of fat in general). Therefore it should invariably be flagged by a key angle (the IC) at death — and this is so. The time and location of death was not noted, and this will marginally affect the rectification, including relocated lunar returns, even if he died only on the other side of town from where he was born. For his death, I have arbitrarily used noon at the location of birth although this certainly won't impact progressions.

The original 5:30 is an inherently suspicious time to begin with — especially for a 19th century chart when spring–driven clocks needed much more frequent adjustment, when synchronization with Greenwich was much less necessary (especially in smaller towns without railroads), and

2nd Pisces Sun	3rd Aries	4th Taurus	5th Gemini
		Ψ ♇	
1st Aquarius Rahu Rx Venus T≈ Ascendant Mercury Te-	MARS Moon beginning on 04/14/1904 RAHU Rahu beginning on 11/14/1904 RAHU Jupiter beginning on 07/26/1907 RAHU Saturn beginning on 12/20/1909 RAHU Mercury beginning on 10/26/1912 RAHU Ketu beginning on 05/14/1915 RAHU Venus beginning on 06/02/1916	6th Cancer Jupiter SE	
12th Capricorn Mars E	RAHU Sun beginning on 06/02/1919 RAHU Moon beginning on 04/26/1920 RAHU Mars beginning on 10/26/1921 JUPITER Jupiter beginning on 11/14/1922 JUPITER Saturn beginning on 01/02/1925 JUPITER Mercury beginning on 07/14/1927	7th Leo Ketu Rx ---
11th Sagittarius	10th Scorpio ⚷	9th Libra Saturn Rx E≈	8th Virgo Moon

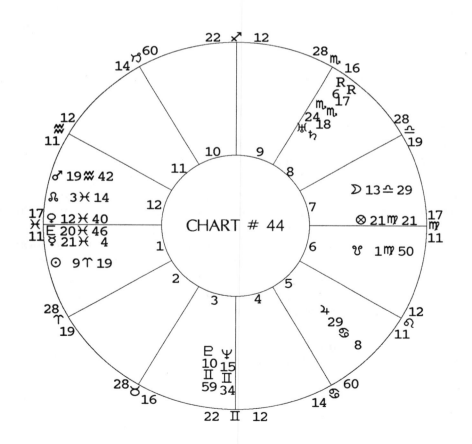

CHART # 44

the general attitude towards time was much more casual than the current era. In any case, this slight rectification has no noticeable effect upon either the tropical or sidereal charts from a purely natal point of view.

Somewhat coincidentally this moves lazy Venus much closer to the Asc (orb is now 4+ degrees). Westerners would call this a 12th house Venus, but Hindu astrology has it in the 1st. This also has Neptune squaring the horizon within 1 degree. As you now clearly know, an exact TOB is necessary for correct angles which is always where the important action is.

A first glance at this chart suggests very impressive planetary powers. For example:

➤ It's a full moon chart which is considered very desirable in Hindu astrology.

> But: the malefic Sun is in the house of food disorders (2nd) and the Moon, ruler of the stomach, is bright in the 8th. The 2nd and 8th houses themselves are very weak via the analytical method of ashtakavarga (the low bindu count is something left to other books, but I just wanted to mention it), yet they contain both lights. The Sun, as ruler of the maraka 7th, is placed in the maraka 2nd and tightly tri-octile to Uranus. And, in the language of co-dependency, powerful "enablers" (7th) must surely have helped him kill himself by delivering massive quantities of food (2nd) to wherever he was, since he clearly would have no mobility.

➤ Powerful Mars is exalted in the 12th in Capricorn within 1/2 a degree of its highest exaltation point (28-CP sidereally).

> But: the suicidal researcher discussed earlier also had a strong Mars in the 12th where a strong Mars typically does quite poorly. From the 12th, the great strength of this Mars attacks the 6th (the house of health owned by the stomach-ruling planet) where Mars is therefore at its weakest even as Saturn closely squares this strength / weakness axis of Mars. In addition, Mars aspects the 3rd, the house specifically ruling desire (and the 6th which rules appetite). Since Mars in fact rules the 3rd, this strong aspect greatly strengthens desires (although deployed in a 12th house self-undoing way).

➤ Jupiter is also powerful since it is less than 3 degrees from its highest exaltation degree in the 6th. Furthermore it has almost no velocity since it was stationary just 5 days before birth.

But the question is: "powerful" how? He moved into his Jupiter Dasa at age 26. A totally stationary natal Jupiter created absurdly extravagant financial expansion for Donald Trump during his Jupiter period. There is a similar 2nd house expansion effect here but with a 6/12 focus. In addition, Jupiter is only stimulated to extreme action by being under full assault from the powerful Mars noted above.

➤ Saturn, ruler of the 1st, is yet a 3rd exalted planet, in this case in Libra in the 9th.

But: powerful Saturn is in a mutual reception with the nearly angular Venus. As Hindu astrology does not attribute to Saturn the power to trine, nearly angular Venus suffers from this association with Saturn (and, for that matter, from Venus' close square to the Neptune/Pluto conjunction). However, since Venus and Saturn are "friends" through their natural respective rulership and exaltation in Libra, the suffering, in this case, is in terms of excessive anabolism.

Progressions

For timing factors, we will see that the Moon (stomach), Venus (anabolism) or Jupiter (excess) was involved in *every* single progressed and eclipse factor at death. In terms of death transits, I have already noted that Mars was exactly conjunct the Asc. Note that T. Pluto was also square the Moon within less than a quarter of a degree.

The following progressions (involving a general benefic) for the birth location were *all* exact within less than a quarter of a degree. Several are within 2 minutes, and some have no orb at all. The P2 date was 4/28/96, and the P3 date was 5/6/97.

- P2 *Moon* conjunct N. Uranus
- P2 Mars conjunct N. *Venus*

- P3 *Moon* tri–octile N. Uranus
- P3 *Moon* conjunct the N. Part of (Mis)fortune
- P3 Saturn octile N. *Moon*
- P3 *Venus* octile P3 Neptune
- P3 Pluto square N. *Venus*
- P3 IC conjunct N. *Jupiter.*

Eclipses

The last two (non–partial) PNE's were 11–PI–27 (sensitizing N. Venus at 12–PI–19), and 24–AQ–31 (square N. Uranus at 24–SC–06). At death, his P2 Pluto was perfectly square the former at 11–GE–29, and his P2 Moon was exactly square the latter at 24–SC–10.

The last two T. eclipses prior to death were 23–CP–21 and 08–LE–06. Matching these at death was P3 Mars at 23–CA–24, the P2 MC at 21–CP–36 (relocation have thrown it 2 degrees), and his P2 Sun was at 08–LE–50.

There was a P3 eclipse about 18 months before death at 28–LE–56. Hitting this at death was P3 Saturn at 28–SC–20. A final eclipse clue is found in the fact that his last P3 station (Jupiter) 10 day/months before death was at 00–VI while his P2 SN at death was the same (00–VI).

In final reference to the malfunction of benefits, note now that some of the ancient Hindu astrology books say that, for Aquarius rising, the Moon and Jupiter are, in general, "functionally evil."

If this case was of interest, readers may also wish to study the death, at age 22, of someone whom the *Guinness Book of World Records* has called "The Biggest Man Ever Born" — although this apparently was not a case of self–induced death through excessive behavior. This is Robert Pershing Wadlow who was born 2/22/18 at 6:30 AM CST in Alton, IL (38N53 & 90W10), and who died on 6/27/40 at 1:30 AM in St. Louis. The Guinness book was apparently referring to height since he was one inch from being nine feet tall, but only made it to about 500 lbs.

CASE 3 (Anorexia Death of Karen Carpenter)

Just for contrast to Case 2, let's look at the example of famous singer Karen Carpenter who died of heart failure related to anorexia nervosa. The work of Carpenter and her brother Richard was extremely popular and, depending on the source, they were said to have sold somewhere between 30 and 80 (most commonly 60) million albums. Many of her smooth, hauntingly romantic, and often melancholic, melodies frequently were at the top of the charting services. Indeed, they had 16 consecutive Top 20 songs.

Anorexia is a lack or loss of appetite. Appetite itself is actually more accurately characterized as a psychological condition dependent on memory and associations, and this is as compared to hunger which is physiologically aroused by the body's actual need for food. It is said that anorexia can be brought about by foods, surroundings or people that are perceived as unattractive. So it could relate in part to a high aesthetic sensitivity. The designator "nervosa" further specifies that the loss of appetite is due to emotional states such as anxiety, irritation, anger and fear.

Heart failure is typically associated with it, but this is not due to any physical defect of the heart other than the absence of its nourishment. Overall, this condition is considered a "personality disorder." It is most frequently found in young adult females, and it is often associated with their ultimately irreversible obsession with losing weight.

Carpenter's registered birth data is 2–Mar–1950 @ 11:45 AM EST in New Haven, CT 41N19 & 72W56 (see chart # 45). Let me show you how hyper–sensitive this TOB is within the Hindu system. Carpenter died on 2/4/83. Using my birth ayanamsha for her of 23–04–27 and a birth time of 11:45, she was in the *last day* of a 20–year Venus Dasa (she was also in a Ketu Bhukti)! If she had been born only seconds earlier, then she would already have been one day into the new Dasa of the Sun at her death. We will be discussing the Sun shortly.

The natal chart presents some very strong features. First, Uranus is exactly conjunct the Asc (and if she were born one minute later it would be nearly perfect). This is going to powerfully associate her physiological environment with her nervous system. Second, Mars is conjunct the mSN (Bhukti factor) within 3 minutes, and this mutually disorders the stressful side of each factor, i.e., the SN contributes to the devascularization of Mars, and Mars pounds the sensitivity of the SN (in the navamsha, the Mars/SN conjunct was in her 6th). To add disorder, Neptune is the 3rd planet in the 4th house with these two.

A third observation is that the Moon, which rules the stomach, is powerful in its own sign in the 2nd house of appetite, and further it is only 2 degrees from Pluto. It also receives exceptional energy from the 8th. Saturn, by the way, is the exact midpoint of Neptune and Pluto, and all three are at the exact same degree (I'll be noting some key direct hits on Saturn). Reinhold Ebertin in his *Combination of Stellar Influences* says of Saturn as a Neptune/Pluto midpoint: "Dark foreboding, pessimism, self–torment. Grievous soul–suffering, the decline of one's powers and

10th Pisces Rahu Rx +	11th Aries	12th Taurus	1st Gemini Ascendant
9th Aquarius Sun ≈--	KETU Saturn beginning on 12/29/1960 KETU Mercury beginning on 02/08/1962 VENUS Venus beginning on 02/05/1963 VENUS Sun beginning on 06/05/1966 VENUS Moon beginning on 06/05/1967 VENUS Mars beginning on 02/05/1969 VENUS Rahu beginning on 04/05/1970 VENUS Jupiter beginning on 04/05/1973 VENUS Saturn beginning on 12/05/1975 VENUS Mercury beginning on 02/05/1979 VENUS Ketu beginning on 12/05/1981 SUN Sun beginning on 02/05/1983 SUN Moon beginning on 05/23/1983		2nd Cancer Moon 0
8th Capricorn Venus RT Jupiter f Mercury Re-			3rd Leo Saturn Rx T≈--
7th Sagittarius	6th Scorpio	5th Libra	4th Virgo Ketu Rx E Mars Rx --

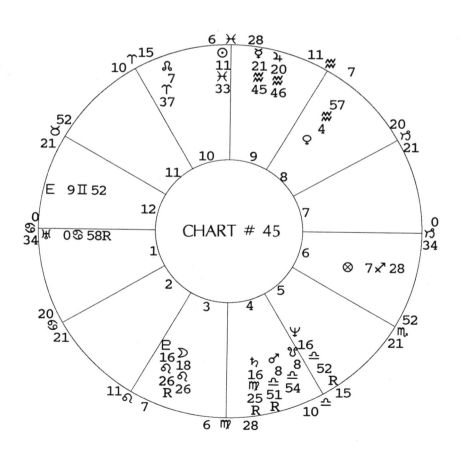

faculties with time."

On the positive side, we have to account for her beautiful musical talent, and what we find is the exact same formation observed in the (admittedly rectified) charts of Elvis Presley and Eric Clapton (see the chapter on rectification). That is, assuming the rectifications are valid, all have a Mercury-ruled sign rising, and Mercury again finds itself merged with Venus into the relatively rare rajayoga condition, and this combination is again found in the 8th house. This Mercury / Venus rajayoga aspects the 2nd containing the Moon in its own sign, and the 2nd in Hindu astrology rules both the voice and writing.

Mercury is also conjunct Jupiter within a degree, but Jupiter is fallen (this inversion of a benefic conjunct the ruler of the 1st reminds me of one of her tentative, and most well-known, songs titled "We've Only Just Begun To Live"). However, this does further strengthen the 2nd where Jupiter is exalted. By the way, the navamsha confirms her musical stature with Mercury, ruler of the 10th, actually in the 10th combined with Jupiter, the ruler of the 1st. Jupiter rules music in most pre-Neptunian systems, although Mercury is often assigned to music by Hindu astrology.

In discussing Eric Clapton, I mentioned in passing that the 3rd and 9th rule the performance of music. In Carpenter's chart we see that the Sun and Saturn (Saturn rules time which is what music is all about) are in each of these houses while they are also in a mutual reception[†].

Now let's look at some timing. Since Carpenter's body was commonly known to be grinding to a halt, we will expect more Saturn-type issues and less Uranus-type issues. For similar reasons, Pluto should not be so apparent except for the progressed tightening of its orb to the N. Moon.

Starting with Venus, the 20-year Dasa planet, by P3 it was now at 6-CA-39 and, in fact, conjunct Uranus at 7-CA-4. Notice that this is now nearly square her N. Mars/SN conjunction at 8-LI-54. This 4-planet square was set off by the last T. eclipse at 8-CA-27. Further, N. Bhukti Ketu (w/ Mars) was conjunct the P2 IC at 9-LI-12, i.e., within 18 minutes.

[†] *I had a client who, as one of the world's top violinists, frequently performed for the Presidents and Prime Ministers of various countries. He had Jupiter and Mercury opposing across the 3/9 axis. They were also in a mutual reception with Mercury fallen in Pisces while Jupiter strengthened it and hence canceled the debility.*

Continuing with the Ketu Bhukti, you will recall my comment that her N. Saturn was the exact midpoint of N. Neptune and Pluto with all being at the same degree. At death, the P3 mSN was at 16-VI-31, right on N. Saturn at 16-VI-25. But to really confirm the hyper-sensitivity of her N. Saturn, during her brief adult life she also had a P3 eclipse, and this was exactly on Saturn at 16-PI-29. As I have stated, and you have now seen a number of times, whenever a progressed eclipse hits a N. planet, it makes that planet extremely fated.

Along this same line, she had her first eclipse 16 days after birth making it a P2 eclipse and thus defining yet another fated point. This was at 27-PI-28. At her death, P2 Mars, proceeding from its N. conjunction with the SN, was at 27-VI-22, and this was square T. Neptune at 28-SA-24. It is also the case that the T. NN was within a degree of being conjunct her Asc/Uranus.

I mentioned that she was within one day of moving into a Sun Dasa, and would have been if born only seconds earlier. This is actually likely since the Sun is in a mutual reception with Saturn and is opposed by it. When we look at the Sun by P3, we see that it is within one applying degree of being conjunct P3 Mars (26-TA-38), and this is square her P3 Asc of 26-LE-48. T. Saturn was itself slow at 4-SC-22 and it would be stationary within a week. This station was exactly square to N. Venus, on what was technically the last day of the 20-year Venus Dasa.

COMMENTS ON OTHER CASES

Excluding the natural draw of celebrities, who may very well be in a temperamental class of their own, a big problem with doing this chapter, or really any case–oriented chapter, is that of trying to find the mythical "average" case in order to make globally "prudent" observations.

A standard "typical" case might be that of a person born 11–Oct–1933 at 4:40 AM EST in Queens, NY 40N45 & 73W57 (chart not shown) who shot himself on 10/21/69. It has these kinds of natal elements: Venus was his Dasa planet. It ruled his maraka 2nd, and was conjunct Mars strong in its own sign of Scorpio (transits from and to Jupiter show its maraka status as ruler of the 7th). Neptune was in his 12th and exactly hit, i.e., sensitized by a PNE. He was born with a powerful Saturn (9-AQ) both stationary and in its own sign (CP). This strong Saturn squared Mercury, ruler of his chart, with a 3–degree orb. At death, a perfect grand cross was further set up against chart-ruler Mercury with the P2 IC at 6-AQ, the P2 Moon at 6–SC and T. Saturn at 6–TA. This is so powerful that it does not even need to be shown.

Perhaps another "typical" natal signature might be that of a person born on 24–June–1941 at 2:20 AM EDT in Bronx, NY 40N51 & 73W54 (chart not shown). Mars rules his chart. At 25–PI it is conjunct his N. SN at 26–PI. This opposes his NN which is itself conjunct Neptune at 25–VI (i.e., he has an exact Mars/Neptune opposition exactly along the nodes with Mars ruling the 1st). This double axis overlay is exactly square his Moon at 26–GE (he shot and killed himself during a Moon Bhukti on 3/19/73). This is the basic shell of highly karmic personal chaos, and other logic supported.

Yet a third case is that of someone born 9–Jan–1950 at 7:03 PM EST in Manhattan, NY 40N46 & 73W59 (chart not shown). Here the Moon rules the 1st. The Moon is with Mars and square Uranus (his P3 Sun was exactly conjunct N. Mars at death). Two planets are stationary in the maraka 7th (Mercury, ruler of his 12th conjunct a fallen Jupiter, and Venus, ruler of his 4th). This stationary Venus is angular at the 7th cusp and is opposed by a perfectly angular Pluto conjunct the Asc, so this was probably a suicide over love. He killed himself during a new Rahu Dasa (with the nodes not far from Neptune). Interestingly, his natal true node was only 5 minutes off the placidus 3/9 axis, and he killed himself by jumping in front of a subway train[†].

Be all this as it may, my research, and indeed research theory, suggests that there really is no such thing as an "average" case, although each case can present its own clear image. This leaves me in the position of having to worry about whether I am selecting cases that simply reinforce my personal arguments or even more general astrological prejudices. That would be very easy to do either consciously or unconsciously. And if I just pulled cases out of a hat, as I have generally tried to do throughout, there would still be the doubters -- including me. But let me say that I have never turned away from a case, or excluded a case, because it did not work.

I would also like to dissuade the reader from any thought that an alleged

---

[†] *I had a female friend with a very self–destructive chart and personal history. Her first romantic boyfriend, at age 12, also killed himself by jumping in front of a subway train.*

natal "grand trine" will prevent suicide. I'll give as one example among many the case of someone born 4-Dec-1937 at 12:05 PM EST in Manhattan, NY 40N46 & 73W59 who shot and killed himself on 12/02/73 (chart not shown). Here Saturn (at 28-PI), ruler of the 1st, is "trine" Venus (at 27-SC) and "trine" Pluto (at 29-CA). Hindu astrology asserts that none of these planets have the power to cast a trine, and indeed he killed himself in the midst of this alleged trine when his P3 Asc was conjunct N. Pluto exactly at 29-CA. By the way, his P2 Asc was exactly conjunct N. Uranus at 10-TA (as was his P3 SN), but here I shall digress no further.

In the end, neither this chapter nor this book can meet a certain type of "scientific" criteria for "proof." Yet this does not mean that its comments are not useful or true. Astrology will probably always remain suspended at that mystical juncture between statistical science and interpretive art (modern medicine is suspended there also). Therefore, in deference to this concern, I will close out this chapter with comments on four cases (randomly selected from what used to be called the Rodden/ISAR database) that specifically emphasize a strong *Jupiter* factor — highly angular, strong by sign, bhukti-activated and/or stationary at birth.

This would seem to be the most counter-intuitive, and therefore will hopefully have some special instructive quality (as opposed, for example, to stationary or angular outer planets with all the expected supporting patterns). Regrettably, I have no facts about the life circumstances of the following four cases. But again: *please do keep in mind* that these final cases are deliberately odd, and will look much more positive and disputable than "standard" suicide charts whose signatures are much more clear. I am specifically trying to pick some "devil's advocate" cases here.

CASE 4 (Exalted Jupiter Conjunct The Moon)

This female shot herself at almost age 15 on 10/10/69. She was born 19-Oct-1954 at 00:20 AM EST in Queens, NY 40N43 & 073W52 (see chart # 46). This Cancer-rising chart is ruled by the Moon in her 1st house. The Moon is strong in its own sign of Cancer. Further the Moon is closely conjunct a strong Jupiter only 1/2 a degree from its point of maximum exaltation. So what is the problem here?

> ➤ She had been in a Saturn dasa almost her entire life. Saturn rules her maraka 7th and 8th. Saturn is strong (exalted in Libra) at the bottom of her chart, and is very near a stationary

9th Pisces	10th Aries	11th Taurus	12th Gemini Ketu D E
8th Aquarius	SATURN Ketu beginning on 10/07/1955 SATURN Venus beginning on 11/16/1956 SATURN Sun beginning on 01/16/1960 SATURN Moon beginning on 12/28/1960 SATURN Mars beginning on 07/28/1962 SATURN Rahu beginning on 09/07/1963 SATURN Jupiter beginning on 07/13/1966 MERCURY Mercury beginning on 01/25/1969 MERCURY Ketu beginning on 06/22/1971		1st Cancer Jupiter ET Moon O Ascendant ♓
7th Capricorn Mars ERT		2nd Leo ♇
6th Sagittarius Rahu D –	5th Scorpio Venus +	4th Libra Sun f Saturn E Mercury Rx S++ ♆	3rd Virgo

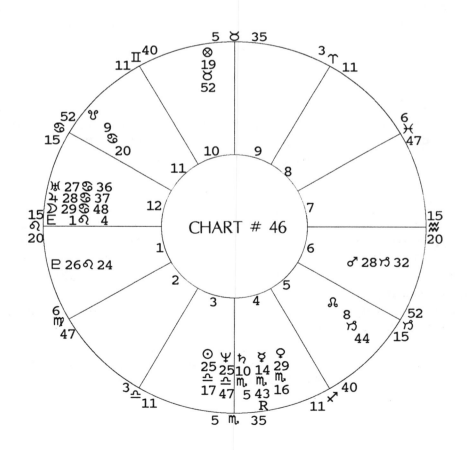

CHART # 46

Mercury which rules her 12th. She had moved into a new Mercury dasa in the year of her death. This stationary planet is in the same house (the 4th) with a fallen Sun which in turn is exactly conjunct Neptune (in fact, her Sun is fallen in 6 of the varga harmonic charts).

➤ She never escaped Saturn since it is now being invoked by its proximity to Mercury[†]. At death, her weak P2 Sun had moved forward the 15 degrees to be exactly conjunct her N. Saturn, and T. Saturn was exactly conjunct her MC.

➤ Pluto is in her maraka 2nd. Her P2 Asc had progressed down the 11 degrees to exactly conjunct it. In turn, this conjunction was being perfectly squared by both T. Neptune at 26-SC and her P3 MC which, at 26-SC-24, was indeed squaring N. Pluto TTM.

➤ When stationary Mercury became Dasa–activated it invoked numerous strong and tightly aspected factors: Saturn of course, then the fallen Sun/Neptune conjunction in hard T-square aspect to the 1st house Moon which is not so great after all since Uranus is only one degree away and this conjunction is being perfectly opposed by a powerful (exalted) Mars from the maraka 7th. So Mercury was just a final point of invocation for all the harsh and emotionally–unstable factors noted to this point.

Once again, we see here a case where, in my opinion, classical Hindu astrology would further enhance its already superior perspective by including the natal placements and function of Uranus and Neptune in this pattern. Many astrologers in India are already beginning to do this.

CASE 5 (Jupiter Dasa)

Hard Moon/Uranus aspects seem to be quite difficult for adolescent females. Here is the case of yet another 15–year–old female who killed herself with a shotgun on 11/01/84 while listening to what was described as "morbid punk rock" music. Her data is given as 23–Aug–1969 at 1:10

[†] *I have a very industrious friend who natally has Gemini rising with Mercury perfectly conjunct Saturn. As expected, Mercury Bhuktis are always much worse than the Saturn Bhuktis which Mercury follows. The Saturn period is oppressive, but the Mercury period is depressive. It is important to master this function of invoking vs. invoked planets.*

AM in Leominster, MA 42N32 & 71W46 (see chart # 47). This presents a bit of a detective problem since my sources indicate EDT, but the Rodden/ISAR database explicitly indicated EST. This raises the question of whether EST was written on the original birth certificate or whether it was just an error in entry. I am showing the EDT charts, but will comment on the EST in the one instance where there is an argument for it. Note that the Hindu house placements and Dasa/Bhukti do not change in either case.

Here the N. Moon rules the maraka 2nd and is located in the maraka 7th. It is almost perfectly angular on the Desc in the EDT chart. When she killed herself another female friend was in the room who also killed herself. This therefore argues strongly for the EDT. This angularity is further activated by the fact that her Moon is perfectly square to Uranus in the 4th, and Uranus is only a few degrees from Jupiter which rules the maraka 7th.

She was indeed in a Jupiter dasa, and now you see that maraka Jupiter had the primary effect of activating her angular Moon/Uranus square. Further, at her death P3 Jupiter was exactly opposing/invoking an exact (and blocked) P3 Mars/Saturn conj. Note also that her N. Saturn is both stationary and only 4 degrees from its most fallen degree (i.e., near 20-AR sidereally). Another argument for EDT is the fact that T. Mars at death was at 19-CP which is the cusp of her Placidus 8th.

In the same house with Jupiter and Uranus is a Mercury/Pluto/mSN conjunction all within 2 degrees (the node is at a sidereal cusp but Rx). The strongest argument for the EST TOB is the fact that natally the tSN would conjunct the IC within 8 minutes of orb which is always karmic and would be more animating of the rolling five-factor cluster (much of this cluster had further tightened up by P2: her P2 Sun at death was exactly square a strong Mars in Scorpio, and P2 Pluto was right on her Mercury).

But this argument is not needed since there are three other factors that activate the meridian and nodal axis. First, the last T. eclipse before the suicide was at 22-SA thus square the mean natal nodes exactly. Second, P2 Mars was coming right up to this at 21-SA and was therefore square the true nodes exactly. Third, she had a P2 eclipse 4 days after birth at 04-PI. This is only 1 degree off the EDT MC, so it had been sensitized in any case.

10th Pisces	11th Aries Saturn Dx	12th Taurus	1st Gemini Ascendant Venus
	Tf		Te++

9th Aquarius Rahu Rx ++		2nd Cancer

KETU	Saturn	beginning on 04/21/1970
KETU	Mercury	beginning on 05/30/1971
VENUS	Venus	beginning on 05/27/1972
VENUS	Sun	beginning on 09/27/1975
VENUS	Moon	beginning on 09/27/1976
VENUS	Mars	beginning on 05/27/1978
VENUS	Rahu	beginning on 07/27/1979
VENUS	Jupiter	beginning on 07/27/1982
VENUS	Saturn	beginning on 03/27/1985

8th Capricorn	3rd Leo Sun M Ketu Rx --

7th Sagittarius Moon +	6th Scorpio Mars 0 Ψ	5th Libra	4th Virgo Mercury Ee Jupiter -- ♓ ♇

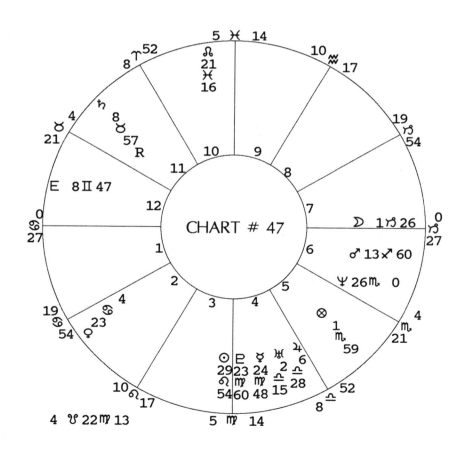

CHART # 47

CASE 6 (Angular Jupiter in Own Sign)

This person stabbed his wife to death and then shot and killed himself on 06/17/87. He was born on 28–May–1951 at 2:45 AM (zone –1ST) in Arras, France 50N17 & 2E47 (see chart # 48). Here, if the TOB was recorded correctly (which I personally somewhat doubt, but I won't go into it) Jupiter is angular very near the Asc in its own sign. This would seem to be highly benevolent for both the 1st and 7th. In addition, he had only one fallen planet in all his varga harmonic charts.

But looking a little deeper we see that:

➤ Uranus is exactly square this from the bottom of the chart thus promoting instability with regard to the relationship symbolism of the horizon.

➤ Saturn is stationary in the maraka 7th, and he was in a Saturn Dasa. Further, T. Uranus was square this N. Saturn station.

➤ Not only is Neptune also in the 7th, it is square Venus, karaka for wife and marriage (with a 2 degree orb).

➤ Three event factors were conjunct this confused N. Venus:

• T. Mars (karaka Mars is natally conjunct his Sun, indicating a latently violent soul),
• P3 Uranus (natally square the horizon as noted above) and
• P2 Mercury (natal maraka ruler of the 7th). P3 Mercury (again, ruler of the 7th) was now exactly conjunct his natally stationary Saturn.

➤ He was in a Rahu Bhukti, and we see exact nodal activity in three ways: A) the T. NN was now exactly conjunct his N. Jupiter/horizon and square Uranus, B) the P2 nodes were square the P2 Asc/Desc, and C) P3 karaka Mars was square his N. nodes TTM.

CASE 7 (Stationary Jupiter)

This is another case of suicide by gunshot. The data is: 12–Dec–1943 at 00:38 AM EWT in Manhattan, NY 40N46 & 73W59 (chart not shown be-

1st Pisces Jupiter Ascendant 0	2nd Aries Mercury +	3rd Taurus Mars T+ Sun	4th Gemini Venus ++ ♓
12th Aquarius Moon T- Rahu Dx	JUPITER Sun beginning on 10/16/1967 JUPITER Moon beginning on 08/04/1968 JUPITER Mars beginning on 12/04/1969 JUPITER Rahu beginning on 11/10/1970 SATURN Saturn beginning on 04/04/1973 SATURN Mercury beginning on 04/07/1976 SATURN Ketu beginning on 12/16/1978 SATURN Venus beginning on 01/25/1980 SATURN Sun beginning on 03/25/1983 SATURN Moon beginning on 03/07/1984 SATURN Mars beginning on 10/07/1985 SATURN Rahu beginning on 11/16/1986 SATURN Jupiter beginning on 09/22/1989	5th Cancer ♇	
11th Capricorn		6th Leo Ketu Dx	
10th Sagittarius	9th Scorpio	8th Libra	7th Virgo Saturn Dx ♆

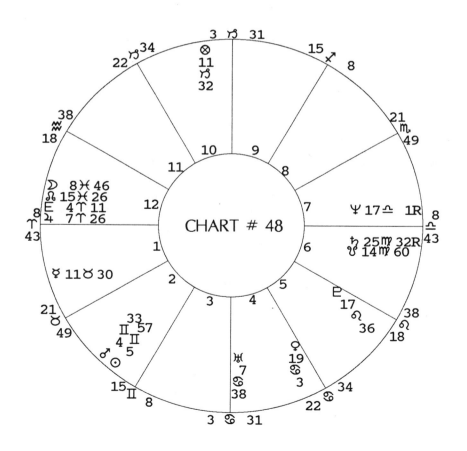

CHART # 48

cause the date of death is not known). This case struck me as quite odd because the person was born on a stationary Jupiter. This usually presents such a level of opportunity in some zone of life that it can usually compensate for any other stressful chart factors. Looking at it strictly as protective from suicide, I would regard such a Jupiter as more positive in the 12th (per his Western chart) than in the 1st (per his Hindu chart) since this would give a type of angelic protection to the unconscious, whereas Jupiter in the 1st could merely create a large or attractive physical presentation.

The Moon is conjunct maraka Saturn within 2 degrees, but there is nothing very odd about that. It is a little more interesting that this Saturn is 6 degrees on one side of the MC, and Mars is 6 degrees on the other side of the MC, thus making the meridian a focal point of frustration. Saturn also does oppose his Sun, which rules his 1st, but the orb of 4 degrees is too wide for my taste. In his navamsha, Saturn is in his 12th in a mutual reception with Venus. In his main chart Venus rules his MC and, at about age 44 (assuming he lived to that age), he had a P2 eclipse exactly square that Venus. Perhaps most interesting to me is the fact that he has Pluto conjunct his NN natally (midway between the true degree and the mean degree), and that Pluto had been exactly hit by a PNE. This makes Pluto very karmic, and it was indeed located in his 12th house.

Suicide is destruction at one's own hand, and this suggests unique 1st house linkages. Any suicide chart should show much more of an inner derangement than a regular death chart, and this suggests an increased focus upon the Sun, the Moon, the nodes and the 12th house. Since this is such a large and complex topic, I recommend research via the high quality IDEA database (formerly the Rodden/ISAR database) for those who would like to give more attention to the matter. It has timed birth data for hundreds of suicides by gunshot, drinking acid, subway train, hanging, jumping from heights, drowning, stabbing, gasses, narcotics, and more. Many of these show much sharper, and more classic, patterns than those I have randomly selected[†].

[†] *For further information, write to IDEA c/o ISAR at P.O. Box 38613 in Los Angeles, CA 90038-8613.*

MURDER

considered not doing a chapter on murder since offhand it would seem to be statistically rare and therefore of only peripheral interest. But, in a way, that is untrue. Every minute around the world someone is being willfully killed by someone else, and of course, this is yet another area of dubious U. S. world leadership. In 1990, 22 people were killed in England by handguns, 68 in Canada and 87 in Japan. But in the U. S., the corresponding body count was 10,567. As of late 1993, murder is the third leading cause of death while at work. A recent network news commentary said, "this gives new meaning to the phrase 'work is murder'." It's also true that murder is the leading cause of death in the United States for certain age group and racial populations.

Another chapter in this book touched briefly on the topic of infant mortality, but here I can make the more specialized observation that, in 1991 alone, more than twice as many American children under the age of 10 were killed by firearms than U.S. troops were killed in the Persian Gulf and Somalia conflicts combined. And between 1979 and 1991 nearly 50,000 U.S. children were killed by guns. This is roughly equal to the number of Americans killed over the entire duration of the Vietnam War. And these are only firearms statistics.

Thanks again to the research and publishing activities of Lois Rodden, I've had the opportunity to look at the charts of hundreds of maniacs across a spectrum of deviance. As a result of this review, I think it's safe to say that standard astrological analytical techniques do not provide a very good vehicle for making any kind of a determination about certain classes of action that result from intent that has historically been characterized as "evil," such as murder, nor for being able to determine such intent.

Of course it is possible to see high frustration, hard energies, power complexes, a lack of solid grounding and/or neural integration, and so forth. But that doesn't necessarily lead to maniacal choices, and such "features" are often seen in the charts of some of the world's most industrious people. As an example, I was once hired to provide astrological Christmas entertainment on a cruise ship for a staff of intensive care nurses. Never have I seen a "worse" set of "maniac" charts! But their occupational choice turns out to be a constructive use of such energy – where patients are often within seconds of dying all around them, where they frequently have to defibrillate people right off of their beds, and so forth.

Obviously the charts of people who extinguish oil well fires will not produce great librarians. Astrology knows little about choices within the context of cycles, nor about chemical disorders, nor why some charts seem to produce birth defects while other seemingly similar patterns do not. It may have to do with certain degree areas, sensitive sub–harmonic patterns (which are useful on the subject of twins) or any number of other productive possibilities. But the whole area is quite speculative at this time.

In the end, some negative characteristics seem to be a fundamental quality of the soul since many of these "evil" traits (that go well beyond standard misbehavior) often show up at a very early age. And these traits often continue to evolve unrelentingly without regard to "causal" parental and environmental factors that often take an unfair brunt of the blame by default in our current behaviorally–oriented era. All "secular humanist" jokes aside, I think it's safe to say that murder is not a behavioral disorder.

Western legal systems make a significant allowance for an impulsive murder that is the momentary result of a seemingly unmanageable passion vs. a calculated one. Wide punishment allowances are made for "intent" as opposed to the mere commission of the act itself. But from an astrological point of view, it is rare to see a murder that does not demonstrate karmic links between perpetrator and victim without regard to its circumstances (although, just to be contrary, I have selected one in Case 2 discussed below).

Therefore, although murder will still exhibit common death features, this chapter will serve to highlight the issue of linkage, or lack of linkage, between perpetrator and victim. Let's review just 2 cases considering that we will actually be looking at multiple charts per case. There is also an entire assassination chapter immediately following this one that further develops many cases closely linked to this topic.

CASE 1 (Mass Family Murder)

My first randomly selected illustration comes from a newsletter I received in November 1993 from the Boston Chapter of the NCGR. The data on this case had been collected from official records by Frances McEvoy who is quite industrious in researching the astrology of tragedies in Massachusetts that have been highlighted in the news. This is the case of a 15-year-old boy, who on the afternoon of October 9, 1993, shot in the head and killed his father, mother and 11-year-old sister. With the volume of data, this discussion could rapidly get out of hand. So I will just highlight some major links and provide the data so that you may further study the case yourself.

The data is as follows:

> *Son/Killer* (b. 24–Apr–1978 @ 10:28 AM EST in New Bedford, MA 41N38 & 70W56) – see chart # 49,
> *His Father* (b. 14–Mar–1959 @ 9:50 PM EST in New Bedford, MA 41N38 & 70W56) –see chart # 50,
> *His Mother* (b. 10–June–1957 @ 2:05 AM EDT in Acushnet, MA 41N41 & 70W54) –see chart # 51, and
> *Sister (Daughter)* (b. 1–July–1982 @ 8:53 PM EDT in New Bedford, MA 41N38 & 70W56) – see chart # 52.

One of the first and most significant links here is the fact that the son, mother and sister *all* had fallen Moons at the *exact* same sign and degree (23–SC). This is zero degrees sidereally, and thus is within 2 degrees of its single most fallen degree (3–SC sidereally). Actually, you will note that the Hindu listings show the Moon for both his mother and sister as being in the last few longitudinal *minutes* of sidereal Libra. Given this location and the Moon's speed, they should be considered in sidereal Scorpio. The ruler of his father's chart is Venus, and Venus is exactly quincunx these three Moons – again within 15 applying minutes of another Mars-ruled sidereal cusp. Venus was also the father's Bhukti period at death.

With this first strong link, let's go back and interrogate the boy's Moon, keeping in mind that what is true of his Moon will therefore have a direct and strong bearing upon his mother's and sister's Moon. We find the following harsh formations to this already fallen position:

➤ With Cancer rising, the Moon rules his chart.

➤ Natally, Saturn perfectly squares it to the minute (further, the Moon and Saturn are exactly contra–parallel at birth within 9 minutes of arc).

➤ This perfectly square N. Saturn was stationary at birth thus further amplifying its effect.

9th Pisces Ketu Rx + Mercury Dx f≈	10th Aries Sun E	11th Taurus Venus O	12th Gemini Jupiter T≈
8th Aquarius			1st Cancer Ascendant Mars RTf≈
7th Capricorn	JUPITER Mars beginning on 10/11/1978 JUPITER Rahu beginning on 09/17/1979 SATURN Saturn beginning on 02/11/1982 SATURN Mercury beginning on 02/14/1985 SATURN Ketu beginning on 10/23/1987 SATURN Venus beginning on 12/02/1988 SATURN Sun beginning on 02/02/1992 SATURN Moon beginning on 01/14/1993 SATURN Mars beginning on 08/14/1994		2nd Leo Saturn Dx e--
6th Sagittarius	5th Scorpio Moon fe≈ Ψ	4th Libra ♅ ♇	3rd Virgo Rahu Rx E

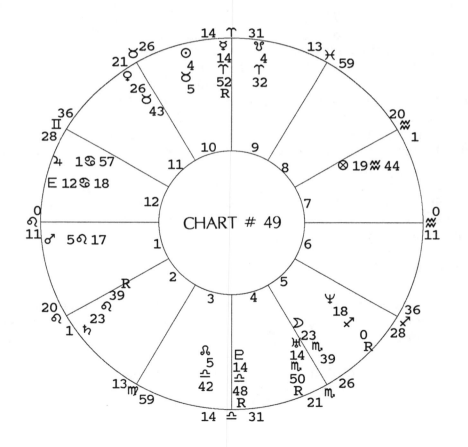

6th Pisces	7th Aries	8th Taurus	9th Gemini
Sun e Mercury Tf Ketu − Venus Ee		Moon M Mars +	

5th Aquarius	MARS Mercury beginning on 11/06/1975 MARS Ketu beginning on 11/03/1976 MARS Venus beginning on 03/30/1977 MARS Sun beginning on 05/30/1978 MARS Moon beginning on 10/06/1978 RAHU Rahu beginning on 05/06/1979	10th Cancer ♓
4th Capricorn	RAHU Jupiter beginning on 01/18/1982 RAHU Saturn beginning on 06/12/1984 RAHU Mercury beginning on 04/18/1987 RAHU Ketu beginning on 11/06/1989 RAHU Venus beginning on 11/24/1990 RAHU Sun beginning on 11/24/1993 RAHU Moon beginning on 10/18/1994	11th Leo ♇

3rd Sagittarius	2nd Scorpio	1st Libra	12th Virgo
Saturn RT+	Jupiter S	Ascendant ♆	Rahu E

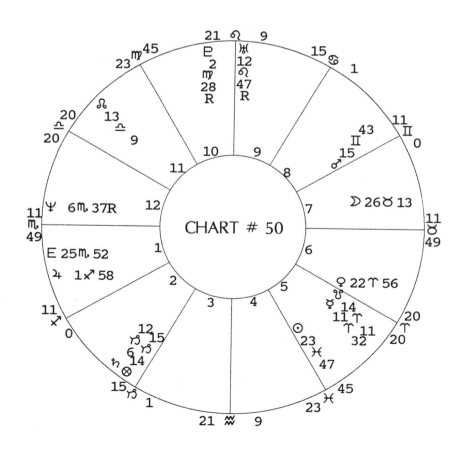

CHART # 50

1st Pisces Ascendant	2nd Aries Ketu D	3rd Taurus Mercury ≈++ Sun	4th Gemini Venus ≈++ Mars Te
12th Aquarius	SATURN Moon beginning on 11/19/1972 SATURN Mars beginning on 06/19/1974 SATURN Rahu beginning on 07/28/1975 SATURN Jupiter beginning on 06/04/1978 MERCURY Mercury beginning on 12/16/1980 MERCURY Ketu beginning on 05/13/1983 MERCURY Venus beginning on 05/10/1984		5th Cancer ♓
11th Capricorn	MERCURY Sun beginning on 03/10/1987 MERCURY Moon beginning on 01/16/1988 MERCURY Mars beginning on 06/16/1989 MERCURY Rahu beginning on 06/13/1990 MERCURY Jupiter beginning on 01/01/1993 MERCURY Saturn beginning on 04/07/1995		6th Leo Jupiter e++ ♇
10th Sagittarius	9th Scorpio Saturn Rx --	8th Libra Rahu D Moon Te- ↵ Ψ	7th Virgo

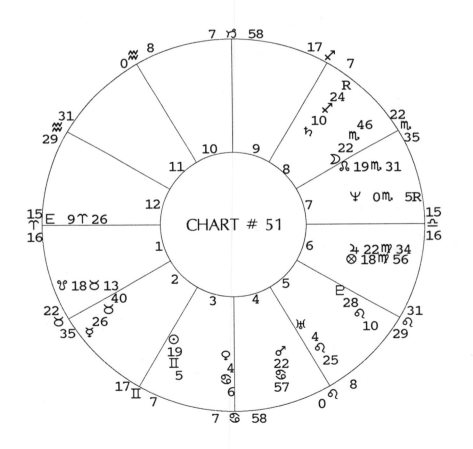

CHART # 51

4th Pisces	5th Aries	6th Taurus Venus 0 Mercury	7th Gemini Sun T+ Rahu Dx E
3rd Aquarius			8th Cancer
2nd Capricorn	JUPITER Mars beginning on 06/28/1983 JUPITER Rahu beginning on 06/04/1984 SATURN Saturn beginning on 10/28/1986 SATURN Mercury beginning on 11/01/1989 SATURN Ketu beginning on 07/10/1992 SATURN Venus beginning on 08/19/1993 SATURN Sun beginning on 10/19/1996		9th Leo
1st Sagittarius Ketu Dx + Ascendant ♆	12th Scorpio ♓ ↙	11th Libra Jupiter S-- Moon e- ♇	10th Virgo Mars T-- Saturn

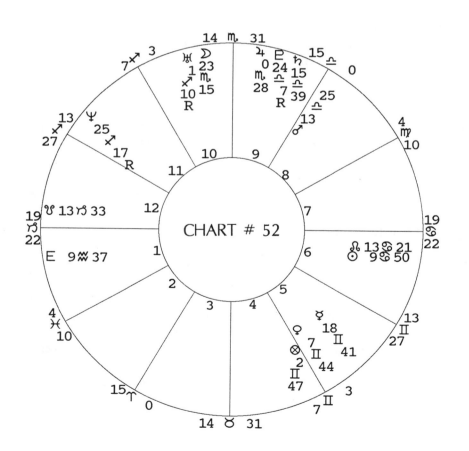

CHART # 52

➤ This stationary (karaka) Saturn rules his maraka 7th (and his 8th), and is located in his maraka 2nd (in his navamsha, Saturn is fallen in his 8th along with the nodal axis and opposing Mars).

➤ As of 1/14/93, he was in a Saturn dasa and Moon bhukti, so we should expect a ripened manifestation of this brutally square and stationary natal condition during this period.

➤ At the murder, T. Pluto was exactly conjunct their Moons (23-SC), and T. Saturn was exactly square it (23-AQ) therefore opposing N. Saturn. Pluto had been conjuncting and stationing around this Moon sign and degree for almost two years.

Further extending this power/frustration/blockage pattern:

➤ His Moon is in a mutual reception with a fallen Mars in his 1st (this fallen Mars is conjunct his mother's Uranus). Mars malfunction is extended through its exact contra–parallel with Neptune, and Neptune is in the same house with the Moon.

➤ And Mars disposes his Sun (the natural atmakaraka or soul indicator) while being in square to it.

His father

Besides the Sun, Mercury is also his atmakaraka (soul indicator) since it is the planet at the highest sidereal degree, and this brings to light another rare formation that links into his father's chart:

➤ The boy's Mercury (14–AR) is fallen in Pisces and also stationary.

➤ It is totally angular at the MC.

➤ This stationary, angular and fallen soul indicator is then exactly opposed by a totally angular Pluto (14–LI) on the IC, and this exact double angularity necessarily externally manifests what might otherwise remain a more internal pattern.

➤ His father's true nodes (14–AR/LI) exactly overlay the son's meridian (and therefore the son's Mercury/Pluto), and we observe that his father was in a Rahu Dasa when murdered by his son. To reinforce the Plutonian link, his father was himself born on a stationary Pluto.

➤ Nodal issues continue to be reinforced in that his father had a PNE at 19-LI and two P2 eclipses at 17-AR and 3-LI. The boy had three exactly overlaying PNE's at 19-LI, 17-AR and 3-LI.

His sister

This Pluto discussion suggests a digression into his sister's chart:

➤ His completely angular Pluto at 14-LI (opposite his fallen stationary Mercury) was jammed into the one degree slot between his sister's N. Mars at 13-LI and N. Saturn at 15-LI, thus animating both.

➤ As a partial consequence of this, and the fact that Saturn rules the house of her brother, she died in a Saturn dasa. Saturn is a maraka for her since it also rules her 2nd and, as noted, is conjunct Mars within 2 degrees with her brother's Pluto as the midpoint. She herself had a Pluto station 3 days after birth (her 3rd P2 year). In the light of these Saturn and Pluto comments, you will now recall that T. Saturn and Pluto were respectively and exactly conjunct and square her Moon (plus brother and mother, of course).

➤ Further reinforcement of this same theme is shown in the fact that her P3 Asc (28-CA-15) was exactly square P3 Pluto (28-LI-23), and this would have been TTM with only seconds of birth time error.

➤ This same P3 Pluto was also exactly octile N. Venus which brings up the following key points.

➤ Venus was her bhukti planet. At her death P3 Venus was at 13-SA-33. So where was the last T. eclipse just before she died? At 13-SA-55, and I've illustrated this progression-to-eclipse issue elsewhere in this book. Further meaning of this Venus bhukti is found in the fact that P3 Venus was exactly opposing her P3 Sun, and her Sun is with her node in the house of relationships. Let's now look at that node, and further extend the eclipse commentary in two ways.

➤ First, you will note that she has her natal node at 13-CP/CA in the

1/7 axis. Well, 5 days after birth (her 5th year) she had a P2 eclipse exactly on this axis thus perfectly reinforcing its karmic relationship message. Second, she had a PNE at 19-CA-14, and this is perfectly conjunct her relationship axis (the "horizon"). At her murder, T. Uranus and Neptune were both at 18+ of CP (i.e., conjunct her Asc) thus animating this pre-stimulated angle. As natal reinforcement of all this, her Neptune, horizon and node were all at the same degree of declination.

➤ Finally, you may note that Jupiter was stationary only a few days before her birth. One may therefore wonder why it didn't provide more general protection than it did. The reason is because Jupiter was not in a position to help her because she herself was a representation of Jupiter since it ruled her chart (she was as completely sweet and considerate as her brother was violent and antisocial). She actually *was* Jupiter in her own chart, and this was at 00-SC-28. You will note she was in a Saturn dasa. So where was P3 Saturn at her death? At 00-SC-02, conjunct the ruler of her 1st. Jupiter was therefore debilitated, and unable to stand up to the other events in her chart.

His mother

Finally let's now review his mother. As you recall, she had the same Moon as daughter and son which was being conjoined by Pluto and squared by Saturn. This Moon was exactly conjunct her Placidus 8th house, and this Moon/cusp was exactly eclipsed pre-natally just before her birth. Let's call this PNE #1. She had three other PNE's, and two of these were exactly conjunct a subsequent natal planet, and one was conjunct a violent T. planet:

➤ PNE #2 at 9-TA/SC was conjunct T. Mars at 8+ SC.

➤ PNE #3 at 10-SA-9 was conjunct N. Saturn at 10-SA-24.

➤ PNE #4 at 25-TA-55 was conjunct N. Mercury at 26-TA-40.

This last (2nd house) PNE on Mercury is especially noteworthy for many reasons. Her son's Venus was also exactly conjunct it at 26-TA-43 as was her husband's Moon at 26-TA-13 (indeed, her husband's P3 IC was at 25-TA-21). In addition, she was in a Mercury dasa thus linking together this entire pattern. Her Mercury was also in a mutual reception with a planet in the same house with Mars while her P3 Mars would be totally stationary within one more day/month (and this P3 Mars was tightly tri-octile to P3 Mercury within 10 minutes).

As a further comment on her Mars, note that it is one of three planets in her chart that is well into the last sidereal degree of a sign. This natally links together Mars, the fallen, tragically-aspected Moon, and Jupiter — with Jupiter (ruler of her 1st and her current Bhukti planet) as the exact midpoint. Her N. Mars at 22-CA-57 is square her P2 SN at 22-AR-30, while 22-AR-53 is her son's P2 Mercury (you remember Mercury in his chart), and 22-AR-56 is her husband's N. Venus (his active bhukti planet at death).

Reviewing karaka Saturn for her, we see that P3 Saturn was exactly opposite (TTM) her P3 Part of (Mis)fortune, and her P2 Desc was well within one applying degree of her P2 Saturn; and this was while her P3 Sun was within 5 applying degrees of her N. Desc. Another Saturn curiosity is that her husband's Saturn had gone fully stationary by P2 only two day/years before, so it still essentially had no velocity. This station was at 7-CP, and that is exactly upon his wife's N. MC, and this angularity again converted this symbol into an event.

Finally, in her chart we also see a typical IC/Neptune death pattern interplay where her P3 IC was conjunct her P3 Neptune within 14 minutes. Her P2 Moon was also tri-octile her N. Neptune TTM, and her P3 Asc was conjunct P3 Uranus.

In closing on this case, and as if it were needed, I will note two additional precipitating factors in the boy's chart. First, his P3 MC/IC axis was tightly square his N. Mars, while his P2 Asc was conjunct his P2 Mars.

CASE 2 (Killed Over A Pack of Cigarettes)

In complete contrast to the intense familial intrigues of the case noted just above, this is the case of two relative strangers, one of whom stabbed the other to death in an argument that began over a pack of cigarettes. The data for this case was again personally researched by Frances McEvoy based upon a news item, and she posted this data in the February 1994 issue of the newsletter of the Boston Chapter of the NCGR.

Bruce Hinckley was the victim who died at age 33. His data is 13-April-

1959 @ 1:25 PM EST in Boston, MA 42N21 & 71W04 (see chart # 53). The young male (yet again 15 years of age) who was convicted of the crime was Thomas Petruzelli. His data is 30–July–1976 @ 6:05 PM EDT in Malden, MA 42N25 & 71W04 (chart not shown). Let's review what you now know to be three classic considerations:

> ➤ Eclipse Action: You may recall from the chapter on natural expected deaths in one's own chart that I clearly linked together the deaths of Arthur Ashe, Willie Brandt and Petra Kelly through exact hits by the T. solar eclipse that occurred on 6/30/92 at 8–CA–57. It turns out that this murder currently under discussion occurred on 7/4/92 – only four days after that same eclipse. Will we find the link once again? Absolutely, and more perfect than ever.

Hinckley (the victim) has Leo rising, so the Sun rules his chart. On the day of this T. eclipse where do you suppose his P3 Sun had arrived at? It was exactly at 8–CA–57 thus conjunct the eclipse TTM. When he was killed four days later, his P3 Sun had only moved on to 9–CA–7. Let me pause here and reinforce this point about how important it is when a T. eclipse happens to occur directly on a key progressed planet.

Critical events often occur immediately when a progressed personal planet or angle is eclipsed by transit. This is currently an aggravating problem for astrologers since it requires them to cross–monitor both transiting and progressed positions relative to each other over time. This is quite demanding since most current software does not assist in monitoring the impact of transiting and progressed positions upon each other. Hopefully this problem will eventually be solved by more synthetic software that emphasizes meaningful patterns over reams of homogeneous data.

Let me use two political illustrations to confirm what I am saying. First, former Vice President Dan Quayle (04–Feb–1947 @ 11:48 AM CST in Indianapolis, IN) has N. Venus in the 8th. By 7/21/90 it had cycled around by P3 to be at 29–CA–09. On that same date there was a total solar eclipse at 29–CA–04. And on that same date his wife Marilyn was rushed to the hospital for emergency gynecological (Venus) surgery.

As a second example, in November of 1993 there was an eclipse at 21–SC–32, and this was exactly square Bill Clinton's P3 IC of 21–LE–43 and opposing his P3 Sun of 21–TA–16 (this is also exactly Hillary's N. Saturn square stationary N. Mercury degrees). I wrote an article forecasting immediate calamity for him because of this and many exact supporting

8th Pisces	9th Aries	10th Taurus	11th Gemini
Mercury Sf Ketu Rx S– Sun e		Venus O	Moon e++ Mars T

7th Aquarius				12th Cancer
	RAHU	Ketu	beginning on 09/19/1972	
	RAHU	Venus	beginning on 10/07/1973	
	RAHU	Sun	beginning on 10/07/1976	
	RAHU	Moon	beginning on 09/01/1977	
	RAHU	Mars	beginning on 03/01/1979	
	JUPITER	Jupiter	beginning on 03/19/1980	
	JUPITER	Saturn	beginning on 05/07/1982	

6th Capricorn				1st Leo
	JUPITER	Mercury	beginning on 11/19/1984	Ascendant
	JUPITER	Ketu	beginning on 02/25/1987	
	JUPITER	Venus	beginning on 02/01/1988	
	JUPITER	Sun	beginning on 10/01/1990	
	JUPITER	Moon	beginning on 07/19/1991	
	JUPITER	Mars	beginning on 11/19/1992	

5th Sagittarius	4th Scorpio	3rd Libra	2nd Virgo
Saturn S+	Jupiter Rx T		Rahu Rx SE

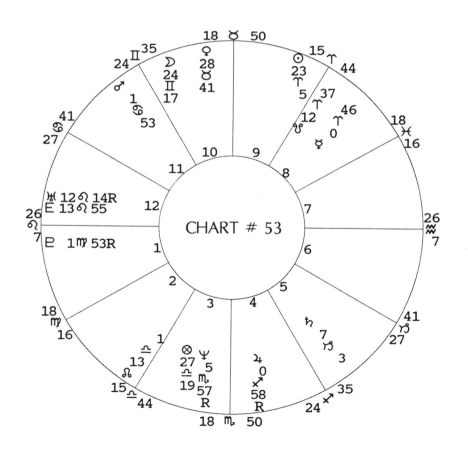

CHART # 53

considerations. Within less than two months (but some starting almost immediately) the following resulted: 1) his "Trooper Sex Scandal" hit the major media, 2) a lunatic unexpectedly won the popular legislative vote in Russia, 3) two Secretaries of Defense resigned, 4) his lawyer was served with a subpoena for the congressional inquiry into his Whitewater investment, 5) he had to issue an apocalyptic warning to North Korea, and 6) his mother died somewhat unexpectedly.

I've seen this on many occasions, so transiting eclipses on progressed points clearly deserve respect. In the JFK assassination case discussed in the next chapter, you will see a slight variation on this, where just before he was killed, a progressed angle arrived to exactly conjunct both a natal angle and a natal planet that had themselves just been exactly eclipsed. Now back to our case.

➤ Marakas: Saturn rules the 7th and Mercury rules the 2nd. These have a further link in that Mercury is fallen in the 8th, and Saturn aspects Mercury. But a standout factor is that both these maraka planets had almost no velocity at birth. Mercury went fully stationary the day before birth, and Saturn went fully stationary three days after birth. Saturn, of course, is also the karaka for death.

Note further that P2 Venus (natally square Pluto with an applying 3 degree orb) was opposing N. stationary maraka/karaka Saturn within 7 minutes at 7-CA-10. The P2 Part of (Mis)fortune was also conjunct N. Saturn within 1/3 of a degree. Switching back to the other maraka, P2 Mercury was at 7-TA and this was exactly conjunct P3 Mars at 7-TA.

➤ Dasa/Bhukti: Jupiter is the Dasa planet, so we ask whether it is suffering significant natal stress. The answer is yes because it is exactly square Pluto natally. Then we further observe a double Pluto problem that ripens this natal situation. First, three years ago at age 30, Mr. Hinckley was in a total P2 Pluto station. Considering the velocity of a P2 Pluto, it was still fully stationary. Second, T. Pluto was Rx at 20-SC-20 thus applying to a conjunction to his N. IC.

By the way, in this regard I was tempted to argue for an adjusted birth time 6 minutes later than the BC (i.e., 13:31) for three reasons: A) this actually would make his IC 20-SC-20 thus perfectly conjunct T. Pluto TTM, B) this would put his Desc at 27-AQ-16 and his killer's P3 Mercury (the killer's Bhukti planet and ruler of the killer's own maraka 7th) was at

27-AQ-31, and C) the victim's adjusted Desc would be exactly square his P3 maraka Mercury TTM. Without regard to these points, I can tolerate the original TOB since the victim's P3 Uranus was at 18-LE-49 thus perfectly square to his N. IC at 18-SC-50 (a few seconds of birth time error would have made it exact TTM). Note also that the killer had N. Uranus at 3-SC and this linked into one of the victim's PNE's at 3-TA.

Meanwhile, what about the victim's Bhukti Moon? Natally it is in the same house as Mars and opposite the house holding stationary Saturn. It thus invoked both of these energies in the context of all the harsh and fated geometry noted above. And perhaps a brief clue is seen in the fact that his P3 Moon had moved into position (24-VI) to be exactly square his N. Moon.

Here are some brief observations on the perpetrator's chart (not shown, but data given above) starting out with four Mercury observations:

➤ He was in a Mercury Bhukti and Mars Dasa. Mercury is a maraka since it rules his Gemini 7th. Natally, Mercury is further in the same house as Mars (confirming its status as a maraka), and indeed, the perpetrator had a more general reputation as a bully (Mars causing stress to others).

➤ His N. Mercury was exactly on a cusp, i.e., at 23-LE-30 it was only 3 minutes from the ayanamsha of his birth year (23 degrees and 27 minutes). His P2 Sun was now conjunct this at 23-LE-6, and this was exactly square one of his PNE's at 23-SC-10.

➤ P3 Mercury (27-AQ-31), ruler of the 7th, was exactly square N. Jupiter (27-LE-15), ruler of the 1st (P3 Jupiter, in turn, was tri-octile N. Pluto TTM).

➤ P2 Mercury (18-VI-17) was octile N. Uranus within 5 minutes, and this Uranus, 2 degrees from the MC, was nearly angular (P3 Saturn was also exactly square P3 Uranus, and this was only a degree from another PNE).

➤ His nodal axis was only a few degrees from Uranus, and the tNN at 7-SC-52 was almost perfectly square his N. Sun at 7-LE-50. This could suggest some karma with regard to his Sun, and indeed, we find his N. Sun in his 8th only 1 degree from N. Saturn (also in the

8th). Thus he was caught up with the issue of death.

➤ With regard to his Dasa planet (Mars), it had moved to 24–VI–39 by P2, and the last T. lunar eclipse that occurred before this event was perfectly square at 24–SA–20.

Overall, I don't have the impression that these two individuals were karmically connected. Rather I think they were just mutually–invoked random agents toward the achievement of each other's chart patterns. Some deaths really are like that, just as many of life's key events, such as a major illness, are not necessarily karmic at all. As usual, the data is provided so that the reader may perceive some pattern that I do not.

Personally, for both charts I'm completely fascinated by the near complete disengagement of the progressed angles which seem to be floating in space. Therefore, this case is quite an anomaly relative to almost all the other cases in this book, and I have no particular hypothesis for that unusual fact.

But wait! I can't brush my hands and walk away from this case just like that. Because that's not the entire story. I mentioned that the killer was in a Mercury Bhukti and Mars Dasa, and I stated that these were both in the same house. But I didn't say which house. It was the 9th. "The 9th," I hear you scream, "I thought that was a great house!" Well, yes it is, but you will further recall that it is also the house of the father (since the 1st is the 5th from the 9th).

Now we further notice that the killer's Sun (as the natural indicator of the father) is also the ruler of the 9th. It is greatly damaged by being in the 8th and conjunct Saturn. *Now* we are starting to get a significant clue about the meaning of the P2 Sun noted above relative to the eclipse hit. Now we see that this whole episode has to do with the *father* in a very fundamental way.

For here is what Paul Harvey, on his nationally syndicated radio show, might call "The Rest of The Story." It further turns out that the father of the boy who committed the stabbing returned to the scene of the argument to help confront the ultimate victim, and the father was armed with a piece of lumber! So now you see what the boy's chart was saying. Even after his son was judged to be guilty, the father went to court to seek an injunction forcing the high school to allow the boy to return to classes until sentenced (the boy eventually received a one year sentence for assault and battery). This case resulted in a new law allowing schools to keep out students charged in a violent crime.

So now we have a wild card. Might it be the case that there was a karmic link between the victim and perpetrator's father? I throw out this possibility as a technical challenge to the reader, and suggest your application of the techniques noted to this point. The data for Anthony Putruzelli (the attacker's father) is: 8–Aug–1953 @ 3:32 AM EDT in Stoneham, MA 42N29 & 71W04 (chart not shown). The more sophisticated reader may want to do some research in the Hindu literature regarding murderous yogas, and see how they may apply relative to the cases noted in this chapter.

ASSASSINATION

Assassination gives another perspective on this topic, as we would expect to see even more clear and arguably fated patterns. Practically speaking, if we can get a better fix upon what factors are likely to precede or be present at an assassination, I'd like to think that executive protective services would be interested in it — if only from the viewpoint of the more efficient allocation of their limited manpower. Even if a relatively good astrologer couldn't say when an assassination *would* occur, he or she should be able to list the extensive periods when it would *not*, and that is very productive information in its own right.

Assassinations may very well have degree linkages that are idiosyncratic to individual countries. An initial hypothesis is that it should tie into the chart of the country at various weak or power points. For example, any U.S. chart (based upon 7/4/1776) had the mSN (always a mundane weak point) at 7–AQ–36 at the formation of the country (true was 6–AQ–36). I'll discuss a TTM hit to this point in the discussion of John Kennedy's chart below, but for now I want to point out where tropical *Mars* was located natally in the charts of various U.S. assassins:

[In the left column in parentheses are the individuals the assassins attacked (but not necessarily fatally). For example, Sara Moore assaulted Gerald Ford, and so forth. In the right column in parentheses I have added some supplemental observations about the assassins' natal charts other than their *Mars* placements which are underlined.]

Moore (Ford)   – <u>07–AQ</u> (02/15/30)
                               (and 06–SC = Moore's south node)

Ruby (Oswald)   – <u>08–AQ</u> (03/24/11)
                               (and 05–TA = Ruby's Saturn)

Ray (King)   – <u>08–AQ</u> (03/10/28)

Oswald (Kennedy) – <u>11–AQ</u> (10/18/39)
                               (and 06–SC = Oswald's Venus)

Tropical astrologers may wish to argue that Mars in Aquarius can produce action driven by ideological fanaticism. However, I see these particular Mars placements as being in sidereal Capricorn where Mars is exalted, i.e., at its most industrious and effective. So from my point of view, I would expect to see a broader derangement in each chart.

Beyond the Mars pattern, here are some related hard links to the mean South Node of the U.S. (6–7 degrees of tropical Aquarius). This is just a cursory attempt to highlight a purely 4th harmonic pattern via a glance at gross untimed birth data of the assassins. Obviously, in every individual case, numerous very precise linkages could be established through progression, perpetrator/victim synastry, return charts, allegedly "violent" stars, and on and on. Again in parentheses are who the assassins attacked.

Sirhan (R. Kennedy) – 06-LE = his natal Pluto
                      05-AQ = his south node (03/19/44)

Guiteau (Garfield)   – 09-AQ = his progressed Mars conjunct
                                 NN (09/08/1841)

Booth (Lincoln)   – 08-AQ = his natal Neptune

Zangara (Roosevelt) – 08-AQ = transiting Saturn

Bremmer (Wallace)   – 06-SC = his natal Mars
                                 06-LE = his natal Venus
                                 (08/21/50)

Fromme (Ford)   – 05-SC = her natal SN (10/22/48)

Hinckley (Reagan)   – No linkage to this pattern (05/29/55), but
                       he was arguably the most clinically deranged.

I've reviewed the charts of several other individuals who committed acts of terrorism or political assassination in other countries, and they had no natal placements at 6–8 degrees of the tropical fixed signs. So astrologers in other countries may wish to investigate whether their assassins had a link into the lunar south node of the chart of their own country. I would also recommend looking at other stress or power points in a nation's chart.

For example, when the U.S. brutally repulsed Iraq from Kuwait on 01/17/91, the T. Sun, Saturn and NN were all at 27–CP (we bombed them again twice in early 1993 – once when Mercury was at 27–CP and again when the Sun was at 27–CP). 27–CP is exactly where Pluto is located in the U.S. chart, and in addition, P3 Pluto was stationary (progression date: 05/

11/1784). The obvious relevance of this U.S. Pluto position is further seen in the following sample reviews of the John Kennedy, Abraham Lincoln, Malcolm X, Robert Kennedy and John Lennon assassinations.

CASE 1 (John F. Kennedy)

JFK's natal chart is almost too good to start with because it is a "classic" illustration of its type. It also clearly demonstrates the value of the concepts being emphasized in this book. What probably makes his chart especially classic is the fact that JFK is fundamentally famous for being assassinated. This should reflect in both the potentials of his natal chart and in the elevation of transiting/progressed factors at death. It does.

Kennedy was born on 29–May–1917 at 3:15 PM EST in Brookline, MA 42N20 & 71W07 (see chart # 54), and was assassinated by Lee Harvey Oswald on 11/22/63 at 12:30 pm CST in Dallas, TX (32N47 & 96W49). This birth time (which is excellent but probably a few seconds late), requires an astrologer to choose between two sidereal Ascendants since tropically, like the ayanamsha, it is at 22+ degrees. For too many reasons to enumerate here (based upon his reputation, health, family, spouse, election wins, etc.) I have chosen sidereal Virgo rising. Tropical astrologers, don't panic! This does *not* mean that he had to look or act like your standard prototype of tropical Virgo rising! Now on to the mechanisms...

Clearly, this chart is "electric" — but electricity flows both ways. Mercury, ruler of the 1st, was stationary at birth in a vitality house (the 8th). In turn, Mercury was conjunct a very powerful Mars in its own sign. This aggressive, high vitality combination was further applying to a conjunction to Jupiter (all three within a five degree orb). Jupiter, in turn, was *exactly* square a *second* stationary planet at birth — Uranus (you will recall that Elvis Presley was also born on a Uranus station).

So essentially a stationary ruler of the 1st (conj violent Mars and fully aspecting a maraka house — the 2nd) was square a stationary Uranus! Saturn, ruler of the political 5th and five degrees from Neptune, was exactly angular at the MC — and exactly opposing U.S. Pluto on Kennedy's IC.

Notice that Jupiter has maraka status as ruler of the 7th, and indeed, T. Jupiter was in his 7th at the assassination (by the way, exactly conjunct the P3 MC within 9 minutes). Jupiter is further relevant because Kennedy moved into his Jupiter Dasa six months after winning the election.

7th Pisces	8th Aries Mars M Mercury D –	9th Taurus Jupiter e-- Sun -- Venus OT	10th Gemini Ketu Rx E ♇
6th Aquarius ♓	MARS Moon beginning on 10/17/1942 RAHU Rahu beginning on 05/17/1943 RAHU Jupiter beginning on 01/29/1946 RAHU Saturn beginning on 06/23/1948 RAHU Mercury beginning on 04/29/1951 RAHU Ketu beginning on 11/17/1953 RAHU Venus beginning on 12/05/1954	11th Cancer Saturn T ♆
5th Capricorn	RAHU Sun beginning on 12/05/1957 RAHU Moon beginning on 10/29/1958 RAHU Mars beginning on 04/29/1960 JUPITER Jupiter beginning on 05/17/1961 JUPITER Saturn beginning on 07/05/1963 JUPITER Mercury beginning on 01/17/1966	12th Leo Moon ++
4th Sagittarius Rahu Rx –	3rd Scorpio	2nd Libra	1st Virgo Ascendant e

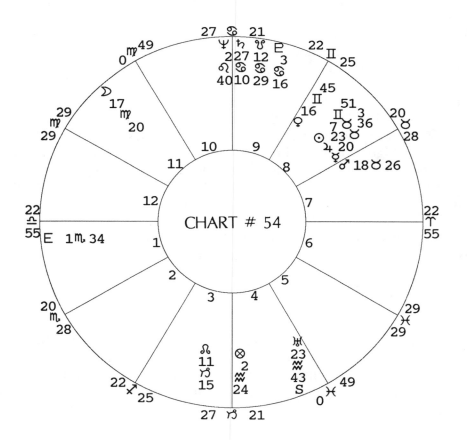

Generally we wouldn't focus upon the maraka status of Jupiter, but in the case of the full set of configurations that apply in this particular chart, we need to confirm that it is capable of permitting death — and it is.

In early July of 1963, Kennedy moved into his Saturn Bhukti. Saturn, ruler of the house of his health and his enemies (6th), is exactly angular natally at the MC. A number of critical things then occurred:

➤ On July 20, 1963, there was a total solar eclipse at 27–CP, exactly on his I.C., U.S. Pluto, and opposite his Saturn.

➤ In November, his P3 Asc cycled around to exactly conjunct this Saturn/MC combination that had just been eclipsed (this triple combination was also exactly quincunx P3 Uranus). This was the key trigger in the context of everything else.

➤ On 11/16 the last new Moon was at 23–SC thus sensitizing, via an exact T–square, the natal square of stationary Mercury (with Mars/ Jupiter) to stationary Uranus[†].

➤ Kennedy went to Dallas. In Dallas, Pluto is *exactly* conjunct his relocated MC of 03–CA and exactly square his relocated Asc of 03–LI.

➤ On the date of assassination, 11/22, his P3 Neptune was now conjunct the U.S. SN TTM (07–LE–36). P3 Saturn was conjunct N. Neptune within 5 minutes. T. Neptune was exactly conjunct (at 15–SC) the last full Moon before Kennedy was born. This, in turn, is where Pluto was when the Movie *JFK* was released about 28 years later which was a progressed Moon and a Saturn cycle in its own right[†].

And so we see a confluence of exact classical considerations which, by their accumulation, precision and importance, made assassination a near inevitability. Conversely, major factors in isolation, do not necessarily yield death. For example, the month before he was shot, President Reagan had an exact eclipse on his natal Sun at 16–AQ. I won't discuss this

---

[†] *For normal lives we would not usually focus upon the last full Moon before birth, but it becomes relevant for people who are potentially involved in national karma.*

because it did not result in death, and President Reagan's time of birth is speculative. But there was an apparent absence of sufficient supporting factors to assure death.

Some final comments on the chart of the U.S. at the death of Kennedy (using one of the common Sag-rising charts of 7/4/1776 @ 16:47 LMT in Philadelphia, PA):

> ➤ The P2 SN was conjunct P2 Neptune,
> ➤ P3 Mars was conjunct the N. Moon (26–AQ), and
> ➤ The P3 IC was conjunct the N. SN.

CASE 2 (Abraham Lincoln)

Abraham Lincoln is the case of another admired assassinated U.S. President who was also born on a Uranus station. And in this case, stationary Uranus was with Mars and the NN in the sidereal 10th. Additionally, the last total eclipse before he was born was within one degree of this Uranus. Amazingly, by the way, the eclipse before that was exactly conjunct N. Mars, and the eclipse before *that* was exactly conjunct N. Saturn; these all occurred during the pre-natal period giving an extremely fated life. Lincoln's data is given as 12–Feb–1809 @ 6:54 AM LMT in Hodgenville, KY 37N33 & 85W45 (see chart # 55). He was assassinated on 04/14/1865 at age 56. The U.S. Moon for the above chart is only a few degrees from both Lincoln's Sun and Asc.

I have personally pushed his TOB back about 2–3 minutes to 6:51 in order to get sidereal CP-rising. To give him AQ-rising would put his Piscean VE/JU conjunction (in exaltation & rulership) in the 2nd house suggesting great wealth potentials that he obviously did not display. However, his third house was quite good. For example, he wrote all his own speeches including the famous Gettysburg Address (but as a technical side note, in Hindu astrology, speech and writing are usually attributed to the 2nd house, and publishing to the 3rd). There are many other reasons to fractionally adjust his TOB that will be seen below. This still leaves a Mercury/Pluto conjunction in Aquarius for those concerned with its alleged "humanitarian" sign symbolism. This fractional adjustment doesn't affect the tropical chart at all.

To briefly digress further on the adjustment: this puts Neptune exactly on his MC (and Saturn only 3 degrees off). This exact angularity was further highlighted by the fact that Neptune went stationary by P2 when

3rd Pisces Jupiter Oe Venus ET	4th Aries Ketu Rx --	5th Taurus	6th Gemini
2nd Aquarius Sun Mercury T+ ♇	RAHU Mars beginning on 12/05/1844 JUPITER Jupiter beginning on 12/23/1845 JUPITER Saturn beginning on 02/11/1848 JUPITER Mercury beginning on 08/23/1850 JUPITER Ketu beginning on 11/29/1852 JUPITER Venus beginning on 11/05/1853 JUPITER Sun beginning on 07/05/1856 JUPITER Moon beginning on 04/23/1857 JUPITER Mars beginning on 08/23/1858 JUPITER Rahu beginning on 07/29/1859 SATURN Saturn beginning on 12/23/1861 SATURN Mercury beginning on 12/26/1864 SATURN Ketu beginning on 09/05/1867	7th Cancer
1st Capricorn Moon + Ascendant e		8th Leo
12th Sagittarius	11th Scorpio Saturn ♆	10th Libra Mars - Rahu Rx ⛢	9th Virgo

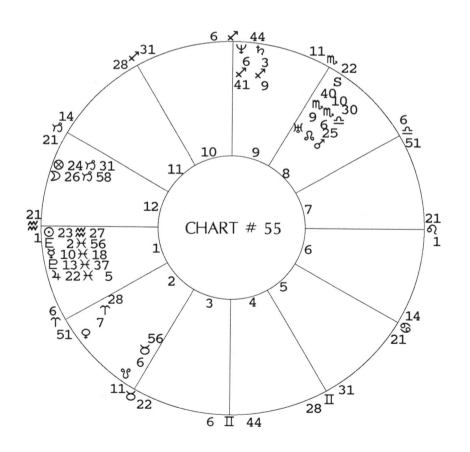

CHART # 55

he was 26, and Saturn went stationary by P2 when he was 30. Thus they were both at low velocity much of his young adult life. Ultimately he had to deal with a Union in chaos, a number of lost elections, his own nearly suicidal depressions (and complete lack of formal education), Marfan syndrome, an illegitimate mother who died when he was 10, a clinically insane wife, a shiftless father, and the death of a son which bothered him so much that he had the child disinterred twice so that he could look at him. As a final comment on the exactly angular Neptune, in the end he himself had to be buried 13 feet underground after his coffin was embedded within six feet of concrete in order to repel grave robbers.

The Moon, as ruler of both the mother and the 7th, is in the 1st. Therefore, Saturn in the 11th aspects the 1st (wife and mother), 5th (son) and 8th. Mars in the 10th also aspects the 1st (wife and mother), 4th (mother) and 5th (son). You may review the chart yourself for supporting considerations.

Back to assassination: Lincoln's natal Moon is at 27–CP which, like Kennedy, *again* has us back to U.S. Pluto. On the day Lincoln was shot, T. karaka Saturn was square it at 27–LI. Lincoln's own P3 Venus had also progressed up to 27–CP (see 3/5/1811). Venus is ruler of both his 5th (politics) and 10th (government rule), and T. Mars was exactly square his N. Venus at death. P2 Mars, ruler of his 4th and his MC (remember: not necessarily the same as the 10th), was exactly octile Saturn (ruler of his 1st, and a maraka as ruler of his 2nd). His P3 Sun, as ruler of his 8th, was exactly conjunct natal Pluto in the 2nd at 13–PI.

Nodal comments: Lincoln's own nodes squared the nodes of the U.S. At death, his P3 Asc was conjunct his P3 SN. Not counting a very partial eclipse three days before he was killed, the immediately prior eclipse was perfectly square his horizon. In this discussion of the last two paragraphs, notice the extensive involvement with the pre–natal eclipse points. Finally, at death his P3 Asc was exactly conjunct his P3 SN (within 3 minutes if you use the true one).

CASE 3 (Malcolm X)

The chart of Malcolm "X" clearly ties in with a number of the main assassination elements suggested to this point. He was not a politician but clearly an influential national leader. Malcolm Little's birth certificate indicates that he was born on 19–May–1925 @ 10:25 PM CST in Omaha, Nebraska 41N17 & 96W01 (see chart # 56). He was assassinated by gun-

4th Pisces ♓	5th Aries Moon + Mercury ≈+	6th Taurus Sun T-- Venus 0	7th Gemini Mars T≈ ♇
3rd Aquarius	SUN Venus beginning on 08/21/1953 MOON Moon beginning on 08/21/1954 MOON Mars beginning on 06/21/1955 MOON Rahu beginning on 01/21/1956 MOON Jupiter beginning on 07/21/1957 MOON Saturn beginning on 11/21/1958 MOON Mercury beginning on 06/21/1960	8th Cancer Rahu Rx ♆
2nd Capricorn Ketu Rx ++	MOON Ketu beginning on 11/21/1961 MOON Venus beginning on 06/21/1962 MOON Sun beginning on 02/21/1964 MARS Mars beginning on 08/21/1964 MARS Rahu beginning on 01/18/1965 MARS Jupiter beginning on 02/06/1966	9th Leo
1st Sagittarius Ascendant Jupiter Rx Me	12th Scorpio	11th Libra Saturn Rx E	10th Virgo

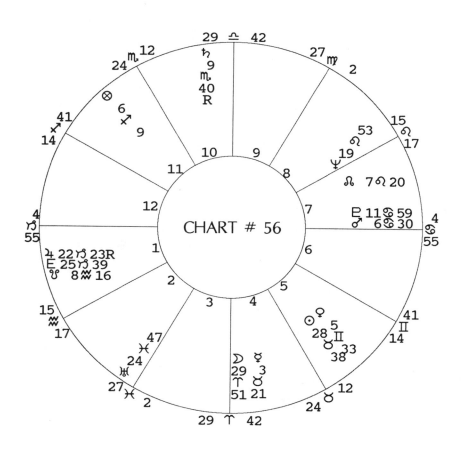

CHART # 56

shot on stage on 02/21/65 after a speaking engagement in Manhattan around 3:15 PM. There is quite a symbolic clue in the fact that a week before that (02/14/65) his house was burned.

Following is some quick background for non–American readers. Malcolm X was a black civil rights leader who, having led a life of discriminatory mistreatment, preached an intense philosophy of black supremacy and an advocacy of racial segregation, although this philosophy was mellowing and shifting towards the end of his life. He had been a member of the Black Muslims, a religious sect, but was suspended as a Muslim minister on 11/23/63 – the day after John F. Kennedy was assassinated.

On 03/08/64 he broke away completely from the Black Muslims to form his own religious sect and a political organization. There was great tension with the Black Muslims thus directing initial attention to them as the likely attack group. In the end the feeling is that a larger and more political group was responsible – possibly by manipulating the Black Muslims.

Without going into detail, suffice it to say that this assassination, like many others, was characterized primarily by vast *confusion* (remember that key word). News reports, eyewitness accounts, grand jury testimony and trial testimony was highly contradictory. The behavior of nearly all key players was strange. There were also many unanswered questions, an incomplete investigation and key persons disappeared. Although there was a confession, the identity of the true killers remains in doubt.

First of all, why all the confusion? Because, just as with the attempted assassination of former President Reagan, T. Neptune was stationary (Rx at 20–SC–00), and this was square to N. Neptune at 19–LE–53. His P2 Asc was at 20–AQ–02, so the assassin, represented by the Desc, was exactly conjunct Neptune. His last eclipse before birth was at 19–LE–39, i.e., also exactly conjunct N. Neptune, and this is a defining consideration. T. Jupiter, ruler of the 1st, was at 19–TA (opposite T. Neptune), and T. Venus, ruler of his MC, was at 20–AQ thus caught up in the perfect cross formation.

Malcolm X moved into a Mars Dasa on 08/21/64 and Rahu Bhukti on 01/18/65, so we will pay special attention to the behavior of these two factors. At birth, Mars (in Gemini) was highly angular being located only 1 & 1/2 degrees from the Desc (Pluto is also 5 degrees from Mars in the 7th). Note that Mars is in what is sometimes referred to as a "paran" formation or "mundane square" with the Moon which is itself perfectly angular since it is exactly conjunct the IC. This has much to do with his internalization of a great anger due to mistreatment from others and contradicts the illusion of a near sextile[†].

It also has much to do with why his house was burned down during the Mars Dasa (Mars also being the dispositor of his moon and IC) and the Rahu Bhukti (the node in Cancer in the 8th — with Neptune —and disposed by the Moon). Very hard mundane squares are unusual and will "act out" more powerfully than other squares which may otherwise even be perfectly square by standard longitude.

Mars is also a maraka, and a warning of his impending death is found in the fact that his P2 Sun was conjunct it. Saturn was another maraka as ruler of the 2nd, and the P3 Sun was conjunct it. Both of these conjunctions were within 10 minutes of orb. Also within 10 minutes of orb was the P3 Moon which was at 06-LI-39 — exactly square natal Mars. Parenthetically you'll note that Mars not only aspects the 1st house but therefore also Jupiter, its ruler. This Mars/Jupiter polarity contributes to why he developed a fanatical philosophy around violence.

So what about the nodal axis (his Bhukti)? I've already mentioned a number of Moon issues as the Moon disposes the node's sign from the 8th. You will also note that his nodal axis is the same as the U.S. (his tSN at 07-LE and mNN at 08-AQ). In this regard I direct your attention back to all the other assassination examples at the beginning of this section. His P3 MC had moved to 10-AR and his P3 SN was now exactly square it at 10-CP (this would be TTM if he was born 1 & 1/2 minutes earlier). P2 Saturn was also exactly square his N. nodal axis (while P3 Saturn was square P3 Neptune and octile N. Pluto). You may wish to note that he was born in a Ketu Dasa and Rahu Bhukti perhaps indicating a karmic destiny.

U.S. Pluto (27-CP-34) was once again involved because when you relocate Malcolm X to Manhattan (where he was killed) his relocated Asc was at 28-CP. In addition his P3 Asc had moved up to 27-CA thereby putting his descendant (the assassin) on U.S. Pluto. So we see the same national themes continuing to emerge.

[†] *As a clarifying technical note, when one natal planet is on the horizon and another on the meridian, they "act out" as a highly dynamic personal combination even if they are technically only 60, as opposed to 90, degrees apart.*

CASE 4 (Robert Kennedy)

According to his office, Robert Kennedy was born on 20–Nov–1925 at 3:11 PM EST in Brookline, MA 42N20 & 71W07 (see chart # 57). On 6/5/68 the likely Democratic presidential nominee was shot and killed in a hotel restaurant pantry area in Los Angeles, CA. Again we see the tNN at 27–CA (exactly conjunct John Kennedy's Saturn) with the mSN at 28–CP again conjunct U.S. Pluto and his own Moon in the 10th within 2 minutes of orb. Robert Kennedy, as U.S. Attorney General, had achieved much fame to this point by his overt pressures upon various elements of organized crime, major labor unions plus the strange embedded Director of the FBI.

The assassin's gun held eight bullets, yet ten bullets were recovered. A group of prominent criminologists agreed that Kennedy was actually killed by a second gun fired from about 2 inches behind his ear, yet the officially designated lone assassin fired from two feet or more in front of Kennedy. This case had many strange elements that I won't go into, including the refusal to test–fire the alleged assassin's gun, the refusal to reopen the case for any reason, and the fact that the frail alleged assassin appeared unsteady and glazed over, could not remember drawing a gun, had no apparent motive, and had never lacked personal responsibility or discipline.

Displaying much charisma and momentum, it appeared that Kennedy was on his way to winning the Presidency. He was in his Jupiter Dasa (10/62) and Mercury Bhukti (6/67). N. Jupiter is conjunct his MC within less than a degree; sidereally it is in its own sign of Sagittarius in the 9th (along with Venus). However, Jupiter is aspected by an exalted Saturn in the 7th, and Mercury is in the 8th in a Mars–ruled sign (Scorpio) exactly octile to Mars.

Aries rises, and its ruler Mars is angular at the Desc within one degree, thus contributing to his reputation for exceptional aggressiveness often characterized as ruthlessness. Indeed, in his navamsha, Mars is also in the 7th house both as a rajayoga karaka and in exaltation! Note that Jupiter is also in a "paran" condition with Mars as both are angular thus producing a powerful type of mundane square (as just discussed in Case 3).

Let's look a little closer at the Dasa and Bhukti planets. Jupiter would seem to be both intrinsically and functionally good. However, it does share rulership of the 12th house, and it is with Venus. Venus is a double

12th Pisces	1st Aries Ascendant	2nd Taurus	3rd Gemini
			♇
11th Aquarius ♓	RAHU Rahu beginning on 10/24/1944 RAHU Jupiter beginning on 07/06/1947 RAHU Saturn beginning on 11/30/1949 RAHU Mercury beginning on 10/06/1952 RAHU Ketu beginning on 04/24/1955 RAHU Venus beginning on 05/12/1956 RAHU Sun beginning on 05/12/1959	4th Cancer Rahu Dx --	
10th Capricorn Ketu Dx ++ Moon +	RAHU Moon beginning on 04/06/1960 RAHU Mars beginning on 10/06/1961 JUPITER Jupiter beginning on 10/24/1962 JUPITER Saturn beginning on 12/12/1964 JUPITER Mercury beginning on 06/24/1967 JUPITER Ketu beginning on 09/30/1969	5th Leo	♆
9th Sagittarius Venus − Jupiter MT	8th Scorpio Sun T++ Mercury +	7th Libra Mars + Saturn E	6th Virgo

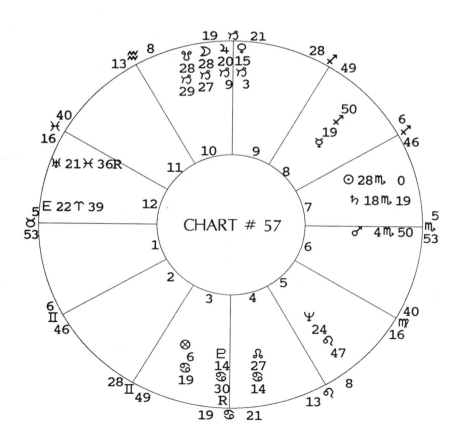

maraka as it rules both the 2nd and the 7th houses. It is also in an "enemy's" sign. It also receives the strongest aspect in his chart as it is opposed by Pluto within half a degree (the T. nodal axis was also exactly square this axis). In Los Angeles, Kennedy's relocated Asc was at 21-AQ. So where was Kennedy's P2 Venus at the assassination? — at 21-AQ exactly conjunct his relocated Asc. The next paragraph will show how Venus may have functioned as a malefic.

A *female* in a white polka-dot dress was seen in the pantry area with the alleged assassin just before the shooting. A female campaign worker had gone out on a balcony to escape the smoke and heat of the evening. She saw the women in the polka-dot dress enter the building with two other people. Later she was "nearly run over" by these three people after the murder. The woman shouted, "We shot him!" When the campaign worker asked who they shot, the woman answered, "We shot Kennedy!" The police later produced a candidate, but the campaign worker said it was not her. Yet the woman the police produced was found dead in a hotel room several days after the alleged assassin's conviction.

What about the Bhukti Mercury (natally with the Sun in Scorpio in the 8th)? P3 Mercury was within one degree of being conjunct N. Pluto (which exactly opposed N. Venus), and T. Mercury was stationary on the day of the assassination. Mercury was fallen in his navamsha.

What about the two strong malefics in the maraka 7th — Mars and Saturn? His P3 moon was conjunct N. Saturn within 3 minutes, and his P2 Moon was square N. Saturn within 1 degree. P2 Saturn was also conjunct within half a degree the last new Moon before he was born (itself at the cusp of Kennedy's 8th house). His P3 Asc was conjunct his natally angular Mars within 10 minutes, and it would have been exact TTM if Kennedy were born 2 minutes later than the given time. P2 Mars and P3 Saturn were at the same sign and degree, as was the P2 Asc and the P3 node.

N. Neptune had almost no velocity since it was stationary only a week after his birth, and T. Neptune was square N. Neptune within 10 minutes. This contributes to the final weirdness and inconclusiveness, and we have already seen the stationary Neptune problem in other attempted and successful assassinations. The mundane shock and brutality were also shown by the fact that T. Uranus and Pluto had both gone stationary only a few days before he was killed. T. Saturn (22-AR-26) had also moved up to within less than a degree of being conjunct the most recent eclipse before the shooting (23-LI-20).

CASE 5 (Luis Donaldo Colosio)

This case is an extension of the RFK discussion immediately above. I'm inserting it here since it replicates many of the same patterns and issues. Since this will be a more limited discussion, I won't be showing his chart. Like RFK, Colosio was the leading, and near certain, candidate for President of Mexico. He was shot and killed by one or more assassins on 3/23/94 under circumstances as equally confusing as Kennedy's. His data is 10-Feb-1950 @ 11:45 PM PST in Magdalena de Kino, Sonora 30N38 & 110W57 (chart not shown).

As an Aries-rising person, Kennedy's two maraka houses were ruled by Venus. With Libra rising, Colosio was a flip of this, with Mars ruling both maraka houses. Kennedy had Mars very angular at the 7th. Colosio had Mars ruling the 7th and stationary natally in his 12th house (to confirm its very malefic status, Mars in his navamsha rules the 7th and is in the 2nd). At the same time that the P3 ruler of his 1st (Venus) came to a complete halt, this natally stationary malefic ruler of his 7th, proceeding from the 12th, was exactly conjunct the MC by P3 — a *perfect* assassination configuration.

We saw a Moon square Saturn issue in Kennedy's chart at the assassination. Colosio also had a fallen Moon located in the maraka 2nd natally square Saturn (but the natal orb is over one degree), and he was in a Sun Dasa and Saturn Bhukti (natally, they are in a mutual reception). By the way, Bhuktis can be broken down into further sub-periods called antara Dasas. On the exact day of the assassination, Colosio had moved into such a sub-period for Ketu — and Ketu is the other factor in his 12th house. Thus it animated issues associated with his powerful 12th house Mars.

I'll add a brief comment on the chart of Mexico. I use the standard constitutional chart of 31-Jan-1917 @ 4:00 PM in Queretaro, MEX 20N36 & 100W23 (chart not shown). Actually, I use a time 25 seconds later. Here are a few standard factors. The Moon and Jupiter are the marakas. At the assassination, Mexico's P3 Moon was at 17-AQ-28 conjunct N. Mars at 17-AQ-39, and square the P3 Asc of 17-TA-25. The P3 Sun (leader) was conjunct P3 Jupiter (the other maraka). P2 Mars at 18-AR-01 was square Mexico's N. Asc of 18-CA-01 TTM. T. Uranus in the 8th exactly opposed N. Saturn in the maraka 2nd, and so forth.

However, the final parallel point I want to make with regard to RFK was the fact that in Mexico's chart, the N. Sun (leader) of 11-AQ-31 was exactly opposed by P3 Neptune of 11–LE–29. And not only that, but P3 Neptune was nearly stationary – as was P2 Neptune. For the U.S. chart I use (noted in the tertiary chapter), U.S. P2 Neptune was totally stationary at the assassination of RFK. As I've said, stationary Neptune, of one type or another, is quite common at assassination attempts.

CASE 6 (John Lennon)

This major world figure in the area of popular culture is yet a final example of the U.S. Pluto effect. Even though he was a British citizen, he was shot and killed at age 40 in New York city on 12/8/80. His Moon (natally in a tight grand trine with Uranus and Neptune) is at 27–CP–25 which puts it only 9 minutes away from U.S. Pluto! Note that the dispositor of his Moon is Saturn which will be shown to be a significant factor in his murder.

Lennon was born on 9–Oct–1940 in Liverpool, England 53N25 & 02W55. His time of birth is doubtful. One biography gives 7:00 AM. His father allegedly gave a birth time of 6:30 PM to Lennon's stepmother, and this was also quoted in another biography. Lennon himself is said to have told an astrological writer, Sybil Leek, that he was born at 8:30 AM. Yet another source said he was born during an air raid, and these allegedly only occurred at night. Various Hindu charts I have seen do not immediately seem to indicate sufficient status to forecast, as they normally do, his wealth and worldwide fame or even his chosen career. A quick scan around the zodiac, changing the birth time every two hours, indicates that initial arguments could be made for several alternative sidereal ascendants.

I don't wish to be dragged into peripheral rectification arguments here, although all of the times given above are certainly wrong as can be clearly seen through progression of the angles, eclipse patterns before death, the relocated angles, and so forth. For purposes of this discussion, I will be using 6:50 AM British Summer Time (see chart # 58). 6:49 is equally plausible. This is only 10 minutes off the time selected by James Braha in his own documented discussions of this chart, and it has sufficient argumentative strength for my purposes.

What we can see here is an extremely fated life with an exceptional amount of exact nodal and eclipse activity. The last new Moon only eight days before he was born was an eclipse at 08–LI. The first full Moon after he was born was another eclipse at 22–AR. As it happens to work out, using

7th Pisces Ketu D +	8th Aries Saturn Rx Tf Jupiter Rx	9th Taurus	10th Gemini
6th Aquarius	MARS Moon beginning on 09/04/1959 RAHU Rahu beginning on 04/04/1960 RAHU Jupiter beginning on 12/16/1962 RAHU Saturn beginning on 05/10/1965 RAHU Mercury beginning on 03/16/1968 RAHU Ketu beginning on 10/04/1970 RAHU Venus beginning on 10/22/1971 RAHU Sun beginning on 10/22/1974 RAHU Moon beginning on 09/16/1975 RAHU Mars beginning on 03/16/1977 JUPITER Jupiter beginning on 04/04/1978 JUPITER Saturn beginning on 05/22/1980 JUPITER Mercury beginning on 12/04/1982	11th Cancer	
5th Capricorn Moon +			12th Leo Venus T
4th Sagittarius	3rd Scorpio	2nd Libra Mercury ++	1st Virgo Mars Ascendant Rahu D Sun

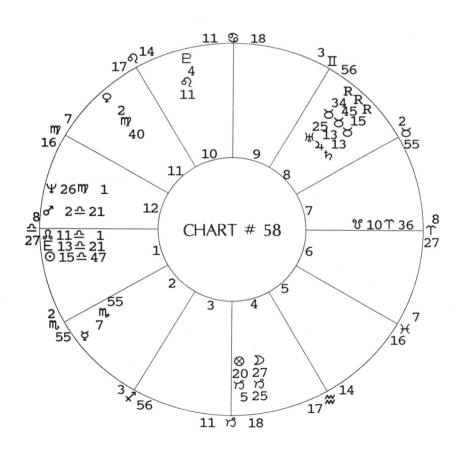

CHART # 58

a birth time of 6:50 gives a tropical Asc of 08-LI — exactly on the PNE of eight days earlier. This therefore makes him a "marked" man. At death, we also find that the P2 nodal axis was at 08-LI. T. Saturn was also at 08-LI. It was also conjunct T. Jupiter — just as both these planets were conjunct at his birth. The P3 Sun was at 08-AR. Indeed, even at his first divorce on 11/8/68 the T. SN was at 08-LI.

At death his P3 Asc was only one degree off of his tNN. The T. mean nodes were square N. maraka Jupiter TTM (and N. Saturn by 1/2 a degree). T. Mars was only one degree from the IC, the P2 moon was exactly square N. Mars, and P3 Mars was exactly square the P3 nodes.

When you relocate Lennon's chart to NYC, the new P3 Asc (02-CP-27) is now only 6 minutes from being square his N. Mars. It could be exact depending upon the NYC coordinate used. Indeed, N. Pluto is also now less than a degree from being square the new MC/IC, and P3 Pluto is only 3 minutes from exact square to the new MC/IC. At death the T. nodes were only 2 minutes from being conjunct the relocated Asc/Desc (13-LE-46). Note that all these comments refer to minutes and not degrees, and they argue for the perfectibility of the slightly adjusted time I have selected. Note also that an eclipse less than five months before his death was exactly conjunct N. Pluto (4 AQ/LE).

After 18 years in the fated-for-fame Rahu Dasa, Lennon went into his Jupiter Dasa in early 1978 and his Saturn Bhukti in May of 1980. As already noted, these two planets were conjunct in the 8th house within half a degree. Hindu astrology says that Saturn wins the contest for dominance because it is in the lower degree of longitude. Westerners might argue that Jupiter wins the war because it is one degree higher in the sky by northern declination. Suffice it to say that they are very locked together, and both fully aspect Mercury in the 2nd which rules both the 1st and the 10th.

His high level of wealth came from the fact that Saturn is exactly conjunct the single most fallen degree for Saturn in the entire zodiac (20-AR). This means that Saturn is aspecting the exactly opposing point in the 2nd house where Saturn would be at its most exalted, plus that point is receiving a further exact full aspect from natal Jupiter. Saturn, which you will recall is also the karaka of the 8th, greatly damages the 8th while we note that Jupiter has status as a maraka (side note: Venus, at 02-VI-40, is the other maraka, and the actual last eclipse before his death was exactly on it at 03-PI-03). When we look at Saturn's progressed condition, other than the points already noted, we see that P3 Saturn was conjunct N. Uranus within 13 minutes indicating that the death is shocking. The 8th is also made more violent because Mars aspects this house which it also rules.

CASE 7 (John Connolly)

You might think that this 27-CP issue would just be related to people with a national linkage into the U.S. chart, but that's not necessarily so. Texas governor John Connolly had national aspirations, but he was invariably frustrated in that regard (he began running a Saturn Dasa in 12/72, switched parties less than a year later, very shortly after was indicted on bribery charges which knocked him out of the 1974 Vice Presidential race, and despite accumulating a huge base of financial contributions, received only one delegate at the 1980 Republican presidential primary).

At the national level, Connolly is perhaps most well remembered for having been in the same car with John Kennedy when he was assassinated. Connolly was very seriously injured, but he survived. There is some thought that Lee Harvey Oswald was actually trying to kill John Connolly since he had written to then Governor Connolly attempting to get his dishonorable discharge from the Marine Corps changed to honorable, but Connolly's office never replied.

I gave Connolly's data and discussed his chart at some length in the chapter on rectification via death (see chart # 8). I concluded that his TOB is actually 13 minutes earlier than the given time which I believe was rounded to the hour. I discussed related death factors in that prior chapter since he eventually died on 6/15/93 at age 76 of pulmonary fibrosis. Now let's look at the assassination issue.

Here is my key point again about 27-CP. In discussing Kennedy, I had mentioned that the most immediately prior T. solar eclipse was at 27-CP-24. So where was John Connolly's P2 Moon? – at 27-CP-24 which is U.S. Pluto again, and conjunct the eclipse TTM! Is this starting to strike you as monotonous?

Here are some supplemental considerations. Staying with eclipses for the moment, the immediately prior T. eclipse was at 14-CP-06. At the shooting, Connolly's P2 tSN was on this eclipse point at 14-CP-16 which is also, by the way, the cusp of his tropical 2nd house (14-CP).

At the assassination, both his P2 and P3 Neptune had very little velocity. T. Neptune (15–SC–53) then moved in to be square to his N. Mercury (15–AQ–47). Twenty–nine years later he ultimately died shortly after entering his Mercury Dasa from lung (Mercury) problems.

This is another example where Hindu astrology would have to struggle unnecessarily to explain why he was shot during a Jupiter Dasa since Jupiter is with the Moon, and Mars does not aspect it. It's true that Saturn does aspect Jupiter in the sign where Saturn is fallen, but what accounts for the extremity of the response? The real missing "Factor X" once again is the fact that "unseen" Neptune is exactly square to N. Jupiter. So when a Jupiter period activates, so does Neptune, and Neptune is in the same house with Saturn which does aspect Jupiter. Neptune and Saturn both also fully aspect N. Mercury which is itself only 5 degrees from Uranus.

By the way, it's not too hard to understand the effectiveness of the Ketu Bhukti period he went into in November of 1963 (the month of the assassination), since Ketu is in the 8th with Pluto, and the consequent Pluto activation is discussed both above, below and in the rectification chapter. This is another example of a "Factor X" which goes unseen from the more purely Vedic perspective.

The partially discussed rectification of his angles at death now continue to be validated by the assassination attempt. For example, his N. Asc is 13–SA–19, and the true P3 NN at the shooting was at 13–SA–13 (T. Pluto had also just hit the square to this at 14–VI). There was also a large clustering of factors and angles at 7 to 8 degrees of tropical mutable signs:

08–PI–10	=	his N. Sun
08–PI–30	=	his N. Mars (ruler of sidereal Scorpio Asc)
08–VI–43	=	his P3 Asc
09–VI	=	T. Uranus
07–GE–28	=	his P3 MC
07–SA–33	=	his P3 Mercury
08–SA	=	T. Mercury

Note also: CA–02 = his N. Pluto and
CP–02 = his P3 Mars (opposing the progressed ruler of the 1st)

It's also interesting that, at the assassination, T. Mars was in his 1st at 20–SA; then, when he was hospitalized 29 years later on 5/17/93 with breathing problems, the P3 Sun had progressed to the exact same point (20-SA). As you may have noticed, he natally has the Sun and Mars exactly conjunct.

CASE 8 (Huey Long)

Lets shift gears a little and take a look at Huey Long. Variously called the "Kingfish" and the "Dictator of Louisiana," he was a popular but corrupt Governor of the state of Louisiana who resigned to join the U.S. Senate in 1931. He was shot in the state Capitol in 1935. Lois Rodden has reported records that say this was on 9/7, but other records I've seen say 9/8. Her resources says he died 3 days later; other records say either 2 days or 30 hours later. It doesn't really matter for our purposes.

Long was born on 30-Aug-1893 in Winfield, LA 31N56 & 92W38. Lois Rodden quotes his TOB as 4:15 AM CST, and this is per a "quote from a personal associate of the Senator." I'm very unconvinced, so I won't show the chart (all the progressed angles are disconnected and floating in space; the natal angles are also without transit and eclipse stress, etc.). I only want to take a look at the two "theme" issues we have seen over and over here of 1) the U.S. nodes at 6-7 LE/AQ and 2) U.S. Pluto at 27-CP.

Long was seemingly shot by a doctor (Carl Weiss) who believed 1) that Long had kept his father-in-law from getting a job, and 2) that Long had implied that some members of Weiss' family were black. Weiss was characterized as an "assassin" in Ms. Rodden's book titled *Astro-Data V*, but was this an "assassin" or "merely" a murderer? Seven witnesses identified Weiss as the killer (Long's bodyguards immediately killed Weiss), and Long himself never disagreed.

However, theories abounded that Long was killed as part of a conspiracy to remove him from power and/or because he posed too much of a threat to first-term President Franklin D. Roosevelt. The case was clouded by the disappearance in 1940 of Weiss' gun, the records of the original investigation, and the fact that no autopsies were performed on either party. But the records and gun were subsequently found with the daughter of the original lead investigator (there was, after all, a Sun/Venus/Neptune conjunct the day of the shooting).

In June of 1992 another investigation concluded, even though all the witnesses were now dead, that the shooting really was just a case of personal revenge. My objective in highlighting this case is merely to question to what extent this was really a national issue.

Since he was a U.S. Senator, there should be some registration to the U.S. chart. And there was. The last T. eclipse sensitized 6-LE-18, and this exactly overlaid the U.S. true nodes within 18 minutes. At the shooting, Long's own P2 Moon was at 6-SC-42. His P3 Saturn was at 6-SC-35 (TTM square the U.S. mean node) while his N. Uranus was at 7-SC-33. And this loops us back to the lists at the very beginning of this chapter.

But, unlike all the above cases, there was really nothing going on at 27–CP, although, of course, we can't be sure since his birth angles are quite certainly wrong. So I am not inclined to see a dark national conspiracy.

How about you?

But speaking of that, let's wrap up with a look at...

CASE 9 (Rajiv Gandhi)

Having attempted to make the case that the U.S. chart may uniquely stimulate assassination activity at 6 LE/AQ and 27 CA/CP due to those points being the nodes and Pluto in our natal chart, I will close with an odd observation on the recent and rather vivid assassination of Rajiv Gandhi, the former Prime Minister of India (some readers may further recall that the former Prime Minister was his mother, Indira, who was herself assassinated on 10/31/84). Rajiv's own assassination only six years later occurred as he got out of his car to speak at a political rally on 5/21/91. A bomb concealed in a bunch of flowers exploded, killing him and 14 others.

Let me begin with the usual general discussion, but first note that I'm inclined to think he was actually born about 2–3 minutes later than his given TOB since, as you will see, numerous indicators run about 1/2 to 1 degree short of where they "should" be. I'll flag the many instances of this with the notation "short". This problem may be slightly further aggravated by his birth location since, according to the *Nehru Journals*, as passed orally through several sources, Rajiv Gandhi was born on 20–Aug–1944 @ 8:11 AM IWT (–6.5) "near" Bombay, India 18N55 & 72E54 (see chart # 59).

His chart immediately shows how he shares a certain instability with his mother. Not only is Mars, as the ruler of his 4th, a maraka in his 2nd, but

8th Pisces	9th Aries	10th Taurus	11th Gemini Saturn ++
		♓	
7th Aquarius	MARS Rahu beginning on 03/06/1975 MARS Jupiter beginning on 03/24/1976 MARS Saturn beginning on 02/28/1977 MARS Mercury beginning on 04/09/1978 MARS Ketu beginning on 04/06/1979 MARS Venus beginning on 09/03/1979 MARS Sun beginning on 11/03/1980		12th Cancer Rahu Rx ♇
6th Capricorn Ketu Rx	MARS Moon beginning on 03/09/1981 RAHU Rahu beginning on 10/09/1981 RAHU Jupiter beginning on 06/21/1984 RAHU Saturn beginning on 11/15/1986 RAHU Mercury beginning on 09/21/1989 RAHU Ketu beginning on 04/09/1992		Sun M Jupiter T Ascendant Moon Venus -- Mercury e
5th Sagittarius	4th Scorpio	3rd Libra	2nd Virgo Mars Te ♆

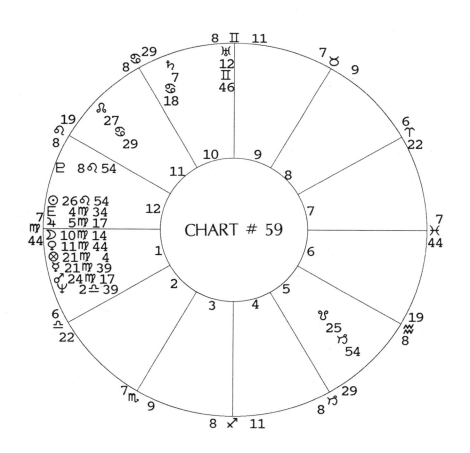

further, the Moon conjunct Venus (near the Asc) is closely square to Uranus (near the MC). So they were both subject to personal shock from the public arena. His MC is 8–GE–11, and the last solar eclipse just before his mother was killed was at 9–GE–26 ("short").

Natally, he has 5 planets in the 1st including the three natural benefics, and also the Sun which is, in fact, the ruler of the 1st. His Sun is at the exact same sign and degree as Bill Clinton's. At 26–LE–54, the ruler of the 1st was closely conjunct by the P3 IC at 27–LE–11.

Recognizing that Venus is inherently unstable due to this natally angular square, we see that the P3 Asc (now conjunct the N. MC) is at 8–GE–58, and this is conjunct P3 Venus at 9–GE–18 (but "short") — and this is right on his mother's former pre–assassination eclipse degree.

Mars is a problem being in his 2nd natally. Now we see that his P2 Asc at 24–LI–8 is conjunct P2 Mars at 24–LI–49 (but "short"), and this is square the P2 tSN at 24–CP–4. And once again the progressed IC is perfectly involved since the P2 IC at 23–CP–42 is conjunct this P2 SN (but "short"). Note further that the last T. solar eclipse was at 25–CP–20, right on his N. mSN of 25–CP–54. This is a cyclic repetition of his last solar PNE at 27–CA–22 (right on his N. tNN at 27–CA–29).

T. Mars at the assassination was fallen at 26–CA — right on this nodal and eclipse congestion and, in fact, he was in a 12th house Rahu Dasa period (Mercury was his Bhukti planet, and Mercury, as ruler of the maraka 2nd, was not even 3 degrees from the obviously very active maraka Mars in the 2nd). Note now that his N. tSN is exactly conjunct U.S. Pluto.

His own N. Pluto was at 8–LE–54, P3 Pluto at 9–LE–29 and P2 Pluto at 9–LE–58 — all on his Placidus 12th cusp of 8–LE–19 (but "short"). And where was the last T. lunar eclipse? Conjunct Pluto at 9–LE–51. And note for the record that this was square to P2 Venus, ruler of his 10th, which was now at 9–SC–17. As the next paragraph shows, further significant and classic activity was occurring only 2 degrees away from this point right on the U.S. nodal axis.

T. Saturn had gone stationary at 6–AQ–50 right on the U.S. SN, and it was even stronger by being stationary in its own sign. It perfectly opposed T. Jupiter at 6–LE–50. This is sidereal Cancer, its exaltation sign, but alas Mr. Gandhi's P3 Mars was exactly conjunct T. Jupiter at

6-LE-35 in its fallen sign — thus giving further strength at the south end where Mars would be exalted and where Saturn was stationary. This combination overpowered Jupiter which was, in addition, the most transitory of the three.

These chart factors raise the questions of whether A) these two degree themes of 27-CA/CP and 6-LE/AQ are generically related to assassination, or whether B) Rajiv Gandhi had special links to the U.S. (with the possibility of hidden intrigues), or C) this is all just random coincidence. There had been occasional allegations that Mr. Gandhi was in the employ of the U.S. CIA. The reader is invited to further investigate this matter on his own.

Parts of Death

I want to make just a quick closing comment on constructed points (often referred to as "Arabic Parts") that have been linked to the issue of death. Specifically, I'm aware of an alleged Part of Fatality (Asc + Saturn - Sun) and a Part of Death (Asc + 8th Cusp - Moon). Well-regarded astrologers Charles Emerson and Barbara Watters also apparently endorsed something called a "Death Point" (Mars + Saturn - the MC).

Parenthetically, I've been told that Barbara Watter's husband, James, was part of a $5-6 million study by The Metropolitan Life Insurance Company to research the hypothesis of a correlation between premature death, crippling disease and inclination towards accidents if born when Mars was at perigee (closest to the earth).

I know of two further "Parts of Assassination." The first is Mars + Neptune - Uranus, and the second is the Asc + Ruler of the 12th - Neptune. Some old Western texts say that one is susceptible to assassination if one has 24 degrees of Capricorn on the natal Asc. This probably proceeded from a very small base of data and, in any case, since we don't know how old this rule is, we don't know within what zodiac it may have any applicability.

In contrast, Robert Granite, in a footnote in his book titled *The Fortunes of Astrology* makes reference to a fixed "degree of assassination" which he says is at 24 degrees of Leo/Aquarius. Granite asserts that in order to activate that degree one *must* have the Sun, Moon, Ascendant or one of the "Parts of Assassination" *on* this degree. It's not clear whether he studied only U.S. assassinations, in which case there could arguably be some kind of national chart link, but there is enough full data here for the reader to test any of these points. This data also presents the opportunity to test the 8th and 12th cusps for various house systems.

Some old books also emphasize the prominent function of Neptune due to the issue of treachery, and this seems to be quite true. As usual, no single factor does it, and many other things must confirm.

EPILOGUE

The day I am completing this chapter (4/1/94) there is a big article on the front page of the *Washington Post*. It states that a "landmark" has been achieved in the new field of genetic medicine because scientists reported today that, for the first time, they have brought about lasting improvement in a patient with a life–threatening disease. The patient had suffered a heart attack at age 16, and she had undergone bypass surgery at age 24. Her rare hereditary syndrome causes cholesterol levels to rise to 10 times normal levels, thus clogging the blood vessels of both her and other family members. Early death is typically assured.

The experimental technique involved the direct replacement of defective genes with normal ones, and it signals that an array of formerly fatal diseases will soon be treatable through direct genetic manipulation. It was very interesting to me that this procedure was said to have been actually carried out in 1992 because that was the year that Pluto actually entered sidereal Scorpio for the first time. I had forecast, in a postmarked article, a major scientific development, fundamental to life's mysteries, as a result of that ingress.

So, in closing out this book, I would like to point out how matters have really come full circle. The reason is because this scientific breakthrough in applied genetics routes us directly back to the full page epigraphical quote by Alice Bailey, the famous channel of Tibetan metaphysics, at the very front of the book. Suppose science is developing the power to block all fatal diseases? Obviously this is no longer a science fiction question.

Under this new circumstance, when does the soul withdraw? To this point it has typically had to deal with a very reluctant body and a fearful personality ego. Bailey, perhaps anticipating this scientific evolution, says that the soul will soon be withdrawing itself under conscious circumstances within an environment that does not support fear.

To the extent that this book increases such consciousness, and therefore defuses spiritual fear about death, I would like to think that it is a tool of constructive assistance in the transition to this new plateau of understanding. May each reader extract from this book whatever values may assist in that regard, and ignore the rest.

No one has a more true sense of life, and its meaning, than people on the front lines of a war or on their deathbeds. The extent to which we try to ignore death is the extent to which we tend to ignore life. Since "death" is the inevitable final fact of all earth–based incarnations, consider leading your life *not* as though "today is the *first* day of the rest of your life," as some pop psychology self–help books propose, but rather as though it were your *last*.

The former method implies a false option to cast off spiritual errors as though they were last year's fashions – instead of last year's building blocks. The latter method will tend more to preempt such errors in the first place in a spiritually logical, and therefore naturally self–correcting, way. From my incense–activated childhood assisting at the Catholic altar, the following frequent refrain now comes to mind: "Pax vobiscum, et cum spiritu tuo" (Peace be with you, and with your spirit).

RESOURCE DIRECTORY

For those who may wish to pursue further research into this topic on a personal computer, here is a partial list of vendors that can provide all the necessary calculations and often much more:

PC Jyotish

Passage Press
8180 S. Highland Drive
Sandy, UT 84093

ph: 800-873-0075

Astral-11

Institute for East-West Studies
803 Rockfellow Drive
Mount Shasta, CA 96067

ph: 916-926-4256

CCRS Horoscope Program

Mark Pottenger
838 5th Avenue
Los Angeles, CA 90005

ph: 213-487-1000

Matrix Software

315 Marion Avenue
Big Rapids, MI 49307

ph: 800-PLANETS

Various Pkgs from ACS, Inc.

P.O. Box 34487
San Diego, CA 92163-4487

ph: 800-888-9983

Haydn's Jyotish

Haydn Huntley
203 West Stone
Fairfield, IA 52556

ph: 515-472-7025

Visual Jyotish

C&D Scientific Software
One Ford Avenue
Lynnfield, MA 01940

ph: 617-334-4967

Parashara's Light

Geovision Software
P.O. Box 2152
Fairfield, IA 52556

ph: 515-472-0855

Astrolabe

P.O. Box 1750
Brewster, MA 02631

ph: 800-843-6682

Goravani Jyotish

211 Crest Drive
Eugene, OR 97405

ph: 541-485-8453

HINDU ASTROLOGY TERMINOLOGY

For those readers who would like to further investigate the original classical texts on Hindu astrology (or even commentary on the classics), below is a list of about 1,700 astrological terms that I have accumulated over the years from a variety of sources. Some of these words clearly seem to be Western, but if I have seen them in a Hindu reference source, I usually captured them. There also seems to be a variety of creative spellings for many of these words. I've tried to show the various combinations that I've seen. I also recognize that the given meanings are generally quite cryptic. But what is here is better than nothing (which is what I personally started out with), and these meanings will often give you a sufficient clue to make improved sense of some particular statement that might otherwise just stop you cold. Finally, I cannot assure the completeness or accuracy of any of these meanings; it's just the best I could pull together. Readers are welcome to submit corrections and additions.

Abda .... Year
Abdadhipathi .... Ruler of the year
Abdaphala .... Yearly forecast
Abhijin Muhurtha ...... Auspicious moment
Abhijit .... "Invisible" 28th asterism
Acharya .... Teacher
Adhana .... Moment of conception
Adhi .... Mental distress
Adhikamasa .... Additional "intercalary" (compensatory) month
Abhukta Moola .... Inauspicious time of birth
Achcha .... Venus
Adhama .... Bad
Adhana .... Conception
Adhimitra .... Good friend
Adhipat(h)i .... Owner; ruler
Adhipathya .... Rulership
Adhis(h)atru .... Great enemy
Adhivarsha .... Leap year
Adhi yoga .... Benefics in 6,7 & 8 from Moon
Adhyaya .... Chapter
Adi .... First
Adrishta .... Unseen; luck
Adya .... 1st house
Aga .... Fixed ("unmoving") signs – TA, LE, SC & AQ
Agama shatras .... "White magic"; Science of temple ritual
Agna .... Command (its chakra is in the brow)

Agni .... Fire
Agni hotra .... Fire ritual
Agni mandala .... Solar ingress into certain stars
Agu .... Lunar north node
Agyna .... 10th house
Ahargana .... # of days elapsed from start of Kali Yuga
Ahas .... Duration of the day
Ahi .... 150 parts of a sign
Ahimsa .... Non-violence
Ahoratra .... Full day measured from sunrise to sunrise
Aja .... Aries
Ajyasparsha .... Mars affliction to the blood
Akal Mrityu .... Accidental death
Akasa .... Space; ether
Akash .... Sky
Akshamsa .... Terrestrial latitude
Akshavedamsa .... 45th harmonic chart
Alpatmaja .... Fixed signs; few sons
Alpayu .... Short life; early death
Alpheta .... Giver of life
Amala yoga .... Benefics in 10th
Amatyakaraka .... Planet in 2nd from highest degree
Amavasya .... Tithi #30 (12–0); new Moon (end of lunar month)
Ambu .... 4th house
Amla .... Sour
Amrita .... Ambrosia which grants immortality
Amsa .... Longitude of planet; part of a sign
Anapha yoga .... Planets in 12th from Moon
Anareta .... Zone or factor having to do with death
Anga .... Part of the body
Angaraka .... Mars
Angas .... Limbs; parts
Anishta bhavas .... Houses 6, 8 & 12
Anisthta .... Inauspicious
Annapras(h)ana .... A baby's 1st feeding
Antaras .... Inter-periods
Ant(h)ara dasas .... Tertiary planetary periods (9 of them)
Antargraha .... Inferior planets
Antaryuti .... Conjunction of inferior planets
Anthara .... Unit of time measurement
Anthyaja .... Untouchable
Antya .... Last
Anupachaya .... Houses other than 3, 6, 10 & 11th from Asc

Anupadesa	Watery places
Anuradha	"After Radha" Asterism #17 (03-SC-20) (SA)
Apachaya	Houses 1, 2, 4, 7 & 8 (some add 12)
Apad	Without legs
Apahara	Stealing
Apasmara	Coma
Apheta	Same as alpheta
Apmandal	Ecliptic
Apoklimas	Cadent houses (3, 6, 9 & 12)
Apourusheya	Impersonal; super-human
Aprakashaka Graha	Shadow Planet (invisible)
Apa	Water
Aputra	Childless
Ara	Mars
Arambha	Start or beginning (point)
A(u)rd(h)ra	"The Moist One" Asterism #6 (06-GE-40) (NN)
Argala	That which aids or obstructs (Jaimini term)
Ari	Enemy
Aridra	Same as ardra; alpha orionis
Arishta	Danger to life; death before age 12
Asishtayoga	Combinations for misfortune
Arka	Sun
Artha	Wealth or materialistic
Aroha	Ascending
Arohana	Same as arohi
Arohi	Ascending from fallen degree to exaltation degree
Aroodha rasi	Sign as distant from ruler as ruler from house
Artha	Financial and practical activities (houses 2, 6 & 10)
Arudh(r)a	Horary rising sign
Arudha rasi	Sign as distant from Asc ruler as Asc is from ruler
Aruna	Sun
Arupa	Shapelessness
Ascendant	Rising sign/degree; related to 1st house
Asha	Desire
Ashadha	4th lunar month (June/July)
Ashad(h)apoorva	See Poorvaashada
Ashad(h)auttara	See Uttaraashada
Ashta	8; combust
Ashtakavarga	8 sources of planetary energy, for transit results (337)
Ashtama rasi	8th sign
Ashtami	Tithi #8 (84-96 & 96-84)
Ashtamsa	8th harmonic
Ashtottari (dasa)	Alternative to Vimsottari of 108 yrs (SN not used)
Ashubha	Inauspicious
Ashwina	7th lunar month
Ashwini	Star that defines zero Aries (see Asvini)
As(h)les(h)a	"The Embracing" Asterism #9 (16-CA-40) (ME)
Aspada	10th house
Asphujit	Venus
Asta	Setting; combust
Astamgata	Combustion
Asterism	1/27th of the visible sky (each is 13.33 degrees)
Asthi	Bone
Astodaya	Helical planetary rise and set
Asu	6 = 1 Pala (see gurvakshara); 4 seconds (sid. time)
Asura	Lunar north node
Asura Sandhi	Twilight
Asura	Demon
Asura yogas	Malefic combinations
Asvattha	Pertains to pipal tree; alternative name for Sravana
Asvini	"Possessing Horses" Asterism #1 (00-AR-00) (SN)
As(h)wini	Same as Asvini
Aswija	(undefined)
At(h)ichar(a)	Acceleration
Atiganda	Sun/Moon yoga #6 (2-6-40 to 2-20-0)
Atimitra	Good friend
Atma	Soul
Atmaghana	Knowledge of self
Atmakaraka	Soul indicator – planet at maximum degree (plus Sun)
Atmasakti	Spiritual force of the soul
Aurdhra	Same as arudhra
Avadhi	Period of time
Avahana	Invocation
Avanati	Depression
Avaroha(na)	Descending from exaltation degree to fallen degree
Avasthas	Planetary states of existence; 12 postures
Avatara	Descent of the Divine birth into form & shape
Avayoga	An inauspicious yoga
Avyakta	Invisible plane
Aya	Income; 11th house
Ayana	Direction; solstice; equinox; half a year
Ayanabala	One of the 6-fold planetary strengths
Ayanams(h)a	(expanding) precession gap between tropical & sidereal
Ayaya	Gains and profits; 11th house
Ayurbhana	8th house
Ayurbhava	8th house

Ayu(rdaya) .... Longevity
Ayurveda .... Vedic longevity system of health/remedies
Ayush (karaka) .... Longevity (indicator); Saturn
Ayush(h)than .... 3rd & 8th houses (the life-giving houses)
Ayushmana .... Sun/Moon yoga #3 (0–26–40 to 1–10–0)
Badha Sthan .... Obstruction house (11,9,7 for Cardinal,Fixed, Mut. Asc's)
Badhak Graha .... Rul. of 11th if Asc is card. (9th if fix, 7th if mut)
Baghya .... Obstructing planet (ruling and in house of obstruction)
Bahir Grahas .... Pertaining to external affairs
Bahiryuti .... Superior planets (Mars on out)
Bahudhanya .... Superior conjunction
Bahukalatra .... 10th year in 60 year cycle
Bala .... Having more than one wife
Balabhadra .... Strength
Balarishta .... Astrological writer
Balava .... Infant mortality (some say to 8; some say 12 or more)
Bal Chandra .... Half of a lunar day
Bali .... Crescent Moon
Balishta .... Retrograde
Balya .... Strong
Bandhana .... Planet in a friend's house
Band(h)u .... Imprisoned
Barhaspathyamana .... Relations; Brother
Basanta .... Jupiterian "year"
Basanta Ritu .... Spring
Basanta Sampat .... Spring Season
Basti .... Vernal Equinox
Beastial Signs .... Lower half of body zone defined from naval to genitals
Beeda .... GE, VI, SA & PI
Beholding Signs .... 1st, 2nd, 4th, 7th, 8th, 9th & 12th
Benefic .... Sign pairs w/same declination (1/6,2/5,3/4,7/12,etc.)
Benefics .... A planet which gives good results
Bhabhog .... Non-dark MO, VE, JU, & ME w/o negative association
Bhachakra .... Remaining portion of a nakshatra yet to be traversed
Bhackakra .... Zodiac
Bhadra .... same as bhachakra
Bhadra Tithi .... 6th lunar/solar month
Bhag .... 2nd, 7th & 12th days of a lunar half month
Bhaga .... Part or division; degree
Bhagan(a) .... Female organ
Bhagini .... Solar revolution; planetary revolutions
Bhagol .... 11th house
                       Sky

Bhagya .... Fortune; luck; destiny; prosperity; 9th house
Bhamsa .... 27th harmonic chart
Bhanga .... Cancel
Bhanu .... Sun
Bharani .... "She who carries" Asterism #2 (13–AR–20) (VE)
Bhaskar .... Sun
Bhaskaracharya .... Famous Hindu astronomer
Bhattotpala .... Commentator of Brihat Jataka
Bhava .... House
Bhava Avsan .... End of a house
Bhava Chakra .... Table of house cusps; cuspal house chart
Bhava Dhipathi .... House ruler or significator
Bhava Lagna .... Ascendant (sometimes of a certain type)
Bhava Madhya .... House midpoint
Bhava Rambha .... Beginning of a house
Bhava Sadhan .... Longitude of house cusp
Bhava Sandhi .... Junction of two houses; their cusp
Bhava Spashta .... Longitude of house cusp
Bhava Sphuta .... Determining house longitude
Bhavana .... House
Bhavas .... Houses
Bhavasandhi .... Juncture point of two contiguous houses
Bhavishya(d) .... Future (regarding the)
Bhavishya Purana .... Book of Future Prophesy (1 of 18 puranas)
Bhavishya ithasala .... Applying aspect
Bhavishya kathan .... Forecasting
Bhayat .... 6th house
Bheda .... Portion of a lunar mansion already traversed
Bheet(h)a .... "Tact"; diplomacy and covert methods
Bheri yoga .... Planet in a debilitated/accelerating condition
Bheetha .... Auspicious combination
Bhiksu .... Condition of a planet during acceleration
Bhinnashtakavarga .... Monk; Beggar
Bhogamsa .... Ashtakavarga of each planet being considered
Bhogya .... Celestial longitude
Bhogyamsa .... To pass time
Bhoo .... Portion of arc yet to be traversed
Bhookendrik .... Earth (earthly element in creation)
Bhookendriya .... Geocentric
Bhooloka .... Geocentric
Bhoomi .... Earth
Bhoomineech .... 4th house
                        Perigee

363

Bhoomyuchcha .... Apogee
Bhoot tatwa .... Elements
Bhouma .... Mars
Bhrahmadamasa .... Planet in same sign in 9 vargas (dignified)
Bhramana .... Planetary axial rotation
B(h)ratrukaraka .... Brother indicator; Mars
Bhratru .... Brother
Bhratrubhava .... 3rd house
Bhratrukaraka .... Planet in 3rd highest degree
Bhrgu .... Venus
Bhu .... To exist
Bhuja .... Distance from nearest equinox
Bhukt(h)a .... Time gained
Bhukt(h)amsas .... Portion already traversed; arc gained
Bhukt(h)i .... Secondary planetary periods (9 of them) after dasas
Bhuktinatha .... Sub-period ruler
Bhumi .... Ice; Earth sphere
Bhutattava .... Earth element
Bhuvana Deepika .... Text on horary astrology
Bhuvarloka .... Astral world
Bij sanskar .... Planetary correction or rectification
Bile .... One of the three humours
Bimba pariman(as) .... Apparent planetary diameter
Bimbos .... Inductive of transitory delight
Bindus .... Beneficial marks or dots in ashtakavarga
Biped .... GE, LI, AQ & 1st 1/2 of SA
Blind signs .... AR, TA & LE at 12 AM; GE, CA & VI at 12 PM
Bodhana .... Mercury
Boreal signs .... Aries to Virgo
Brahma (#1) .... Unique planetary distinctions by dispositors
Brahma (#2) .... God (of Trinity) of creative/anabolic force
Brahmacharya .... Sun/Moon yoga #25 (10–20–0 to 11–3–20)
Brahma dasa .... Period when disciple completes spiritual training
Brahman .... Alternate method of timing events
Brahmana .... The highest/first/spiritual class/caste; water signs
Brahmana .... Same as brahman
Brahmanda .... Universe (macrocosmos)
Brahma rasi .... Sign occupied by Brahma
Brahmin .... Same as brahman
B(h)ratrukaraka .... See same above under "Bratr..."
Br(i)haspati .... Jupiter/Thursday
Brihat Jataka .... Classical astrological text
Brihat Samhita .... Classic text on natural phenomena

Buddhi .... Reason or intelligence
Budha .... Mercury
Buddha .... Same as Budha
Candra .... Moon
Cara .... Cardinal ("moveable") signs (AR, CA, LI & CP)
Caput draconis .... North node of the Moon
Cauda draconis .... South node of the Moon
Cazimi .... In the heart of the Sun (perfectly conjunct)
Chaitra .... 1st lunar/solar month (March/April period)
Chakra .... Chart; wheel; cycle; spinal center
Chakra dasa .... Alternate method of timing events
Chamara yoga .... Ruler of Asc in own sign or exalted
Chandal .... A low caste/class
Chandala .... North node
Chandas .... Rhetoric
Chandra .... Moon; feather; vedic hymn
Chandra Grahan .... Lunar eclipse
Chandra Lagna .... As though the Moon defined the 1st house
Chandra Masa .... Lunar month
Chandra Mangala .... Moon/Mars interplay (conj or mutual reception)
Chandra Mas .... Lunation
Chandrasta .... Setting of the Moon
Chandra Varsha .... Lunar year
Chandrodaya .... Rising of the Moon
Chapa .... Arc
Chara .... Same as cara
Chara bala .... Sign strength
Chara dasa .... Variable Jaimini period system based upon signs
Charakarakas .... Changeable significators based only on degree rank
Charakhanda .... (undefined)
Charana .... Phase; pada; 1/4 of a nakshatra
Chat(h)urhamsa .... 4th harmonic chart
Chat(h)urasra .... 4th (& 8th?) house(s)
Chaturdas(h)i .... Tithi #14 (156–168 & 24–12)
Chaturthamsa .... 4th harmonic chart
Chaturthi .... Tithi #4 (36–48 & 144–132)
Chatushpada .... Four-legged ("quadruped") signs
Chat(h)ushtaya .... Quadrants (houses 1, 4, 7 & 10)
Ches(h)ta .... Motion
Ch(h)aya .... Shadow
Ch(h)aya grahas .... Rahu & Ketu
Chhayasunu .... Saturn (son of Chhaya who is spouse of the Sun)
Chhidra .... Defect; 7 kinds of inauspicious planets (usually re:8th)

Chitakasha .... Stirring of the mental space causing vibrational waves
C(h)itra .... Star Spica – Asterism #14 (23–VI–20) (MA)
Chitta .... Same as c(h)itra
Chittottha .... 7th house; mental illness
Climacteric Conj .... Jupiter and Saturn conjunctions
Combustion .... Weakened because too near the Sun (distance varies)
Configuration .... Three or more planets in one house
Conjunction .... Two planets in the same sign (w/o regard for orb)
Constellation .... 1/27th of zodiac (same as asterism & lunar mansion)
Cosmic cross .... T–Square
Critical degrees .... Card (0/13/26); Fixed (9/21); Mut (4/17) – lunar motion
Dainik .... Daily or diurnal
Daiva .... Unknown factor; past karma
Daivagyna .... Astrology
Daivajna .... Astrologer
Dakshina .... South
Dakshina Gola .... Southern hemisphere
Dakshinayana .... Southern route of the Sun (CA to SA)
Dakshinayana bindu .... Summer solstice
Dana .... "Temptation", use of incentives such as money
Danaveiya .... Venus
Danda .... "Punishment", use or threat of force
Dara .... Wife (or husband)
Darakaraka .... Planet in 7th highest degree
Daridra .... Poverty
Dasa .... (primary) Planetary period or cycle (9 of them)
Dasa chid(h)ra (#1) .... Period of a defective or damaged planet
Dasa chid(h)ra (#2) .... End of a dasa
Dasama .... 10th house
Dasanatha .... Ruler of the dasa period
Das(h)amsa .... 10th harmonic chart (career)
Dash(a)mi .... Tithi #10 (108–120 & 72–60)
Dashavarga .... Ten divisions of a sign (see dashamamsa)
Dasra .... Same as Ashwini
Dasvargas .... Divisions of a sign
Dattaka .... Adopted
Day Signs .... LE, VI, LI, SC, AQ & PI
Decanate .... 1/3 of a sign
Deaf signs .... LI & SC (before noon); SA & CP (after noon)
Deekshita .... Performer of sacrifice
Deen(a) .... Fallen or debilitated placement
Deept(h)a .... Exalted
Deepthamsa .... Combustion arc

Deer .... Symbol for 1st half of Capricorn
Deergha .... Long
Deerghaya (or yu) .... Long life
Deha .... Sun or Asc
Deity planet(s) .... Jamini term giving status to 3 planets
Desha .... Last nakshatra before one's natal one
Deshantar rekha .... Terrestial longitude
Deva .... 5th house
Deva loca .... World of immortals
Devanagari .... Script
Devas .... Gods
Devendra .... (undefined)
Devara .... Husband's younger brother
Deveiya .... Jupiter
Devi .... Goddess
Dhairya .... 3rd house
Dhana .... Wealth; 2nd house
Dhanakaraka .... Jupiter
Dhanis(h)t(h)a .... "The Wealthiest" Asterism #23 (23–CP–20) (MA)
Dhanu(s) .... Sagittarius
Dhanurvidya .... Archery
Dhanya .... Method of timing events
Dharma .... Duty; one's proper task(s); righteousness; nature
Dharmabhava .... 9th house
Dharmasthana .... same as dharmabhava
Dharma karmadhipa .... Conjunction of rulers of 9th & 10th
Dharma trikona .... Same as trikona (1st, 5th & 9th)
Dhata .... Libra
Dhatu(s) .... Metals and minerals; semen; elementary force
Dhee .... 5th house
Dhipat(h)i .... Owner(ship); Ruler of
Dhoomaketu .... Comet
Dhriti .... Sun/Moon yoga #8 (3–3–20 to 3–16–40)
Dhruva (#1) .... Pole; Pole star; time in right ascension
Dhruva (#2) .... Sun/Moon yoga #12 (4–26–40 to 5–10–0)
Dhumaketu .... Comet
D(h)usthanas .... 6th, 8th & 12th
Dhruvanadi .... Nadi astrology (Satyacharya)
Dhuma .... (undefined)
Dhwaja .... Ketu
Dig .... Direction
Digbala .... Directional strength (planet in "best" house)
Digits .... Phases

365

Dik	Direction or strength
Dik Bala	Same as digbala
Dina	Diurnal duration
Dinakrita	Sun
Dinardha	1/2 of the daylight period
Dinmana	Natural day
Dirgha	Life of 100 years
Disha	Direction
Ditya	Sun
Diurnal signs	LE, VI, LI, SC, AQ & PI (strong during day)
Diva	Day
Divarathri bala	Part of Shadbala
Dolan	Oscillation
Dosh	Evil humour
Dosha	A net quality of obstructive or weakening blemish
Drashta	Apparent
Drashta graha	Aspecting planet
Drekkana	3rd harmonic chart; decanate (1/3 of sign)
Dreshkana	Same as drekkana
Drigbala	Strength of an aspect
Drig dasa	Alternate method of timing events
Drik	Aspect
Drishta	Aspected or aspecting
Drishti	Aspect (by planets to certain other planets & houses)
Drishti Kshitija	Visible horizon
Drishtiphala	Result of an aspect
Drishtipinda	Total of all aspects
Drishya	Visible
Drishyardha	Visible hemisphere
Druk bala	Aspect strength
Drusya	Aspected
Dumb signs	Water signs (CA, SC & PI)
Durga	Goddess as demon-slayer; Goddess of destruction
Duruva	Time of right ascension
Dushchikya	3rd house
Dusht(h)a marana	Violent death
Dustha	Planet in malefic sign
Dus(h)t(h)anas	Malefic Houses (6, 8 & 12)
Dussthan	Same as dushtanas (or trik)
Dusthanas	Same as dushtanas (or trik)
Dvadasamsa	Malefic house
Dvisvabhava	Dual, mutable or common (signs) – GE, VI, SA & PI
Dvisvabhta	Same as dvisvabhava

Dwadas(h)amsa	12th harmonic chart
Dwadashaka	12th house
Dwadashi	Tithi #12 (132–144 & 48–36)
Dwaita	Plane of duality
Dwaja	South node
Dwandwa	Gemini; dual signs
Dwara rasi	Sign being considered
Dwipada rasis	Two-legged signs (common/mutable)
Dwirdwadasa	Mutual 2nd/12th house planetary positions
Dwirwadasa	Planet being disposed
Dwiswabhata	Same as dvisvabhata
Dwriswabhava	Same as dwiswabhata
Dwiteeya	Tithi #2 (12–24 & 168–156)
Dwitiya	Same as dwiteeya
Dyuna	7th house
Eadhipthya	Ashtakavarga reduction due to joint ownership
Easarapha	Combination unique to Tajaka System
East	Indicated by 3 fire signs
Ecliptic	Apparent path of the Sun around the Earth
Ekadasamsa	11th harmonic chart
Ekadashi	Tithi #11 (120–132 & 60–48)
Ekadhipat(h)ya	Planet owning 2 signs
Ekadhipat(h)ya haran	Ashtakavarga reduction due to joint ownership
Ekadhipat(h)ya hrasa	Same as above
Ekadhipat(h)ya s(h)odhan(a)	Same as above
Elarata	Saturn's transit of 12th, 1st & 2nd from Moon
Ether	5th element (fire, earth, air, water, ...)
Exaltation	Best sign position
Ephemeris	Book containing daily longitude of planets
Eswara	Ruler
Eunuch planet(s)	Mercury (and sometimes Saturn)
Even signs	Earth & water signs (same as female or gentle)
Faladesh	Interpretation
Female signs	Earth & water signs (same as even or gentle)
Familiarity	Mutual reception
Flavors	Note: planetary flavors differ much from East to West
Flexible	Mutable
Friends	Positive planetary relationships (e.g., VE & SA)
Gajakesari (yoga)	Mutual reception of Moon & Jupiter in quadrants
Gamana	7th house
Ganapathi	An element of cosmic forces
Ganda (#1)	Sun/Moon yoga #10 (4–0–0 to 4–13–20)
Ganda (#2)	Certain poor birth combinations at nakshatra cusps

Gandanta (#1)	Moon or Asc in last 1/9th of a water sign (negative)
Gandanta (#2A)	The point where a nakshatra & sign end simultaneously
Gandanta (#2B)	Cusp of water and fire houses
Ganesh	Elephant-faced god (related to Jupiter/knowledge)
Ganita	Astronomical calculations; Hindu mathematics
Garga	Famous sage
Gati	Motion
Gaurava	Respect
Gayatri	Mystic formulas based on Law of 7
Gayat(h)ri mantra	Chanting
Geha	4th house
Geniture	Birth
Gentle signs	Earth & water signs (same as even or female signs
Ghana	Knowledge
Ghanta	Hour
Ghata	Aquarius
Ghatana	Event
Ghatanahshana	Epoch
Ghati	1 = 24 minutes (= 60 palas) X 60 = 1 day; 2 = 1 muhurtha
Ghatika	Same as ghati
Glou	Moon
Gna	Mercury
Gnana	Wisdom, higher knowledge or discrimination; 10th house
Gnat(h)i	Relatives
Gnathikaraka	Planet in 6th highest degree
Go	Transit(s)
Gochara dasa	Progression
Gocharaphalam	Result of transits or progressions
Godhuli	Sunset
Gokula	Taurus
Gola	Hemisphere
Golardha	Spherical astronomy
Gole	Hemisphere
Gopuramsa	A planet well placed in 8 harmonic charts
Gouri	Goddess consort of Siva
Gowri	Same as Gouri
Graha	Planet (i.e., something able to grip or seize)
Graha aperan	Planetary aberration
Grahagunakar(a)	Planetary factors
Grahakrant rasish	Dispositor
Grahana	Eclipse

Grahanagata Pinda	Eclipsed body
Grahana Seema	Ecliptic limit
Graha Nikaya	Solar system
Graha Pinda	Product of bindus
Graha Sphuta	Regarding planetary longitudes
Graha Yuddha	Planetary War (see this definition)
Grahiya Ayana	Precession
Grahiya Kaksha	Orbit
Grahiya Siddhanta	Planetary Theory
Grandi (yoga)	Produces fatal disease
Granthi	Knot
Greeshma	Summertime
Griha	4th house
Grishma	Summertime
Gulika (#1)	Son of Saturn; a secondary/tertiary planet
Gulika (#2)	Jaimini sensitive Asc point at end of Saturn period
Guna	Qualities
Gunakara	Factors
Guru	Jupiter; a spiritual guide
Guruvar	Thursday
Gurvakshara	10 = 1 Asu
Hala	Plough
Happy	When a planet is in a friend's house
Harsha	Ruler of 6 in 6
Harshana	Sun/Moon yoga #14 (5-23-20 to 6-6-40)
Hast(h)a	"The Hand" Asterism #13 (10-VI-00) (MO)
Heena	Mean
Heli	Sun
Hemanta	Mild winters
Hershel	Uranus
Hibuka	4th house
High tide	Moon from IC to Desc or MH to Asc (Moon is strong)
Homa	Fire ritual
Hora	Planetary hour; 1/2 a sign
Horadhipathi	Ruler of 1/2 a sign
Hora lagna	Planetary ruler of the hour
Horamakaranda	Ancient astrological text
Hora Sastra	Science of time (astrology)
Hour	Equals 2 & 1/2 ghatis
Hras(a)	Reduction
Hyleg	Allegedly sensitive zones related to life & death
Indra (#1)	Uranus
Indra (#2)	Sun/Moon yoga #26 (11-3-20 to 11-16-40)

Indrachapa	Alleged planet
Indramsa	Planet dignified in 6 different vargas
Indriya	5 organs of sensation
Indu	Moon
Intercalary	(undefined)
Induputra	Mercury
Iravat	Strong in 9 divisions
Ishta	Time of birth from sunrise; a favorable period
Ishtadeva	Deity
Ishtakala	The given time
Ishtam	Time of birth ("wished for", "desired")
Ishtapinda	Accumulation of beneficial factors
Issue	Children
Ithasala	Combination in the Tajaka system
Jadya	Disease
Jagrit	Awake
Jaimini	Ancient author of a system of astrology
Jala	4th house; the liquid water element
Jala graha	Moon & Venus
Jalatrikona	Water signs
Jamitra	7th house
Jana	Men
Janaardana	The Collective Man
Janma	Birth
Janma lagna	Birth ascendant
Janma nakshatra	Nakshatra of birth Moon
Janma rasi	Natal Moon sign
Janmarksha	Natal Moon constellation
Japa	Penance; repetition of a mantra or divine name
Jaraja	Illegitimate child
Jataka	Nativity, judgement of a
Jataka Chandrika	Ancient astrological text
Jataka Desamarga	Ancient astrological text
Jataka Parijata	Ancient astrological text
Jataka Rnava	Ancient astrological text
Jataka Tatwa	Ancient astrological text
Jathaka	Horoscope
Jati	Last asterism before the one containing your Moon
Jaya	Spouse; 7th house; victory
Jeeva (#1)	Jupiter
Jeeva (#2)	Living things (insect to human; life, individual soul
Jeevaka	Monks whose behavior is somewhat frivolous
Jeevanopaya	10th house
Jhasha	Pisces
Jiva	Jupiter
Jooka	Libra
Judwan	Twins
Jyes(h)tha (#1)	3rd lunar month
Jyes(h)tha (#2)	"The Eldest (Antares)" Asterism #18 (16–SC–40) (ME)
Jyoti	Light
Jyotish(a)	Science of Light (Vedic/Hindu astrology)
Jyotishi	Astrologer
Jyotisha marthanda	Sun of astrology
Kadamba	Ecliptic pole
Kahala	Important
Kaksha	Orbit; term or division
Kaksha hras(a)	Reduction in longevity
Kaksha vriddhi	Increase in longevity
Kakshya	1/8 orbit of a sign
Kala	Time; life/death; 30 = 1 ghati (see kashtha)
Kala Bala	Temporal strength (of a planet)
Kalachakra	Time cycle; a system of period, planets & signs
Kala hora	Re: rulers of each hour of a day
Kalakrama Vigyan	Chronology
Kala Purusha	Time personified (w/houses as body components)
Kalatra	Wife
Kalatra bhava	7th house
Kalatra karaka	significator of 7th house (spouse)
Kali	Dark form of goddess (related to Saturn); strife
Kali Yuga	Dark (iron) age started at death of Krishna (2/18/–3102)
Kalki	10th (next) avatar of Krishna
Kalpa	Brahma's Unit of time (4.32 billion sidereal years)
Kama	Desire; 7th house
Kanada	Rishi who discovered the atom ("anu")
Kanina	Son born before marriage
Kantanka	Quadrant
Kanthirava	Leo
Kanya	Virgo
Kapha	Biological water humour; phlegm(atic)
Karaka	(planet) Significator of certain matters/houses
Karakamsa	Sign occupied in navamsha by rasi Asc ruler or atmakaraka
Karakatwas	Significations
Karana	Half of a tithi (each has a name recycled 8 times/month)
Karka	Cancer
Karkata	Same as karka

Karkataka .... Same as karka
Karma (#1) .... Philosophy/Law of cause & effect; rebirth; deeds
Karma (#2) .... Career; 10th house
Karma karaka .... Jupiter
Karmarksha .... 10th asterism from natal lunar asterism
Karna .... Ear; 3rd house
Kartara .... "Scissors" or planetary bracketing of various kinds
Kartika .... 8th lunar month
Kartikeya .... Son of Shiva
Karyapa .... Significator
Karyasiddhi .... Success
Karyesa .... Same as karyapa
Kashaya .... Mixed taste
Kashta Pind .... Total of malefic aspects
Kashtha .... 30 = 1 kala (see nimisha)
Kataka .... Cancer (sign of); conception
Katibandha .... Zone
Katuka .... Bitter
Kaumara .... Planet in its own house
Kaurpi .... Scorpio
Kavya .... Venus; poetry
Keeta .... Scorpio; insect
Kemadruma .... No planet either side of the Moon
Kendra .... Angular/cardinal houses (1,4,7 & 10); quadrants
Kendra bala .... Strength due to angularity of a ruler
Keraleeya .... Collection of astrological works
Kesava .... Author of Tajaka system
Kesava Paddhathi .... Ancient mathematical astrological text
Ket(h)u .... Lunar south node; dragon's tail (quality of Mars)
Kha .... Sky; Sun; 10th house
Khagola .... Celestial sphere
Khagoliya Kshitija .... Celestial horizon
Khagrasa Grahana .... Total Eclipse
Khahi .... Astringent
Khala .... A condition of debility
Khanda .... Section or division
Khara .... Hot or pungent
Khavedamsa .... 40th harmonic chart
Kirana .... Ray
Kirthi saham .... Significators ruling fame
Kona .... 5th or 9th house; trine
Kranti .... Declination
Krantipata .... Equinox

Kranti Vritta .... Ecliptic
Kranti Vrittaki Tiryakata .. Obliquity of the ecliptic
Krishna .... Hindu God
Krishna Paksha .... Dark half of the lunar month (waning;occidental)
Krishneeya .... Ancient astrological text
Kris(s)amsa .... Degrees of planets in ascending order (w/o signs)
Kr(i)ttika .... "The Cutters" Asterism #3 (26–AR–40) (SU)
Kriya .... Aries; a religious action
Kronos .... Saturn
Krura rasis .... Cruel (signs i.e., masculine)
Kruranetra .... Mars
Krurodaya Haran .... Having to do with a reduction in longevity
Kshaitija .... Horizontal
Kshana .... Unit of time (48 minutes)
Kshata .... Wound; 6th house
Kshatriyas .... Warrior caste (2nd level); fire signs
Kshaya .... Loss; the disease of cancer
Kshepa .... Celestial latitude
Kshetra .... Quarter; sign; zone
Kshetrabala .... Residential strength
Kshetra sphuta .... For fertility
Kshiti .... Earth
Kshitija .... Horizon
Kuja .... Mars
Kujadosha .... An afflicted Mars house placement for marriage
Kulata .... Woman without virtue
Kulira .... Cancer
Kumar .... Mercury
Kumbha .... Aquarius
Kundali .... Horoscope chart; map; diagram
Kundalini .... The "coiled spring" in man
Kuta .... Mars
Kutumba .... Household; family; 2nd house
Labh(a) .... Gain; 11th house
Laghu (grahas) .... Inferior (planets i.e., Mercury & Venus)
Lagna(m) .... Ascendant or 1st house ("attached to")
Lagna dhipat(h)i .... Ruler of the Ascendant
Lagna sphuta .... Longitude of Ascendant
Lagnayus .... Longevity based upon the strength of the Ascendant
Lahiri .... Ayanamsa Committee (approved 23–25–25 for 1/1/69)
Lakshana .... Signification
Lakshmi .... Goddess of beauty/fortune (related to Venus)
Lame .... Saturn (plus Sag & Cap at twilight)

369

Lankodaya .... Equatorial Ascendant
Lavana .... Salt
Laya .... Destruction
Leya .... Leo
Ling(am) .... Male sex organ; gender
Lipta .... Period of arc or time
Loka .... World; people; planetary heavens; "to see"
Lomasa .... Ancient astronomer
Long signs .... LE, VI, LI & SC
Lopa darshana .... Combustion; setting
Lord .... (planetary) Ruler/Owner of a house
Loukika .... Worldly
Low tide .... Other than high tide locations for the Moon
Luminaries .... Sun and Moon ("the lights")
Lunar Mansion .... Asterism; constellation
Lunar Month .... Averages 29 days, 12 hours & 44 minutes.
Lunar Signs .... AR, TA, GE, CA, AQ & PI (milder, safty–seeking)
Lupta .... Conjunct; lost
Madhura .... Sweet
Madhuayu .... Middle period of life
Madhya .... Middle; Midpoint of 10th house
Madhyahna .... Noon
Madhyama .... Ordinary; average
Madhya ravi .... Mean Sun
Madhya Vindu .... Midpoint
Madhyayu(s) .... Same as madhuayu
Madhyamayus .... Same as madhyayu(s)
Magha (#1) .... 11th lunar month
Magha (#2) .... "Bountiful" Asterism #10 (00–LE–00) (SN)
Maha Dasha .... Primary planetary period
Mahants .... Priests
Mahapurusha Yogas .... Yogas that give strong personalities
Maharaja .... ruler or king
Maharishis .... Great Indian sages
Mahatmya .... Greatness
Mahayugas .... Very large cycles of time
Maheswara .... (undefined)
Makar(a) .... Capricorn
Makar Rekha .... Tropic of Capricorn
Makha .... Same as magha
Makuta .... Crown
Malavya yoga .... Venus in angle & (exalted or in own sign)
Male signs .... The fire and air signs

Malefic .... Negative or stressful in effect
Malefic planets .... SU, dark MO, MA, SA, Nodes & ME if w/MA or SA
Mana .... Measure; weight; 10th house
Manaka .... Standard
Manaka Samaya .... Standard time
Manas .... Mind; potential for feeling
Manchaka .... A raised seat dais resting on columns
Manda .... Saturn
Mandagraha .... Superior or slow-moving planet
Mandapa .... Ceremonial religious canopy
Mandi .... Son of Saturn
Mandochcha .... A celestial force
Mandooka dasa .... Alternate method of timing events
Mangal(a) .... Mars
Mangal(a)dosha .... Same as kujadosha
Mantras .... Vibrational equasion with special powers
Mantravadi .... Magician
Mantreshwar .... Ancient astrological author
Mantri .... Jupiter
Manuja .... Man
Manushya .... Two–legged; human
Manushya Jataka .... Ancient astrological text
Maraka .... Planets empowered to "kill"
Marana .... 8th house
Maranasthan .... Certain defective placements for health
Mardala .... A type of drum
Margas(h)ir(sh)a .... 9th lunar month
Margi .... Direct in motion
Markesh .... Same as margasira
Masa .... Lunar Month
Mathamaha .... Maternal relation
Mathas .... Monasteries
Matru .... Mother; 4th house
Mat(h)rukaraka .... Planet in 4th highest degree
Matsya .... Fish; Pisces
Mauline .... Appearing in the morning
Maya .... Illusion
Meena .... Pisces
Mes(h)a .... Aries (starts at the star Ashwini)
Meshurana .... 10th house
Mina .... Same as meena
Misra .... Mixed (i.e., mutable) signs
Mithra Ksherthra .... Friendly sign

370

Mithuna .... Gemini
Mitra .... Friend; Sun
Mlechchas .... Non-Hindu
Moksha .... Spiritual liberation; enlightenment; salvation
Moola .... Minerals; plants, trees & shrubs; also see Mula
Moolatrikona .... Portion of own sign better than remainder of own sign
Moonga .... Coral
Moti .... Pearl
Moveable (signs) .... Cardinal signs
Mridanga .... Air-filled leather musical instrument
Mridwamsa .... Sensitive sign point
Mriga .... Deer (as symbol of Gemini)
Mriganka .... Moon
Mr(i)gas(h)ira(s) .... "Deer's Head" Asterism #5 (23-TA-20) (MA)
Mrigasya .... Capricorn
Mrigendra .... Leo
Mrita .... Dead; planet in fall
Mritya .... Death
Mrityu .... 8th house
Mrutyu .... Same as mritya (death)
Mrutyunjaya .... Conqueror of death
Mudhita .... Friendly place
Mudit(h)a .... Condition of a planet in a friendly house
Muhurt(h)a (#1) .... Right Moment i.e., electional astrology
Muhurtha (#2) .... 30 = 1 day (see ghatika)
Mukta .... Pearl
Mukta atma .... Liberated soul
Mula .... "The Root" Asterism #19 (00-SA-00) (SN)
Mulatrikona .... Same as moolatrikona
Muntha .... (undefined)
Musala yoga .... All planets in fixed signs
Musaripha yoga .... Yoga unique to Jataka system
Mushita .... Combust
Mute (signs) .... Water signs
Mutual Reception .... When two planets exchange signs (strengthening)
Nadi .... Channel; Branch of astrology for fated events
Nadika .... 24 minutes of time
Nadi Vritta .... Celestial equator
Manu .... 1st ruler of the human race
Naga .... Stones
Naisargika .... Permanent
Naisargikabala .... Natural strength
Naisargika Karaka .... Natural significator

Nakshatras .... 27 (28? 33?) lunar mansions; constellations; asterisms
Nakshatra Dasa .... Alternate method of timing events
Nakshatra Dina .... Sidereal day
Nakshatra Divasa .... Sidereal day
Kakshatra Kala .... Sidereal time
Nakshatra Pada .... 3 degrees & 20 minutes of a constellation
Nakshatra Samaya .... Sidereal time
Nakshatra Varsha .... Sidereal year
Nakta Yoya .... Yoga unique to Tajaka system
Namakarana .... Giving a name; baptising
Nandana .... Son; 5th house
Napunsaka .... Eunuch
Narada .... Rishi associated with Nadis
Naradeeya .... Ancient astrological text
Naraka Lokas .... Interior regions (hells) denser than matter
Nara Rasis .... Human signs
Nasasthanas .... 6th, 8th & 12th houses
Nashta .... 12th house
Nasa .... Nose
Natha .... Meridian distance
Nature .... 10 different classes of instinct (airy, godly, hot, etc.)
Nautch .... Dancing Girl
Nava .... Nine; 9th house
Navami .... Tithi #9 (96-108 & 84-72)
Navams(h)a .... 9th harmonic chart ("relationships")
Navamsa Dasa .... Alternate method of timing events
Nayana .... Eyes; 2nd house
Neecha .... Debilitated planet in fallen (i.e. worst) sign
Neechasthana .... Depressed/fallen planet
Neechabhanga .... Cancelling effect of a fallen condition
Neechabhilashi .... Planet in the sign before its fallen sign
Neelakantha .... Ancient Hindu astrologer
Neelama .... Blue sapphire
Netra .... Eyes
Nica .... Fall
Nikrishta .... Worst
Nimisha .... 11 = 1 kashtha
Nipeeditha .... Conquered in war
Nirayana .... Sidereal zodiac
Nirdesha Kshana .... Epoch
Nirdhana Yogas .... Combinations for poverty
Nirguna murti .... Formless state of God
Nirukta .... Text on the Vedas

371

Niryana .... Departure
Niryana Sula Dasa .... Method of Timing Death
Nisheka .... Conception; consummation of marriage
Nisheka Lagna .... Conception ascendant
Nocturnal signs .... AR, TA, GE, CA, SA & CP (strongest at night)
North .... Indicated by 3 water signs; ruled by Mercury
Nriyugma .... Gemini
Obhayachari .... Planets on either side of Sun (excluding Moon)
Ochcha .... Exaltation
Ochchabala .... Exaltation strength
Ochchabhaga .... Exaltation degree (for each planet)
Ochha .... Exaltation
Ochha kendra .... Arc of exaltation
Odd signs .... Same as male signs
Oja .... Odd
Ojamsas .... Odd navamsas
Ojapada .... Odd group
Oopa(n)chaya(s) .... Same as Upachaya(s)
Own sign .... Remainder of sign that is not part of moolatrikona
Pada .... Quadrant (1/4 part); foot
Paddhati .... System
Padma .... Lotus
Paka rasi .... Same as Dwara sign
Paksha .... Half a lunar month
Pala .... Unit of time; one pala = 24 seconds (and 60 vipals)
Palabha .... Geographical latitude
Panap(h)ar(as) .... Succedent houses (2,5,8 & 11)
Panchaka .... Inauspicious period; 5th house
Panchami .... Tithi #5 (48–60 & 132–120)
Panchamsa .... 5th harmonic chart
Panchanga .... Hindu Ephemeris/Almanac ("five constituents")
Panchasiddhantika .... Ancient astronomical text
Pandita .... Knowledgeable
Panna .... Emerald
Papa .... Malefic (planet); sin (papi means "sinful"); 12th house
Papagraha .... Sinful planet (malefic)
Papakart(ha)ri .... Bracketed between malefics
Papa lagna .... Same as Arudha ascendant
Papargala .... Malefic combination
Para .... Unit of time = 4 seconds
Parabhava .... 8th house
Paradara saham. .... Adultery indicator
Paradesa .... Foreign country indicator

Paragala .... Malefic agency
Parakrama .... Courage
Paramaneecha .... Perfectly fallen (to exact degree)
Paramayus .... Maximum longevity
Paramochcha .... Perfectly exalted (to exact degree)
Paras(h)ara .... Ancient author/rishi of most popular astrology system
Parasari .... Parasara's astrology system
Paratpara .... Same as para
Paravthi .... Political power
Paridhi .... Circumference
Parigha .... Sun/Moon yoga #19 (8–0–0 to 8–13–20)
Parijata .... A standard astrological work
Parijathamsa. .... In own varga sign twice (positive)
Parikramana. .... Revolution
Parivara .... Family; household
Parivart(h)ana .... Exchange of places (signs/houses)
Parvagana .... Number of lunations
Parvathamsa .... In own varga sign three times (positive)
Paryaya .... Cycle; synonym
Pasa yoga .... Unfortunate combination
Paschad .... Western
Paschadasthamba .... Setting toward the West
Paschchagamana .... Retrograde
Pashchima .... West
Pashu .... Beast
Pata .... (undefined)
Patala .... Abyss
Patha .... Course; celestial force; 60 years
Pathala lagna .... Lower meridian
Pathona .... Virgo
Pati .... Husband; 7th house
Patni .... Wife; 7th house
Patyamsa .... Krisamsas subject to certain reductions
Pausha .... 10th lunar month
Peeda .... Affliction
Peedita .... Afflicted
Peedya .... Planet in last degree of sign (weak;unhappy)
Peenasa roga .... Nasal disease
Phala .... Effect (of)
Phalabhaga .... Astrological interpretation
Phala Deepika .... A standard astrological work
Phalitbhaga .... Astrological prediction
Phalguna .... 12th lunar month (last before Spring)

Phanin .... Rahu
Pidya .... Same as Peedya
Pinda .... Body; total
Pinda anda .... Microcosmos
Pit(h)a .... Father
Pit(h)amaha .... Paternal relation
Pit(h)ru .... Father; 9th house
Pithrukaraka .... Indicator of paternal affairs
Pitta .... Biological fire humour; bile
Planetary War .... Two planets conjunct within 1 degree (excludes lunar cycle)
Pluta Varsha .... Leap year
Poorna Grahana ...... Total eclipse
Poornayu .... Full life
Poornima .... Tithi #15 (168–180); full Moon
Poorva .... East
Poorvabhadrapada ... See purvabhadrapada
Poorvabhaga .... Eastern; 1st portion
Poorvaphalguni ...... See purvaphalguni
Poorva Mimamsa Sastra ... Karmic philosophy of Maharishi Jaimini
Poorvapunya .... Past life efforts getting credited in this life
Poorvashadha .... See purvashadha
Porphyry .... Modern system of house division (uses meridian)
Pournima .... Full Moon day
Prachhaya .... Umbra
Prachi .... East
Prag .... Eastern
Pragandanta .... Twilight
Pragast(h)amb(h)a ... Setting towards the East
Prajapati .... Uranus; star Rohini; sexual function
Prakasha .... Light
Prakasha Varsha .... Light year
Prahkyati .... 10th house
Prakrit(h)i .... Nature; the principle of inertia
Pralaya .... Destruction of the apparent objective world
Pramadhi .... (undefined)
Pramuditi .... Planet in friendly circumstances
Prana .... "Breath", life force; bio–electricity
Pranapada .... Sensitive point
Pranayama .... Control of prana (not really breath\shwaasa)
Prapeedita .... Condition of being defeated in a planetary war
Prarupa .... Unit of measure of time/arc
Pras(h)na Chinthamani ..... Ancient astrological text
Pras(h)na Deepika ... Classic astrological text on horary astrology

Pras(h)na (Shastra) .... Query; horary (chart based upon time of query)
Prashnakarta .... Querent
Prashnalagna .... Querent
Pras(h)na Marga ... Ancient astrological text
Prasuti .... Maternity
Prateeka .... Symbol
Pratipada .... 1st day of a lunar month
Pratipat .... Tithi #1 (0–12 & 180–168))
Pratyak .... Against
Preethi .... Love, affection
Prekshana .... Observation
Premanidhi .... A commentator
Prerana .... Promoting
Preshya .... Servant or service
Pristhodaya .... Rise with hind portion first (AR, TA, CA, SA & CP)
Prishta .... Buttocks
Prishthatogamana ... Retrograde
Prithuroma .... Pisces
Prithvi .... Earth
Priti .... Sun/Moon yoga #2 (0–13–20 to 0–26–40)
Prthive .... Earth
Progression .... A Western method of forecasting w/time substitutions
Puja .... Ritual (worship)
Pukhraja .... Precious yellow stones
Punarbhava .... Son born of a woman who has remarried
Punarbhu .... Woman
Punarvasu .... "Two prosperous again" Asterism #7 (20–GE–00) (JU)
Punarvasya .... Same as punarvasu
Punya .... Goodness; moveable sign
Punya saham .... Religion significator
Purana(s) .... Ancient literature\wisdom preceding the Vedas
Purnayu .... Long life
Purnendu .... Full Moon
Purusha .... Cosmic Being; the active principle
Purvab(h)adrapada ... "Former of Lucky Feet" Asterism #25 (20–AQ–00) (JU)
Purvabhaga .... 1st half
Purvap(h)alguni ..... "Former Reddish One" Asterism #11 (13–LE–20) (VE)
Purvapunya .... See poorvapunya
Purvas(h)ad(h)a ..... "Former Invincible" Asterism #20 (10–SA–20) (VE)
Purvapunyasthana ... 5th house
Pushana .... Sun
Pushkala .... Ruler of Moon in kendra or friendly house
Pushparaga .... Precious yellow stones

Pus(h)ya .... "Nourishing/Lucky" Asterism #8 (03–CA–20) (SA)
Putra .... Son; 5th house; children
Putrakaraka .... Planet 5th highest in degree
Quadrants .... see Kendra (the four angular houses)
Radha .... "The Delightful" – see Visakha (same as that)
Radix .... Birth chart
Rahu .... Lunar north node; dragon's head (quality of Saturn)
Rahukala .... Period of time influenced by rahu
Rakshasa .... Demon or evil being
Raja .... King (sometimes refers to the Sun); exalted condition
Rajapadmansa .... Planet in same sign in 7 vargas
Rajasa .... Virtues of royalty
Rajasaguna .... Courage and love of the arts
Rajaspada .... 10th house
Rajayogas .... Positive and powerful ("royal") planetary "unions"
Rajasic .... Agitated
Rajasika .... Interested in money, pleasure and related distractions
Rakshasa .... Super–human evil demon
Rakta suvarna .... Reddish yellow
Rama .... 7th avatar of Vishnu; divine warrior (related to Sun)
Ramani .... Virgo; a beauty
Ramayana .... Epic story of Rama
Rana .... 8th house
Randhra .... 8th house
Rapt motion .... Apparent daily motion due to earth's rotation
Rasa .... Taste; flavor
Rasat(h)ala .... Lower meridian (IC); 4th house
Rashmi .... Ray
Ras(h)i .... Sign (of the zodiac); "cluster" or "heap" (of stars)
Rasi Chakra .... Primary natal horoscope; the zodiac
Rasi dasa .... Ruling period of a sign
Rasi Gunakara .... Zodiacal factors
Rasi Hrasa .... Reduction or loss of a sign
Rasi Kundali .... Zodiac chart
Rasi Mana .... Time of oblique ascension
Rasi Vriddhi .... Increase or gain of a sign
Ratna .... Gem or precious stone
Ratri .... Night
Ravi .... Sun
Ravineecha .... Perihelion (the closest a planet gets to the Sun)
Raviuchcha .... Aphelion (the futhest a planet gets from the Sun)
Ravivara .... Sunday
Rajya .... 10th house

Reka .... Denying wealth
Rekna .... Malefic points in ashtakavarga
Revati .... "Wealthy" Asterism #27 (16–PI–40) (ME)
Riksha .... Asterism; sign
Rina .... Debt; 12th house
Ripha .... 12th house
Ripu .... Enemy; 6th house
Rishi(s) .... Ancient Vedic seers
Ritu .... Season
Ritukala .... Menstrual period
Roga .... Disease (roga yogas cause disease); 6th house
Rohini .... "Growing/Red One" Asterism #4 (10–TA–00) (MO)
Rudhira .... Blood
Rudra .... Fierce form of Shiva; a positional distinction; Pluto
Rudramsa .... 12th harmonic chart
Ruminant signs .... Signs of ram, bull & goat (AR, TA & CP)
Runa .... 6th house
Rupas .... Units of strength measurment (planet/house)
Ruthu .... Season
Sabhayam Vasati .... Secures a distinguished public position
Sadhaka (graha) .... Result–producing planet
Sadhe Sati .... "7 & 1/2 years" Saturn's transit of 12, 1 & 2 from Moon (bad)
Sadhya .... Sun/Moon yoga #22 (9–10–0 to 9–23–20)
Saguna murthi .... "Frozen form" of God
Sahachara .... Companion
Sahaja .... Siblings; 3rd house
Saham .... Ability
Sahama .... 50 in number (hard to explain!)
Sahams .... (undefined)
Sahasrara .... Causal time
Sahodara .... Brother; 3rd house
Sahottha .... 3rd house
Saimhikeya .... North node of the Moon
Saivamsa .... Planet in same sign in 11 vargas (positive)
Saka .... (undefined)
Saka yoga .... Jupiter in 6th from the Moon
Sakina .... Female deity
Sakranti .... Sun's entry (into a sign)
Sama .... "Good Counsel", mild appeal to reason; 1 year
Samadhi .... Divine hypostasis; deep yoga trance
Samagama .... Conjunct the Moon
Samakshetra .... Neutral sign
Samapada .... Even group

374

Samarsingh	Ancient author on prenatal astrology
Samasaptaka	Mutual opposition
Samaya	Time
Samb(h)and(h)a	Planetary relation (re: occupation;ownership,aspect)
Sambasiva	Same as Siva
Sambhu Hora Prakasika	Ancient astrological text
Samhara	Destruction
Samhara Khanda	Catabolic portion of the zodiac (Sag through Pisces)
Samhita	Interpretation of omens; re: mundane astrology
Samikara	Equation
Samkranti	Solar ingress into a sign
Sampat	Equinox
Samptata	Same as sampat
Sampatik Saura	Tropical year
Sampurna	Full, complete
Sampvatsara	Annual constant
Samrajya yoga	Similar to raja yoga
Samudaya	Community
Samudra	Ocean; sea
Samvat	Period or era
Samvatsara	60 year cycle
Sanchar Desha	Dwelling place
Sandhi	Cusp of Sagittarius & Capricorn (a lame point)
Sandhya	Twilight; dawn
Sandhya tara	Venus rising in West after sunset
Sanghatika	16th constellation from birth one
Sani	Saturn
Sanketa	(undefined)
Sanketnidhi	Indication
Sanskara	Ancient astrological text
Sankramana	Solar ingress
Sankranti	Same as sankramana
Sanskrit	Ancient "name = form" language of classics
Santana	Occupying favorable divisions
Santa	Children; 5th house
Santapa	Sorrow
Sanyasa	Ascetic
Santha	Condition of planet in beneficial shadvargas
Sanyasa yogas	Combinations for asceticism
Saptama	7th
Saptami	Tithi #7 (72–84 & 108–96)
Sapt(h)amsa	7th harmonic chart

Sapta padi	7 steps of circling sacred fire (marriage–related)
Saptarshi	7 stars in Big Bear for 7 sages
Saptha Varga	Same as saptamsa
Sarani	Table (for example, of houses)
Saraswathi	Learning (music, language, mathematics)
Sarat	(undefined)
Saravali	Ancient astrological text
Sarga	Re: origin of space, time & elements
Sarpa	North node of the Moon
Sarvashtakavarga	The ashtakavarga of all planets combined
Sasa yoga	Saturn strong and in a kendra
Sastra	Branch of learning, science, scripture
S(h)at(h)ab(h)is(h)a(i)	"Having 100 Physicians" Asterism #24 (06–AQ–40) (NN)
Sati	Virtuous wife
Satwikaguna	Pious nature
Satkarma	Good deeds
Satru	Enemy; 6th house
Satrukshetra	Unfriendly house
Satruvarga	Negative sub-harmonic chart
Sattvic	Spiritual (in effect)
Sattwa	Purity
Satva (guna)	Excellent qualities
Satva (vela)	Excellent time period
Satvic	Creative; pure; life-sustaining
Satwika	Of pure thoughts, inclinations and deeds
Satya	Truth
Satyaloka	Realm of final truths
Satya Yuga	Golden age of truth
Saubhagya	Sun/Moon yoga #4 (1–10–0 to 1–23–20); fortune
Sauramana	Solar month
Saumya (rasis)	Mild/even (signs) – i.e., feminine
Savana	Two consecutive sunrises
Savana dina	Apparent solar day
Savya	Direct (opposite of apasavya); clockwise; dexter
Sayan(a)	Tropical zodiac
Seeghra	Fast moving planets; inferior planets
Seeghrochcha	A celestial force; apogee
Setting	At the descendant (in the 7th house)
Shadow planets	Lunar nodes
Shadbala	System of 6 kinds of planetary strength & weakness
Shadbala pinda	Summary of the 6 kinds of strength and weakness
Shadgraha yoga	Yoga involving 6 planets
Shadvargas	6 main harmonic charts

Shakata .... Having to do with the Asc/Desc axis
Shakta .... Far from the Sun in longitude
Shakuna .... Omens
Shakra .... Category of monks
Shanaishcharya .... Saturn
Shani .... Saturn
Shaniwara .... Saturday
Shankara .... Shiva
Shanmukha .... 6-faced son of Siva
Shanta .... Beneficially-placed planet
Shanti .... An act of religious propitiation
Shara .... Celestial latitude
Sharad .... Autumn
Sharasana .... Sagittarius
Shas(h)t(r)a .... Science; 6th house
Shastamsa .... 6th harmonic chart
Shastashtaka .... Relationship to 6th and 8th
Shashthi .... Tithi #6 (60–72 & 120–108)
Shastiamsas .... Unit of strength
Shastri .... Learned master
Shastyamsa .... 60th harmonic chart
Shatpanchasika .... Ancient horary astrological work
Shatru .... Enemy (Mars); 6th house
Shatrukshetra .... Enemy territory
Shatruta .... Enmity
Shayana .... Bed; sleep
Sheeghrochcha .... A celestial force
Sheetadyuti .... Moon
Sheetaritu .... Winter
Shesha .... Balance
Shiksha .... Hindu phonetics
Shirobindu .... Zenith
Shirsha .... Head
Shirshodaya .... Rise with the head first (GE, LE, VI, LI, SC & AQ)
S(h)iva (#1) .... God (of trinity) of catabolism/destruction
Shiva (#2) .... Sun/Moon yoga #20 (8–13–20 to 8–26–40)
Shobhana .... Sun/Moon yoga #5 (1–23–20 to 2–6–40)
Shodana .... (undefined)
Shodas(h)amsa .... 16th harmonic chart
Shodasavarga .... Same as shodasamsa
Shoola .... Sun/Moon yoga #9 (3–16–40 to 4–0–0)
Short signs .... AR, TA, AQ (& PI?)
Shraddha .... Faith

S(h)ravana (#1) .... 5th lunar month
Shravana (#2) .... See sravana
Shubha (#1) .... Sun/Moon yoga #23 (9–23–20 to 10–6–40)
Shubha (#2) .... Auspicious (factor); benefic; 9th house
Shubhagrihi .... Essential dignity
Shubha lagna .... Auspicious time
Shubha marana .... Easy/peaceful death
Shubhargala .... Helpful factor
Shubha yoga .... Benefics in the 1st house
S(h)udras .... Menial/"untouchable" caste; ME & SA
Shukla .... Sun/Moon yoga #24 (10–6–40 to 10–20–0)
Shukla paksha .... Waxing/brightening half of the month
S(h)ukra .... Venus
Shukravara .... Friday
Shushka (planets) ..... Mars and Saturn
Siddha .... Sun/Moon yoga #21 (8–26–40 to 9–10–0)
Siddhamsa .... 24th harmonic chart
Siddhanta .... Mathematics
Siddhi (#1) .... Sun/Moon yoga #16 (6–20–0 to 7–3–20)
Siddhi (#2) .... Perfected state of mystic merger
Siddhis .... Miraculous powers of yogis and saints
Sidereal (zodiac) ..... Zodiac based upon fixed star positions
Sign .... "What's your sign?" means Moon (or Ascending) sign!
Sikhi .... South node
Simha .... Leo
Simhananamsa .... Planet in own varga sign 4 times
Simhasanabsa .... Same as simhananamsa
Sirodaya .... Ascendant
Sirshodaya .... Signs rising by the head
Sisira .... (undefined)
Sita .... Venus
Siva .... Same as Shiva
Skanda .... War god (related to Mars)
Sodya Pinda .... Total of sign & planet pindas
Solar signs .... LE, VI, LI, SC, SA & CP (assertively brave)
Soma .... Moon
Somavara .... Monday
Sookshma .... Further proportional subdivision of bhukti periods
Soumua .... Same as saumua
Soumya .... Mercury
South .... Indicated by 3 earth signs
Soucha .... Deep exaltation
Sparsha .... First contact in an eclipse

Spashta	Celestial longitude (planetary or house)
Sphuta	Same as spashta
Sphinx	Related to the fixed signs
Sraddha	Devotion
S(h)ravana	"Hearing"/"One who limps" Asterism #22 (10-CP-00)(MO)
Sravist(h)a	"Most Famous" Asterism #23 (23-CP-20)) (MA)
Srimukha	7th year of 60 year lunar cycle
Sripathi Paddhathi	Ancient astro-mathematical text
Sri Rama	Hero of the Ramayana
Srishta	Creation
Srishti	Universe; creation of all living forms
Srishti Khanda	Anabolic portion of zodiac (Aries through Cancer)
Srishtyadi Ahargana	# of days since creation
Srnga	Cusp of the Moon
Stambhana	Station; stagnation
Sthana	House (good)
Sthanabala	Positional strength
Sthaneeya samaya	Local time
Sthira	Same as aga (fixed signs)
Sthira bala	Strength due to 1 or more planets in a sign
Sthira dasa	Fixed Jaimini dasa system used to forecast death
Sthiti	Protection
Sthiti Khanda	Sustaining portion of zodiac (Leo through Scorpio)
Sthniti	Existence
Stones	84 of these (5 major prec; 4 minor prec; 75 semi-prec)
Stree Jataka	Astrology unique to females
Stri	Same as soumya; feminine?
Stri Jataka	Same as stri jataka
Subbmarama	Natural death
Subha	Same as stri; 9th house
Subha drishtis	Beneficial aspects
Subha Parivanthana	Beneficial mutual reception
Subhargala	Providing beneficial assistance
Subhavesi Yoga	Benefics in 2nd house from Sun
Subrahmanya	Hindu god; equivalent of Michael
Sudarshana	Predictive system using 12 signs as first 12 years of life
Sudarshan(a) Chakra	"Grand splendid wheel"
Sudhanshu	Moon
Sudra	Agriculture
Sudras	Farmers and serving caste (4th level); air signs
Sukarma	Sun/Moon yoga #7 (2-20-0 to 3-3-20)
Sukha	Comfort & happiness; 4th house
Sukla Paksha	Bright half of the lunar month
Sukra	Venus (same as shukra)
Sukranadi	Ancient astrological text
Sukshma	Invisible plane
Sukshma Sarira	Man's astral body
Sula dasa	Alternate method of timing events
Sun/Moon Yogas	Add longitudes of both to get sign/deg/min (27)
Sunya	Zero
Suptha	Inimical sign
Suracharya	Jupiter
Surya	Sun
Suryakendriya	Heliocentric
Suryamsa	12th harmonic chart
Surya Siddhantha	Ancient astronomical text
Suryaneecha	Perihelion
Suryochcha	Aphelion
Suryodayadi	Time from sunrise to birth
Sushputi	Sleep
Sushumna	Spinal cord
Suta	Son
Sutakshaya	Death of own children
Sutra	Aphorism
Suvarna	Gold; "good sounds" (letters)
Suveerya	Increasing in strength
Sva	Self; 2nd house
Svati	Golden star Arcturus – Asterism #15 (06-LI-40) (NN)
Svavarga	In own harmonic
Swa	Same as sva
Swabhava	Character; nature
Swagotradevi	Personal family deity
Swakshetra	Planet located in the house it rules
Swami	Ruler; owner
Swapna	Dream
Swargabalamsa	In same varga sign 5 times
Swastha	Planet in its own sign
Swasthya	Health
Swati	Same as Svati
Swavarga	Own division
Synastry	Comparison of two charts for compatibility
Synodical	Two planet cycles beginning at the same point
Tajak(shastra)	Lesser annual forecasting system w/12 sign divisions
Tajik	Study of events
Tajika	Same as tajaka
Tamas	North node of the Moon

Tamasic .... Of a lazy, greedy, angry or harmful nature
Tamoguna .... Mild nature; having qualities of the devil?
Tamovela .... Most inauspicious time division (1 of 3)
Tantra .... Basic universal forces
Tantra mantra .... Sorcery
Tantra yoga .... "White magic"
Tanu .... Body; 1st house
Tapa .... Penance; 9th house
Tapana .... Sun
Tarabala .... (undefined)
Tarakas .... Stars
Tarakatav .... Protectiveness
Taraprachhadana .... Occultation
Taraghar .... Planetarium
Taranitanaya .... Saturn
Tarka .... Logic
Taruni .... Virgo
Tatkalika .... Temporary
Tatkalika mitra .... Temporary friend
Tatpara .... Measurement unit of arc or time
Tatwas .... Elements (5)
Tauli .... Libra
Thama .... North node
Thamas .... Of an evil nature
T(h)anu .... Same as tanu
T(h)ridos(h)as .... 3 primary bodily humours
Thrikalagnana .... Knowledge of past, present & future
T(h)ithi .... 1 lunar day (i.e., 12 degrees); #'d 1-14 + 15 & 30
Thrimsamasa .... 30th harmonic chart
Thrirasyadhiparhi .... Ruler of the year
Thula .... Libra; scales
Tilak(a) .... East point marked by females between the eyebrows
Tithiphalam .... Effect of being born on any particular tithi
Torana .... An arched doorway
Toyadhara .... Aquarius
Toyashraya .... "Dependent on water" (TA, GE, VI & AQ)
Transits .... Forecasting based upon physical location of planets
Trayodashi .... Tithi #13 (144-156 & 36-24)
Treta Yuga .... Silver (3rd) age
Tridosha .... 3 humors (of ayurveda)
Triguna .... Same as tridosha
Trik .... Houses 6, 8 & 12 (same as dusthana)
Trikala .... 3 time periods – past, present & future

Trikalagna .... Astrologer
T(h)rikona .... Trine houses (1, 5 & 9) – most fortunate
Trikona Dasa .... Alternate method of timing events
Trimsamsa .... 30th harmonic chart
Trimsamsaphalm ..... Effect of each of the 30 degrees of a sign
Trimurthis .... Trinity of Brahma, Siva and Vishnu
Tripadarksha .... Constellations 3/4 in 1 sign and 1/4 in next sign (JU ruled)
Triteeya .... Tithi #3 (24-36 & 156-144)
Tritiya .... Same as triteeya
Tritrikona .... Houses 1, 5 & 9
Tropical (zodiac) ..... Western zodiac based upon the 1st moment of Spring
Truti .... Error; moment?
Tula .... Same as thula
Turyamsa .... 4th harmonic chart
Ubhayalingi .... Hermaphrodite
Ubhayodaya .... Pisces
Ucc(h)a .... Exaltation
Ucchasthana .... Same as ucca
Uch(c)ha .... Exalted (planet in its best sign)
Uchchabhilashi .... Desiring to enter next sign (of exaltation)
Udaya .... Rising; 1st house
Udu dasa .... Alternate method of timing events
Udupati .... Moon
Udvasana .... Dissolution
Uksha .... Taurus
Unmeelana .... Reappearance
Unnatamsa .... Altitude
Upachaya .... Houses 3, 6, 10 & 11 (OK with malefics) "increasing"
Upagrahas .... Planetary satellites
Upanayana (#1) ...... Sacred thread ceremony (to infuse divine knowledge)
Upanayana (#2) ...... 3rd eye (upa = extra, and nayana = eye)
Upantya .... 11th house
Upapada .... Sign as distant from 12th ruler as ruler is from 12th
Upa Veda .... Text on the Vedas
Upaya .... Antidote to a planetary affliction
Upaye .... Same as upaya
Utpanna .... 5th constellation from natal lunar constellation
Uttama .... Planet strong in 3 divisions
Uttara .... North
Uttara ayananta ...... Northern solstice
Uttara b(h)adrapada .. "Latter of Lucky Feet" Asterism #26 (03-PI-20) (SA)
Uttara gola .... Northern hemisphere (celestial)
Uttara Kalamrita ...... Ancient astrological text

Uttara kranti — Northern declination
Uttara prosthapada — Same as Uttarabhadrapada
Uttara p(h)alguni — "Latter Reddish One" Asterism #12 (26–LE–40) (SU)
Uttara s(h)ad(h)a — "Latter Invincible" Asterism #21 (26–SA–40) (SU)
Uttara yana — Northern course of the Sun (Capricorn to Gemini)
Uttarayana bindu — Winter solstice
Vachaspati (or y) — Jupiter
Vahanakaraka — Venus
Vahanast(h)ana — 4th house
Vageesha — Jupiter
Vahana — Vehicle; conveyance
Vahana yogas — Yogas for owing a car
Vaidhriti — Sun/Moon yoga #27 (11–16–40 to 12–0–0)
Vais(h)akha — 2nd lunar month
Vaiseshika — Hindu physics
Vaiseshikamsa — In same varga sign 12 times
Vaishnavamsa — In same varga sign 10 times
Vaishyas — The trading caste (3rd level); air (or earth?) signs
Vaishya planets — Moon & Mercury
Vaisya — Business or trade
Vajpeya — Sacrificial ceremony
Vak — 2nd house
Vakra — Mars
Vakrachesta — Regrograde
Vakramargatva — Retrograde
Vakratva — Retrograde
Vakri — Retrograde
Vakyasthanadhiparhi — 4th house ruler
Valaya — Ring; girdle
Vali — A fold or wrinkle; curly
Valsakha — 2nd lunar month
Vamana — Dwarf
Vana — Forests
Vanaprastha — Monk who dwells in natural settings without clothing
Vanchanabheeti — Fear and suspicion
Vani — Speech
Vanic — Trade or trader
Vanik — Libra
Vara — Weekday
Varaha — Boar; mythical rhino–like animal
Varahamihira — Hindu astrologer
Varga — Divisional/harmonic chart (16 of these)
Vargesa — Varga ruler

Vargikarana — Classification
Vargottama — Planet in same sign in both rasi & navamsha (positive)
Variyana — Sun/Moon yoga #18 (7–16–40 to 8–0–0)
Varja — Sun/Moon yoga #15 (6–6–40 to 6–20–0)
Varna — Caste; color
Varnada dasa — Alternate method of timing events
Vars(h)a — Year
Vars(h)aphala — Annual results
Vars(h)apravesha — Solar return
Vars(h)arambha — Beginning of the new year
Vars(h)aritu — Rainy season
Varsheshwara — Ruler of the year
Vartamana — Present
Varuna — Water (the God of); urinary function
Varuni — Neptune
Vasanta ritu — Spring season
Vasara — Day of the week
Vastu — Object
Vata — Biological Water humour; wind
Vaya — Age
Vayu — Air (the God of) or movement
Veda(s) — "Word of God" in four parts
Vedabhamsa — 24th harmonic chart
Vedamsa — 40th harmonic chart
Vedanga jyotis(h)a — Ancient astronomy
Vedanta — Philosophy of self–realization
Vedha(s) — Obstruction, points of planetary affliction
Vedi(ka) — Altar
Veerya — Semen; 3rd house
Vela — (Period of) Time
Vibhava — 2nd of 60 year cycle
Vidya — Education/learning; knowledge; 4th house
Vigata — Past
Vighati — 24 seconds (1/60th of a ghati)
Vihaga — Bird
Vikala — Combust
Vikrama — Courage; 3rd house
Vikshepa — Celestial latitude
Vilagna — 1st house; Ascendant
Viliptha — Unit of time/arc measurement
Vims(h)amsa — 20th harmonic chart
Vipala — Unit of time measurement
Vivaha — Marriage

Vimshottari ... 120 year dasa cycle of fixed planetary periods
Vinasha ... Destruction; 8th house
Vipareeta ... Sinister
Vipat ... Danger
Virama Sandhi ... End point of a house
Virupa ... Unit of time/arc measurement
Visha ... Poison
Vishaghatika ... Very inauspicious time
Visakha ... "Forked/Two-Branched" Asterism #16 (20-LI-00) (JU)
Vishama ... Odd (vs. even)
Vishamapada ... Odd group
Vishavrekha ... Terrestrial equator
Vishkumbha ... Sun/Moon yoga #1 (0-0-0 to 0-13-30)
Vishnu ... God of trinity who preserves/sustains equilibrium
Vishuva ... Equinox
Vishuvad Rekha ... Equator
Vishuvad Vritta ... Equator
Vishuvamsa ... Right ascension
Vishva ... World; Aries
Vishwakarma ... Shape-builder or geometrician
Vit ... Mercury
Vitta ... Finance; 2nd house
Vivaha Saham ... Marriage indicator
Vivasa ... Unclothed
Viyoga ... Opposition
Viyuti ... Same as viyoga
Vraya ... Loss; expenditure; 12th house
Vriddha ... Old
Vriddha Yavana ... Ancient astrological author
Vriddhi (#1) ... Increase
Vriddhi (#2) ... Sun/Moon yoga #11 (4-13-20 to 4-26-40); 4th house
Vrischika ... Scorpio
Vris(h)a(bha) ... Taurus
Vritta ... Circle
Vrsa ... Taurus
Vrscika ... Scorpio
Vyadhi ... Physical ailments, pain or disease
Vyaghata ... Sun/Moon yoga #13 (5-10-0 to 5-23-20)
Vyakta ... Visible, tangible world
Vyapara ... Business; 10th house
Vyasa ... Prophetic visionary rishi
Vyatipata ... Sun/Moon yoga #17 (7-3-20 to 7-16-40)
Vyaya (#1) ... Malefic

Vyaya (#2) ... Loss and expenditure; 12th house
Wara ... Week day
Waterless Regions ... Traversed by AR, LE, LI & SA
Watery signs ... CA, SC, CP & PI
West ... Indicated by 3 air signs
Yama ... Pluto; God of death
Yamaghanta ... Jupiter's satellite
Yamakantaka ... same as yamaghanta
Yamyottara ... Meridian
Yana ... Vehicle
Yantra ... Lucky talisman
Yantras ... Mystic diagrams or ideograms
Yasa ... Fame
Yatpinde Tatbrahmande ... As above, so below
Yatra ... Campaign astrology – electional along with natal
Yauvana ... Planet in moolatrikona
Yoga ... Union; 27 combinations; addition; spiritual practices
Yogakaraka ... A positive planet due to good ownership conditions
Yogaphalam ... Result of different yogas
Yogardha dasa ... Alternate method of timing events
Yogee ... Hindu saint
Yoni ... Shape (of a woman's reproductive organs); species
Yuddha ... (planetary) War
Yugas ... Four major world ages constituting a Mahayuga
Yugma(nava)msas ... Even navamsas
Yugmarasis ... Even signs
Yuti ... Conjunction
Yuva ... Young (planet in 12-18 degrees of a sign)
Zenith ... Directly overhead

INDEX

4th Pisces Mercury f Mars T≈ Sun Te	5th Aries	6th Taurus Rahu Dx ++ ♅	7th Gemini
3rd Aquarius Venus	RAHU Jupiter beginning on 11/22/1973 RAHU Saturn beginning on 04/16/1976 RAHU Mercury beginning on 02/22/1979 RAHU Ketu beginning on 09/10/1981 RAHU Venus beginning on 09/28/1982 RAHU Sun beginning on 09/28/1985 RAHU Moon beginning on 08/22/1986		8th Cancer Saturn -- ♇
2nd Capricorn	RAHU Mars beginning on 02/22/1988 JUPITER Jupiter beginning on 03/10/1989 JUPITER Saturn beginning on 04/28/1991 JUPITER Mercury beginning on 11/10/1993 JUPITER Ketu beginning on 02/16/1996 JUPITER Venus beginning on 01/22/1997		9th Leo
1st Sagittarius Ascendant Moon +	12th Scorpio Jupiter Rx ≈ Ketu Dx --	11th Libra	10th Virgo ♆

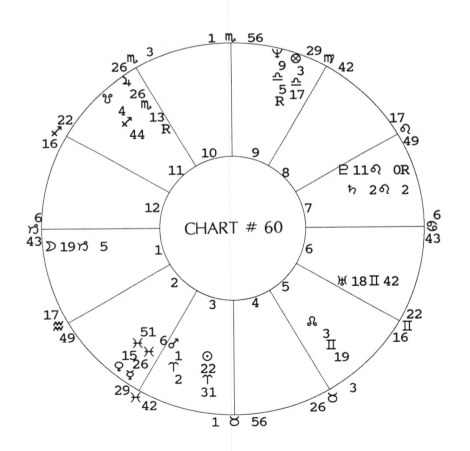

About The Author

Richard Houck is President of ARC Associates, Inc. in Washington, DC. Its charter is to provide performance-based astrological research and consulting services to enhance the specialized time cycle management requirements of corporate, political and professional clients. He has spoken to numerous groups about astrology under a variety of auspices, from psychotherapy students to country clubs and monasteries. Mr. Houck has a special interest in documented and unequivocal forecasting, and he has a recognized, and highly accurate, reputation in this regard, especially in the area of political events. He has been interviewed at length on radio and television, and is the author of over 100 postmarked articles distributed primarily to other astrologers, both nationally and internationally. He has been quoted in non-astrological newspapers and in publications such as *Today's Investor*. His astrological work was featured twice on the cover of *Leaders* magazine, a closed-circulation periodical that is only distributed to the 40,000 top world leaders.

Among his many related activities, Mr. Houck has offered a performance-based contract (with the financial odds stacked against him) to the NIH Office of Alternative Medicine. In this challenge, he offered to statistically prove the "astrological effect" under a medical scenario where the random odds would technically, and indisputably, be a trillion to one against his success. NIH would not accept the challenge citing inadequate resources and the fact that they do not engage in "betting." In 1994 ARC Associates was also the sole sponsor of the largest Hindu astrology conference ever held on the east coast of the United States. Mr. Houck has 15 years of experience as an astrologer, and owns a unique 500-book astrological library. He also publishes a restricted-circulation newsletter that is only distributed to clients with whom he has a retainer relationship. His degree is in Philosophy.

Several years prior to the incorporation of ARC Associates, Mr. Houck worked primarily in the corporate arena as an investigative assurance specialist in the security, integrity and control of very large automated systems. He was Manager of the 24-person Advanced Computer Auditing Techniques group for the Washington, DC office of Arthur Andersen & Co, and he was also one of their top international trainers in this specialty area. His computer security reports went to the Board Committee level of numerous "household name" corporations across the full range of major industrial classifications. He has been the Senior Information Officer for Intelsat, the international governmental consortium that runs the world satellite network. He has also been a Director in the Information Technology Division of an executive recruiting firm, President of the largest computer security association in Washington, DC, and an independent consultant to other private companies and the Federal government.

WOULD YOU LIKE TO LEARN MORE ABOUT EASTERN ASTROLOGY?

These recommended books are available from your local bookseller (or you can order them directly from Groundswell Press).

Hindu Astrology Lessons - (0-9641612-6-5) This is a very popular, 250-page anthology with brief, entertaining articles by 36 dedicated writers, many of whom are very well known in the field of Jyotish. It covers a spectrum of topics and interests while addressing skill levels from beginner to advanced. It contains hundreds of unique tips and clues to strengthen your understanding of Vedic astrology concepts. *Hindu Astrology Lessons* also contains direct networking access to all contributors worldwide (addresses, phone numbers, email, etc.). Cost: $16.95 + $2.95 S&H.

Digital Astrology - (0-9641612-7-3) by Richard Houck. Did you know there is a strong transit forecasting system from India that was specifically reserved for the "age of metals" (i.e., *computers*)? That it is an ancient *binary* system based upon *bit switches* (called "*bindus*") being turned "on" or "off"? That these bit switches are clustered into groups of *eight* (now known as a *byte* of data)? That this automated pointing system summarizes information in *spreadsheets*? "Westernized," and with many amazing examples, it is scheduled for 1998. Cost: $16.95 + $2.95 S&H.

Special Sidereal Ephemeris - (no ISBN) Groundswell Press is the Exclusive Manufacturer of this unique 100-year (1920-2019) sidereal Ephemeris. It basically flags three important phenomena: 1) All solar and lunar *eclipses*, 2) All *stations* of Jupiter ↔ Pluto, and 3) All sign *ingresses* for Jupiter ↔ Pluto. With this efficient and focused resource, you can quickly spot changes of condition that can strongly impact your forecasting work. An "underground favorite," this booklet works well with techniques highlighted in *The Astrology of Death*. Cost: $10.00 (S&H is free).

Eastern Systems For Western Astrologers - (1-57863-006-1) Another anthology (350 pages), but the articles are more in depth. Four are from the Indian, or Vedic, perspective featuring James Braha, Hart deFouw, Dennis Flaherty, and Richard Houck. The other four are: Astrology & The Chakras, The Degrees of The Zodiac & The I-Ching, Chinese Five-Element Astrology, and Tibetan Astrology (respectively by Ray Grasse, Robin Armstrong, Bill Watson, and Michael Erlewine). The introduction is by Thomas Moore. Cost: $19.95 + $3.95 S&H.

Ancient Hindu Astrology For The Modern Western Astrologer - (0-935895-04-3) by James Braha. This is the 350-page book widely recognized as having originally stimulated the stampede of interest in Vedic astrology. Now in its 9th printing, this classic is as popular as ever due to its clarity, comprehensiveness, practicality and usefulness. It is also beautifully executed. Cost: $21.95 + $3.95 S&H.

OTHER RECOMMENDED BOOKS

We receive frequent queries wanting suggestions for even more books on Indian astrology. Consider these—many writers have multiple works—and they will lead you to other writers worthy of your time:

Light on Life by Hart deFouw and Robert Svoboda (Penguin)

Fundamentals of Astrology by M.R. Bhat (Motilal Banarsidass)

Fundamentals of Vedic Astrology by Bepin Behari (Passage Press)

Predictive Astrology of the Hindus by G.K. Ojha (Taraporevala Sons & Co.)

How To Judge A Horoscope by B.V. Raman (Motilal Banarsidass)

Astrology, Destiny & The Wheel of Time by K.N. Rao (Vani Graphics)

Constellational Astrology by Robert De Luce (De Luce Publishing Co.)

Timing of Events by Sumeet Chugh (Sagar Publications)

Divisional Charts by V.K. Choudry (Sagar Publications)

New Techniques of Prediction - Part II by H.R.S. Iyer (Publisher Unknown)

Essentials of Horary Astrology or Prasnapadavi by M.R. Bhat (M. Banarsidass)

There is also useful information in the many books by: K.N. *Rao*, Dr. K.S. *Charak*, K.S. *Krishnamurti*, J.H. *Bhasin*, and K.T. *Shubhakaran*

<u>SOME CLASSICS</u>:

Brihat Parasara Hora Sastra translated by G.C. Sharma (Sagar Publications)

Phaladeepika translated by Kapoor (Ranjan Publications) [or Sareen (Sagar Publications)]

Brihat Jataka translated by P.S. Sastri (Ranjan Publications)

Uttara Kalamrita translated by P.S. Sastri (Ranjan Publications)

Bhrigu Sutram translated by G.S. Kapoor (Ranjan Publications)

Bhrigu Nandi Nadi translated by R.G. Rao (Ranjan Publications)

Sarvartha Chintamani translated by J.N. Bhasin (Sagar Publications)

Jaimini Sutras translated by B.S. Rao (Ranjan Publications)

Some recommended US sources for these books are:

East US	- Nataraj Books	- 703-455-4996
Middle US	- JDR Ventures	- 330-263-1308
West US	- Astrology Center of America	- 805-641-2157
Internet	- www.astroamerica.com	(and many others)

See also *21st Century Books* in Fairfield, IA and *The Bodhi Tree* in Los Angeles, CA

TYPICAL SERVICES AVAILABLE FROM RICHARD HOUCK

Following are some common Astrological Services for *Individuals*

Basic Natal Chart The unique features, strengths & weaknesses of the natal chart covering all the fundamental areas of life. For mature adults, this is most useful in the context of a cycle review.

Detailed Identification of Life Cycles Select: lifetime, 5-year, 2-year, 1-year or monthly. As periods shorten, the commentary becomes more granular & specific. Annual reviews (on birth days) are *very* popular; they are quite useful for detailed planning vs. your specific goals that year.

Rectification As the *Astrology of Death* demonstrates, an accurate birth time is critical. We receive many national referrals for this work. The fee is based upon hours expended (factors: the range of potential birth time error & the quality of client inputs).

Relocation Certain locations can radically change your life for better or worse (career, relationships, health, investing, etc.). This should only be done in the context of *Eastern* chart strengths and cycles. We receive many referrals for this work— including from the organization that really started it all.

Relationships Invest a modest sum on the front end, or possibly be among the 50% that spend *many* thousands of dollars (and much time and heartache) "undoing" their partnerships on the back end. There is much unique information in this. Need we say more?

Childhood Development Children have the same cycles as adults, and equally intense, but children have no ownership authority over their environment. Hence complex symbolic patterns are often internalized and/or projected onto the family (representing society). Child psychologists use the phrase "acting out" — but acting out what? Astrology often presents the true symbolic mechanism.

Augmentation of Therapies We have assisted the healing professions in the acceleration of therapeutic insights, but mostly at the psychological level. We are interested in more cycle involvement at the physical level.

"When" Questions These are called *electional* ("*muhurtha*") and *horary* ("*prashna*") charts. For quality purposes we prefer to do these only for clients whose annual reviews have already been done. This way such charts are yet another reinforcing support layer.

TYPICAL SERVICES AVAILABLE FROM ARC ASSOCIATES, INC.

Astrological Services for *Corporate, Political & Professional Clients*

- Attention <u>Politicians</u>: Did you spend millions running for office when a competent astrological consulting firm could have told you that you couldn't win in the first place? (Attn: <u>Attorneys</u>: this is the same as the course of a court case.)

   (We've *never* been wrong in forecasting a political election, *and* our work is *documented* via postmarked newsletter, or in public media such as newspapers.)

- Attention <u>Marketers</u>: Have you ever spent $10,000 on a major marketing presentation only to move *backwards* in the eyes of the important client?

   (It happens *all* the time, and it's *absolutely* preventable.)

- Attention <u>Personnel Departments</u>: Do many of your employees seem like square pegs in round holes? Indeed, are you paying for employee crisis counseling when the issue may be mostly cyclic?

   (These are often misdiagnosed and stigmatized as "mental health" problems.)

- Attention <u>Investors</u>: The stock market is soaring, but you are going bankrupt? Can you possibly still believe that general market cycles have anything at all to do with your financial cycles?

   (As they say: reload your clue box. There's no link.)

- Attention <u>Medical Doctors</u>: Ever go through periods of misdiagnosis and really weird patients?

   (Knowing these periods will greatly impress your malpractice insurance company.)

- Attention <u>Millionaires</u>: We like performance challenges that let us put your money where our mouth is. This cuts through claims and theory to the heart of the matter.

   (You pay a doctor whether you fail to get better or even get worse. You pay a lawyer whether or not you go to jail, and so forth. But ARC Associates, Inc. will generally financially *guarantee* the quality of its work. Call to discuss this.)

Why has Rick Houck's work been featured twice on the cover of what Paul Harvey has called "the world's most exclusive magazine?" Why, of all astrologers, was Rick Houck selected by NBC for an evening prime time interview? How many astrologers can produce references on international kidnapping cases? Why, in a book he wrote, did a former Morgan-Stanley VP cite Rick Houck as a "nationally recognized political astrologer?" Check out the practical level of former "real world" accomplishment in the last paragraph on the "About The Author" page. Stop wondering if astrology works; instead, put it to use. The only real questions are whether you have a real astrologer, and how far can you push astrology. The "value added" invariably exceeds the retainer. Please call to discuss it.

FOR MORE INFORMATION...

A copy of *your* **Hindu astrology chart**, keyed to the same codes as in this book, and including the navamsha, dasamsha, ashtakavarga, shadbala, dasa/bhuktis, etc. is available for $10 (with postage prepaid). Please supply complete and accurate birth data.

If you are anticipating, or already experiencing, a **difficult life challenge** (or a great opportunity), please be advised that we have a relationship with an ashram of priests in India who are trained to perform very **specialized Vedic prayer rituals** called *yagyas* to enhance favorable circumstances and neutralize unfavorable circumstances. These *can* last as long as a week and *can* involve as many as 108 priests. The fee is related to duration, number of priests involved, and other considerations, but we can assure you that powerful, and often amazing, results have been reported over and over again. Please call to discuss this.

Check payment for all products and services *must* be expressed in US dollars and *must* be drawn upon a US bank. Any Postal Orders must reflect international postal agreements. International orders: *Please add* the necessary additional postage amount for any products you would like shipped outside the US (especially airmail). Currently (1997) we still do not accept credit cards. If you would only like to be put on our **mailing list**, just let us know.

Richard Houck may be contacted directly for research, consultations, etc. (see just prior pages). Write to him at ARC Associates, Inc., 11324 Rambling Road, Gaithersburg, MD 20879-3412 USA. Phone/fax is: 301-353-0212. Email: RichardHouck@worldnet.att.net. [Note: within the next few years Richard Houck plans to relocate to Pensacola, FL. As necessary, call information there (555-1212). The current area code is 904.]

"So ... it comes down to this."